Art and Politics in
Have Gun—Will Travel

Art and Politics in
Have Gun—Will Travel

The 1950s Television Western as Ethical Drama

KATHLEEN L. SPENCER

McFarland & Company, Inc., Publishers

Jefferson, North Carolina

Frontispiece: Paladin (Richard Boone) in working gear

LIBRARY OF CONGRESS CATALOGUING-IN-PUBLICATION DATA

Spencer, Kathleen, 1947–
Art and politics in Have gun—will travel :
the 1950s television Western as ethical drama /
Kathleen L. Spencer.
p.   cm.
Includes bibliographical references and index.

ISBN 978-0-7864-7884-2 (softcover : acid free paper) ∞
ISBN 978-1-4766-1774-9 (ebook)

1. Have gun—will travel (Television program)
2. Masculinity on television.   3. Sex role on television.
4. Boone, Richard—Biography.   5. Television actors
and actresses—United States—Biography.   6. Western
television programs—United States.   7. United
States—On television.   I. Title.
PN1992.77.H35S64 2014   791.45'75—dc23   2014031848

BRITISH LIBRARY CATALOGUING DATA ARE AVAILABLE

On the cover: Richard Boone in a publicity photograph
for *Have Gun—Will Travel* (CBS/Photofest)

Printed in the United States of America

McFarland & Company, Inc., Publishers
Box 611, Jefferson, North Carolina 28640
www.mcfarlandpub.com

To Richard Allen Boone, 1917–1981,
actor, teacher, visionary

Table of Contents

Acknowledgments

In 1986, I went to the movie theatre to see *Stand By Me*, the film adaptation of the Stephen King short story "The Body," about four 12-year-old boys who go on an expedition to look at the body of a kid killed by a train. As the boys march along on their quest, they begin to sing lustily: "The Ballad of Paladin," the theme song of a television Western immensely popular in 1960, when the story is set. Hearing the familiar tune and words, I was instantly carried back to my own childhood on a tide of nostalgia almost too poignant to bear. Even though I had watched the series with my family every Saturday night for a couple of years, I hadn't thought of the show in more than 30 years. But that song brought Paladin vividly into my mind, with all his contradictions: his rich laugh contrasted with his sometimes ominous demeanor, his furious anger balanced against his tender compassion for the weak, his universal competence, and, always, his passionate concern for justice. Wow— Paladin! At ten, I aspired to be Paladin when I grew up, undeterred by the minor handicap of being a girl. Then the scene on screen shifted, and I was swept up in the film again, moved by the powerful story and the skill of the four young actors.

But long after the movie was over, I found myself returning in my mind to Paladin, wondering if the series had really been as good as I remembered. At the time, I had no way to answer that question, but it lingered at the back of my mind through the next eight years. Then, in 1995, after years of academic gypsying from one institution of higher learning to another, I gratefully landed a tenure-track job at a community college in Cincinnati, Ohio. That same year, Columbia House Video began to release the episodes of *Have Gun—Will Travel* on VHS. To celebrate my new economic security, I splurged and ordered the videos. Every five or six weeks, a new tape arrived with four more episodes selected from the six seasons of the series in no apparent order.

As I watched, I was gratified as well as astounded to realize that the series was indeed as good as I remembered. Though not every episode rated an A+, quite a few did, along with plenty of episodes only a little lower in quality. Though the special effects were rather primitive by 1990s standards, the writing, the directing, and, above all, the acting were, on the whole, highly impressive. There were a handful of disappointments, of course: weak scripts, illogical plots, moments of melodrama or sentimentality, historical anachronisms, experiments that didn't work. But overall, the quality was consistently high. Further, I was struck by how many of the episodes dealt sympathetically with racial and ethnic minorities, and—more remarkable still, given the time period—the number of women in strong, non-traditional roles. That certainly didn't match my expectations for a television show from the 1950s. As both a Boomer in good standing and a student of popular culture, I was impressed, and intrigued. What had made such a series possible in a mass medium like television?

During the rare crannies of free time in a heavy teaching load, I began looking for answers, studying the Western as a genre and its connection to issues of masculinity, investigating the early history of television, and continuing my professional study of gender and race issues, meanwhile eagerly watching new episodes as they arrived. Once I possessed the complete series, I went back through them in broadcast order, looking for patterns, and eventually making detailed transcriptions. Then I realized that the story would be incomplete unless I compared *Have Gun* to its most popular competitors, so my research branched out to include *Gunsmoke, Wagon Train*, and *Bonanza*—the three other most popular, longest-running Westerns of the period. Fortunately for me, all these series were being released on video and DVD for home viewing: more episodes to watch and annotate.

When retirement finally gave me the leisure to begin researching and writing in earnest, I got immeasurable assistance from two books on the series: (1) *The Have Gun—Will Travel Companion* by Martin Grams, Jr., and (2) *Richard Boone: A Knight Without Armor in a Savage Land* by David Rothel, both published in 2000. These books proved invaluable to my work, particularly the numerous interviews with Boone's family members and co-workers, which provided me with insight into the actor and his values and methods that I could have obtained from no other sources, since most of these interviewees have died in the last few years. I am grateful to both Mr. Grams and Mr. Rothel for preserving this material and making it publicly available, and even more grateful for their gracious permission to quote selectively from their interviews.

One challenge of researching topics in popular culture is that most of the material comes from articles and interviews published in mass media sources like *TV Guide* and *Saturday Evening Post*, and in newspapers across the country. For finding me copies of these 50-year-old articles, I am grateful to the interlibrary loan specialists at Cincinnati State Technical and Community College: first, Briana Conroy provided me with cheerful and dedicated support for many years, and later, Myra Justus picked up the baton and soldiered on for me. This is the perfect place to express my thanks to *TV Guide* for permission to quote from Richard Gehman's three-part article on Richard Boone published in their pages in January 1961, and to Richard Schickel for permission to quote from his article about Boone and *Have Gun—Will Travel*, "TV's Angry Gun," originally published in November 1961.

Finally, like anyone who undertakes the Herculean labor of writing a book, I owe debts of love and gratitude to the many friends and family members who took this journey with me, indulging my obsessions, reading drafts, and watching innumerable *Have Gun* episodes with me, often more than once. Among the many, two stand out for Devotion Above and Beyond: Betty Jean Skinner, longtime friend, head cheerleader and Editorial Reader Supreme, who could always see what needed fixing when I was too close to recognize problems; and, in the end as in the beginning, Doug Morriss, king of my heart, champion dance partner, husband and best friend, Merit Badge winner in the Care and Feeding of Authors, whose generous forbearance and cheerful encouragement made those long days in the study so much easier, and who for the duration took so many household chores on himself without murmur or complaint. You've cheered me on and cheered me up every step of the way. This one's for you, babe.

Introduction

Almost every Saturday night from September 1957 to August 1963, the man called Paladin rode across our TV screens. Embodied by craggy-faced actor Richard Boone, Paladin was an anomaly among television Western heroes. Raised in the East as a man of culture and education, a West Point graduate and a Union Army officer during the Civil War, Paladin by the mid–1870s resided in an elegant suite in San Francisco's Carlton Hotel. He kept box seats at the opera, the ballet, and the theatre, visited the best restaurants, and patronized the finest vintners, tobacconists, tailors, and haberdashers. He was most often found with a beautiful, elegantly-dressed woman on his arm—a different woman each time.

But periodically a plea for assistance would arrive at the Carlton by letter, telegram, or in person, or one of the regional newspapers Paladin subscribed to would report a problem that intrigued him. Then Paladin would send the lovely lady home, change into his black trail clothes, strap on his gun with the silver figure of a chess knight on the holster, and ride out to battle the forces of ignorance, arrogance, and greed—for the standard fee of $1,000. He knew the deserts and mountains of the West from Mexico to Alaska. He knew the far-flung frontier towns, cattle ranches, mining camps, and Army posts of this vast region as well as he knew the streets of San Francisco, and displayed a respectful familiarity with the many different cultures and peoples to be encountered there: Mexicans, Indians of various tribes, Chinese, blacks, along with the occasional Easterners and European visitors who ventured into the American frontier.

Paladin shared many characteristics with the typical Western hero: a strong sense of ethics, skill with numerous weapons, including his fists, and a willingness to use those weapons to defend himself or those who were weak and deserving. And, of course, he shared a gender: Western heroes were, by definition, male. But in other ways, he stood apart from the familiar image. Where the traditional Western hero was reserved, even somber, a man whose actions spoke for him, Paladin was erudite and articulate, a master of literature, of rhetoric, history, and law. For him, words could be more powerful than guns. It was only when words and reason failed that he turned, reluctantly, to violence. Supremely self-assured, Paladin did not have to react to every challenge to his competence or his honor. While real threats merited a serious response, a braggart's insolence might provoke only a laugh—a full-bodied, assertive shout of amusement or derision. No other Western hero laughed as often or as richly as Paladin.

Though literally a "hired gun," Paladin was not a gunfighter in the traditional, and pejorative, sense of that term. He did not use his prowess with a gun to establish a reputation or gratify his ego. Nor was he a conventional bounty hunter, another despised occupation for a man with a gun. Typically, bounty hunters were in it for the money: if a fugitive was wanted "dead or alive," it was easier to bring in a corpse than a living man. But for Paladin, money was less important than the principles of law and justice. An accused man was entitled to a trial, if at all possible; a convicted man was entitled to a legal execution rather than a trail-side assassination, if Paladin had any choice in the matter. His strength and his skill with weapons gave him great power, but he always acknowledged the responsibility to use that power appropriately. Week after week, audiences watched Paladin make calculated judgments, identifying those who deserved his help, whether or not they could pay for it (on more than one occasion, Paladin reduced his usual $1,000 fee, or even offered his services free if circumstances warranted). He also had to decide on the form his help should take to produce the optimum outcome—not necessarily just what his current employer had asked him to do. He could never be hired to kill someone, not even a criminal under a death sentence. What employers were actually hiring was not Paladin's gun, but his brain: the gun was merely one of the tools at his disposal. He, not his employer, determined the methods to be used to solve the problem, and he was capable of resigning or even switching sides in the middle of a job if his employer proved unreasonable, unethical, or dishonest.

Despite his independence, Paladin was no lone wolf taking the law into his own hands. As a matter of principle, he worked with and through local law officers (when there was one), as long as the partnership could produce the justice that was his goal. But on the frontier, law could be a tenuous thing, only as strong as the lone individual who embodied the law in any given community. While some sheriffs were both competent and virtuous, others lacked one or more of the qualities needed to create a just and orderly society. They might be too old or too young to control the local troublemakers, or they might be interested only in drawing their salary and preserving their own skin. Some were paid servants of the local Big Landowner, while a few lawmen were themselves the problem, openly abusing their power for their own advantage. When the local authority prevented a just solution instead of facilitating it, then Paladin stepped in to redress the balance, reinforcing the weak and fearful, inspiring the community to unite against the greedy and corrupt, or appealing over the sheriff's head to a higher authority. Paladin's true job, then, was to shore up the fragile system of frontier law wherever he found it needing help.

But his greatest and most unique asset among Western heroes was his skill as a mediator, his ability to listen. Time after time, Paladin would meet with a client, learn their tale of trouble, and then hear the anxious demand: "What are you going to do to solve my problem?" His characteristic reply: "I won't know till I hear the other side of the story." Paladin's choices are governed by this fundamental belief: that there is always another side, another perspective, that he must understand in order to resolve the conflict properly. That is, Paladin defines success not as achieving his employer's wishes, but as creating a just solution to a dispute. He never set himself up as the sole arbiter of justice, but because Paladin was a clear-eyed objective outsider to each dispute, his judgment always carried significant weight.

The only other continuing character on *Have Gun—Will Travel* was Hey Boy, the Chinese porter at the Carlton. As a hotel employee, Hey Boy performed varied services for Paladin, but he was also Paladin's friend and occasional co-conspirator. Though their relationship was unquestionably hierarchical, it was grounded in mutual appreciation, even affection. In his daily interactions with Hey Boy, Paladin demonstrated knowledge of, and respect for, Chinese culture and language. He might tease Hey Boy from time to time, but he also relied on his assistance, and when a crisis occurred in Hey Boy's life, Paladin rode swiftly to aid his friend.

For six seasons, Paladin continued his efforts to spread civilization and justice in the west. At the end of the sixth, Richard Boone, burnt out on the character and exhausted from the grueling production schedule (39 episodes per season in which, as the sole star, he appeared in almost every scene), moved on to other projects.

Television Westerns of the 1950s

Of course, *Have Gun—Will Travel* was only one of many Westerns on television in these years. Between 1955 and 1964, Westerns dominated American television programming to a degree that is almost inconceivable now.[1] In those eight seasons, the three national networks—ABC, CBS, and NBC—debuted 45 different original Western series, to say nothing of the syndicated shows, reruns, and the Hollywood movies that added more hours of Western programming per week. Though half of these series were quite ephemeral—12 lasted one season or less, another 11 went off the air after two seasons—some of the most successful survived for six, eight, fourteen seasons or more. The phenomenon hit its peak in the 1959–60 season, when 28 first-run Western series were broadcast each week—17.5 hours, almost one quarter of all evening programming. Since, in these early days of television, a season was typically 39 weeks long (two to three times the length of a 21st century season), that meant the number of new Western stories airing during the year was truly astounding.

Westerns weren't new on television in 1955, but at first the genre was aimed exclusively at children. Shows like *The Lone Ranger* (1949), *Hopalong Cassidy* (1949), *The Gene Autry Show* (1950), *The Cisco Kid* (1950), and *The Roy Rogers Show* (1951) taught simple moral lessons to young viewers in the guise of adventure stories. In 1952, *Death Valley Days* moved to television after 22 years on the radio, offering stories about the lore and legends of the country's most famous desert. But that was a syndicated show rather than a network offering, and therefore only available in selected locales, while many of the stories were little more than anecdotes.

Then out of the blue, in September 1955, each of the national networks premiered a Western for adults in prime time. On Sunday nights, NBC offered *Frontier* (like *Death Valley Days,* a 30-minute anthology series—stories with different characters each week). *Frontier's* stories were relentlessly unglamorous, emphasizing the real difficulties people encountered moving into and settling a new, often inhospitable territory. As the narrator, Walter Coy, announced each week: "This is the West. This is the land of beginning again. This is the story of men and women facing the frontier. This is the way it happened."[2] On Tuesday nights, ABC offered two series. First was the half-hour *Life and Legend of Wyatt Earp,* starring Hugh O'Brian, based substantially on the facts of the historical marshal's life. Following that came the hour-long *Cheyenne,* starring Clint Walker as a solitary adventurer wandering the West after the Civil War.[3] And on Saturday, September 10, 1955, CBS premiered *Gunsmoke,* the story of Marshal Matt Dillon and his friends Doc, Chester, and Kitty in Dodge City, Kansas, in the 1870s. *Gunsmoke,* already popular on the radio since 1952, gained quick acceptance from the new television audience, and ultimately ran for twenty consecutive years, becoming the longest-running continuing-character series in television history.[4]

In 1956-57, two more adult Westerns were added: *The Adventures of Jim Bowie* on ABC, loosely based on another real-life figure, and *Dick Powell's Zane Grey Theatre* on CBS, an anthology series specializing in the Western stories of Zane Grey. But then the proverbial floodgates opened: in 1957-58, ten new Western series were introduced; the following year, another nine; and in 1959-60, twelve more. Of course, a number of the earlier series disappeared as the new ones arrived, but that still left the schedule crammed with Westerns.

The sheer number of programs was significant, but even more telling was the popularity of the genre with audiences. In 1956-57, there was only one Western in the top ten programs: *Gunsmoke* in its second season, tied for seventh place with the game show *I've Got a Secret*. The following year, there were five Westerns in the top ten, including *Gunsmoke* now in first place. By 1958-59, seven of the top ten programs on television were Westerns, including all of the top four: *Gunsmoke, Wagon Train, Have Gun—Will Travel* and *The Rifleman*. For each of the next three seasons, Westerns claimed the top three spots in the ratings.

Then, as suddenly as it arose, the craze passed. Westerns fell out of favor. Partly, they were undone by public concerns about the level of violence portrayed on television screens, especially with so many children watching. More significantly, as TV research companies like Nielsen produced ever more detailed information about the viewing audience, networks learned that Westerns appealed primarily to older people, while by the early 1960s the most coveted demographic—young adults and children—much preferred situation comedies.[5] By 1962-63, only two Westerns were found in the top ten shows: *Bonanza* in fourth place and *Gunsmoke* in tenth, with only another two in the top twenty-five—*Rawhide* at twenty-second, and *Wagon Train* at twenty-fifth. Although one of the few surviving Westerns, *Bonanza*, would rise to the top slot in 1964 and stay there for three seasons, clearly the Western as cultural phenomenon was over—so thoroughly over that there have been only a handful of successful Western series in the intervening fifty years.[6]

Scholars of American popular media have published numerous studies of television Westerns, trying to explain this dramatic rise and fall of the genre. Books by John G. Cawelti, J. Fred MacDonald, Lee Clark Mitchell, Horace Newcomb, Martin Pumphrey and Gary Yoggy give us a broad overview of the TV Western, surveying typical themes, characters, and story lines; however, these studies pay more attention to general patterns than to specific series. More recently, detailed episode guides have been published to four of the most popular and longest-running Westerns of this period: *Gunsmoke* (1955–1975), *Wagon Train* (1957–1965), *Have Gun—Will Travel* (1957–1963), and *Bonanza* (1959–1973).[7] Unlike the academic studies, these episode guides are aimed primarily at fan audiences. Each provides background and production histories of the series, along with biographies of the stars and other important figures like series creators or producers, but the primary emphasis is on broadcast schedules, plot synopses, production details of cast, directors, and writers, and anecdotes from participants in the series. While these guides provide valuable information, particularly the broadcast data and the interviews with series participants (most of whom have since died or are otherwise unavailable), there is little analysis of the politics, sociology, or psychology of the series, and even less discussion of its aesthetic quality. For each of the fan authors, the merit of the series they're cataloging is a given, needing no justification or analysis.

My study aims to fill the gap left between these two different types of studies, raising the questions neither the scholars of the genre nor the fans of the specific series have addressed. Part I explores the contexts that shaped the series: the sociological factors that made the Western so popular in this period, the development of television from a creative playground into a lucrative business, and the values and attitudes that Boone brought to his series, in contrast to the values that guided *Have Gun*'s most popular and longest-running competitors, *Gunsmoke, Wagon Train* and *Bonanza*. Part II analyzes the episodes themselves, identifying the most prominent themes and patterns in the series in order to identify what they contributed to an ongoing conversation about American values.

Though *Have Gun* was one of the most well-regarded Westerns of the period, since the end of the Western craze it has received far less attention than these other three shows. Yet the series represents a remarkable cultural achievement. In a socially conservative genre, the Western; in a socially conservative medium, television, which had to appeal to the broadest possible audience in order to be profitable; above all, in a socially conservative era like the 1950s, when cultural upheaval made many people long for simple answers and black-and-white moral judgments, *Have Gun* instead challenged its audience to ponder some of the difficult questions facing the country. The series used Western adventure stories to raise questions about the proper use and abuse of power, about the complex relationship between law and justice at the ragged edge of civilization, about the place of minorities in a dominant culture—racial, ethnic, religious minorities, or other groups considered inferior or suspect, as women were in the 1950s. In a genre that celebrated independence and self-reliance, *Have Gun* examined the role of communities, what people needed from communities and what communities needed in order to function constructively. It even used this most macho of genres to examine the 1950s American model of manhood. In an era when culture, art, and intellectual pursuits were often considered effeminate, the charismatic and virile Paladin quotes poetry freely, rejoices in opera and ballet, plays chess for fun, and reads classic literary texts in their original language, challenging contemporary assumptions about what it means to be a man.

The focus of the series was determined largely by its star, Richard Boone, who quickly became the dominant voice in shaping *Have Gun*. Because of Boone's extraordinary control of the series, and his absolute commitment to artistic quality, the producers sought out the most innovative writers, the most creative directors, and the best-trained actors in Hollywood and New York. As a result, *Have Gun* stands out as politically the most liberal, and intellectually and aesthetically the most sophisticated television series of the period, certainly among Westerns, and arguably among TV shows of any genre in the late 1950s and early 1960s. Within the limits of a mass medium, Boone managed to create genuine, serious art—if not in every episode, then in a remarkably high percentage of them. How the miracle was wrought, and why it was significant, is the topic of this book.

PART I: CONTEXTS

An Overview

The first half of the book explores the three crucial factors that prompted and shaped the Western craze on 1950s television. First, the *message*: since popular culture by definition addresses the psychic concerns of its audience, what compelling need did the television Western speak to? Why were so many broadcast hours a week devoted to Westerns? Second, the *medium*: from its first decade (1945–1954) to its second (1955–1964), television changed profoundly, both in its technological aspects and in its business model. How did these changes affect the kind of entertainment TV offered its audiences? Third, the *men*: the creators, producers, and stars involved in these four series shaped the productions to reflect their own values and concerns. How did their divergent priorities affect the series they dominated?

The Message: The Westerner as Man of the Hour

The mass media give us the heroes and the villains we need to help make sense of the world in a particular time and place. Judging by the prime-time television schedule, between 1955 and 1963 the hero Americans needed most was the Westerner. This pattern raises important questions for the cultural historian. What qualities did the Westerner possess, in his various guises—cowboy, lawman, cattle baron, gunfighter—that spoke to the psychic needs of the audience? What features of American society in these years prompted such a surge of television series about the Old West?

The popular impression of the Fifties, looking backward, is of an orderly era with a minimum of social dissent. Prosperity was widespread, good jobs were plentiful, and (for the first time in history) everyone with a good job could afford to own a house. The nuclear family was the dominant institution, untroubled, serene to the point of boredom, the young people mostly "square" and quietly conforming, and everyone dressed very formally: men wore suits, women wore dresses and high heels, and in public, hats were considered essential for adults of both genders. As David Halberstam observes in *The Fifties*, "In that era of general good will and expanding affluence, few Americans doubted the essential goodness of their society. After all, it was reflected back at them not only by contemporary books and magazines, but even more powerfully and with even greater influence in the new family sitcoms on television." In this period, he continues, traditional authority was still respected. Not only did Father Know Best, but Americans "trusted their leaders to tell them the truth, to make sound decisions, and to keep them out of war."[1]

However, when we look more closely, the fifteen years between the end of World War II and John F. Kennedy's election as president are less monolithic and a good bit less serene than this nostalgic image suggests. In fact, the period is marked by wrenching paradoxes and tensions. In particular, two great anxieties confronted the people of the United States. One concerned the position of the nation in the world: a decade after its decisive victory in World War II, America was threatened by enemies both external and internal. The other anxiety concerned the position of men in America—their manliness, their ability to properly fill the male gender role. Many commentators in this period were convinced that the masculinity of the nation's men had been seriously undermined, leaving the family and the country vulnerable. Chapter One will analyze both these great anxieties to explain why, for many Americans, the television Western provided such comfort and reassurance.

The Medium: Television's Growing Pains

From its earliest days, television was at least as much a business enterprise as it was an entertainment medium. The primary focus of most network executives was less on broadcasting good shows than on building a lucrative industry whose resources they could control. But in that first decade, when nobody knew what television could do, the creative staff experimented freely with a variety of programs, learning television's capabilities and its limitations. This process was facilitated because, in that first decade, television was restricted to fairly small, often elite audiences, mostly on the East and West coasts and in major Midwestern cities like Chicago. But by 1955, a significant transformation had occurred: television, now found in most American living rooms, had become both a lucrative business and a medium for mass entertainment. In order to understand the Western craze of the 1950s, we need to understand how the business aspects of television affected what viewers saw on the screen: how series were adopted and scheduled by the networks, and how they were financed. What constraints did the financial powers—networks, sponsors, and production companies—impose on the programming they broadcast? We also need to examine what the audience contributed to the pattern. What did viewers want from television in this period? This history is the subject of Chapter Two.

The Men in Charge: Richard Boone and His Competitors

Authority and power can come from many different sources on a TV series. Sometimes it is the series creator who controls the overall vision, other times it is the producer, while the stars of the series often gain considerable influence over time. On *Gunsmoke*, aside from the first television season (1955-56), the creators of the original radio series most directly shaped what appeared on the screen.[2] For both producer Norman Macdonnell and writer John Meston, creating authentic unsentimental stories about the West and the real people who populated the region was a high priority, though the constraints of TV forced them to soften the original harsh vision of the radio *Gunsmoke*.[3] But over time, as the four stars— James Arness as Matt Dillon, Milburn Stone as Doc Adams, Dennis Weaver as Chester, and Amanda Blake as Miss Kitty—settled into their characters, they began to exert their own influence over the scripts, defending their characters' consistency. Blake recalled years later,

> We were possessive about the show. We had a property that we loved.... It was, "Don't mess
> around with Miss Kitty." Or, "Miss Kitty wouldn't say that." Or, "Chester wouldn't say
> that to Matt Dillon." We wanted to keep the character relationships in the right perspec-
> tive and we just guarded this jealously.[4]

In particular, as Arness grew into the role of Matt Dillon, he often edited down long eloquent speeches into a few simple words, arguing that Dillon was not a talker but a man of action. Most observers on the set agreed that the changes made the scene more effective.[5] Once Macdonnell and Meston left the series, about halfway through its record-setting twenty seasons, the stars provided the passion and the continuity of vision that kept *Gunsmoke* a popular show for most of its long run.

By contrast, *Wagon Train* was not the product of a personal passion, but a network creation designed to fill a specific purpose. In order to compete in the Western sweepstakes, NBC wanted a series that combined the popular adult Western format with a weekly "star" vehicle, like *GE Theatre*, to attract major performers known for their work in other genres, especially movies, to the television screen. So the producers' highest priority was creating juicy guest-star roles that would entice well-known actors to *Wagon Train*.[6] However, as the central continuing characters, the series stars—Ward Bond as wagon master Seth Adams and Robert Horton as scout Flint McCullough—had the most compelling interest in what happened on the screen. Bond in particular came to exercise virtual veto-power over the scripts. On one occasion, production was delayed for two days while Bond and the show's staff rewrote 63 pages of a 70-page script that he found "offensive." As the public face of *Wagon Train*, Bond was determined that the show would reflect his values.[7] After Bond's sudden death in November 1960, halfway through filming the fourth season, the show lost momentum; when Horton left at the end of the fifth season, *Wagon Train* limped on for another couple of seasons, adding characters, changing days and times, expanding to 90 minutes, even filming in color, but with no one to carry on the vision, the show slowly died.

Bonanza, on the other hand, was from the beginning a labor of love for its creator and producer, David Dortort. Dortort had two priorities for his series: first, he wanted something different from the familiar "one man and his gun" western, a grander vision about a prominent family running a large Western estate. For Dortort, the ideal family consisted of the powerful father and his three grown sons—four strong men who loved each other in a clean, manly way, to counter the 1950s situation-comedy image of fathers as fools and bumblers.[8] His second priority was a specific setting, Nevada Territory in the late 1850s, a crucial place and time in American history which would allow him to tell stories combining education with entertainment.

For *Bonanza*'s entire 14-year run, Dortort controlled every aspect of the series. He not only developed and cast the show but modeled two of the four characters on the personalities of the actors he picked for the parts—Michael Landon as Little Joe and Dan Blocker as Hoss[9]; and his hand was heavy on all the scripts. Though he wrote or co-wrote only four scripts in the first season, Dortort spent several weeks with the writer of each episode before shooting began, fine-tuning the script; he then worked through the script with the director for at least three days to make sure there was no doubt about what he wanted done with it.[10] Unfortunately, the scripts produced by this process were often a disappointment to the four stars, who had no hesitation about confronting the producer with their objections, though seldom with much effect. Over time, however, the actors were able to make a few changes. By the third season, Lorne Greene finally persuaded Dortort to make his character, paterfamilias Ben Cartwright, warmer to his sons and more reasonable to his neighbors—but only by threatening to leave the series.[11] Pernell Roberts, as oldest son Adam, struggled for six unhappy years before he left the series. After his escape, youngest son Joe dropped the "Little" from his name and took over many of Adam's roles. Other continuing characters were added over the years, creating opportunities for new story lines, but when Dan Blocker died suddenly in May 1972 of post-surgical complications, *Bonanza* suffered an irrecoverable blow which even Dortort could not solve, and finally closed down three months later.

But in the case of *Have Gun—Will Travel*, star Richard Boone was the man with the vision—a vision not about the show as a Western but about maintaining high artistic standards in a mass medium, and addressing key social issues of tolerance and justice. As producers came and went (a total of six over six seasons), Boone dictated nearly every aspect of the series, choosing scripts, writers, directors, actors, even costumes, though in a much more collaborative fashion than Dortort. By the third season, he began to direct as well, 28 episodes out of 225—more episodes than any other director but Andrew McLaglen, who directed 116, over half the total. A man of fierce intelligence and strong political principles, a visionary who believed in the transformative power of the theatre and was unselfishly committed to giving everyone involved in the enterprise a chance to do their best work, Boone drew on every aspect of his personality and a lifetime of experiences to shape *Have Gun—Will Travel*, both what viewers saw on the screen and what the cast and crew experienced on the set while making each episode. Chapter Three traces the personal qualities and the life experiences that made Richard Boone the man he became, while Chapter Four examines life on the set of *Have Gun—Will Travel*, in contrast to those of its three main competitors, to show how Boone's values and priorities determined what the audience saw and heard on their television screens.

ONE

The TV Western: American Manhood in Crisis

The Leader of the Free World

As the leader of the victorious Allied forces, the U.S. emerged from World War II a major international power. That prominence created opportunities for the nation but also brought serious challenges in dealing with allies, with former enemies, and (in the case of the Soviet Union) with a one-time ally turned enemy. Many Americans, especially the well-educated and experienced young officers returned from the war, faced these challenges with confidence and resolve. But others retreated to a terrified isolationism, convinced that the wartime alliance with the Russians had been a terrible mistake all along. Through that alliance, America had won the war, but—in the isolationists' eyes—we had lost the peace. These isolationist sentiments not only impeded international cooperation but, within America's borders, fueled the virulent anti-communist witch hunts and blacklists that poisoned the country from 1947 until well into the 1960s. Dissent or protest in any form was construed as treason and punished severely. In particular, the growing agitation over civil rights for African Americans was viewed as evidence of Communist attacks on American civilization.

By the later 1950s, the anxieties about communism shifted from fears of ideological subversion to terror of actual military attack. It was offensive enough to see the success of "godless Communists" who rejected the religious faith so central to America's sense of its identity; when the Soviet Union developed nuclear weapons of its own, along with long-range missiles capable of delivering those bombs to most major American cities, the fear rose to hysterical levels. Many American families built bomb shelters in the back yards of their new suburban homes; at school, children practiced "duck and cover" drills to protect themselves in a nuclear attack. The Soviet Union also launched spy satellites and put a man into space orbit ahead of American efforts. As a result of all these developments, many Americans were convinced that we were locked in a life-or-death struggle with a ruthless enemy—and that our victory was by no means assured. How were we to deal with such threats? What models could we use to guide our actions in our new role as world leader? These were questions that desperately needed answering.

American Manhood at Risk

On the domestic front, as on the national one, the 1950s was a paradoxical era, a public face of success and security masking profound anxiety. On television, happy white middle-class families offered an idealized role model for the viewing audience, but at the same time, anxiety about families filled the pages of popular media and psychological research alike. Much of that anxiety concerned the role of men in society. In the eyes of many commentators in the 1950s, the masculinity of American men seemed dangerously deficient. According to psychologist Hendrik Ruitenbeek, summing up what many other scholars thought at the time, American men were actually in a state of crisis, whether they recognized it or not.

> The average man may not yet be aware that he is in crisis. He believes that as a male his position—social, economic, and sexual—makes him superior to the female. Nevertheless, all through American society, the male's behavior shows that he actually is experiencing a change which affects his traditional roles as father, lover, and provider. This change may be summed up in a single word: emasculation.[1]

This view of American men in crisis, which dominated the culture from the 1930s through the 1970s, derived from a new psychological theory about gender roles. According to Joseph Pleck in his groundbreaking study, *The Myth of Masculinity,* sex roles were traditionally defined by a rigid separation of the sexes into different social spheres. Men's domain was the larger world of business and politics, women's the home and family. The social institutions of a culture, imposing this rigid segregation of the sexes, justified and explained the customary gender roles. Individual personalities, tastes, capabilities, or desires were immaterial. By "nature," men did what men were supposed to do; women did what women were born to. There was, in theory, no overlap and no confusion between the two roles.[2]

However, in the late nineteenth century, women began to make their way into the world outside the home, invading once all-male settings like colleges, social clubs, political groups, and especially the workplace. Their intrusion destabilized the entire system and its prescriptions about the nature of women and of men, producing enormous anxiety about men's place in American society. That anxiety grew particularly intense and widespread in the 1930s and again in the 1950s. In an earlier age, Pleck explains, "males became men by participating in all-male social life and holding a job," but in the increasingly "heterosocial" world of the 1930s, that traditional path to manhood was gone. Especially in the grim circumstances of the Great Depression, when men could no longer count on a job that would allow them to support their families, they needed an alternative way to demonstrate their masculinity. Psychologists stepped into the cultural breach with a new theory of *sex role identity,* which replaced the old external system of institutionally-defined gender with an internalized, psychologically-based mechanism.[3] That is, unlike the old ideas, the new model argued that men may be born *male,* but they have to be *made* into men—and the task is both difficult and uncertain.[4]

According to this new theory, heavily influenced by some of Freud's early hypotheses, the fundamental task of an individual's psychological development is to establish the proper "sex role identity"—that is, to become a normal man or normal woman. However, the theory also postulates that sex role identity is "the extremely fragile outcome of a highly risky developmental process, especially so for the male."[5] Why is it harder for males? According to the psychologists, an individual's sex role identity derives from his or her relationship with the same-sex parent, but since both boys and girls receive their earliest parenting primarily from the mother, the boy has a far more challenging task than his sister: he must at some point transfer his identification from his mother to his father. According to the theory, what makes this shift in allegiance especially difficult for American boys is a too-common pattern of absent fathers and overdominant mothers.

In light of these theories, psychologists were convinced that many American men would fail to achieve masculine sex role identity, or at the very least, would struggle with serious feelings of inadequacy.[6] They pointed to one "proof" of their theory: the increasing number of homosexuals in America. Homosexuality, they argued, resulted from "insecurity" in the male sex identity, caused by a man's inability to shift his identification from his mother to his father. That is, a homosexual was attracted to other men rather than to women because internally he identified himself as female. Other common cultural ills—delinquency, violence, and hostility toward women—were also explained by men's "insecurity" in their sex role identity.[7] The widespread acceptance of this theory helps explain why so many people worried about the "deficient" masculinity of American men in these crucial decades.

Of course, the theory was both shaped and reinforced by historical events. The Depression, with its unemployment rates of twenty-five percent, created an unprecedented challenge to the traditional male role of family economic provider. Men who could no longer support their families lost status, lost pride, and above all, lost faith in themselves as men, having failed in their gender-defining responsibility. World War II restored much of this traditional manhood, especially for those men who performed military service; but it also sent many women out of their homes and into war work, in order to free more men for combat. Although some worked in traditionally female roles, like nursing or clerical work, a significant number of women found jobs in fields previously restricted to men—in chemicals, rubber, petroleum, steel, aircraft, shipbuilding, and munitions. In such fields, women found themselves earning more money than they could have imagined. Equally significant, they earned respect for their abilities as workers. Government and industry, recognizing the importance of the work being performed by women—many of them mothers of young children—established subsidized child-care facilities to make it easier for the women to do their work without worry or distraction. These experiences had a profound impact on family dynamics when the war ended and the men returned home.

At the end of the war, the culture could have chosen to extend these more egalitarian trends into peacetime. But instead, there was a dramatic reversal into ultra-domesticity: bread-winning fathers and stay-at-home wives and mothers devoting all their energy to a large brood of children, double the family size of the pre-war norm. The decade of the 1950s, exemplified by the cheerful, middle-class white suburban families that dominated television comedies, has come to be regarded with fervent nostalgia as the golden age of family normality, the last hurrah of a treasured and now lost domestic Eden. However, as Arlene Skolnick explains in *Embattled Paradise: The American Family in an Age of Uncertainty*, the deviant model is not the current family dynamic (smaller families, mothers working outside the home, more egalitarian gender roles) but the patterns of the 1950s. What is so puzzling about that period, she argues, is the extreme form of the nuclear family: "a birthrate that approached that of India, the insistence that marriage and motherhood take up the whole of a woman's identity, and the increased emphasis on gender difference."[8] The 1950s family is set apart, a throwback to the old Victorian model, and dramatically different from the family both of the first quarter of the twentieth century, and the last.

So the question arises: What were the conditions that made this old-fashioned family model seem appropriate, even desirable, to the society as a whole and to the individual men and women who made up society? More important, how did this style of family, with gender roles so distinct and separate, affect the people who lived in them? Critiquing the effects of the 1950s family model on women, a process which began famously with Betty Friedan's *The Feminine Mystique* (published as a book in 1963, but based on research she started in 1957), formed the foundation of second-wave feminism in America. But the effects on men, though less often analyzed, also deserve attention. The 1950s family model, so apparently advantageous to men, in fact burdened them with contradictory demands that created serious challenges and stresses.

1950s Gender Roles

Naturally, after the long traumatic years of combat and absence, the returning veterans were eager to re-establish themselves in a normal life of work and family, but there were many other factors at the end of the war encouraging a throwback to older patterns of family life, not least among them women's patriotism and genuine gratitude to the soldiers who had sacrificed and suffered so much. Though large numbers of women were simply fired from their well-paying war jobs, many voluntarily, even eagerly, returned home to "normal" family life.[9] True, there were heavily promoted media campaigns to encourage this process, but as Skolnick observes, "Effective advertising and propaganda work not by injecting alien ideas but by striking responsive chords, appealing to wishes and fears that are widely shared. The yearning for home and family in the immediate postwar era had deeper roots than media manipulation could have provided."[10] There was also the effect on their men to consider. Even though many women had enjoyed the prestige and independence of a paycheck and wanted to continue working, wives who kept their jobs after the men returned from war would have made their husbands look like incompetent providers. In light of the lingering wounds to these men's confidence already inflicted by the Depression, few women would have wanted to undermine their husbands' self-esteem in such a way.[11]

In addition, a potent combination of cultural carrots and sticks reinforced the new family ideology. First, a "stick": at the end of the war, all the subsidized child-care centers were summarily closed, making it much more difficult and expensive for mothers to continue working outside the home. On the "carrot" side, two postwar government policies encouraged a return to the traditional family model. In addition to paying college tuition for the returning veterans, the G.I. Bill granted them subsistence allowances—which were increased by fifty percent if they had dependents, thus encouraging unmarried veterans to marry and married ones to have children even while still in school. In addition, the bill provided veterans with low-cost mortgages, laying the groundwork for the dramatic increase in the American middle class. The Federal Aid Highway Act of 1956, which built extensive networks of highways between and around cities, facilitated the rapid development of suburbs where the veterans could find affordable housing in the necessary quantities. Thus, as Sylvia Hewlett points out in *A Lesser Life*, in the postwar period the government subsidized "to the tune of several thousand dollars a year per household, a particular kind of family—one that comprised a bread-winning husband, a homemaking wife, and one or more children."[12]

Other cultural factors also reinforced this family model. One of the most unexpected of these factors is the Cold War. On the psychological level, the anxieties of the Cold War produced a deep hunger for security and comfort in the home, especially after the long years of the Depression and the war in which such comforts had been rare and fragile. Pragmatically, too, the Cold War influenced Americans' choices. The existence of a post-war draft encouraged some young men to marry and produce children quickly as a way to avoid military service, particularly during the Korean conflict (June 1950–July 1953). But beyond that pragmatism, the 1950s family also became a potent propaganda weapon in the Cold War. The working wives who had been such a crucial component of the war effort, and the institutionalized child care which had supported their work, now were widely denounced as Communist ideas. The ultra-domesticity of the 1950s family thus became additional evidence of American superiority over the Soviet Union.[13]

Psychological theories also served to reinforce the new domesticity, with its rigid separation of gender roles. Psychoanalysts in the postwar period tended to focus on the problems of women, as Freud's theories about women's biological nature became widely influential. The popularized versions of these theories insisted that "normal" women found fulfillment only in "marital sexuality and mothering. Any inclination toward independence, interest in work outside the home, or dissatisfaction with the roles of wife and mother were seen as signs of neurosis and 'penis envy.'"[14] Women's magazines and television shows reinforced these messages, glorifying dutiful mothers and wives. Only upbeat stories were allowed in these magazines, where glossy photos showed "relentlessly happy" women, "liberated from endless household tasks by wondrous new machines they had just bought." According to the new postwar definition of femininity,

> The American woman first and foremost did not work. If she did, that made her competitive with men, which made her hard and aggressive and almost surely doomed to loneliness. Instead, she devotedly raised her family, supported her husband, kept her house spotless and efficient, got dinner ready on time, and remained attractive and optimistic; each hair was in place. According to studies, she was prettier than her mother, she was slimmer, and she even smelled better than her mother.[15]

But another crucial factor supporting the new domesticity was the resurgence of the "sex role identity" paradigm. Now that the war was over, psychologists again raised the alarm about the embattled masculinity of American men. American families, they asserted, needed the firm commanding presence of the fathers who had so long been forced to be away. The psychic health of American children was seriously threatened by the situation the war had created—a combination of dominant or working (masculinized) mothers on the one hand, and absent fathers on the other. There was a widespread concern in particular that American boys were growing up less than manly, or that, alternatively, they were becoming juvenile delinquents—the new "national problem" trumpeted in all the women's magazines and other mass media. Book after book, article after article reinforced the message: a father's dedicated attention was all that stood between his boy and a lifetime of deviance and misery. The American father of the 1950s was urged fervently to spend time with his sons, play with them, share his manly hobbies with them, laugh at their jokes, and listen to their problems in order to teach them to be men. Only in this way could he save them from turning into either sissies (most fatally into the ultimate sissy, the homosexual), or into juvenile delinquents.[16] *Life* magazine proudly proclaimed 1954 the year of "the domestication of the American man."[17] In May of that same year, *McCall's* magazine offered an editorial describing the ideal family in which men, women, and children were creating "a new and warmer way of life." The same issue featured an article on a paper-mill executive who "not only shared the household chores with his wife but helped decorate the home and was very involved in day-to-day care of his three young children."[18]

This emphasis on "family togetherness" was something new. In agrarian cultures and in the early days of the Industrial Revolution, the family was primarily an economic unit rather than an emotional one. From a young age, children worked alongside their parents, performing small but economically useful tasks. Parents were expected to provide food, clothing, and shelter to their children, to educate them to be productive members of society, and to arrange appropriate marriages for them, but the children's happiness or personal fulfillment was not considered the parents' responsibility in any social class.[19] But in 1950s America, for the first time in history, parents were held responsible for the psychic health of each child. More, the nuclear family was expected to constitute an entire universe of "satisfaction, amusement, and inventiveness" for all its members. As historian Elaine Tylor May comments, the American family of the 1950s was supposed to "create a home that would fulfill virtually all its members' personal needs through an energized and expressive personal life."[20] The "good life" was invariably focused on family fun and togetherness, a pattern reinforced by the middle-class television families of the period—the Nelsons of *The Adventures of Ozzie and Harriet* (1952–1966), the Andersons of *Father Knows Best* (1954–1963), the Cleavers of *Leave It to Beaver* (1957–1963)—all dwelling in the suburbs in domestic comfort and security.

Yet at the same time as men were being urged to this intimate emotional involvement with their children, they were also expected to fulfill the role of the strong Victorian-era patriarch. The same issue of *McCall's* which celebrated the virtuous paper-mill executive with his small children contained an editorial which insisted, "For the sake of every member of the family, the family needs a head. This means Father, not Mother."[21] This demand created an irresolvable contradiction for men. On the one hand, as Skolnick points out, the literature of marriage and the family, echoed by the women's magazines, insisted that "the strongest families and the happiest marriages were 'democratic,'" but fathers in popular culture who failed to fulfill the strong patriarchal role were shown as emasculated or henpecked (like Dagwood Bumstead in the comics or the father of James Dean's character in *Rebel Without a Cause*). These men were mocked for not standing up to their wives and for depriving their sons of manly role models.[22] Expected to be simultaneously the dominant *pater familias* and the sensitive nurturing dad, no wonder many American men were confused and anxious about their masculinity.

And all of these ideals were enforced with an intense pressure for conformity. In the 1950s, any deviation from established behavioral norms was subject to severe criticism. In the arena of marriage and the family, Skolnick describes a totalitarian intolerance that directed deep suspicion against anyone who dared to deviate from the ideal: "the unmarried adult, the working woman, the childless couple, the 'effeminate' male."[23] The pressures to be perfect—the perfect husband, the perfect wife and mother, the "perfect family"—mounted, and the stakes grew ever higher.

Manhood and Conformity

In the workplace as well as the home, conformity became the mantra and the mandate of this period, a conformity that undermined the individual autonomy and social freedom supposed to be the birthright of American men. But this pressure to conform was not accepted unquestioningly. As David Halberstam observes, conformity became the subject of a major intellectual debate in the 1950s. Watching the modern corporation become ever larger and more impersonal, many feared that the dramatic increase in living standards had been purchased at the sacrifice of freedom and individuality, that America was "losing its entrepreneurial class to cautious, gray managers, men afraid to make mistakes and take chances."[24] Throughout the decade, a number of influential books were published on the subject. Sociologist David Riesman's *The Lonely Crowd* (1950) was a study of the social psychology of conformity. C. Wright Mills' *White Collar* (1953) and William H. Whyte's *The*

Organization Man (1956) both analyzed the status of the legions of corporate employees. The subjects in these studies, far from the strong independent men of the American myth, are emasculated drones.[25] The fiction of the period also echoed these anxieties: J.D. Salinger's *The Catcher in the Rye* (1951), Richard Matheson's *The Incredible Shrinking Man* (1953), Sloan Wilson's *The Man in the Gray Flannel Suit* (1955)—all reflect an aching awareness that the average man's freedom of action and self-expression was seriously constrained, another experience undermining his sense of his own manhood.

As Michael Kimmel argues in *Manhood in America*, the workplace has always been central to American men's definition of themselves and their worth. However, by the 1950s modern corporate capitalism had transformed American culture "from a nation of small entrepreneurs—Self-Made Men—into a nation of hired employees."[26] The "Organization Man" labored for his company, one of dozens or hundreds or thousands of men indistinguishable from himself, a cog in a wheel: "small, insignificant, in many cases unappreciated, hemmed in by the mundane oppression of conformity and the vicissitudes of everyday life," as sociologist Martin Nussbaum observed in 1960.[27] In C. Wright Mills' description, the "White Collar Man," newly professionalized and thus officially elevated in status, is paradoxically too weak to threaten anyone. In fact, he is not even able to "practice an independent way of life."

> He is pushed by forces beyond his control, pulled into movements he does not understand; he gets into situations in which his is the most helpless position. The white collar man is the hero as victim, the small creature who is acted upon but who does not act, who works along unnoticed in somebody's office or store, never talking loud, never talking back, never taking a stand.[28]

American men struggled with a serious dilemma. Work was essential to the definition of manhood—work at a career that provided a decent livelihood for his family. But too many men's jobs offered them nothing beyond money, no opportunities for demonstrating any of the other prized qualities of manhood—courage, independence, pride, skill.[29] In this era of exalted domesticity, the home could fill some of these needs. In his role as a father, for example, a man could find the kind of autonomy and significance he was typically denied at work. But the domestic sphere provided no opportunity for adventure and excitement, no way to put manhood to the test. Under these conditions, Kimmel asks, "How could men remain responsible breadwinners and not turn into docile drudges? How could men become active and devoted fathers—to make sure their sons did not become sissies—and not turn into wimps themselves? How could men let their hearts run free with a wife and kids to support?"[30] The contradiction between the ideal of manhood and the daily experience of life, both at work and at home, was creating fierce stresses on many American men. No wonder that many men—burdened with such conflicting instructions, and bearing the entire responsibility for the family's welfare on their "manly" shoulders—should begin to feel that their family was as much a burden and a trap as a source of companionship and love.

By mid-century, the alternatives to domestic life that American men had traditionally turned to for adventure and renewal of their manhood were no longer available. The frontier was officially closed. The war, which had been both terrifying and transcendent, with its life-and-death choices, intense action in a moral cause, and intimate bonds with a "band of brothers," was a decade in the past. According to Kimmel, fraternal orders like the Elks, the Masons, or the Shriners, once a dependable site for male companionship heightened by ceremony and ritual, had become the subject of ridicule, like the lodge attended by Ralph Kramden and Ed Norton on *The Honeymooners*.[31] True, in this period, physical fitness re-emerged as a road to enhanced masculinity, promoted by passionate spokesmen like Jack LaLanne, but not all men were willing to work so hard at escape. As a result, fantasy became the outlet of choice for many American men in the 1950s. "So long as they remained breadwinners and devoted dads, [middle-class men] could become wild and adventurous *consumers*, savoring real men's 'true' adventures or grabbing fantasy thrills with traditional heroes like cowboys or with those delinquents with hearts of gold that Hollywood was fond of creating"—like Brando's character in *The Wild One* or any character played by James Dean.[32] The 1950s saw the development of numerous magazines for men to supply the missing adventure, like *Real: The Exciting Magazine for Men* (1950) and *Impact: Bold True Action for Men* (1957). The same decade also saw the creation of *Playboy* (1953) and James Bond, the ultimate spy, creations which spoke to men of a very different fantasy life, of adventure clothed in suave urbanity, cultural sophistication, and effortless seduction of the most desirable women in the world.

But the 1950s also saw the resurgence of the Western, in fiction, film, and especially on television. The Western proved to be ideally situated to address the anxieties of Americans—and in particular, American men—domestically as well as politically. It gave the audience a model both for America's role in the world and for men's role in America.

Icon for an Age: The Marlboro Man

As David Halberstam tells the story, in the early 1950s, American tobacco companies faced a difficult challenge. Mass-circulation magazines had begun to publish articles on possible links between smoking and cancer (as *Reader's Digest* did in July 1954). In response, the Federal Trade Commission forced cigarette makers to remove the health claims that had long featured prominently in their advertising. To counter consumers' health concerns, cigarette makers introduced filter-tip cigarettes. Marlboro was the brand that Philip Morris Co. chose as their entry in the new competition. However, to be successful in this new market, Marlboro needed some serious rebranding. Not only were filter cigarettes already stigmatized as effeminate (apparently, "real men" didn't worry about lung cancer), but Marlboro, developed in the 1920s, had originally been marketed to women. So Philip Morris planned an entirely new advertising campaign to target the brand at men.

They entrusted this campaign to Leo Burnett, a crusty straight-talking Midwesterner who kept his ad agency in Chicago, proudly distant from the over-sophisticated environs of New York. Burnett brainstormed with his best people to find the most masculine symbol in American life. Concluding it was the tattoo, the agency created a series of ads with rugged men from different backgrounds (sea captains, athletes, gunsmiths, cowboys, and so on), all sporting tattoos on their hands that became highly visible when they lit a cigarette. The first ad ran in January 1955, beginning what would prove a stunningly successful campaign. That year, Marlboro made $5 billion in sales; by 1957, the figure was $20 billion.[33] But one ad in the series so stood out—the cowboy with his craggy, weather-beaten face—that he soon replaced the tattoo as the theme of the campaign. The Marlboro Man, sexy and solitary, home on the range as he smoked his cigarette, became the ultimate symbol of "masculinity, adulthood, vigor, and potency."[34]

Nine months later, the first television Westerns for adults debuted: *Frontier, Cheyenne, The Life and Legend of Wyatt Earp,* and *Gunsmoke*.[35]

The Western to the Rescue

Dr. Ernest Dichter, who offered socio-psychological advice to advertisers, explained the value of the television Western in modern society. In September 1957, he argued that such series provided a defense against the frustrations of modern society. Most people, he claimed, felt a great hopelessness about the world's problems, but in Westerns, "the good people are rewarded and the bad people are punished. There are no loose ends left.... The orderly completion of a Western gives the viewer a feeling of security that life itself cannot offer."[36] As Erik Barnouw points out, Dichter's explanation also has political implications, suggesting that "the American people, exasperated with their multiplying, unsolved problems, were looking for scapegoats, and that telefilms provided these in quantity; also, that frustrations were making Americans ready for hero solutions—a [Wild Bill] Hiko[c]k , an Eisenhower."[37] In addition to consoling viewers struggling with personal anxieties, the Western also gave them a model for America's new role in the world, confronting the threat of worldwide Communism. The genre encapsulates what Americans believe most fervently about their national character. According to Ralph Brauer, among many others critics of the genre, "The Western is America; it is a fable of our identity, our image of ourselves."[38] In 1893, an obscure young historian named Frederick Jackson Turner delivered a lecture on the Frontier and American identity at the Chicago World's Fair. Jackson declared that the Frontier, "the meeting point between savagery and civilization," was the true birthplace of the American character. Americans, he argued, began as Europeans, civilized and respectful of authority, but as they moved west, the frontier stripped off their civilized habits, breeding a new "tendency" to be "anti-social" and an "antipathy to control." The end result of this process was a distinctive new national character—informal, crude, violent, but also democratic and full of initiative, valuing nationalism, mobility (both geographic and social), and egalitarianism. For over a century, though not without challenge and controversy, Turner's theory has shaped thinking about the role of the frontier in the American character.[39]

Of course, like most nationalist myths, ours was carefully framed to emphasize the positive aspects of our history. As J. Fred MacDonald observed, "The video West was all American, and that meant Caucasian, most likely Anglo-Saxon, and usually Protestant."[40] Placing the "story of America" after the Civil War and west of the Mississippi River allowed us to be silent about the treatment of blacks during and after slavery, while the many Westerners of Mexican heritage largely disappeared from view (aside from the occasional péon or vicious bandito, and certain television Westerns for children which presented Mexican characters in a highly sympathetic light, like *The Cisco Kid* (1950–56), *Zorro* (1957–59), and *The Nine Lives of Elfago Baca* (1958–1960), the latter two both produced by Walt Disney. The genocidal campaigns against the Indians could be presented in heroic guise as the story of brave settlers defending themselves (with the help of the Army) against bands of brutal, unreasoning savages. With the proper framing, no inconvenient facts or uncomfortable perspectives need disturb the Sacred Narrative, and its power as a source of comfort and reassurance could remain untainted.

But beyond feeding nationalist pride, the Western provided the country with a model to explain our role in the Cold War. The Western was typically framed as a contest between Good and Evil: the sheriff against the outlaws, the Army against the Indians, the lone hero against the gunfighter. As MacDonald explains, the American narrative of the Cold War drew unconsciously on the familiar patterns of the Western. The Russians could readily be cast as the Bad Guys—the "global outlaws forcefully grabbing other people's countries, undermining world stability, threatening the future of mankind." America, of course, was the selfless Hero, "advocate of freedom, protector of the downtrodden, champion of Free World democracy, proponent of bourgeois capitalism," whose mission it was to defend the world from the ruthless outlaws. The analogy with the Western, MacDonald argues, unconsciously shaped the American response to Soviet expansionism: "Like those innocent ranchers and townspeople in countless Westerns who found their parochial existences threatened by das- tardly outlaws, unassuming Americans at this time of global tension were compelled to defend themselves, their possessions, and the values for which they stood. A noble cause had been thrust upon them. Failure to act heroically might have been tragic." As a result, America's traditional isolationism melted away, and "the Policeman to the World" was born.[41]

What a Man's Got to Do

As Norman Mailer put it, "Masculinity is not something one is born with, but some- thing one gains. And one gains it by winning small battles with honor."[42] This notion of masculinity not as something innate but as something to be achieved, as well as the connec- tion between masculinity and honor, is a truism, one which is central to the Western as a genre. Lee Clark Mitchell observes, "From the beginning the Western has fretted over the *construction* of masculinity."[43] Significantly, the genre's popularity increases dramatically in those periods when gender roles are called into question—for example, during the period of suffragist agitation between 1880 and 1920, and again in the 1950s.[44] Under the placid surface of post-war suburban life, decades of stress on gender roles was accumulating pressure. The dramatic resurgence of the Western in this period suggests both the level of concern with gender and the relevance of the genre to those concerns. For many American males of the 1950s—anxious, repressed, powerless, burdened by domestic responsibilities and starved for adventure—the Western Hero became both a role model and a potent escape fantasy.

The Westerner, whether in fiction, film, or television, is independent, fearless, self- confident, and above all, free. Commentators from the 1950s use quite similar language to describe this archetypal figure. For Robert Warshow in 1954, the Western hero is notably "a figure of repose." Though lonely and even a little melancholy, "his loneliness is organic, not imposed on him by his situation but belonging to him intimately and testifying to his completeness."[45] That is, his solitariness is a choice, a source and measure of strength rather than a weakness. No crowd dictates his actions; he is self-contained and self-sufficient. In a 1955 interview Clint Walker, star of the new TV Western *Cheyenne*, identified some of the same themes in describing the special heroism of the cowboy: "It's the kind of heroism that makes it possible for a man to live alone and at peace with himself, or to do what seems right whether it comes easy or comes hard, to stand up for what he believes in, even if it's going to be the last time he stands up."[46] In 1960, sociologist Martin Nussbaum described the Western hero as characterized by "his restlessness and freedom of action. He can 'pick himself up' whenever he desires and, like the wind, drift on, because he is not troubled with family ties or attachment to a permanent home." In contrast to the domesticated family man and corporate drone of the 1950s, Nussbaum sees the Western hero as "a drifter, a vanishing sym- bol of individualism in an age of togetherness and conformity." With a gun strapped to his thigh as an overt symbol of his masculinity, the Westerner is "uninhibited, decisive, fearless, and noble."[47] Martin Pumphrey, who encountered the TV Western heroes of the 1950s as a child, describes them as "*self-dependent* individualists and non-conformists. They are loners and outsiders, needed by society but not tied to it. In the mind's eye, they know how to handle themselves, have superior powers of perception and the skills, knowledge and experience to take control and succeed whatever the odds."[48]

To these qualities of independence, knowledge, discipline and skill, the Western hero adds something more important. Above all, he is a man of probity and principle. Breaking the rules—drawing first in a gun duel, shooting a man without warning, or worse, in the back—would destroy the hero in a way that death could not. Warshow argues that, fundamentally, what the Westerner fights to defend is

> the purity of his own image—in fact, his honor. This is what makes him invulnerable. When the gangster is killed, his whole life is shown to have been a mistake, but the image the Westerner seeks to maintain can be presented as clearly in defeat as in victory: he fights not for advantage and not for the right, but to state what he is.... The Westerner is the last gentleman, and the movies which over and over again tell his story are probably the last art form in which the concept of honor retains its strength.[49]

Horace Newcomb, like Pumphrey, draws on his experiences growing up with the Westerns of the 1950s. For him, Western heroes reliably offered "a safe haven for those needing protection, the compendia of wisdom for those needing instruction, the strong, sometimes violently capable arms for those needing action. They stood against the unruly, irrational, immoral, excessively and illegally violent villains, outlaws and psychotics who threatened life on the fictional frontier."[50] All of these descriptions, with their emphasis on *honor*, exalt the Westerner as a hero out of the old tales—knight errant, champion of the powerless, dedicating his life to service of his fellows with no thought of reward. No wonder, then, that the Western hero was an appealing figure, especially to male viewers whose daily lives offered so little in the way of honor, so little opportunity to demonstrate heroic qualities, so little control over their own fate and that of their community.

One feature of the Westerner's life seems to have been especially enviable in the oppressively domesticated 1950s—the fact that he lives in a world free of domestic ties, free of responsibilities to home and family; or, more precisely, free of women and their demands and expectations. This feature looms large in virtually every commentary on the Western hero. As James Arness, *Gunsmoke*'s Marshal Dillon, memorably put it in 1958, "People like Westerns because they represent a time of freedom. A cowboy wasn't tied down to one place or to one woman. When he got mad he hauled off and slugged someone. When he drank he got good and drunk." People watch Westerns, he claimed, "to escape from conformity. They don't want to see a U.S. marshal come home and help his wife wash the dishes."[51]

In fact, based on the popular Western series on television, viewers did not want to see the hero come home to a wife at all, even if she didn't ask his help with the housework. The Western was a world which belonged essentially to men, a world in which male values and gender codes were the uncontested norm. In the Western, men's most significant relationships were almost always with other men. As Mitchell points out, the Western was an "environment that encouraged, indeed prized, intense male bonding"—and did so "without the conventional justification of military need."[52] He is speaking particularly of movies, but consider our four television series. On the Ponderosa, the closeness of the four Cartwrights is justified by blood ties—father to son, brother to brother; but on *Gunsmoke* the relations between Matt, Chester, and Doc could scarcely have been closer if they had been related by blood. The same is true for the regulars on *Wagon Train*: the connections between Major Adams, scout Flint McCullough, Assistant Wagon Master Terry Hawks, and cook Charlie Wooster, though signaled by reciprocal teasing, are based on well-earned trust and deep, if unarticulated, affection. Even Paladin, much closer to the traditional solitary figure of the Western hero, has Hey Boy as a reliable presence in his life.

Significantly, despite the genre's pattern of intense relationships between men, there is never any suspicion of homosexuality in the Western, any more than in the intimate bonding of wartime buddies. It is likely that the homosocial environment of these genres is so traditional, so taken for granted, that the very notion of homosexual desire seems inconceivable. Of course, some of this absence might be attributed to censorship, whose ubiquity in 1950s television is hard to overstate. The sexual prudery of networks and sponsors was so intense that even respectable married couples on television had to be shown sleeping in twin beds. But in the TV Western of the period, we can easily see where heterosexual sex has been downplayed, in those instances when women are present at all. Homosexuality, rather than being downplayed, is simply unimaginable.

The only regular female character in any of these four major series is *Gunsmoke*'s Miss Kitty, and, as a saloon entertainer (the family-friendly version of the prostitute a real-life Kitty would have been), she carries none of the taint of domesticity the Western rejects so firmly. And once she becomes the owner of the Long Branch, she moves even further away from that domestic status. But as Robert Warshow points out, in the Western the prostitute or saloon girl always exists outside the traditional feminine structure, due to her "quasi-masculine independence": "nobody owns her, nothing has to be explained to her, and she is not, like a virtuous woman, a 'value' that demands to be protected."[53] Therefore, unlike a wife, she puts no constraints on the hero.

So on one level, the Western offered viewers—especially male viewers—a world which seemed simpler and clearer in its expectations of men. However, examined more closely, even this simpler version of manhood is not as simple as it appears. As Mitchell argues, the Western's commitment is not to resolving the contradictions in the male gender role, but "to *narrating* all those contradictions involved in what it means to be a man, in a way that makes them seem less troubling than they are."[54] The Western hero, it turns out, faces many of the same contradictory demands as the 1950s American father: to be strong, confident, independent—his own man—and at the same time to be responsible, nurturing, and self-sacrificing. He must be self-controlled, restraining his passions, while at the same time acting decisively to protect his family and his community. These contradictions come to a head around the issue of violence.

The Paradoxes of Violence

As J. Fred MacDonald points out, violence is inevitable in the Western given "the scenario of a world where adult men moved about their society with firearms strapped to their hips and rifles and shotguns holstered on their saddles. This was the visualization of a civilization on the verge of anarchy."[55] In real life, such a social climate would have little appeal (or so we might have thought before the mass shootings of the last decade, the spread of concealed-carry laws allowing weapons in churches, schools, and even bars, and the proliferation of "Stand Your Ground" laws), but in imagination, violence can be more exciting than frightening. As historian W. Eugene Hollon observes in *Frontier Violence: Another Look*, "Generations of Americans have grown up accepting the idea that the frontier during the closing decades of the nineteenth century represented this country at its most adventurous as well as its most violent."[56] Many fans of the Western even took a kind of nationalist pride in this violence as something distinctively American, a strain of lawlessness that identifies the American character as bold, independent, and fearless. James Truslow Adams, Pulitzer Prize–winning social historian in the 1920s, describes the law on the frontier as tenuous: "In the rough life of the border there is scant recognition for law as law. Frequently remote from the courts and authority of the established communities left behind, the frontiersman not only has to enforce his own law, but he elects what laws he shall enforce and what he shall cease to observe."[57] Thus in the popular vision of the West, men with guns strapped to their hips ran roughshod over the respectable citizens cowering behind their locked doors, barroom brawls were a regular occurrence, poker games routinely exploded into violent confrontations, and every day at noon saw a gun duel in the main street. In these lawless surroundings, the only protection a man had was the gun on his own hip.

In *Gunfight: The Battle Over the Right to Bear Arms in America*, UCLA law professor Adam Winkler traces the history of gun rights and gun control in America, including in the West during the later nineteenth century. The frontier, he demonstrates, especially after the Civil War, was indeed awash in guns—not just the long guns (rifles and shotguns) that had been commonplace in America from colonial days but, more significantly, the small repeating handguns developed in the 1850s, and sold cheaply and in mass quantities by Samuel Colt.[58] Therefore, the ubiquitous presence of these guns in movie and television Westerns is based on fact. However, examined more closely, the historical record reveals some startling discrepancies between the myth of the West and the actuality. Research into frontier violence led historian W. Eugene Hollon to conclude that the Western frontier was "a far more civilized, more peaceful, and safer place than American society" in the third quarter of the twentieth century.[59]

Winkler found additional support for Hollon's argument in Robert Dykstra's study of the famous cattle towns of the frontier. Despite their fearsome reputations, these "wide-open" towns had surprisingly low rates of murder and other crimes. Consider Dodge City, Kansas (the setting for *Gunsmoke*): between 1877 and 1886, at its height as a cattle town, Dodge recorded only fifteen homicides, an average of 1.5 per year. Its most violent year, 1878, saw a total of five murders. Tombstone, Arizona, also recorded five in its worst year, 1881—but three of the five were on a single day, in the famous shootout at the OK corral between the Earps and the Clanton gang. In the rough mining town of Deadwood, South Dakota, the highest single-year murder toll in this period was four—a far cry from the picture painted by the recent highly-acclaimed HBO series about the town. Granted, the population of these towns was small enough that the murder rate might not have differed that much from the larger cities of the East. But even so, the number of deaths is dramatically lower than the image of the "lawless" frontier would suggest.[60] Virginia City, Nevada (setting for *Bonanza*) had a notorious reputation: rumor had it that someone was gunned down there every day before breakfast. But the truth was that, by 1900, "most cowboys admitted that they had never even seen a killing, much less killed a man themselves."[61] Though the open countryside was indeed a dangerous place, where outlaws, Indians, and wild animals menaced the traveler, within the city limits not only homicides but crimes like armed robbery, petty theft, rape, and assault were remarkably rare.

The primary reason for the low homicide rate, Dykstra reports, is that frontier towns routinely proscribed the carrying of weapons, particularly concealed weapons. While almost everyone carried firearms out in the wilderness, in town all comers were required to surrender their weapons to the local law officer, or leave them at one of the major entry points into town, or stow them in the livery stable with their horses. A photo taken in Dodge City about

1879 shows a large wooden billboard posted in the middle of the main road through town: "The Carrying of Firearms Strictly Prohibited." Dykstra's research revealed that, if the most common cause of arrest in these towns was "drunk and disorderly," the second most common was illegal possession of concealed weapons, a statistic that indicates lawmen in the Old West took their gun control ordinances seriously.[62]

Although this fact is wildly at odds with our image of the frontier West, it makes perfect sense. These small towns on the edge of the frontier were striving to become bigger, more civilized towns where people could pursue their lives in peace and security, raising families and building businesses. If the towns had been as lawless as the Western stories depicted them, settlers would have refused to come, investors would have taken their money elsewhere, and the urgently-desired growth and development would never have occurred.

So, if the reality was comparatively tame, where did the stories of the lawless frontier come from? According to Winkler, one crucial source was Buffalo Bill Cody's Wild West Show. In Cody's vision of the West, cowboys were always the good guys whose guns saved the day. His star attraction was Annie Oakley with her spectacular marksmanship and trick shooting, but Cody surrounded her act with mock shootouts, Indian attacks, and stagecoach robberies, all staged with maximum drama for the delight of the crowd. As Winkler remarks, "For entertainers, emphasizing violence on the frontier was a surefire way to sell tickets."[63] What was true for Buffalo Bill Cody in the 1890s was still true for Western movies in the 1920s and '30s—and for television Westerns in the 1950s.

Significantly, American audiences accepted this violence (quite sanitized by today's standards, though intense for the time), partly because they believed it to reflect historical accuracy, and partly because they thought the level of violence depicted was an appropriate response to life-threatening events like Indian attacks, cattle rustling, fence-cutting, and outlaws with guns.[64] But more important, audiences seem to have recognized that the violence in the Western existed not just for its own sake, but in service of a philosophical dialogue. As Horace Newcomb and Robert S. Alley argued, the Western is "America's primary story of social authority, of the legitimate and illegitimate uses of violence in the process of creating order, making civilization."[65]

So the key question becomes: what factors make violence legitimate and acceptable in the Western? To answer that, we have to ask a larger question about American attitudes toward violence and state authority generally.

The Rules of Self-Defense

The original American colonists brought with them the traditions of British common law. A key doctrine of that law is the "duty to retreat," by which persons who are attacked must do everything they can to avoid the confrontation before they are justified in defending themselves with violence. Only if retreat is impossible (if the victim's back is literally "to the wall") and the attacker is threatening "grievous harm," only then does fighting back count as legitimate self-defense.[66] The legal logic is clear: it takes two persons to fight. If one of them retreats, death will be avoided and the conflict can then be resolved in a court of law. One key function of the "duty to retreat," then, is to allow the state to keep a monopoly over the resolution of conflict between individuals—in short, to keep a monopoly on legitimate violence. Such a monopoly, by discouraging citizens from taking the law into their own hands, provides the foundation for a society of civility.

However, as a nation America early developed a different attitude toward this issue. In the nineteenth century, in what law professor Richard Maxwell Brown calls "one of the most important transformations in American legal and social history,"[67] the United States rejected the English common-law doctrine, instead asserting that standing one's ground to kill in self-defense was legally justified. In part, this change developed because, for nineteenth-century Americans, the "duty to retreat" came to be considered a doctrine of cowardice. This attitude was particularly pronounced in the Southern states where, throughout the nineteenth century, each gentleman was expected to defend his honor at the slightest offense. If one man insulted another publicly or cast doubts on his honor, the victim was expected to instantly challenge his offender to a duel—although some men shortened the process by pulling out a concealed weapon and shooting their opponent to death on the spot. One historian of gender and violence reports that, in the antebellum South, "courts and juries routinely acquitted those accused of homicide; it was an act of self-defense to shoot your enemy when you saw him, because he might shoot you the next time."[68] Even though many Southern states passed increasingly stringent laws against carrying concealed weapons, along with measures to control the sale of such weapons, the custom of the duel persisted in the region long after other parts of the country had given it up.[69] Like Southerners, Westerners in the nineteenth century also routinely took justice into their own hands, but for quite different reasons. On the frontier, men settled their quarrels themselves because they often had no alternative: the legal system was too tenuous and too thinly spread to intervene effectively.

But the two imperatives—the right to self-defense, and the conviction that violence is essentially uncivilized—persist in American culture, held in irresolvable tension. Anthropologist Margaret Mead described the contradictory cultural messages that confront American men: "We teach them to be tough and to stand up for themselves, and, at the same time, teach them that aggression is wrong and should be suppressed, and, if possible repressed."[70] In response to this contradiction, Mead observed, American boys develop a habit of wearing a "proverbial chip on the shoulder." Though they are forbidden to *start* a fight, if they can manipulate their opponent into knocking that chip off, they are entitled to respond aggressively, granted full sanction to "stand up for themselves." In this way, they can fulfill both halves of the contradiction, proving their manhood while still keeping the moral high ground.

The same contradiction is, of course, embodied in the rules of the classic Western gun duel: as long as the hero is not the first to draw, he can shoot his opponent without guilt. We see here the source of one of the major tropes of the Western: the bully who tries to provoke the hero into fighting, while the hero demonstrates his superior manhood by resisting such provocation as long as possible. As Mitchell explains, this heroic restraint is a key component of the Westerner's character; in fact, it is "essential to our most fundamental ideals of selfhood." However, the aesthetic problem for the Western is that restraint—a refusal to act—is very difficult to dramatize. It only exists dramatically in the presence, or potential presence, of violence.

> The Western signals restraint always *through* the body, in its vacillations and hesitations under the threat of danger—in eyes alerted to peril, or shoulders stiffened in response to a verbal slight, or the gesture of a hand hovering over a gunbelt. Before restraint can be said to exist dramatically, in other words, it needs to be needled, stretched, otherwise exacerbated by the continuing threat of violence.[71]

So the Western hero needs the villain's threatened violence in order to demonstrate his own moral superiority, and to allow the audience to appreciate both his courage and his restraint. As John Cawelti explains,

Particularly in a culture where social values are so confused and ambiguous about the relation between the individual and society, where some values place a great emphasis on individual aggressiveness and others emphasize social responsibility and conformity, the
fantasy of the hero who reluctantly, but nobly aids the cause of social order by acts of individual violence probably corresponds to a widespread fantasy of legitimated aggression.[72]

Thus in the Western, both audience and hero eventually get their needs satisfied. Inevitably,
the antagonist pushes too hard, freeing the hero to respond violently, and the audience gets
a two-fold reward: first the long-delayed adrenaline rush as aggression is released, then gratification at the moral superiority of our hero, his violence sanctioned and legitimatized.

In the 1950s, of course, ordinary middle-class men not only did not challenge each
other to gun duels, they seldom confronted antagonists with any kind of physical violence.
Real-life penalties for such aggression (particularly against a hierarchical superior) would
have been too severe. But the gunfight on the TV Western made an excellent fantasy substitute. As John Evans argued in 1962, "Through his vicarious position in the powerful and
final act of the gunfight, the factory worker or the organization man symbolically shoots
down all the individual officials and impersonal forces that restrict, schedule, supervise,
direct, frustrate and control his daily existence."[73]

Ironically, even while critics were celebrating the effectiveness of TV gunfights as a
vicarious release of tensions, the Western's popularity helped move the handgun from television fantasy to everyday reality. By 1958, MacDonald notes, weapons manufacturers were
turning out 10,000 Western-type guns monthly to meet consumer demand.[74] This new pattern must not have been without critics, for one handgun manufacturer in 1958, while admitting that the TV Western had materially influenced these numbers, insisted that "Western
TV shows, as well as Western movies, should be judged not on the fact that guns are
employed, but on whether the basic plot brings the Golden Rule out convincingly to young-
sters who are watching it."[75] That is, as long as the dramatic context emphasizes morality
and restraint, the resulting violence should be accepted as legitimate.

In any case, the violence in the Western had been effectively sanitized for the audience,
not only because the frontier was distanced in time, but because its era was so limited—a
few decades at the end of the nineteenth century. As Cawelti points out, the audience
knows—even as it watches the gunfights, the Indian raids, the outlaws attacking the town—
that civilization will shortly triumph. Unlike the challenges of contemporary life, the Western
gives us "a fictional justification for enjoying violent conflicts and the expression of lawless
force without feeling that they [threaten] the values or the fabric of society.... However
threatening he may appear at the moment, the Indian is vanishing and the outlaw is about
to be superseded."[76]

Weighed down by anxieties they were largely helpless to resolve, audiences in the 1950s
craved simplicity and clarity. The Western gave them a world in which social problems could
be solved by direct action, including violence if necessary. As MacDonald explains,

> What the TV Western was offering was open warfare, a protracted battle between obvious
> legality and illegality. At stake was control of civilization. There was neither time nor rea-
> son for studied response. The answer to each dilemma was obvious: enough strategy,
> enough muscle, enough gunpowder. Through the concerted application of the brains and
> brawn of good men, this form of adult entertainment showed, indeed advocated, an effi-
> cient way to tame the savage and rescue humanity.[77]

In the process of exploring such issues, the TV Westerns of the 1950s and 60s collectively
provided models for how a man was supposed to act: protecting the weak, facing down the

brigand (whether outlaw, marauding Indian, or tyrannical cattle baron) to prevent them from abusing the innocent, even while restraining his own violent impulses within the boundaries of a rigorous ethical code. The Western hero, in his purest form, sacrificed himself to make a better world for others, to transform a nearly-lawless frontier into a place where civilization could take hold. In a time of roiling anxiety about the masculinity of American men and the role of America in the world, these lessons of manhood spoke both to individual men in their families and to America as a champion of democracy and justice worldwide.

There is no way to know how many viewers took these lessons to heart and acted on them in the real world. Perhaps some of the idealistic college students who risked their lives to fight for civil rights for blacks in the south were inspired in part by the Westerner; certainly (as anecdotes reveal) some small but real percentage of the young men who volunteered to go fight in Vietnam were motivated by the television heroes of their childhood and adolescence. But even those who did not act on the lessons of the Western in such dramatic ways got comfort from seeing conflicts resolved so satisfactorily, and resolved, too, in 30-, 60- or 90-minute periods, week after week. As Dr. Dichter had assured advertisers, American viewers liked Westerns because, reliably, the good are rewarded and the bad punished. Above all, the conclusions are *tidy*; no loose ends are left hanging to provoke discomfort or reflection.

However, where Dr. Dichter sees gratifying simplicity, later critics of the genre see ambiguities. As Horace Newcomb observed, in the TV Western, often "the problems were far more believable than the solutions" offered at the end of the episode. "There was almost always one more dramatic beat following a gunfight or other violent confrontation," a hesitation, implying that the problem was not so much resolved as simply tabled, with no further discussion possible at that time. "Indeed," Newcomb continued, "the actual endings were often exclamation points on insoluble dilemmas."[78] Naturally, this pattern was more marked on some series than others—and on none more than *Have Gun—Will Travel*. Paladin (and, behind him, Richard Boone) is profoundly aware that violence solves nothing important. Though sometimes unavoidable, violence always signals a failure rather than a solution. More often than any other series of its time, *Have Gun—Will Travel* refused to offer its audiences false consolation or fairy-tale endings. Boone trusted that his viewers would be willing to contemplate uncomfortable ideas, if presented to them in the proper artistic form—and, in large numbers, they were.

Television viewers of the late 1950s and early 1960s struggled with significant psychic burdens. Anxious, pressured to conform in all aspects of life, threatened both by external enemies and internal fears of failure, no wonder they greeted the Westerns with enthusiasm, especially those which offered them more comfort and reassurance than challenges. But the psychic needs of the audience only partly explain the flood of Western series inundating television in this period. The rapidly changing priorities of the television industry made the Western an appealing choice for all three networks in the later 1950s, purely for business reasons. The next chapter explores those business reasons, and how the practicalities of television production in this period shaped our four series.

TWO

Television in the 1950s

In order to understand the place of the TV Western, we need to understand, at least in outline, how, and *why*, television changed between 1945 and 1960.[1]

Although the technology for broadcasting moving pictures and sound had been invented in the 1920s and '30s, development of television as a commercial entertainment system had to wait till after World War II. But once civilian affairs assumed priority again, the television industry developed rapidly, driven by the same ferment of energy and innovation that was transforming so many other aspects of American society in these years. By 1947, each of the oldest commercial networks, NBC, CBS, and ABC (along with a fourth, DuMont, which collapsed in 1956), were broadcasting a few programs, but those shows went out to only a small number of stations, mostly clustered in the large cities of the Northeast and the West Coast, plus a few Midwestern urban centers, like Chicago. The coaxial cable did not link the coasts until September 1951, and the system did not fully incorporate Southern stations till the mid–1950s.[2] When Eisenhower took office as president in 1953, there were no more than 108 television stations nationwide, while only twenty-four cities had two or more stations, allowing their residents a choice of programming.[3] In 1949, just ten percent of American families owned television sets—huge cumbersome cabinets with seven-inch picture tubes whose grainy black-and-white images often flickered or rolled or were obscured by the white dots of visual static called "snow."[4]

And what kinds of shows appeared on those tiny screens? During this period of experimentation, programming was wildly eclectic, produced by the sponsors rather than the networks. In the beginning, the networks' function was mostly technical: they supplied the trained personnel, the studios, cameras, and transmission equipment that delivered shows to viewers' television sets. It was the sponsors who chose their favorite performer or entertainment format and "bought" a time slot from a station or network (say, 9–10 p.m. EST on Sunday) in which to broadcast their show and advertise their products. Sporting events initially drew the greatest numbers of viewers (which is why the first television sets were mostly found not in private homes but in bars), but there were also numerous comedy and variety shows featuring the premier entertainers of the period, like Milton Berle, Jimmy Durante, Sid Caesar, Eddie Cantor, Dean Martin and Jerry Lewis, Abbott and Costello, and Bob Hope. There were also children's programs, talent shows, cooking shows, quizzes and game shows, and news. And, most prestigious of all, live drama—ten to fifteen hours per week of live drama in the early 1950s. But in television's first years the majority of shows, whatever their format, shared two characteristics: they were broadcast live, and most of them originated from New York City.

By 1960, virtually all of these conditions had changed. In less than fifteen years, the networks had become well-established and economically powerful. Starting with a handful of affiliate stations, each of the networks had built a nationwide organization that brought their programming into every state and every decent-sized city. The total revenue of networks and stations increased from $1.9 million in 1947 to $744.7 million by 1955, and to $1.16 billion by the end of the decade.[5] And the audience had expanded as well: by 1959 domestic television ownership had grown from ten percent of American families to ninety percent.[6] In ten years, TV had gone from a rare luxury to an essential feature of American cultural life.

Most dramatic of all, however, the type of programming available on television changed. Between 1953 and 1960, as the networks gained control and power at the sponsors' expense, TV shifted from a norm of live programming to a preponderance of series on film, and from anthology programs (featuring a different story and characters every week) to continuing-character series, whether in the action-adventure mode or domestic comedies. The production center shifted from New York to Hollywood, which represented not just a geographical relocation, but a wholly different set of technological processes and production values.

Underlying these major changes in the industry was a dispute about the proper role for the medium in American culture. In 1953 Sylvester "Pat" Weaver, the visionary head of programming for NBC from 1949 to 1956 (creator of *The Today Show* and *The Tonight Show*), urged NBC affiliates to see television not as a "living-room toy" but instead as the "shining center of the home."

> For if we keep this great service vital, if we make our programming serve all elements of our population, if we use entertainment to keep everyone watching, and use showmanship combined with scholarship to make that viewing have a positive influence through the inclusion of cultural and informational and enriching, enlightening material, then we, as much as any group of men in all the world, will affect the fate of the future. Television, by itself, can influence the world for good beyond all present thinking.[7]

But others took a less idealistic view. For them, television was a business, nothing more nor less than the greatest marketing medium in the world. With this perspective, Oliver Treyz, president of ABC television from 1956 to 1962, pulled his network out of a dismal third place and into financial solvency by filling his prime-time schedule with youth-oriented action-adventure series like *77 Sunset Strip, The Rifleman, Adventures in Paradise,* and *The Untouchables*, series which shared an emphasis on predictable plots, handsome leading men, and abundant violence. As Treyz saw it, Pat Weaver with his cultural ambitions had been "programming for people who shopped at Saks Fifth Avenue. I was programming for the people at Sears, Roebuck. There are more of them. They have the right to attention, too."[8] As the television system expanded in the mid–1950s to include the Midwest and the South, largely suburban and rural regions dominated by socially conservative viewers, the kinds of "Saks Fifth Avenue" programs Weaver advocated had become controversial. What Treyz called the "Sears, Roebuck" viewers complained about too-deep cleavage on women performers, about too many risqué jokes, too many dramas featuring "unsuitable" people— those who were working class or even poor, or socially deviant, or from an ethnic or religious minority. In the face of such reactions, sponsors grew nervous. Their object in sponsoring programs was to promote their products or their company to a broad public. If the programs offended too many viewers, the company would lose customers. Sponsors soon realized they would sell more cars, soap, cigarettes, floor wax and refrigerators by supplying a middle-brow audience with light entertainment than by satisfying a small cohort of high-culture viewers. It came down to a conflict in values, symbolized as the difference between New York and Hollywood: between live theatre and mass-market movies, between cultural adventurousness and conventionality, between art and entertainment.

By 1960, the conflict was over: Treyz and Hollywood had won, hands down, and television was confirmed as a mass medium appealing to a mass audience.[9] This transition from New York values to Hollywood laid the groundwork for the Western to dominate the television schedule in the latter half of the 1950s.

Hollywood and Television

In the 1940s, when television was still only a concept for the future, Hollywood's relationship to the incipient industry was a mixture of interest and anxiety. As William Boddy tells the story, on the one hand, many observers were convinced that film was the logical choice for filling most broadcast hours (some speculated as high as 90 percent). The major movie studios, with their technical expertise and their decades of experience in movie making, were in an ideal position to provide such programming. On the other hand, many worried that the standard-length movie would be much too long for viewing in a home setting. In fact, some critics argued that even an hour would be too long. Based on the model of radio programs, they believed the optimum program length for television was thirty minutes, which led them to predict that television would revive vaudeville, with its series of short variety acts.

Economics was also a serious concern. The per-minute cost of even low-budget Hollywood films was so high that it seemed prohibitive for television; sponsors, it was argued, would never agree to pay such prices. Compounding the problem, critics at the time were convinced that viewers would have no interest in watching programs a second time, so each expensive film would be broadcast only once and then consigned to a vault, with no opportunity for additional earnings—making them even less cost-effective.[10]

Despite these issues, in the 1940s the studios were sufficiently interested in television to invest in television research and in television production companies, broadcasting stations, and networks. They also explored the possibilities of pay television and "theater television"—the notion of broadcasting certain programs made for television on movie screens, in order to make television a more lucrative proposition.[11] Nor were the studios then opposed to the idea of producing original material for the new medium, though creating the right deal proved to be more challenging than anticipated. The studios naturally wanted the best prices they could get for their services, and threatened to withhold their talent and their story materials until they got a good deal. Just as naturally, companies like RCA wanted to acquire filmed programming for their future television ventures under conditions most favorable to them, and threatened in turn to cut the major studios out of the loop by turning to independent producers if the majors refused to cooperate.

In addition to the difficulties of the deal, there were other considerations calling for careful thought. Certainly the new medium created opportunities for Hollywood, but it also offered potentially serious competition. In providing material for television, the studios would be undercutting the profits from showing their movies in theatres. How many people would go out and buy tickets for something they could now get for free in their living rooms? Of course, for the studios, reduced movie income would be at least partially balanced by the money they earned from television productions; but for the movie theatre owners, the new scenario was pure disaster. Fewer movies to show meant less money for them. Their distress at the studios' flirtation with producing for television grew so intense that they threatened to boycott the films of any studio that supplied too much product to the new medium.[12]

This struggle mattered because, in the early years of television, there was a genuine market for filmed programs. For the new station operator, filmed programs were not only cheaper to acquire, but required less expensive technology and far fewer personnel to broadcast than the live programming supplied by the networks. So the standoff between the studios and the theater owners created opportunities for small independent producers to fill the gap. By 1949, numerous companies had sprung up to supply shows for television; unfortunately, the shows they created were mostly low-budget formula productions, either situation comedies or action-adventure genres like juvenile westerns, science fiction, crime and mystery, all built on stock characters, formulaic plots, moral oversimplification and the low-brow pleasures of spectacle and melodrama. The shows were created in assembly-line fashion, written by large stables of writers and shot very quickly—a sixty-minute episode in three days at most, thirty-minute shows often in less than a day. As Frederick Ziv, producer of *The Cisco Kid* (1950–56), admitted, "cheap" was the appropriate word for these productions, "not inexpensive, but cheap."[13] Despite these cost-saving measures, producing filmed series for television in those early days remained financially tenuous at best. Even though each episode may have been cheap, creating a successful series involved substantial up-front expenses. In order to sell a series to a sponsor, the producer would need at least thirteen, or even twenty-six episodes in the can, and even if the series sold, the producer might wait two or three years to recoup his original investment, as such syndicated programs were relegated by the networks to less favorable time slots with lower advertising revenues. No wonder producers reduced costs in any way possible. It was the only way to stay in business.[14]

As cheap as they were, in the early 1950s, these series were what represented Hollywood values on television: the old "B" film mentality. As Frederick Ziv explained:

> It was obvious to all of us who had our fingers on the pulse of the American public that they wanted escapist entertainment.... We did not do highbrow material. We did material that would appeal to the broadest segment of the public. And they became the big purchasers of television sets. And as they bought television sets, the beer sponsors began to go on television. And the beer sponsors, for the most part, wanted to reach the truck and taxi driver, the average man and woman. They were not interested in that small segment that wanted opera, ballet or symphony.[15]

Under these conditions, no wonder the prestige entertainment in television in the early 1950s was live drama rather than filmed series.

The Golden Age of Television

The sponsors who poured money and energy into the new medium created many different kinds of shows to advertise their products, but they lavished the greatest attention and money on the live drama anthologies, sponsored by prominent companies like Kraft Foods, Ford, U.S. Steel, General Electric, Armstrong, Alcoa, and Philco. Every week in the early 1950s, viewers could watch a dozen hours of adaptations and original dramas, 30 or 60 minutes long, a different story and different characters each week (hence the "anthology" label). A number of factors combined to make this kind of program the most highly regarded on television. To begin with, the earliest programs were mostly adaptations of classic liter-

ature—novels, short stories, and plays, from Shakespeare to the most recent Broadway hits—
or dramatizations of important historical events. This source material became a key selling
point for the anthologies. Edmund Rice of the J. Walter Thompson advertising agency
explained how the agency convinced audiences to tune in to *Kraft Television Theatre*. "The
actors were not top stars and the play was usually unfamiliar, so we attempted to get our
audience to expect a good story."[16] The tone of Rice's comment suggests that a "good story"
was not seen as a common feature of the other programs being broadcast at the time.

Second, the live drama anthologies attracted legions of talented artists, some from the
world of New York theater and some from the movie studios of Hollywood. A dramatic
downturn in Hollywood movie production after 1948, combined with the ominous spread
of blacklisting in the industry, led the studios to cancel standing contracts with hundreds of
skilled artisans.[17] Displaced and anxious, many of those people went to New York to look
for work in television: directors, writers, designers, technicians, and—probably most significant from the audience point of view—actors. Although television was technologically too
primitive and too limited by small budgets to attract Hollywood royalty (the Cary Grants,
the Clark Gables, the Jimmy Stewarts, the Marilyn Monroes), many actors in the second
tier, especially character actors and those who were beginning to age or who were stuck in
a typecasting rut, eagerly turned to television to refresh their careers and replenish their
bank accounts.[18] In addition, many of New York's established stage actors—drawn by the
prestige of the shows and the quality of the scripts—also performed on these programs,
either between productions, or even while they were appearing on stage, on Sunday nights
when their regular shows were dark. (This was possible because the television dramas had
a short rehearsal period, only six to eight days, and were performed just once). In addition
to providing showcases for such established professionals, the anthology shows became a
virtual theatrical stock company for a group of up-and-coming young actors, providing them
with intense training and experience in a wide variety of roles. Many of these performers
later became major stars in Hollywood, people like Paul Newman, Joanne Woodward, Rod
Steiger, Charlton Heston, Grace Kelly, and Jack Lemmon. Other less exalted names also
used these shows to establish solid acting careers, among them Richard Boone.[19]

In the early 1950s—described by director Arthur Penn as television's "fervent years"—
the energy and excitement of the creative team for these shows was intense.[20] Producing a
new 30- or 60-minute drama every week for 39 weeks of the season demanded all the
resources of everyone involved. The work hours were brutally long, the pressure unrelenting,
the learning curve steep, the pay low, the risk of failure often high, but the psychic rewards
of creating a dramatic production that viewers and critics applauded were likewise enormous.
It was an exciting time to be involved in television drama.[21]

Within a couple years, however, producers of the live drama anthologies encountered
a serious challenge: they were running out of works to adapt. The stories of popular Hollywood films were off-limits to television, protected by copyright, as were any recent Broadway
plays that had been turned into film, like William Inge's *Picnic*.[22] And, with so many anthology shows on the air, there was soon a glut of similar stories being broadcast. In desperation,
the producers began to solicit original scripts, and a group of bright ambitious young writers
responded enthusiastically, men like Paddy Chayefsky, Rod Serling, Reginald Rose, Gore
Vidal, Horton Foote, J. P. Miller, and Robert Alan Aurthur.[23] In February 1951, only 45
members of the Writers Guild of America reported working in television. By the end of the
year, that number had grown to 110. Fred Coe, legendary producer of *Philco Television Playhouse* who pioneered this strategy, had little money to offer the young writers; instead he

offered them his enthusiastic support and free rein to create their own stories.[24] In this atmosphere of trust, they created dramas of great power and variety. Of course, not every script produced in the Golden Age was brilliant. Given the vast numbers of plays involved—in the 1954-55 season alone, there were 343 plays produced on live network series,[25] plus another 400 or so on filmed anthology series—many would of course be pedestrian and conventional. But the number of memorable plays was astonishingly high in these few years. Many were later turned into stage plays or movies or both, including Paddy Chayefsky's *Marty,* Reginald Rose's *Twelve Angry Men*, William Gibson's *The Miracle Worker*, and J. P. Miller's *Days of Wine and Roses.*

Live Drama on Television

When television turned to live drama, the production teams quickly realized that the format shared certain features with the stage and others with movies, as well as a few with radio. These features dictated the kinds of stories best suited to television and the skills performers needed for the new medium. Live television drama demanded actors with stage training. As in a stage production, actors had to know all the dialogue cold, and had to be able to sustain the character from the beginning to the end of the performance. They also needed the skill to improvise their way out of emergencies. Actors who had only worked in movies were therefore at a serious disadvantage in live television. On film, the actor's work is done not in two-hour blocks but in tiny increments, sometimes only a couple of seconds long, and usually out of narrative order, so there is no need to remember large stretches of dialogue or business. Even more important, movie actors were accustomed to the safety net of multiple takes; if the first attempt, or even the second or third, was not successful, the scene could be redone as often as necessary. In live television, there were no retakes.

There were other technical challenges to performing drama live on television that determined which stories were appropriate for the format. First, the number of sets had to be severely limited because the early TV studios were tiny (most were former radio studios) and crowded with cameras and lights and other bulky equipment. Most of those sets needed to be interiors: outdoor sets on television, unlike the movies, inevitably looked artificial.[26] In any case, the panoramas and large-scale action scenes which the movies did so spectacularly were almost impossible to create in a television studio. Time constraints also created significant factors that the creative teams had to work around. As playwright Tad Mosel remembered:

> We learned to write pure Aristotelian plays with unity of time, place, and action because we had to. Take clothes, for example: if there wasn't a legitimate way to keep your actor off to change from a fur coat to a bathing suit you didn't do it. That meant you had to telescope time, and the same actor had to wear the same suit all the way through, so the play could not cover ten years. It was best to cover one or two days and focus on a single dramatic event.[27]

Time also presented another sort of challenge for live television. As with radio productions (and unlike the stage), the total run time had to be precisely calibrated to the second. But while the length of a radio play could be calculated fairly easily by counting the words (usually 140–150 words per minute), television plays typically included visual sequences with no words, so the timing could vary wildly from one rehearsal to the next.

Cast, director, and crew had to be prepared to speed up or slow down, to cut a scene or pad it, in order to fill the time exactly.[28]

The key feature which live television drama shared with the movies was the camera and the centrality of the close-up, that intimate connection with the face of the actor in which the tiniest changes in expression carried the story: a lifted eyebrow, a hesitant smile, a narrowing of the eyes, a trembling or tightened lip revealed everything the character was feeling. In television, this emphasis on close-ups was partly pragmatism: one of the easiest ways to cover a set change or conceal an action from the viewers—for example, to allow a "corpse" to walk invisibly off the set—was to shift to close-ups, so that one or two actors' faces filled the screen. But this technique also suited the style of plays being done on live television, where "the human face became the stage on which drama was played."[29] Fortunately for the producers, in the early 1950s a new generation of American actors had passionately adopted Method acting. In contrast to older acting traditions, which relied on external techniques of body and voice to convey the character's emotional state, Method acting emphasized matching the actor's emotional state to that of the character. For the Method actor, the small changes in facial expression and the gestures that convey emotion appear naturally in response to the character's mental state. Method acting, then, proved the ideal approach for taking advantage of the camera's penetrating scrutiny.

Despite these technical challenges of time and space, as Erik Barnouw argues, the creators of these dramas—producers, directors, and writers alike—"were not inclined to think of live drama as a limiting factor; it merely influenced the kind of drama to be explored. They found its niche in compact rather than panoramic stories, in psychological rather than physical confrontations."[30] That is, television proved ideally suited to an intensified dramatic realism requiring nothing but a handful of characters on the simplest sets. Character was more important than plot, language more vital than action. As a script editor observed in 1953, "Live TV is limited in scope: that is, it cannot depend upon broad panorama, colossal montages, or the thrill of the hunt or chase to help the limping script. Literally, the 'words are the thing,' and in nine out of ten TV shows, the climax depends upon what the characters say rather than what they do."[31]

Kitchen Drama: Marty

Paddy Chayefsky, one of the most distinguished of the Golden Age playwrights, devoted considerable thought to the qualities that made a good television play: "In those days, practically anything made a story—it was a kind of miniature work that was required, the equivalent of a short story. You could take any impulse and make a show of it." Chayefsky points out, "There is far more exciting drama in the reasons why a man gets married than in why he murders someone."[32] A case in point: Chayefsky's first big hit, *Marty* (1953), considered by many critics the best TV drama of the period. *Marty* tells the story of a young unmarried butcher, short and stocky (he calls himself a "fat little man"), thirty years old and still living with his mother, who pushes him to find a wife. Marty reluctantly goes to a dance at a ballroom, where he meets Clare, a skinny schoolteacher. Though his friends and his mother run Clare down and discourage his interest, Marty finally decides to defy them and pursue the relationship. That's the whole story. Neither in setting, tone, nor character does this play resemble a typical Hollywood romance: there is no trace of glamour or of the conventional issues of romantic relationships in the movies. As part of his philosophy of dramatizing the lives of ordinary people, Chayefsky often deliberately chose protagonists like Marty and Clare (played on television by Rod Steiger and Nancy Marchand) who defied Hollywood standards of beauty. Like the story and characters, the language of the play is utterly ordinary. Chayefsky explains, "I tried to write the dialogue as if it had been wire-tapped."[33] For example, when Marty and his unmarried pals gather on Saturdays, their conversation is plain, prosaic: "Well, what do you feel like doing tonight?" "I don't know. What do you feel like doing?"

Some critics dismissed such stories as "ashcan drama" or "kitchen drama," lacking in glamour and exciting action.[34] But Chayefsky argues, "What we did was to dramatize the lives of those people out there in the audience, and we contributed what any artist is supposed to contribute, some sort of understanding. It's the job of the artist to let his audience have some insight into its otherwise meaningless pattern of life."[35] Audience reactions to *Marty* indicated that Chayefsky had succeeded in his goal, although nobody involved with the show realized it at first. Ten minutes after the broadcast ended, the studio was empty, the sets down, everybody gone home. But the next day, the influential *New York Times* reviewer Jack Gould devoted his whole column to *Marty*. Although the review was not a rave, it was a serious analysis in a time when television drama seldom got much attention.[36] Even more important was the reaction of ordinary viewers. Years later, Rod Steiger recalled the morning after the broadcast. As he walked to the coffee shop for his breakfast, people repeatedly greeted him: "What are we going to do tonight, Marty?" Steiger would return the line in character: "I don't know, what do you want to do?" After the third or fourth such encounter, Steiger knew that something special had happened: "This play touched the core of loneliness in the average man and swept across the country." Delbert Mann, who directed the production for *Philco Television Playhouse* (and later the Hollywood film) agreed: "That show brought more phone calls and letters than any show we ever did. They were universally, 'My God, that's the story of my life. How could you have played it so truly?' People were crying on the phone."[37] Something powerful was happening on American television.

And, as all the commentators agreed, the writer was at the center of that power, the key to the artistic promise of live television drama.[38] Partly, this emphasis on the writer was a simple acknowledgment of the truth: when drama is focused so heavily on character rather than plot or action, obviously the writer's craft gains prominence. However, pragmatic considerations also led to the highlighting of the writer's role. Small production budgets made it impossible for producers to hire big-name actors, and, with a different story each week, there were no continuing characters to draw audience loyalty, so they needed another way to attract attention. An inspired press agent for NBC's *Philco Television Playhouse* told producer Fred Coe, "You know, Fred, you can't afford stars. Publicize the playwrights."[39] Advertisements would promise, "Another Rod Serling story tonight," "A new play from the author of *Marty*." The fact that writers were creating original works especially for television marked the drama anthologies as "an arena for individual, distinctive artistry," in contrast to mass-produced Hollywood movies.[40] As a result, despite the minuscule financial rewards (before 1955, a 60-minute script netted its author between $500 and $1,500),[41] television playwrights in the "Golden Age" of the 1950s had nearly as much prestige as the playwrights of the legitimate theatre.

Unlike the Hollywood screenwriter who (then as now) was regarded as the least important member of the production team, seldom mentioned in the publicity and given no say over the script once it was submitted, the television playwright was granted considerable control over any changes to the script and treated as an honored contributor during the rehearsal period. Until the moment of broadcast, the work "belonged" to the writer. Even more important, after the broadcast, he could find himself widely discussed, even famous, his work analyzed seriously by critics in major publications. Such attention could make a writer's career. Consider the experience of Rod Serling, whose first major teleplay, "Patterns," was praised so highly by the *New York Times* that it was immediately given an unprecedented second live staging. Within two weeks of the broadcast, Serling had received twenty-three offers for television writing assignments, three offers to write motion picture screenplays, and fourteen requests for interviews from leading magazines and newspapers, plus two offers from publishers to discuss novels.[42] Although his was the most extreme example, he was far from alone in receiving such attentions. With such exhilarating approval from so many sources, it must have been easy to believe that the Golden Age of television would flourish for a long time.

The End of the "Golden Age"

But Golden Ages are often short-lived, and this one was no exception, all too soon undermined by an irresistible combination of forces: first, by the timidity of the sponsors; second, by the ruthless financial interests of the networks; and third, by the complacence of the audience, willing to settle for formulaic entertainment of the most undemanding kind. In this handful of years, Pat Weaver's idealistic vision of television elevating and enlightening American audiences while entertaining them was replaced by a philosophy of appealing to the lowest common denominator—and audiences accepted the change with little protest.

The slide started with the sponsors. At first, the advertising agencies who represented the sponsors' interests had paid little attention to the drama shows, because relatively few people were watching. But by the end of 1953, the shows began to garner serious attention. They were winning Emmy awards for their writers, directors, and performers, and the ratings soared. But even more significant, the television critics began to write frequently about the dramas. Where a filmed series like *I Love Lucy* (1951–1961) or *Dragnet* (1952–1970) might be reviewed only once or twice a season, a live drama series might get forty national newspaper reviews, usually at least twenty-five per season. Indeed, according to an NBC survey, the newspaper space devoted to television increased 500 percent between 1953 and 1955, and much of that reporting was focused on the live dramas.[43] Once the advertising agencies realized audiences were watching, they began to pay more careful attention to the shows. As director Arthur Penn remembered, "It started with, 'Oh, God, is she going to say that?' or 'Can you get her not to have such a dirty nose?' Then it went to 'Can we see the scripts before rehearsals begin?' The pressure got worse and worse." Delbert Mann concurred: the sponsors of *Playhouse 90*, he said, wanted "more conventional drama," in place of what they had started to call the "neurotic playhouse."[44]

Despite the favorable reactions of audiences and critics, the advertising agencies hated what they saw on the live dramas. As Erik Barnouw points out, the reasons for their distress are not mysterious:

> Most advertisers were selling magic. Their commercials posed the same problems that [*Marty*] dealt with: people who feared failure in love and in business. But in the commercials there was always a solution as clear-cut as the snap of a finger: the problem could be solved by a new pill, deodorant, toothpaste, shampoo, shaving lotion, hair tonic, car, girdle, coffee, muffin recipe, or floor wax. The solution always had finality.
>
> Chayefsky and other anthology writers took these same problems and made them com-

plicated. They were forever suggesting that a problem might stem from childhood and be involved with feelings toward a mother or father. All this was often convincing—that was the trouble. It made the commercial seem fraudulent.[45]

Worse, the protagonists of the live dramas, so ordinary, so plain, so often working class or marginal for some other reason, were not the right sort of people for the advertisers' purposes, nor living in the right neighborhoods with the right lifestyle. As one advertiser explained, in refusing to support a series of telecasts based on Elmer Rice's Pulitzer-prize–winning play *Street Scene*, no agency would want to have its products associated with the squalid atmosphere of Rice's slum setting. "On the contrary, it is the general policy of advertisers to glamorize their products, the people who buy them, and the whole American social and economic scene.... The American consuming public as presented by the advertising industry today is middle class, not lower class; happy in general, not miserable and frustrated."[46]

Naturally, sponsors wanted their products shown in a favorable light on the television shows they supported financially, and often mandated extreme conditions to produce this end: for example, one coffee manufacturer forbade the mention of tea on any program it sponsored, and certain cigarette makers insisted that no other tobacco products, like cigars or chewing tobacco, be referred to on their shows.[47] Sometimes sponsors even objected to ordinary English words that seemed to refer to a competitive product. As Rod Serling explained in 1960, "You can't 'ford' a river if it's sponsored by Chevy; you can't offer someone a 'match' if it's sponsored by Ronson lighters."[48]

But the impulse to control went deeper than product treatment. Most sponsors were also anxious to avoid any suggestion of controversy in their shows. This is not really surprising: the formative years of television, 1948–1952, were also the heyday of Senator Joseph McCarthy and the blacklist. The witch hunt atmosphere, especially intense in Hollywood and the New York theatre community, could not but impact television at a time when its program patterns, business practices, and institutions were being shaped. As Erik Barnouw observed in a memorable metaphor, television, "evolving from a radio industry born under a military influence and reared by big business, now entered an adolescence traumatized by phobias. It would learn caution, and cowardice."[49] Rod Erickson, a long-time advertising man for Procter and Gamble, the largest advertiser on television, explained the thinking of his company: "Controversy divides your audience. Half the people will hold it against you. The other half will think you're wonderful but they won't buy your product, so what's the purpose? Procter bent over backwards to avoid controversy. They don't want one box of something not to be bought."[50] As the advertising manager for Procter and Gamble elaborated to the FCC in 1961,

> The writers should be guided by the fact that any scene that contributes negatively to the public morale is not acceptable. Men in uniform shall not be cast as heavy villains or portrayed as engaging in any criminal activity. There will be no material in any of our programs which could in any way further the concept of business as cold, ruthless and lacking in all sentiment or spiritual motivation. If a businessman is cast in the role of villain, it must be made clear that he is not typical but is as much despised by his fellow businessmen as he is by other members of society.[51]

In the mid–1950s it seemed that practically every topic of substance could be construed as controversial. Subjects with even the faintest hint of sexual implications, more strictly censored on television than on the radio, led the list of taboos. Political issues were off-limits, especially anything referring even obliquely to race relations. No character could express an antisocial attitude, unless it was immediately contradicted by other characters. Labor and the workplace were beyond the pale of acceptable topics for drama; even irony and satire were viewed with suspicion.[52] In fact, one advertising director defined "controversial" programs for the FCC as stories which represented "one group in conflict with another."[53] The advertising director for General Motors went further, informing the Office of Network Study in 1960 that his company's definition of unacceptable controversy included too much emotional intensity, even if the eventual outcome was satisfactory: "Generally speaking, it would certainly be desirable not to have commercial placement in a program where the first act or second act might end at a very high emotional pitch, or a show that is constantly one of a highly emotional nature."[54] When all these injunctions were obeyed, writers were left with a very narrow range of stories they could tell, and almost none of any social significance.[55] Small wonder that many of the best writers, in despair and disgust, turned away from television to write for less constricted (and better-paying) venues. The way was being cleared for a very different kind of programming: not the realistic problems of ordinary people, but stories of adventure and excitement—like the Western.

The Networks Take Control

The networks, too, contributed substantially to the radical changes in the schedule. Essentially, by the mid–1950s, they had finally grown powerful enough to take control of programming away from the sponsors. Instead of a schedule over which the networks had little control, in which sponsors put their chosen program into a time slot they "owned," now the networks began to create and license the programs they wanted, and to schedule those programs on the days and times that gave them maximum competitive advantage. When sponsors paid for a whole program themselves, they could dictate the content; in the new model, networks sold commercial inserts in each of their programs to many different sponsors, diluting sponsor control. Thus empowered, the networks quickly dropped the prestigious live drama anthologies and the comedy/musical variety shows they had championed to turn to alternative programming. Why the change? Though there were several factors involved, the short answer, of course, is money. The comedy/variety shows, with their large casts and crews and many expensive headliners, had grown increasingly costly to produce; the live dramas, so often controversial, required burdensome oversight, especially when each live show could be broadcast only once. As a result, the networks were eager for more efficient and cost-effective alternatives—and this time, Hollywood was ready to negotiate with its rival.

The turning point came in 1953, when ABC-TV, trailing far behind NBC and CBS in ratings, merged with Paramount Theatres, thereby acquiring not only a large cash infusion but also executives who understood film.[56] The following year, ABC beat out the other networks to create the first arrangement with a major studio to produce shows for television. In a mutually beneficial deal, Disney Studios agreed to produce a series of lavish movie-style series for ABC, while the network, above and beyond the generous purchase price of $50,000 for each episode, invested $500,000 in the amusement park Walt Disney was building in Anaheim, California—a little place to be called Disneyland.[57] As a result of this deal, Disney Studios was able to reach a mass audience to promote both its theatrical movies and the new theme park, and ABC acquired a highly popular and profitable product. In the first few months of the deal alone, the three episodes of *Davy Crockett* made an overnight star of Fess Parker, sold coonskin caps and Davy Crockett lunch boxes by the millions, and catapulted "The Ballad of Davy Crockett" to the top of the music charts, while ABC's ratings soared. The transformation of television had begun.

In 1955, ABC made a deal with a second studio, Warner Brothers, which netted the network series like *Cheyenne*, *Maverick*, *77 Sunset Strip*, and *Bourbon Street Beat*. This arrangement, too, benefitted both network and studio. Because the shows were being produced by major studios, sponsors and ad agencies were initially deferential, reducing pressures for control of content, and allowing the networks to mandate that series stars be spared an obligation to do commercials. For the studios, the economics of filmed episodic television were strikingly advantageous: per-episode budgets were tiny, and since at the time there were no agreements about sharing residual receipts with the artists, the studios walked away with the bulk of the profits.[58] In the wake of these deals, other major Hollywood studios also began producing film series for television. It was, as J. Fred MacDonald argued, the "triumph of industry economics over television aesthetics."[59]

As filmed series arrived in greater numbers, the live drama anthologies that had been the heart of the television schedule began to disappear—dwindling from fourteen in 1955-56 to seven in 1957-58, down to only one, *Playhouse 90*, in 1959–60. In their place came more and more episodic filmed series with continuing characters, mostly Westerns, crime shows, and situation comedies. As a result, between 1955 and 1959, American television programming reached an unprecedented level of homogeneity.[60]

This change created many advantages for the networks: not only were filmed series less expensive to acquire and broadcast, but the networks did not have to undertake the risk or expense of developing new series themselves. They could push those costs off onto the production companies, while retaining a percentage of the revenue generated by a successful series for themselves, and at the same time, they could reduce the power of sponsors and advertisers to control programming.[61] In addition, using filmed series solved the many technical challenges of broadcasting a live program across multiple time zones. A show broadcast live in New York at 9 p.m. Eastern time would either have to air live at 6 p.m. in California—no one's definition of "prime time"—or could be shown at 9 p.m. Pacific time only by broadcasting a kinescope of the performance. To make a kinescope, the originating studio simply aimed a camera at a monitor and recorded the performance on 16 mm film. Then the kinescope would be flown to stations further west in time to be rebroadcast at 9 p.m. local time. But the visual quality of kinescopes was significantly inferior to the live broadcasts, and the entire process was both cumbersome and expensive, whereas series on film could be rebroadcast as many times as the network wanted (or the audience would accept). Film also created opportunities for the kinds of action and spectacle that were impossible to create in a live studio production—for example, in the Western. By 1955, shifting from live programming to film was a proposition that no businessman could afford to overlook—as long as audiences continued to watch.

What the Audience Wanted

The primary purpose of television programming was (and is) to attract sufficient viewers to watch the sponsor's advertisements. That is what the sponsors pay the networks for, and what drives network choices about which series to purchase, to broadcast—or to cancel.

Ratings quickly became the ultimate determinant of television success. Beginning in 1950, television research companies like A.C. Nielsen, Arbitron, and others began to supply the measurement statistics that networks and sponsors relied on to guide their decisions. Originally, each network attempted to create a "balanced" schedule, with shows that appealed to a variety of audiences. If the network's shows averaged decent audiences across the whole schedule, that was considered satisfactory. But eventually a new mandate came down from the executive suites: the objective now must be to win every time period.[62] Once that became the measure of success, a series that drew low numbers of viewers compared to the competing shows on other networks in the same time period—even if its audience rated in the millions, and came from a desirable demographic—would be cancelled as insufficiently profitable. In the ratings game, quantity soon outranked quality.[63]

And what was it audiences wanted, based on the ratings? By the later 1950s, it was clear that the visionaries who had celebrated television as a medium for education and innovation had misjudged their viewers. As J. Fred MacDonald observed, "To the mass audience, television was an escapist utility, not a pedagogical device. As a simple way to transcend the complications of daily living, most Americans preferred programming that was trivial or facile or silly."[64] In the early 1950s, while sophisticated viewers were applauding the live drama anthologies, the mass audience wanted situation comedies. For three seasons in a row (1952–5), *I Love Lucy* was the number-one-rated show in the country.[65] According to numerous commentators, this preference for the "trivial and facile" reflects the dominant American culture at the time, which demonstrated a marked unwillingness to confront serious problems. Charles Winick wrote in 1959 that TV represented "a fairly accurate mirror of the more conservative values of our society. As a result, the medium has difficulty in treating many subjects that have been artistically rewarding in other media."[66] Playwright Reginald Rose seconded this judgment, observing in an interview years later that most of the criticism of the live drama anthologies came from the right wing, from conservatives.[67] Barnouw describes this same phenomenon in overtly political terms. During the Eisenhower years, he argues, television was dominated by the values associated with the Republican party: pro-business, pro–traditional family, a white middle-class mainstream Protestant middle–America, exemplified most clearly in the domestic comedies of the period, like *The Adventures of Ozzie and Harriet, Father Knows Best,* and *Leave It to Beaver.* The affiliation was so close in these years that, as Barnouw put it, the broadcasting industry became virtually an arm of the government: "Prime-time programming, in particular, reflected the alliance—not only in its restraints and taboos, but also in ideas it furthered. And 'entertainment,' rather than news programs, seemed to play the dominant role."[68]

With all its potential as a journalistic and educational tool, television in the 1950s had been allowed to become almost exclusively an instrument for light entertainment and commerce. The networks devoted only 15 minutes a night to national news (the programs did not expand to 30 minutes nightly until 1963). Another handful of shows, like the CBS documentary series *See It Now* with Edward R. Murrow, attempted to address larger cultural or political issues, but by mid-decade such programs were carefully excluded from prime time, shunted off to late-night slots or Sunday afternoons, when few people were watching. The result, Barnouw concludes, is that American TV viewers in the 1950s were not only largely unaware of the problems facing the country, but were unaware that they were unaware, not realizing that anything significant had been left out of the national discourse.

This was particularly true for younger viewers, who seldom watched the news. They learned about the larger world, about what constituted "the good and great" (in Barnouw's words) not from the news but from the filmed series they watched for five or six hours every day. The domestic comedies taught them that all families were white and securely middle class, that all parents were loving, and that any problem could be solved in thirty minutes. The action-adventure series taught other lessons. As Barnouw put it, "Telefilms rarely invited the viewer to look for problems within himself. Problems came from the evil of other people, and were solved—the telefilm seemed to imply—by confining or killing them."[69] The telefilms of the 1950s taught viewers to look for scapegoats, and for heroes who would subdue the villain of the week, preferably by force. Sex and violence suddenly dominated the action-adventure series of the period, a pattern promoted by Robert Kintner, president of NBC, as a way of attracting a younger audience—although in this prudish atmosphere, "sex" meant showing Clint Walker of *Cheyenne* with his shirt off as often as possible. Before this period, as one network executive commented, "You didn't see male bodies on network TV."[70]

The action-adventure series followed a predictable formula: "handsome people in violent or potentially violent situations, moral dilemmas easily comprehended and resolved, a physical setting that gratified the audience [like the Old West, or an exotic locale like Hollywood or Hawaii or New Orleans], characterization that invited viewer identification, and memorable mannerisms that carried over from episode to episode."[71] Generally upbeat, the stories featured uncontroversial social values and recurring characters played by attractive performers. As a result, the shows provided the audience with a feeling of comfort and security. As Eric Barnouw notes, "Each program [of an episodic series] was a variation of an approved ritual. Solutions, as in commercials, could be clear-cut."[72]

This audience desire for the familiar and predictable partly explains why television can be defined by a succession of programming trends: first came the comedy-variety shows, then the filmed situation comedies, then the quiz shows, then the Westerns, each genre a set of variations of a basic formula. This pattern, called *recombinance*, is characteristic of an industry that is more interested in marketing the proven than in taking risks. As media sociologist Todd Gitlin explains, "Consumers want novelty but take only so many chances; manufacturers ... want to deploy their repertory of the tried-and-true in such a way as to generate novelty without risk."[73] We still see it in television today: a new hit program prompts the creation of additional series with the same features (whether that feature is doctors, lawyers, private detectives, or police) until a drop in ratings suggests viewers have gotten bored with the formula, and then a new trend emerges, and the pattern repeats.[74] The formula of *Wagon Train* could be transformed into *Riverboat*, and later into *Star Trek*, famously described as "*Wagon Train* to the stars." The Warner Brothers series *77 Sunset Strip* (1958–1964), whose formula included a pair of clever attractive detectives plus a comic sidekick, soon got translated into different locales as *Hawaiian Eye*, *Bourbon Street Beat* (set in New Orleans), and *Surfside Six* (Miami).[75] The series were so closely related that actors could be moved from one show to another, and occasionally even the characters from one series put in guest appearances on a sister series.[76]

Recombinance also offered economic advantages to the industry. As MacDonald points out, because television required hundreds of hours per month of new programs, the studios needed urgently to maximize the use of production facilities and personnel in order to turn out enough film. If a quarter of the shows being produced were all of the same genre—Westerns, for example—then sets used on one series could easily be used on others. If a genre demanded performers with a specific set of skills, like riding horses and quick-drawing pistols, it was easier to collect a set of actors and stuntmen with those skills if there were numerous series to support their work. This desire for economy and cost-effectiveness affected many decisions about series. For example, following Universal's successful movie about a riverboat gambler (starring Tyrone Power), Warner Brothers was approached to turn it into a series. Bill Orr, head of television for Warner Brothers, objected, "We don't have a riverboat or a lake. We'd have to build them. We have a lot of Western sets. Make him a Western gambler."[77] Just that easily, *Maverick* was born. In short, MacDonald argues,

> Nothing less than the rationalization of a new industry was occurring in the late 1950s. Standardization of product, reliance on familiar formulas, use of mass production techniques by the film studios and networks: national TV, like national culture, was emerging as an efficient, streamlined reality that existed to please the majority, a majority that in great part it had helped to create. Programmers were bringing regularity and controllability to their fare. No surprises here, with regularized genres, regularized plots, and regularized characterization. Everything was being brought under control so advertisers could be enticed to spend billions of dollars in a safe and predictable medium.[78]

The Western is a classic example of recombinance in action—and also an object lesson in its dangers. By the fall of 1959, there were twenty-eight Western series on network prime-time, nearly a quarter of prime time programming. In the late 1950s, it seemed that every series idea brought to the networks was turned into a Western. *Have Gun—Will Travel*, in fact, had originally envisioned a trench-coated soldier-of-fortune in 1950s New York, and had to be translated to 1870s San Francisco in order to win acceptance from the network. At the peak of the phenomenon, sixty million viewers were watching these Westerns each week. However, despite the success of some of these series, a large proportion of them failed, cancelled after only one or two seasons, or even less. The formula had been repeated too often and spread too thin. In their inexperience, the networks pushed a single pattern too intensively. The result? Inadvertently, "The networks had allowed regularization to become monotony. When the Western began its decline by 1960, it collapsed rapidly and definitively."[79]

The Triumph of Hollywood

Once the bulk of television production shifted from New York to Hollywood and from live to film, the production values changed entirely. The shift to film allowed for more action, more spectacle than had been possible with live drama, but also prompted an emphasis on melodrama rather than the more subtle psychological studies of the live dramas, and considerably more violence. As Bill Orr of Warner Brothers acknowledged, in Hollywood "we probably didn't make as good theatrical efforts as they did in New York, but let's put it this way, the audience got bigger and bigger, so I guess it was for the better."[80]

The heaviest impact of the change fell on the actors and the writers. Where the live dramas depended on skilled actors with stage experience, the filmed series, according to Orr, needed only "attractive people with good personalities. They didn't have to be good actors. That wasn't what was selling our shows."[81] Rod Steiger, with much experience in both live television and film work, commented that the shift to film "made it possible for a lot of actors who weren't ready to survive because they could always do it over. I think it lowered the level of professionalism."[82] As a woman, Bethel Leslie experienced the contrast of values in a particularly pointed way: "When I went out to Hollywood, the first thing they did was fit me with falsies that went out to here. The whole atmosphere was different. In New York, there was always a sense that what was important was the work and the performance. Out there, the hair and the lighting was most important."[83] Anne Howard Bailey, who wrote for television both in New York and Hollywood, commented sourly on the quality of many Hollywood actors involved in these series, even some of the stars. She singled out Troy Donahue, cast successively on *Surfside Six, Hawaiian Eye,* and *77 Sunset Strip,* who "couldn't remember how to say hello. It would take ten takes for him to learn to say two lines because he couldn't remember them. None of those people ever learned their lines. It was just madness."[84]

As for the writers, the change from live drama to episodic television cost them both professional prestige and satisfaction in their work. By definition, the episodic series was formulaic and as rigidly structured as a sonnet. Each script, whether 30 or 60 minutes long, had to be built to exacting rhythms: a brief "teaser" at the beginning to catch the audience, a strong climax at the end of each "act" to hold viewers through the commercials that followed, and a "kicker" at the end, either to wrap up the episode or provide a preview of the next week's installment. Not only was the structure rigid, but the content was highly constrained. The main characters, themes, and basic plot possibilities of a series were defined in the pilot, and subsequent episodes were required to conform to those outlines, duplicating the patterns with only minor variations. The continuing characters in a series needed to maintain their defining personality traits week after week, while creating the impression that they were developing and growing. Certainly they could never die, or take any action that would change their lives irreversibly—by getting married, for example. So the audience knew that, whatever terrible dangers might threaten Matt Dillon or Little Joe Cartwright or Paladin in a given week, the hero would survive to return in the next episode, significantly unchanged. Nor, living in an eternal television present, would the leading characters even retain memories of the dramatic events that we had watched them survive. Therefore, the variety that audiences also craved must come from "guest" characters who are able to do the things that the heroes cannot—develop, change, or even die, while the hero functions as a catalyst in their action.[85] This pattern gives audiences what they most desire (now, as in the 1950s): the familiar well-loved characters, whom we feel we know from watching them week after week, engaged in exciting new adventures which display the characters' most valued personality traits.

Though audiences were satisfied, the move from New York to Hollywood cost television writers dearly. With so many constraints on their work, writers dwindled from respected independent artists to minor craftsmen, useful but little respected, and only marginally rewarded financially. Although substantial money was available for the writer who could create a marketable concept for a continuing-character series, thereby acquiring a share in its syndication and subsidiary revenues, the writer of an individual script for a series received only a flat fee per script—no name recognition, and no continuing involvement with the script. Unlike the live dramas, there was no rehearsal period for rewrites, and the writer was kept off the set during production.[86] The networks' view of the writer's role was stated quite baldly. Ross Davidson, director of Program Services at NBC, described the successful TV writer circa 1961: "Our candidate is a healthy, and probably young, realist who has ... discarded *for the moment* any idea of revolutionizing television so that it works for *him*. He is an adaptable artist."[87] The same year, ABC executive Daniel Melnick observed that the new action-adventure programs called for "a different type of television writer, one who doesn't have a burning desire to make an original statement."[88]

By 1958-59, there were few options available for television writers except action-adventure series. The *Television Market List* for that winter, published by the Writers Guild of America-West, listed 103 series, 69 of them in the action-crime-mystery category.[89] Faced with such similar formulas, the writers not only stole plots from Shakespeare and the classics, they borrowed from other series. Writer Douglas Heyes commented, "A couple of my *Maverick*'s turned up on *77 Sunset Strip*. All they did was take it out of the West and put it on Sunset Strip." Marion Hargrove, another experienced television writer of the period, admitted he frequently borrowed the plot of Agatha Christie's classic *Ten Little Indians* for his scripts, including one he wrote for *Maverick* (an episode called "Black Friar").[90] Clearly, the move to the west coast had changed the television writer's job, and not for the better, from the writers' point of view. As Anne Howard Bailey lamented, "In New York, we really tried to come up with quality scripts. In Hollywood, you quickly understood that all they were concerned about was mass appeal, to feed America's limitless desire for cheap, quick entertainment. Nobody ever wanted anything out of the ordinary. I tried to sell controversial stuff, but they never wanted anything that had to do with a racial problem, for example."[91] Another television writer, Manny Rubin, complained, "TV writing has become a hack job. It has conformed too readily to commercial restrictions, and of all the giants who bow before the magniloquent power of the camera, I believe the writer's loss is the greatest of all."[92]

So, in the latter half of the 1950s, television drama moved west and adopted a whole new set of values and priorities, designed to appeal to a mass audience looking for light entertainment rather than intellectual challenge or enlightenment. The Western series of the period largely reflected those new values. However, within the constraints of mass market episodic television, the creators and producers of *Gunsmoke, Wagon Train, Have Gun—Will Travel*, and *Bonanza* tried to do more than pander to the audience's lowest instincts. They strove to offer their audiences something of value. Each series, in its own way and within the limits of the producers' imagination, used the Western context to speak to the concerns of its contemporary viewers. What makes *Have Gun* stand out from its competitors is the intellectual rigor and high aesthetic standards maintained by the series, the insistence on excellence in writing, acting, and directing that grew directly from the influence of its star and de facto producer, Richard Boone, especially his experience in live television drama. In Chapter Three, we'll examine the qualities that Boone brought to the series, and the life experiences that shaped him.

THREE

Richard Boone:
An Unreasonable Man

"Nothing has ever been accomplished by a reasonable man."
—Richard Boone[1]

In the fourth season of *Have Gun—Will Travel*, columnist Richard Schickel described the character of Paladin, highlighting two key traits—his competence, and his anger.

> There is no masculine skill, including a way with the ladies, which he has not mastered to the point of graceful, almost indolent, ease. And there is no meanness of the human spirit, however unimportant it may seem to the objective observer, which does not bring a well-bred twist of contempt to his lips and the glare of ice to his eyes.[2]

Those same traits, Schickel observes, could also be found in the athletic actor with the "magnificently ruined face" who had created the character. Indeed, everyone who knew Richard Boone agreed: he *was* Paladin. Paladin's fierce intelligence, his passion for justice, his huge laugh, his intense and disciplined will, all were part of Boone long before Paladin; likewise Paladin's sensitivity to the underdog, his love of art, theatre, dance, and classical music, even his appreciation of handsome women, good whiskey, and fine cigars. Though Richard Boone traveled a winding, indirect road to Paladin, ultimately he drew on every aspect of his personality and the experiences of a lifetime to create *Have Gun—Will Travel*.

A Quest for Purpose

There was no hint in Boone's early life that he would end up an actor. Indeed, his father would greet the idea with horror as a profession unsuited to a serious man. A third-generation Californian and seventh-generation nephew of Daniel Boone, Richard Allen Boone was born in Los Angeles on June 18, 1917, the second of three children of Kirk and Cecilia Beckerman Boone. Kirk had been born in San Francisco in 1892 where his father, Bower, was a famously flamboyant character who made and lost several fortunes, including one in China.[3] At various times in his up-and-down career, Bower had been a saloon keeper, a gold miner, and owner of a stable of twenty-seven race horses. As Richard later reported, "When grandfather was in the chips, he'd buy a silk shirt in the morning and throw it away at night. If I have any peculiar characteristics, you can blame them on Bower."[4] When Kirk was seven, his mother died of tuberculosis; Bower immediately handed the boy over to his grandparents and headed to Alaska to prospect for gold. In the next years Kirk was passed from relative to relative, though fortunately many of them treated him well. With support from one family in particular, Kirk was quite successful in high school. Bright, hard-working, and responsible, he was president of the student body and captain of the football team. Despite these achievements, his grandfather forced him to leave school before graduation, telling him, "Sorry, Kirk, but you can't finish high school. You have to go to work, go get a job." Perhaps as a result of these experiences, Kirk grew up the opposite of flamboyant, a conservative man with a strong desire for security and respectability.

Kirk found a job at Title Insurance Company, where he met a charming, creative and very beautiful young woman named Cecilia Beckerman. Though they were both quite young, Cecilia about 17 to Kirk's 21, they soon married and started a family: oldest son William, followed soon after by Richard, and nine years later by Betty Lou (known in the family as B'Lou).[5] While working full time in insurance, Kirk put himself through law school at night at the University of Southern California, and ultimately became a corporate attorney, a contract specialist for the oil industry. This professional advancement dramatically improved the family's financial status, but it also reinforced Kirk's conservative tendencies. One of her father's rules, B'Lou explains, was absolutely no talking about family secrets—for example, Bower's colorful past as a gambler and saloon keeper in San Francisco. But the deepest secret of all was Cecilia's Russian Jewish background. Neither of the parental Boones was religious; the family never attended church as the children were growing up, and, as B'Lou remarked, "I can't remember God ever being discussed." Though the grandparents who raised Kirk were devout Baptists, even as a child Kirk had refused any connection to the church, while Cecilia was a "non-practicing Jew" from a family that was only minimally observant. Despite this assertive secularity, Kirk made it clear to the children that Cecilia's Jewishness was never to be mentioned. In the 1920s and 30s, as B'Lou observed, "Jewish was not in the oil business, let me tell you, *really* not."

In the Boone children's young days, according to B'Lou, oldest son Bill was the family stand-out, an excellent athlete and "the life of the party," with the gifts of a stand-up comic. Richard, by contrast, seemed a bundle of contradictions: an intense, sensitive boy with his father's strong will and his mother's aesthetic sensibilities, combined with off-the-charts intelligence and a wild impulsiveness. According to his mother, even at three and a half Richard had a deep voice, and "at five spoke big sentences with great solemnity."[6] Despite his fierce, almost-uncontrollable energy and a surface gregariousness, Richard was actually quite shy. One factor in his shyness may well have been self-consciousness about the adolescent acne that had scarred his face severely. Another factor may have been his close relationship with the charming, artistic, perfectionist mother he so much resembled in temperament. Until B'Lou's birth when he was nine, Richard had reigned as Cecilia's "most-favored child," much as she tried not to have favorites. Being displaced by a baby sister was at first a challenge for him, though he soon outgrew the resentment. By the time B'Lou reached girlhood, Richard was a generous and indulgent older brother.

Conflicts with Authority

As he advanced in school, Richard's willfulness became more evident. B'Lou thought part of the problem was that Richard was "too smart" to be in a public school; she reports that he had the highest IQ ever recorded at Hoover High School in Glendale, and found little at school to challenge him. In fact, Richard once got so bored in Latin class that he simply left his desk and climbed out the window, to the astonishment of the school authorities.[7] Such incidents convinced Kirk to send both his sons to the Army and Navy Military Academy in San Diego in 1929 in order to learn some discipline. However, after two and a half years, the Academy refused to accept further shenanigans from Richard, and much to his own satisfaction, he returned to public school. However, at home, confrontations between father and son resumed full-strength. As Richard later observed, "I was born with a lot of horsepower. There was a lot cooking inside me, a lot of energy, and Dad was a strong man by will and intelligence, and the combination of us was almost bound to result in periodic explosions. He and I disagreed politically, very violently, and things would be hectic around the house."[8] Heated political debates between the then-liberal son and the conservative father became a regular feature of the Boone family dinner hour.

When Richard entered Stanford in 1934, his wild impulsiveness continued to get him in trouble. His studies came easily to him, due to the combination of a high I.Q. and a near-photographic memory.[9] As a result, his good grades cost him minimal effort, leaving plenty of time (perhaps too much) for non-academic activities. He joined the college boxing team and won the intercollegiate light-heavyweight championship twice, which made him a widely-known character on campus. That social prominence, plus his high spirits and natural charisma, made him a leader among certain groups of students. But at that time, his leadership often lacked wisdom. As Boone himself explained, "I had a raging lust for life, for excitement, without the judgment to control it."[10] The trouble came to a head in his junior year. As a prank, he and some of his Theta Xi brothers created a life-size dummy of rags and bottles. Then one dark night they smeared it with ketchup and left it on a sharp curve in the road in front of the fraternity house. When a passing car inevitably ran over the dummy, Boone rushed into the road screaming, "You've killed him! You've killed my brother!" Unfortunately, the driver who emerged from the car—an elderly woman so distressed by the incident that she stumbled and sprained her ankle—turned out to be Mrs. Herbert Hoover, Stanford's first lady. As Richard's son Peter later observed, the stunt was typical of his father, who liked "things that were dramatic and caused people to respond in unusual ways."[11] In this case, he got more drama than he intended. Though the joke may not have been meant maliciously, the resulting scandal caused Richard to be expelled from Stanford, an event that further strained his relationship with his father. Kirk, a self-made man who had worked hard for everything he got, was appalled that his son would throw away such an opportunity for so foolish a reason.[12]

Seeking His Own Path

Richard never returned to college. Through his father's contacts, he found work in the Southern California oil fields as a roustabout and truck driver, and attended night classes at the Art Students League in Los Angeles to study painting. As Boone explained, "In painting I found a wonderful method of self-expression. But there was one thing wrong. I had no talent."[13] At the school, he met a serious young painter named Jane Hopper. In 1937 they married and moved up the California coast to Carmel, to join the artists' and writers' colony that Jane's father, San Francisco journalist James Hopper, had founded in the 1920s. Getting to know the people in this community was the beginning of Boone's real education. Under the influence of the artists and writers there (people like painter James Fitzgerald, actor and art collector Vincent Price, and poet Robinson Jeffers), Boone began to read seriously, and learned to love symphonic music. He got involved with the Carmel little theatre, painting sets for them while experimenting with canvases in the Impressionist style. He also wrote short stories in a "semi–Hemingway" vein. "I was dying to do something to express myself," he explained later, but at none of these activities did he live up to his own standards, describing himself as "a lousy painter and an even worse writer."[14]

Meanwhile, the marriage, which Boone called a "three-year pitched battle up and down the Pacific Coast," was soon in trouble. Coming from a wealthy background, Boone cared nothing about money (though he was always too proud to accept handouts from his family).[15] But Jane, tired of supporting both of them, kept pressuring Boone to contribute some income to the marriage. He took a series of odd jobs—bouncer, adobe bricklayer, bartender—which provided a little money; once Jane found him a position as a Santa Claus in a Monterrey department store. Furiously resentful about that job, he made sure it didn't last long: he soon got himself fired for giving all the toys to the poor children and none to the rich ones. It was typical Boone: with one gesture, he could both get out of a job he didn't want, and fight for those who could not defend themselves, to redress the injustices of the world to the extent of his power. B'Lou believed that during that time in Carmel, her brother was looking for something, "perhaps his place in the world," but then in 1941 "the war came along, and that took care of everybody's direction." Richard and Jane divorced, and Richard joined the Navy.

Boone spent the war in the Pacific as a tail gunner in a torpedo bomber.[16] Though tail gunners were normally no larger than 5'10", the muscular 6'2" Boone folded himself into that cramped space and flew mission after harrowing mission over the Marianas, the Marshalls, Okinawa, and the Japanese mainland. One after another of the carriers he was stationed on came under attack: the *Enterprise* was bombed, the *Intrepid* was torpedoed, and the *Hancock* was dive-bombed by kamikaze planes. After the war, he could joke about it, telling reporter Richard Gehman, "We began to think somebody was trying to kill us,"[17] but at the time, it must have been deeply distressing to such a sensitive man to escape physically unscathed while he saw his friends dying. As Boone's wife Claire commented, "He just knew he was leading a charmed life."[18] Late in the war, his plane was shot down on a remote Pacific island, where he was forced to engage in hand-to-hand combat with Japanese soldiers in order to survive. He later told his son about the experience of holding people in his arms when they died, and how he felt about the human lives he had taken. While sparing Peter the explicit detail of the incidents, Richard accepted full responsibility for his own violent acts. Though killing enemy soldiers had been "something that had to be done," part of his duty as a soldier "to stop the enemy from taking over our country," Boone never minimized the moral costs of his actions.[19]

Other details of Boone's wartime experiences reveal the continuity of his character. In the Navy, he continued his boxing career successfully, winning every bout except the one he fought with broken ribs.[20] He also maintained his complicated relationship to authority. Repeatedly offered a commission, he turned it down every time. "I don't want to be with those stupid officers," he explained; "I want to be with the men."[21] The young man who had so urgently sought a means of self-expression continued to feel that need. Because "you can't carry an easel on a torpedo plane," Boone turned to writing to express his feelings—mostly short stories, plays, and poetry, but he also generously used his gift for words to help his shipmates write letters home to their wives and girlfriends. Discharged from the Navy in 1946, he came home from the war with a series of notebooks and manuscripts, plus a large collection of medals which he promptly threw away (his mother retrieved them from the waste basket). He also came home with what we now call post-traumatic stress disorder. Claire describes him as a "psychiatric case" when he returned: "He would wake up screaming some nights. He was a total mess emotionally. He tried to get psychiatric help, but he had to go through so much red tape that he gave up." And it was over fifteen years before he could force himself to get on a plane again.[22]

Finding His Way

Once safely home, Boone wanted to write plays about his wartime experiences, but he recognized that he didn't know how to write dialogue for actors. So, against the fierce opposition of his father,[23] who thought he was wasting his superior intellect on trivial matters, he took his G.I. Bill benefits to the Neighborhood Playhouse School of the Theatre in New York City, long recognized as the premiere training school for theatre arts in the country. And here at last, Boone found the purpose he had been seeking for so long. As soon as he began working with the student actors, he recognized his true calling: "I became an actor in eighteen seconds. I was hardly in the door of the Playhouse and already I was intrigued."[24] Boredom, his lifelong enemy, was vanquished; he threw himself passionately into a craft which demanded all his immense resources—physical, intellectual, and emotional.

One of the most influential figures at the Playhouse School was Sanford Meisner, head of the acting faculty from 1935 through his retirement in 1990. As Foster Hirsch explains in his history of the Actors Studio and its important forerunners, Meisner's philosophy of acting grew out of his experience as one of the original members of the Group Theatre (1930–1941). This legendary company transformed the American theatre during its brief but influential existence. Drawing inspiration from Stanislavski's central principles—his emphasis on internal truth in acting, and his creation of an ensemble of actors working together in a unified style—the Group Theatre radically reimagined what American theatre could be. They rejected the reigning system which placed the star at center stage, surrounded by deferential actors cast strictly according to "type" (ingénue, heavy, leading man, and so on). In such a system, actors never had the opportunity to grow artistically or technically; they were simply "commodities" in a "capitalist industry."[25] The leaders of the Group Theatre—Harold Clurman, Robert Lewis, and Cheryl Crawford—dreamed of a permanent ensemble of creative artists, trained in Stanislavski's methods and thus enabled to grow to the limits of their own talents. This ensemble would produce plays which would speak to the spiritual needs of both the company and the society, productions in which every element would be integrated aesthetically into one organic whole. As David Garfield explains in *A Player's Place*, his history of the Actors Studio, though the Group Theatre only survived for eleven years, killed off by a lack of good plays to produce and by the strains of sustaining such a demanding artistic enterprise during the Depression, its ideals persisted in those who had shared the experience.[26] Those alumni were now determined to pass on their ideals to new generations of theatre artists.

The traditions from the Group Theatre that Meisner offered his students at the Playhouse were particularly valuable for Richard Boone. First, the vision of actors as members of a community working together for a common goal gave him an idealistic sense of his new profession that appealed to his ardent spirit. Second, the acting techniques that Meisner taught provided Boone with a disciplined method of expressing himself, a way to channel his intense emotions in support of a larger purpose. At the school, he studied improvisation, voice and speech, and various kinds of movement, including modern dance, taught by Martha Graham, the preeminent American dancer and choreographer. Graham's radically new approach to dance proved a logical fit with the aims of the Playhouse. She saw dance as an inner emotional experience whose purpose was to bring about an increased awareness of life and a greater understanding of human nature. For actors, such heightened awareness of their bodies gave them a powerful tool—first, for understanding themselves, the interplay of their minds and their bodies; and second, for communicating with an audience, for expressing emotions and states of mind through movement alone. Graham had been teaching dance at the Playhouse school since its founding in 1928[27]; however, in the years just after World War II many of the students at the Playhouse, like Boone, were combat veterans. For most of these men, the idea of studying dance felt like a threat; they were "afraid they might be put in tutus." But they soon discovered there was nothing effeminate about Martha Graham's kind of dance. After a single hour of her training, as Peter Boone explained, his father and the other tough young ex-soldiers "just crawled to the door; they couldn't even walk after Martha Graham had finished with them." Though few of them became good dancers, that was not the point of the training. As Graham told Boone bluntly, "You can't dance at all— but you can act with your body."[28] The training Graham provided, combined with his years of boxing experience, gave Boone skills that would prove crucial, especially in the many action scenes that filled the rest of his career. It may also explain the otherwise surprising number of scenes in *Have Gun—Will Travel* when Paladin dances.[29]

"The Method"

At the end of the two-year program, in Meisner's judgment, Boone was one of the Playhouse's "most successful acting products."[30] However, the course at the Playhouse was only the beginning of his training as an actor. Even while starting to get professional experience playing small parts on Broadway and in live television, Boone was invited to join the Actors Studio in order to continue his study of Method acting. Unlike the Neighborhood Playhouse, the Actors Studio was not a school for beginners.[31] Founded in October 1947, it was an organization for professional actors, a place where they could get together once or twice a week as a community to work on their skills, to experiment with techniques and solve individual problems of the craft in privacy, away from the view of the public.

The driving force behind the Actors Studio was Elia Kazan. In the six years after the demise of his beloved Group Theatre, he became one of the most exciting and successful directors in America, directing a dozen major plays on Broadway, including *The Skin of Our Teeth* (1942), *All My Sons* and *A Streetcar Named Desire* (both in 1947), plus two highly honored films, *A Tree Grows in Brooklyn* (1945) and *Gentleman's Agreement* (1947), for which he won an Oscar as best director. But all these plays and films, however successful, proved frustrating to him in one key regard: the success of the productions was achieved not through his actors, but in spite of them. The problem wasn't that the actors were untalented, but that each of the actors he worked with, from the most experienced professionals to the beginners, came to his production not only with different levels of ability, but with widely divergent acting styles. They had no common language, no common technique and, above all, no understanding of the kind of ensemble work the Group Theatre had cherished. Worse, they had no place to go where they could study, practice, and improve their skills.

The Actors Studio, inspired and founded by Kazan with support from his Group Theatre colleagues, Robert Lewis and Cheryl Crawford, became that place. As Kazan explained his purpose, "We want a common language so that I can direct actors instead of coach them ... so that we have a common vocabulary. It is not a school. Actors can come and actors can go. It is a place to work and find this vocabulary."[32]

The source of that common vocabulary was the Method, derived from Stanislavski's techniques and exercises for actors. Those exercises were designed, first, to help them relax and concentrate on stage, and second, to draw on their own emotional experiences so that the characters' reactions would attain a higher level of credibility.[33] The job of the actor, as Lee Strasberg said, is to create real experience in response to imaginary stimuli—that is, to take the circumstances of character and situation as given by the playwright and present the audience with a fully-fleshed out human being responding realistically within those parameters. Method acting was simply "a pragmatic way of working to create both the interior life and the logical behavior of a character—a way that can be taught, practiced, monitored, and corrected."[34] The Actors Studio also transmitted the key principles of the Group Theatre to its students—principles learned in turn from Stanislavski's Moscow Art Theatre. First, "there are no small parts, just small actors." For a Method actor, playing a minor courtier in *Hamlet* is no different from playing Hamlet: every role deserves the same dedication, thought, and focus. The second principle is "Love art, not yourself in art." Actors should dedicate themselves to the needs of an ensemble performance rather than self-aggrandizement. Finally, "All disobedience to the creative life of the theatre is a crime." Theatre was a high calling, in some senses a religion, and the actors and other artists that made the theatre what it was should serve that creative life with their highest energies, their utmost honesty, and greatest unselfishness.[35]

The first year, 1947-48, the Actors Studio offered two classes, an advanced class taught by Robert Lewis for actors already trained in the Method, and a beginners class taught by Elia Kazan for actors who were professionals but were unfamiliar with the Method. However, by the end of the first year, Robert Lewis resigned over a conflict with Kazan, and Kazan himself was too busy with directorial jobs to teach his classes on a regular schedule. The need for some additional teachers became obvious. In the fall of 1948, Kazan brought in Lee Strasberg, a fellow alumnus of the Group Theatre, who proved to be an inspired and often inspirational teacher. At first Strasberg taught only part-time, but in 1951 he took on the title of Artistic Director. For the next thirty years, until his death in 1982, he determined the shape of the Actors Studio, for good or ill, and became the single most influential—and controversial—teacher of acting in the country.[36] That same fall, Kazan brought in Sandy Meisner from the Neighborhood Playhouse School to teach a third class of relative beginners whom Meisner himself would invite— among them, Richard Boone.[37] At the Actors Studio, Boone finally found the community he had been longing for; in time, he would become a Life Member.

A Career Begins

Even during his studies, Boone began to get professional experience in a succession of small roles in live television, about 175 parts from 1947 to 1949: roles on assorted live dramas, repeated jobs on the children's television show *Mr. I. Magination*, and even a recurring role as a reporter on a short-lived television series of *The Front Page*. He also got small parts in several Broadway plays, but if Boone was one of the Playhouse's most successful graduates, he was, as Meisner also said, "one of its most pugnacious."[38] Even at the beginning of his career, Boone's highest priority was to maintain his artistic integrity, no matter the cost. For example, in 1947 when John Gielgud was casting Judith Anderson's production of *Medea* on Broadway, the Playhouse sent Boone to the great British actor with a letter of introduction. Gielgud offered him some tea, then suddenly pointed at his visitor, demanding abruptly: "Why can't you play Jason in *Medea*?" Boone was thrilled with his opportunity, but afterward Gielgud decided to play the role himself, and Boone became Gielgud's understudy. He learned a lot from backstage conversations with the great actor, and from watching Gielgud's masterly performances night after night, but since the star never missed a performance, Boone had no chance to play the role himself. When Gielgud finally left the show, Boone thought his opportunity had come, that he would be promoted to the lead. Instead, another actor was brought in to play Jason. Rather than continue as the understudy, Boone simply walked away from the production, unwilling to settle for less than he believed his due.[39]

Even in small roles, Boone always insisted on his own judgment. In 1948, cast as a minor Scottish nobleman in a production of *Macbeth* headlined by Michael Redgrave, Boone soon managed to get himself fired. There are competing stories about the cause of his firing. To one reporter, Boone simply observed that he "didn't like Redgrave very much. I guess that contributed some to getting my tail booted." But Boone told reporter Lee Edson that during a dress rehearsal he had laughed at something Redgrave did. In response, Redgrave "offered to smash him in the nose." When Boone only laughed harder, he was fired, although his nose remained unpunched. Jan Merlin, who studied with Boone at the Playhouse, tells the most vivid (and most likely) version of all. According to Merlin, Boone was fired because "he insisted on falling down the stairs while making his entrance. He kept saying, 'That's the way I feel it. I'm coming on with this great rage, and I'm going to do it like this!'" It was a classic Method actor's response, investing a small part with as much thought and intensity as a large one. But the producers were not impressed. As Merlin reported, "They said, 'Well, you're not going to do it like this because we don't want it.'" When Boone refused to yield, he was let go.[40] In these early years, Boone walked out on parts in no fewer than six Broadway productions. The values he had learned at the Playhouse School and the Actors Studio encouraged him to trust his own standards: "You have to come to a point where you say, 'This is me; if I'm not good enough for you, then the hell with you.' Once you hit that level, a kind of relaxation comes over you. You find that you're not desperately striving for applause to prove that you're good."[41]

In between his other roles, Boone took a job hosting a series of live sports telecasts for CBS from places like Ebbets Field, Belmont Park, and Madison Square Garden. "After those seventy-five ad-libbed shows," he later remarked during his *Have Gun — Will Travel* days, "I knew that nothing in TV could ever frighten me. Without that experience I don't think I could ever face the camera head on as I do."[42] The same year, 1949, he also made a second brief attempt at matrimony with a red-haired singer named Mimi Kelly, but less than a year later they filed for divorce.

Westward Ho

In all, 1949 proved a year of enormous changes for Boone, professional as well as personal. One day while Boone was sitting in the lobby at the Actors Studio, an actress named

Lenka Peterson asked for his help. Hollywood director Lewis Milestone at Twentieth Century–Fox wanted to give her a screen test, and she needed someone to feed lines to her. Good-naturedly, Boone agreed; seated with his back to the camera, he read the Gentleman Caller's lines from Tennessee Williams' *The Glass Menagerie* while the young actress gave her all to Laura. Then Boone dismissed the incident from his mind; it had nothing to do with him. In the end, Milestone was unimpressed with Peterson, but had been intrigued by her unseen partner. Elia Kazan told Boone that they wanted him in Hollywood. The actor was startled: "But that's crazy. My back was to the camera!" "Yes," Kazan agreed, "but you talked. Lewis Milestone likes your voice." When Milestone saw the hard-bitten face that went with the voice, he immediately offered Boone the role of the nerve-wracked colonel in *The Halls of Montezuma* (1950). He was on his way in Hollywood.[43]

But, in characteristic Boone fashion, he went on his own terms. He boarded the plane to California carrying the pages on which he had completely rewritten his part in the film, along with a return ticket. As he later explained, "If the production had not approved what I had done, I would have gone right back to New York. One cannot afford, particularly in the beginning, to do less than one's best. To be forced to compromise at that point is wrong. Better to be fired, better to quit, better to scream the house down than let one's basic talents be abused. If you begin that way, you'll end that way." However, on his first take on his first motion picture, Boone demonstrated the gifts that would serve him so well in the rest of his career: he nailed a complicated seven-page scene perfectly.[44]

As a contract player for Twentieth Century–Fox, Boone made twelve films in the next three years, mostly Westerns and World War II pictures. However, the relationship between actor and studio was testy. As Boone summed it up drily, "At Fox they treated me fine. They gave me big parts in all their bad pictures, and lousy little parts in their good ones."[45] In 1953, the conflict with Fox came to a head during filming of *The Robe*, Hollywood's first CinemaScope production (a new technology designed to give Hollywood an edge over the upstart medium, television). Richard Burton starred as a drunken, dissolute Roman centurion transformed by winning Christ's robe in a dice game after the crucifixion; Boone played the small but crucial role of Pontius Pilate. In the middle of filming this high-prestige project, the studio pushed Boone to start shooting another movie called *Vicki* at the same time. On principle, he refused to work on two pictures at once. When Fox insisted, Boone simply walked out, closing down *The Robe*. Studio scouts finally tracked him down on the beach, sunbathing. As Boone gleefully recounted the story, the studio men "murmured something about holding up progress on a movie that would revolutionize cinema. Then they muttered something about suing this crazy New York actor. Finally they gave in."[46] He returned to the set and completed *The Robe*, then went on to do *Vicki*, but his rebellion cost him. In subsequent pictures, his parts grew smaller and worse, increasing his eagerness to escape from Fox; but that was a virtually impossible goal in those days of iron-clad seven-year contracts, which allowed the studios to dictate every move an actor made. Under these contracts, refusing a part meant than an actor would be suspended (without pay) for the duration of the film's shooting, while those months would be added to the contract.[47]

Meanwhile, Boone did everything he could to continue his professional training. Filming *The Halls of Montezuma*, Boone met fellow cast member Jack Webb, and the two men became friends. Despite objections from Fox, Webb soon cast Boone on half a dozen episodes of his popular radio show, *Dragnet*. Working on *Dragnet* also introduced Boone to Peggy Webber. Webber, only 21 at the time but already an experienced radio actress,[48] took pity on the eager, awkward neophyte and helped him learn the radio business, even such basic techniques as how to turn script pages without making noise. He also quickly recognized how crucial good enunciation was for a radio actor. Alert to every opportunity to perfect his craft, Boone used *Dragnet* to work on his vocal techniques, which paid off handsomely in his later television roles.[49]

In those days, when Boone was still brand new to Hollywood, Webber remembered him as "very effusive, very effervescent … so full of himself that you would have thought that he was just eighteen or twenty years old. He was just ecstatic to be an actor and to be doing what he wanted to do, and it was just a lot of fun to be with him because he was so excited and so thrilled by everything."[50] They dated for awhile, decorously, Boone comporting himself like "the perfect gentleman" with this woman twelve years his junior. For one thing, Peggy, who described herself as "quite a prude and very straitlaced about life" in those days, still lived at home with her mother. For another, as Boone confessed cheerfully to Peggy, Webb and the other members of the *Dragnet* company had warned him that if he "touched" her, he would have to answer to them. However chaste this romance with Webber was, it seems to have been more than a trivial flirtation. True, in typical Boone fashion, he enjoyed shocking her with the details of his past: he told her of his two tempestuous marriages, bragged of a mistress in New York and another someplace else, and claimed to have once killed a man in a barroom brawl.[51] But he also took her to dinner at his parents' home and, more significantly, he told her about his emotional breakdown after the war, an experience he revealed to very few people. At one point, he even asked her to move in with him—an offer that, as a proper young woman of her time, she naturally refused.

Honing the Craft

However, Webber was not just a romantic interest for Boone; she was also a professional he respected so much that he asked her to help him start a workshop for actors in Hollywood—in effect, an Actors Studio-West, to continue the work on the Method he had pursued in New York. (The official Actors Studio-West would be opened fifteen years later, in 1966.) Being new to Hollywood, he needed her help to find just the right people for the group, those with the right training and the right attitudes—that is, no radio actors or newly-minted movie stars, only theatre actors from New York, the same sort of people he had worked with at the Actors Studio. Warren Stevens, a friend from the Neighborhood Playhouse School and the Actors Studio, who had found himself a contract player at Fox only a few months after Boone, eagerly joined the project. When James Whitmore, another Actors Studio member, arrived in Hollywood a little later, Boone and Warren invited him to help them run the workshop. According to Stevens, early members of the group included Lamont Johnson (who later became a director), Ernest Borgnine, Patricia Neal, and Dennis Weaver.[52] Meeting in a rented room at the Brentwood Marketplace, about thirty actors rehearsed and performed scenes for each other, working on roles they would never be allowed to play professionally in order to stretch themselves as actors. In all his activities, Boone "carried the banner for the Method." Webber commented, "He believed in it so totally, and it had done such wonders for him that he was really a very good teacher." As Webber remembered, from the beginning Boone was "so totally dedicated to the arts that nothing was going to stop him, and he had a sensitivity that was beyond the average actor that I had worked with, and I felt that he was willing to go to extremes to achieve what he had been taught. I truly admired that. I thought he really was going to be great; I knew that he had the greatness within him." However disappointing his movie career might have been in the early 1950s, his professional development as an actor and director was proceeding in gratifying ways.

Love and Marriage: Third Time's the Charm

His personal life, too, was gaining a new stability during these early years in Hollywood. In November 1950, Boone went to Australia to make his second movie with Lewis Milestone, a film called *Kangaroo*, starring Peter Lawford and Maureen O'Hara. Milestone's wife, Kendall, had accompanied him to Australia as the first stage of a round-the-world trip, bringing with her an attractive young woman named Claire McAloon, the soon-to-be ex-wife of Kendall's nephew. Despite the pending divorce, the two women remained close, and Kendall had invited Claire to join her on this trip with the object of finding a "prince" to be Claire's next husband. In Australia Kendall achieved her goal—though not quite in the way she anticipated, and without benefit of the world tour.[53]

The day his actors arrived in Australia, Milestone threw a big party for them but, exhausted from the long trip, none of them came. Annoyed, Milestone told Claire to call the actors and order them to show up for dinner. As Claire explained to David Rothel, "I got on the phone with my little girl's voice and this gorgeous voice answered the phone. I said, 'This is Lewis Milestone's niece and we're down here waiting for you. When are you coming?' And the gorgeous voice said, 'Lewis Milestone's niece, we'll be right down.'" At the director's house, Boone burst through the door and demanded in his booming voice, "Where is Lewis Milestone's niece?" Claire, sitting off in a corner, waved at him shyly. He barely said hello to anyone else at the party, instead spending the entire evening talking to Claire, a former actress and ballet dancer who, at 4'11", barely reached his shoulder.

For both of them, it was love at first sight. Claire immediately moved in with Dick, despite the fact that "people didn't do that" in those days, and abandoned her plans for world travel. Boone bought her an antique gold band, and promised they would be married as soon as they returned to America. Though Kendall was furious with her for throwing herself away on a mere actor, sure that the affair was merely "one of those location things," Claire knew she had found what she wanted, and so did Boone. Actually, since neither of their divorces was complete, they were not free to marry till April 27, 1951, but they always celebrated their anniversary as November 1, 1950—the date they met in Australia. In the next two years, Claire suffered several miscarriages, but finally in August 1953 their only child, Peter, was born. Boone, who would prove a devoted and supportive father, was ecstatic. Though the marriage was not without its dramas, essentially it was a happy and stable relationship that lasted to the end of Boone's life. In Peggy Webber's view, Boone found "something very pure and sweet and good" with Claire,[54] who provided the balance and the calming influence that he needed so badly to offset the roar and whirl inside his own skull.

A Doctor in the House

Even while Claire was pregnant with Peter, Boone's career took another fortuitous turn, thanks again to Peggy Webber. One of the young writers for *Dragnet*, James Moser, created an idea for a radio show called *The Doctor*, designed to do for medicine what *Dragnet* had done for the police, using fact-based medical dramas to inform the public. In the summer of 1950, one trial episode was broadcast, about an old woman, played by Peggy Webber, who comes to talk about her kidney problems to a doctor played by Richard Boone.[55] No further episodes were broadcast, but a determined Moser continued to research and develop the idea. In the summer of 1951, Webber married a real doctor and moved with him to Japan, where she was frequently able to watch her husband at work, in emergency rooms, performing operations, even doing autopsies. Back in Hollywood for a Christmas party in 1951 or 1952,[56] Webber spent hours talking with Moser about her experiences with her husband's medical work, arguing that he should aim *The Doctor* at television rather than radio. Not only would the series be an ideal educational tool, allowing the public to get actual medical information through the dramas, it would also be valuable for viewers to see doctors not as gods who must never be questioned, but as human beings with strengths and weaknesses, talking with each other, arguing and raising questions and solving complex medical problems. Webber also told Moser emphatically that, if he took the show to television, he should hire Richard Boone. Moser objected on the grounds that Boone was "so ugly," but she only laughed: "Yes, but he looks like a real doctor. There are a lot of ugly doctors out there." She added that, because Boone did everything in such an "honest, realistic way ... people would really believe that he is a doctor." Moser followed her advice. In September 1954, Moser's show, now titled *Medic*, premiered on NBC television with Richard Boone as Dr. Konrad Styner.

As the series was constructed, there was no single continuing character in every episode; the medicine became the "star."[57] Each week presented a different doctor-patient drama, focusing on a variety of medical problems and issues, both historical and contemporary. The show was meticulously researched and realistic: each episode examined the details of disease and injury, but also explored the social and psychological ramifications of these medical problems for patients, their families, and their communities. Every case was drawn from the files of the Los Angeles County Medical Association and filmed in real operating rooms and other medical facilities around Los Angeles. In exchange for this access, the Medical Association was granted final say over all the medical details, and ultimately endorsed the series for its authenticity. Boone, as Dr. Konrad Styner, narrated every episode, and played a significant role in about a third of the episodes. The show was an instant critical success; less than three months after its premiere, it won top honors in the fourth annual Sylvania Television Awards, and Boone would twice be nominated for an Emmy for his performance as Dr. Styner.[58]

An astounding number of viewers, even some doctors in the audience, were convinced that Boone was a real doctor rather than an actor.[59] In part, their belief was a credit to his Method-actor's commitment to realism: as Peggy Webber had told Moser, Boone always looked honest and real in whatever he did on stage. That was also why he preferred location shooting to sound-stage work. Because *Medic* placed its actors in real hospitals and operating rooms, Boone observed, "You take a deep breath and it smells like antiseptic. There's a different pace involved in working around actual doctors and nurses [who not only served as consultants but sometimes played extras in the episodes] and the perspiration is honest— not glycerin!"[60] On the down side, realism in this particular subject matter caused him personal distress: he had a lifelong hatred of hospitals and, worse, was a dedicated hypochondriac who came down with the symptoms of each disease the show featured. "Every time I had a heart case, I got all the murmurs," Boone admitted to *TV Guide* in 1961. "When I was performing an ear operation, my own hearing went sour. I won't discuss brain damage—some of my friends might say I had that long before Styner."[61] Despite these challenges, Boone never shirked his responsibilities to the role, often watching repeated real-life surgeries like the ones he would be called on to simulate in the episode to make sure he would look authentic.

These conditions made shooting the pilot particularly harrowing for Boone. The story concerned a young woman diagnosed with rapidly-advancing leukemia while pregnant with her first child. She chooses to forego treatment of her disease in order to give her child a chance to be born; in the end, the doctors perform a caesarean section to save the baby. At the exact moment Boone was preparing for this episode by watching a series of such operations at L.A. County Hospital, Claire was scheduled to undergo a real caesarean for Peter's birth. In addition to Boone's normal medical anxieties, Claire's previous miscarriages no doubt exacerbated the worries for both Boones about this latest pregnancy. When Claire came successfully out of her surgery, the new father looked at his healthy son, then went in to see his wife. He told her, "You have borne me a son; you can do no wrong," sat down in a chair beside her bed, and promptly fainted.[62]

Medic improved Boone's professional life dramatically. Perhaps most significantly, the series helped him escape his hated seven-year contract with Twentieth Century–Fox, which still had four years to run. However, as Boone pointed out, the studio heads were only too delighted to get rid of one of their most troublesome and irritating contract players.[63] Boone was even happier than Fox. Not only would he be earning more money as Styner, but at last he could escape the studio's rigid typecasting. As a movie actor, Boone acknowledged, he was limited to playing heavies in Hollywood action films, explaining to a reporter in 1955, "I didn't blame Hollywood. With a face like mine, there are very few big parts a guy can get.... [The producers] have an investment to protect, and it's always safer to use a handsome leading man."[64] But in the role of Dr. Styner, his appearance was in his favor.

In addition to a healthy regular paycheck, the series and its honors also gave Boone a new visibility which boosted his movie career. His salaries doubled, and he now got offered featured roles in much better films than Fox had given him—not "A" list movies, certainly, but some strong "B" features, like *Man Without a Star* (Universal, 1955), starring Kirk Douglas, which featured a vicious all-out slugging match between the two men. Other respectable films he made in these years included *Away All Boats* (Universal, 1956), based on a true story of a World War II battleship under kamikaze attack (an event Boone had experienced personally); *The Garment Jungle* (Columbia, 1957), in which Boone played a ruthless syndicate boss out to break a union; *Lizzie* (MGM, 1957), starring Boone as a psychiatrist (essentially a version of Dr. Styner) treating a young woman with multiple personality disorder[65]; *The Tall T* (Columbia, 1957), where he played a complex, textured villain to Randolph Scott's heroic rancher and Maureen O'Hara's newlywed-in-danger; and a highly-regarded little suspense film, *I Bury the Living* (United Artists, 1958), in which Boone played the new chairman of a cemetery where many of the living owners of pre-purchased plots begin to die mysteriously.

The First Acting Class

Medic introduced Boone to the rigors of shooting a weekly television series, though it was a comparatively gentle introduction: his role as Dr. Styner was much less intensive and time-consuming than Paladin would be a few years later, leaving him plenty of time for movie work. It also gave him time for another project close to his heart. In 1955 he began teaching the first of what would be a lifelong series of acting classes. The best information we have about this first class comes from Robert Fuller, who went on to a long career on television in Westerns and action series.[66] In late 1954, while Fuller himself was still serving in Korea as a Marine, a couple of hard-working Hollywood actors (in fact, Fuller's stepfather and one of Fuller's best friends, Chuck Courtney) were so impressed with Boone's work on *Medic* that they wrote him a letter, begging him to teach an acting class. After meeting with them, he agreed. By early 1955, he was teaching a group of ten to fifteen students, among them Courtney. For $30 a month, Boone worked with his students two nights a week, four to five hours a night, passing on the training he had received from Sandy Meisner and Elia Kazan. That spring, Fuller returned to California and civilian life. Before he was drafted, he had earned occasional money as a stuntman and actor, but in 1955 he had no thoughts of an acting career. However, Courtney was full of enthusiasm for this new class, and encouraged Fuller to come meet Boone: "This man is fantastic; you're going to love him. You've got to come and sit in on our class." So Fuller came. Near the end of the session, Boone offered him a chance to improvise a scene with one of the other students, and Fuller agreed. Though the young ex–Marine had no training at all, Boone saw real potential in his performance, and invited Fuller to join the class if he was serious about acting. For almost four years, Fuller studied with Boone. In 1956, through Boone's connections, Fuller even spent six months at the Neighborhood Playhouse working with Meisner.

One of Fuller's stories effectively illustrates Boone's gifts and methods as an acting teacher. Back in the mid–1950s, Fuller remarks, every young (male) actor thought he was James Dean, himself included. As a result, for about four months, no matter what character he was playing, he found himself looking down at the floor with his thumb in his ear, channeling Dean. Nothing Boone suggested could break the habit. Finally Boone announced that Fuller's next scene assignment was *Hamlet*, the closet scene where the Prince confronts his mother. Fuller would play Hamlet, with Boone's old friend Peggy Webber as Gertrude.[67] Fuller was terrified: "My God, I can't even pronounce the words in that, Dick. You can't do this to me." Boone was adamant: Fuller had to do the scene or leave the class. Fuller read the play, hopelessly lost; then he got the recording of the play with Laurence Olivier and started listening, over and over. Slowly, the play began to make sense to him. Then his father and Courtney offered an inspired suggestion. At the end of his tour in Korea, Fuller had been in the honor guard and in excellent physical shape, so his fatigues were skin-tight and very good-looking. Following their recommendation, he dyed his fatigues black, donned cowboy boots to make himself stand up taller, and put on a sword. No more slouching, no mumbling, no staring at the floor with diffident thumb in ear. He did the scene for Boone twice, then did *Romeo and Juliet*, "and I became Robert Fuller again and knew what I was going to do as an actor for the rest of my life. And I owe it all to Dick for doing it. He saved me right there."

This acting class, the first of many, would continue till early 1959, by which time the demands of *Have Gun—Will Travel* became so great Boone was forced to give it up. But, driven by two imperatives—dedication to the art of the theatre, and a passion for helping young people—Boone always started another acting class whenever and wherever he found himself, even returning to the Neighborhood Playhouse School as a teacher in his last years.

He also used the free time his *Medic* schedule allowed him to pursue another interest: directing for television. Offered a chance to act in the Western anthology series, *Frontier*, he quickly recognized an opportunity. He agreed to star in this episode for a greatly reduced salary in exchange for the chance to direct a second episode. As he told *TV Guide*, "I got $650 out of the deal, and paid $1,200 to join the Directors Guild. But I consider it money well spent."[68]

By the middle of *Medic*'s second season, Boone had become so thoroughly identified with Dr. Styner that, fearful of being type-cast, he announced he would leave the show at the end of the season. In the end, though, Boone did not have to leave the show; a controversy over one episode featuring a caesarean birth led NBC to cancel the series at the end of the second season. The "caesarean birth" dispute was quite public, and garnered considerable discussion; however, a second controversy—one that long remained unknown to the public, but was deeply upsetting to Boone personally—also contributed to the decision to cancel the series. They had shot a powerful episode about a black doctor who had been working in Canada, but decided to return home to the South to start a practice there. But when Southern affiliates refused to run the episode because it featured a black actor, NBC again caved to the pressure, pulling the episode in order to avoid controversy.[69] As late as 1970, Boone was still fuming about the decision, despite the undeniable progress of blacks on television since 1956. These incidents were Boone's first experience of the politics of television; they would not be his last. But the end result was that after two years as Konrad Styner, Boone was once again at loose ends, professionally speaking.

Have Gun—Will Travel: *Landing the Role*

Soon after *Medic* was cancelled, however, opportunity unexpectedly came his way. As Boone was playing the heavy opposite Randolph Scott in *The Tall T*, Scott was offered the lead in a new Western TV series, memorably titled *Have Gun—Will Travel*, about an elegant soldier of fortune based in San Francisco in the 1870s. Having no interest in television, Scott passed the script of the pilot to his co-star. After only ten pages, Boone was eager to claim the role for himself. As he explained to *TV Guide* in October 1957:

> This Paladin is no mere observer. He's a participant who lives like a king, with a need to make the most of every moment, whether it's drinking a glass of wine or hunting some-body down. I read the scripts for 14 different series looking for a character with the right humor and complexity—something as far from Styner as I could find—and the minute I read this one I jumped up and yelled, "This is for me."[70]

Part of his excitement must surely have been a response to Paladin's way of talking, his erudition and his rhetorical gifts. As series creator Sam Rolfe remembered thinking, Paladin was a great character, "but who'll buy this radical? Worse, what cowboy actor can play a high–IQ gunslinger and get away with it?"[71] But Paladin was a role tailor-made for Boone, who had both an equivalent IQ and the skill to render realistically any character he chose. But it was not just the character's language that caught him. As Boone later told reporter Richard Schickel, he felt an almost immediate empathy with Paladin. The character's fierce manner and his determination to pursue justice in isolated corners of the West, Boone argued, must mask some hidden wound: "This man has to have made a hell of a mistake sometime." It was a psychological pattern the actor recognized—perhaps, Schickel suggested perceptively, due to hidden wounds of his own. Boone was willing to admit the possibility: "There have always been a lot of things boiling around inside me, and my problem has been to channel them. I don't know what they are. I could probably find out if I went through analysis, but I haven't, and I probably won't."[72] In truth, whatever demons haunted Boone, his art seems to have given him all the tools he needed to deal with them. As long as he was involved in meaningful theatrical endeavors, either as actor or director, he had no need for therapy.

Despite the strong resistance of CBS executives, who insisted that Boone "had never played anything but doctors,"[73] he argued his way into a screen test for the part. His performance was so compelling that Al Scalpone, CBS's West Coast head of programming, hired him on the spot, wiring the New York office rhetorically, "WHAT DO YOU THINK OF RICHARD BOONE?" The East replied, "RICHARD BOONE IS THE UGLIEST ACTOR IN HOLLYWOOD." Scalpone wired back, "YOU HAVE JUST SIGNED THE UGLIEST ACTOR IN HOLLYWOOD."[74]

His face may have been ugly, but his body suited him ideally to play an action hero. Actor Rayford Barnes, a frequent guest actor on the series, described Boone in these days as very strong and "agile. He walked like a cat. He wasn't an enormous man, but he was very well built, a big-shouldered guy, and he moved like an athlete." As one film producer commented, "Dick's the most physical actor I know. When he plays anger, some of the other actors actually back away from him. But I think that's where his appeal lies. You want to be on his team, even if he does scare you. Or maybe because he does."[75] Andrew V. McLaglen, who directed over half the *Have Gun* episodes, praised his star's ability as a screen fighter. With his natural athletic ability, years of boxing experience, and the dance training he got from Martha Graham, Boone gave McLaglen some of the best fights of the director's long career, seldom needing a double except for the most extreme stunts.[76] Lee Edson, observing the star on the *Have Gun* set, also commented on Boone's physical intensity, the Method actor at work:

> Before he pulls a gun he limbers his fingers, and before he plays a violent scene he seems lost in thought. He acts with such intense realism—his stance, for instance, is sometimes taut like that of an animal bunched for a spring—that he has the ability to evoke great performances from others.[77]

But before he could begin to shoot actual scenes for his new series, Boone needed to acquire certain skills in order to play a Western hero convincingly. Most crucially, he had to learn how to ride a horse—or, more accurately, as he put it, "how to make it appear as if I was riding a horse," since he was quite aware that actually learning to control a horse was a years-long process. He had worked on his riding briefly in 1950 in preparation for filming *Kangaroo*. Now he arranged to work with Ben Johnson, rodeo champion, stuntman, and member of John Ford's informal acting company who was, hands down, the best horseman in Hollywood. Boone immediately liked and respected his teacher so much that he later cast Johnson in several episodes of the series. Despite his admiration for Johnson, spending so much time in the presence of horses—let alone on their backs—was a serious psychological challenge for Boone, whose feelings about horses went "beyond simple distaste into complicated loathing." He frequently remarked, "Turn your back on a horse and you're in danger."[78] The fact that he eventually managed to look comfortable on horseback is a testament both to his courage and his acting ability. However, he used his star status on the series to make sure he spent as little time as possible on a horse (a neat trick in a Western).

The other immediate challenge was to learn the quick-draw of a six-gun. For this he studied with Rod Redwing, one of three professional shooting teachers in Hollywood at the time. Redwing called Boone a star pupil, because he rapidly mastered not only the quick draw but the classic moves of flashy gunplay common to the Western movies: fanning—holding one finger on the trigger and using the other hand to slap the gun hand to fire; the Stage Coach Shift, in which the gun is flipped rapidly from one hand to the other, and the Border Roll, where the gunman pretends to surrender his gun by offering it butt first, but uses a finger hooked backwards in the trigger to flip it around and point it at his former captor. To complete his costume for the series, Boone commissioned a specially-made .38 with a seven-inch barrel, plus a hand-tooled holster, for the then-extravagant sum of $182.50.

The Premiere

On Saturday, September 14, 1957, the first episode of *Have Gun—Will Travel* was broadcast to the nation from 9:30–10 p.m. EST, just before *Gunsmoke*. For the first time, the show's powerful opening appeared on the screen. Against a dark background, in close-up, the bas-relief of a chess knight, silver on a black leather holster. The camera pulls back to reveal a man dressed in black, standing in profile—not his face, just his hands and his body from waist to thigh, the holster filling the center of the screen. Slowly, deliberately, the man draws and cocks the gun, then turns it to point directly at the camera. The accompanying theme music is dark, ominous: a series of tense drumbeat chords on muted brass, four minor chords that start low on the scale and drop lower: bum-bum—bum–BUM; bum-bum—bum–BUM, followed by a sustained vibrato chord. Bernard Herrmann, on staff at CBS, had been entrusted with the job of writing the theme.[79] As the audience stared into the barrel of that gun, a rich powerful voice spoke. The yet-unnamed, unknown Paladin announced coolly: "I'd like you to take a look at this gun. The balance is excellent; this trigger responds to the pressure of one ounce. This gun was handcrafted to my specifications—and I rarely draw it unless I mean to use it." As the drumbeat chords repeat, the gun is slammed back into the holster, and the gunman's hands wrap firmly around his gunbelt, confident and controlled. A sequence of four quick descending notes in a minor scale is repeated several times as the titles appear in tooled-leather lettering: "*Richard Boone* in /*Have Gun—*/*Will Travel*."[80]

In this first episode, "Three Bells to Perdido," Paladin is hired to bring back Dave Enderby (played by Jack Lord), who had ruthlessly killed 21 members of the posse pursuing him and seriously wounded its leader, Jesse Reed. Enderby has fled to an outlaw sanctuary in Mexico with Reed's daughter Nancy, who has fallen in love with the handsome young outlaw. Rather than fighting an entire town to get Enderby, Paladin outsmarts his quarry: he rides away with Nancy, realizing Enderby's ego will make him leave the sanctuary in order to reclaim his "property." Once the outlaw is away from his sanctuary, Paladin can easily capture him and take him back to face trial, while reuniting the chastened Nancy with her father.

So the episode belies the ominous iconography of the opening, which is deliberately structured to play with the audience's expectations. In 1957 everybody knew that, in a Western, the man wearing black was the villain. A mustache also signaled villainy; the hero was always clean-shaven. The opening of *Have Gun* plays into those expectations: gun, music, voice, black garb, all are designed to create alarm. The opening speech often sounds threatening, even grim: but viewers soon realized that the threats are always addressed to Paladin's opponents, to those with evil or misguided intents. Despite his black clothes and mustache, Paladin is the hero, as his very name reveals.[81] A paladin is a knight—originally, one of the twelve champions of Charlemagne, the King of the Franks whose medieval court invented chivalry. Paladin's name, along with the chess knight adorning his holster and his calling card, proclaims him the defender of the weak and the deserving. Each time the card appears on the screen, announcing "Have Gun, Will Travel. Wire Paladin, San Francisco"—which it does once, and only once, in each episode—Herrmann's four-note theme is heard, in a wide variety of orchestrations and tempi, to suit the mood of the moment. The card and its slogan, the chess knight, and the musical theme thus form the leit-motif of the character.

The first episode also establishes Paladin's other side—his elegant San Francisco lifestyle, his voracious consumption of newspapers, and his eye for the ladies (in the opening moments of the episode, he exchanges an intimate flirtatious smile with a young woman in fancy evening dress—a young woman who appears, astonishingly, to be of mixed black and Chinese heritage). And it introduces Hey Boy, though only in passing. When Paladin meets his first employer, Jesse Reed, he reveals himself as an expert in military history and tactics—probably schooled at West Point (though this is not confirmed until a later episode). He also reveals a reluctance to talk about his own past. Once he arrives in the Mexican outlaw town, Paladin demonstrates his comfort with the Spanish language and Hispanic culture, along with a striking politeness in his interactions with people of all social classes. Above all, we learn the central lesson: though Paladin is a "gun for hire," he is not an assassin, and cannot be paid to murder someone, however much they may deserve killing. He chooses strategy over violence whenever possible.

The initial reviews were, at best, moderate in their enthusiasm. On September 18, 1957, *Variety* commented (in typical *Variety*-speak): "In contrast to TV westerns of the past couple of seasons and many to come this fall, "Have Gun, Will Travel" makes no pretense at being an 'adult western,' which is to say it's strictly an actioner. There's no overlying psychological motif—it's strictly business, as is its lead character, who when he's not living it up in San Francisco, puts his gun out for hire. But a well-done action series can prove just as rewarding as a well-done 'adult' oater." However, they admit that Boone is "authoritative and commanding in his role." Later in the first season, Joe Morhaim reviewed the series in *TV Guide* in more dismissive terms.

> *Have Gun—Will Travel*, CBS's western series starring Richard Boone as a character with the single, improbable name of Paladin, strives mightily to be different. But, like a fish crossing a desert (that's different, too), it flops around painfully.... In actuality, Mr. Paladin (is it a first or last name?) is just another Superman (western edition). He meets and solves all problems with a monumental self-confidence and impassivity. When he sets out to do a job, there is no doubt about the outcome. He will triumph and then, smugly, move on to the next chore.

Morhaim concluded that the series "would certainly have a better chance of being an artistic success if it weren't so self-consciously arty."[82]

But despite this skepticism on the part of the entertainment media, audiences quickly warmed to the new series, and by the end of the season, it ranked fourth in the Nielsen ratings, and—infallible sign of success—Paladin merchandise began selling briskly in the toy stores.

Daily Life on Have Gun—Will Travel

During the six years of *Have Gun*, the series dominated almost every aspect of Boone's life, and his family's as well. Five days a week he was up at 5 a.m. and on his way to the studio, where he breakfasted and got into make-up, and the work began. Typically, it was 9 p.m. before he returned home and promptly went to bed so he could do it again the next day. Mondays they rehearsed; Tuesdays through Thursdays, they filmed; Fridays were reserved for publicity work. Despite this grueling schedule, the family did find ways to spend a little time together. During the week, Claire and Peter often joined Richard at the studio for lunch. But because he was so unavailable during the week, Boone reserved the weekends religiously for his family, and especially for Peter, though Peter reports that by Sunday his father was often too exhausted to do very much.

In later seasons, though, when the *Have Gun* company went out for extended location shoots, there was more family time for all the people involved. Three summers in a row, the crew spent a month in Bend, Oregon, shooting multiple episodes. Boone not only brought Claire and Peter, but insisted that the crew members should likewise bring their families— wives, children, even girlfriends. At first the crew was rather horrified, as Claire reported; traditionally, going on location meant the freedom to have "wild times." But then, as the families got to know each other, everyone began to look forward to it; the strong relationships that developed made it all more fun. There were regular activities for the families—picnics, barbecues, even baseball games, and frequent group dinners. These location excursions also gave Peter a chance to watch his father working, which made up for some of the absences during the year. As Peter grew older, he was even allowed to play small roles in a couple of episodes, to test whether he wanted to follow in his father's footsteps. (As it turned out, he didn't.)[83]

According to Claire, Dick always had a lot of friends on the set—a fortunate thing, since during filming he had little time to socialize with anybody else. In fact, this observation about friends on the set was true in two senses. In the first place, as the sole star of the series, Boone developed a lot of control, particularly over casting, directors, scripts, even costumes. He typically gave preference to actors he had known from the New York stage, from his previous Hollywood films, from *Medic*, and from the Brentwood Marketplace group, though others he had not worked with before quickly became favorites and were invited back frequently. Many of the directors, too, were people he had known and worked with in other venues, while Andy McLaglen, who directed the pilot and most of the first season, worked so well with Boone that he ultimately helmed over half of the show's 225 episodes, and quickly became a close personal friend of Boone's. But aside from such friends, as Claire observed, Richard's strongest relationships were not with the other actors but with the crew[84]—probably for the same reasons that, during the war, he was happier spending time with enlisted men than with officers. All his life, he seems to have preferred the company of skilled but unpretentious working people to that of higher-status members of society, even in his own profession.

In contrast to the epic battles he fought with producers and network "suits," Boone earned the love and admiration of most of the crew who worked with him. Having carefully selected his crew for their skills, especially unit managers and heads of technical departments (special effects, costumes, lighting, and so on), he treated them both as friends and as professionals, with fairness and with respect for their expertise. As actor Rayford Barnes commented, "Boone's idea was that if you have a happy crew, you'll have a better show, everyone pulling together as a team. Let's make this product by everybody working together without any jealousies or envies between departments." In the midst of the fourth season, *Have Gun*'s chief grip (head electrician), Wilbur Kinnett, who came to the series after a long career with Gene Autry, Roy Rogers, and Republic Pictures, declared, "I've never seen a happier company than this. And it's all due to Dick. He's a fine guy to work with."[85]

It wasn't that Boone's temper magically grew serene and easy-going as soon as the "suits" left, for there were still outbursts, some of them unreasonable. But most of the people who worked with him regularly understood that his anger was not a star's egotistic temper tantrums but instead reflected both the enormous stress he was under, and his commitment to the highest standards for his show. They also recognized that his temper was generally reserved for those who had earned it. Harry Carey, Jr., a frequent guest on the show, remarked, "I'd see him get nasty once in awhile when somebody didn't do his job right, you know. He wasn't moody, but he might blow his stack over something." Actor/songwriter Johnny Western agreed: "Dick's theory was, 'If you come to work and do the best job that you're capable of, that's fine.' But if you were a professional and you come to work and do an amateur job, look out 'cause he's going to be all over you like a cheap suit."[86] And Carey added, "You didn't feel, however, that you were under his thumb; you weren't subservient to him in any way."[87]

Boone also made it clear that he was not the only person on the set allowed to express anger. In any community that works so closely together and under such intense pressure, anger must be a fairly common occurrence. Uncontrolled, it could have been disruptive, but Boone devised a technique for transforming anger into humor. As Harry Carey tells the story, the head of men's wardrobe, a short dapper man named Joe Dimmitt, periodically went into rages on the set. In response, Boone procured an apple box which he had painted red, white, and blue. Then, said Carey, "When Dimmitt would go into one of his rages, Boone would make him stand on top of this apple box and make his speech. Anybody who started to lose his temper had to get on that apple box."[88] Though Carey does not indicate whether the star used the box himself, Boone's ritual allowed anger to be simultaneously expressed and detoxified, giving it a recognized place while turning it into an amusing performance for the crew.

According to all the witnesses, fun was a key aspect of life on the *Have Gun* set, making the long hard hours of work more tolerable. Carey observed that Boone had the most "exquisite sense of humor I have ever seen on a guy. He just liked to laugh at things."[89] Another key factor in the atmosphere was that, whether in town or on location, the *Have Gun* set was remarkably egalitarian. Contrary to Hollywood custom, there was no "star table"; everyone ate lunch together, star, cast, and crew alike. As actress Fintan Meyler remembered, "We all sat at the studio commissary ... around one or two tables; [we were a] very family oriented show, much like *Gunsmoke*, not common for the other television shows." Johnny Western recalled frequent lunches in the restaurants around the studios, when Boone typically picked up the tab for the whole group; there would be drinks, and lots of jokes and laughter, Boone's the heartiest laugh of all. And, unlike other series, where the wrap party was a once-a-year affair, the *Have Gun* crew held a wrap party every week. According to Peggy Rea, an old friend of Boone's from the Brentwood Marketplace Group as well as *Have Gun's* production secretary, these wrap parties typically started on the saloon set on stage and worked their way up to Paladin's Carlton suite. Claire usually came in to join Richard for these parties and the dinner that followed. Occasionally, the whole group moved down to the Chinatown restaurant owned by the family of Kam Tong, the actor who played Hey Boy.[90]

Under Boone's influence, sometimes these after-work parties turned into spontaneous excursions. As Andy McLaglen tells the story, Boone was "a little bit crazy! He'd finish shooting one day and say to a couple of cast members and the director, 'Come on, let's fly up to San Francisco.' 'What?' 'Yeah, let's fly up there; we'll be back by tomorrow morning.'" And always, Boone would pay for the trip out of his own pocket. Frank Pierson, who became producer in the fourth season, recounts what surely must have been the most memorable of these excursions. Arriving early at the studio one morning, he found actor William Conrad, the guest star of that week's episode, sitting on the sidewalk waiting for him. Conrad explained the situation: "Well, you've got no star, you've got no cameraman, and the stunt man's gone too." The night before, filming had ended a little early, and Boone had taken a small group, including Conrad, in search of a Chinese dinner. In those days, Los Angeles rolled up its sidewalks quite early in the evening, so it was hard to find a place to go out and eat. Boone's solution was to fly the whole group to San Francisco. Unfortunately, by the time they reached their chosen restaurant, it was closed, so back they went to the airport. By this time, Pierson observed, they had already been drinking for hours, so instead of flying home, they decided to charter a plane to Hawaii. That was when Conrad left the party, returning to LA while the rest went on without him. With this much of a clue, Pierson started calling around and finally located his wandering star at an airport in Hawaii, "trying to get to Hong Kong for a Chinese dinner." He laughed, "You can imagine how drunk they were at that time."[91]

Indeed, alcohol was always a significant feature of the after-work socializing of the *Have Gun* crew, as it was for much of society in the 1950s and 1960s—and not just the beer and wine that are common now; in those days, the social custom was cocktails and hard liquor flowing freely. However, all the commentators agree that the partying was never allowed to affect the next day's work. As Harry Carey put it, Boone "made drinking a kind of sport and fun.... Dick was amazing. Despite all the drinking that he did, I never saw him when he wasn't absolutely sharp as a tack at work, and I never saw him miss a line of dialogue." Every actor, even the most skillful, blows a line from time, Carey pointed out; "they forget a line here or there or they say it wrong. I never saw Boone do that." Though a hangover might make work unpleasant—especially an early-morning call on location in the desert, with the sun hot and bright—still, everyone was there and ready, if occasionally grouchy. And, Carey explained, help was always close at hand. At Boone's instructions, the first aid crew always stocked hangover remedies to make the sufferers feel better. Rayford Barnes explained the rules: however much alcohol got consumed,

> you had better be ready the next morning. If I'm a special effects guy on a team of three guys and I'm depending on the others and they are depending on me, and you come in half corked, out drunk, and can't do the job right, you could kill somebody. The same thing was true of the stunt men. The same with the actors; if you come in half drunk and can't remember your lines and are missing your marks, you're affecting the whole scene, and other actors wouldn't like it.[92]

Peter Boone later observed thoughtfully that his father did sometimes drink more than was good for him, but added, "I never saw it get in the way of his work." But he also offered a crucial insight into Richard's temperament: "He couldn't stand to be bored.... As long as he had projects going, things to be thinking about—whether it was writing a screenplay, working on something in Hawaii with kids [where the Boones moved after *The Richard Boone Show*], or even fishing—if he had something to occupy himself, then everything was fine, and the partying was great and good fun." In later years, Peter admitted, when the good roles dried up and the movers and shakers in Hollywood had forgotten Richard's name, his father's drinking grew heavier and began to take a serious toll on his health.[93] But during the Paladin years, Boone was working well, and the partying was still fun, still under control.

It can be difficult for a twenty-first–century audience, when drunkenness has become socially unacceptable (though far from uncommon), to understand its casual acceptance fifty years ago. There is also no question that the long-range costs of the custom were high for many people, including Boone himself. But it is important to keep the stories of the *Have Gun* after-work parties in the context of the time, to see it as it was seen then—as nor-

mal and customary, and remembered afterward largely for its intense sense of fun and camaraderie.

Daily Life Off the Set

Aside from such socializing on the set, Richard Boone lived a remarkably quiet life for
a television star of his magnitude. He and Claire avoided the Hollywood party circuit; Claire
had had her fill of that life with her first husband, and Richard, who was surprisingly shy
away from his work, generally preferred a quiet dinner alone with his wife, or with one or
two close friends—Andy McLaglen and his wife Sally, Lewis and Kendall Milestone, a few
other couples. The Boones also celebrated the holidays with a circle of friends in Hollywood.
As Claire remarked, though Richard was not at all religious himself, he was interested in
both Judaism and Christianity, and quite knowledgeable about both traditions. His study
of Judaism was partly motivated by mother's heritage: in fact, as the child of a Jewish mother,
he was technically a Jew himself, though this was a point no one emphasized. Besides, as
Claire pointed out, most of the Boones' friends in Hollywood were Jewish. In a spirit of
community, Richard, Claire and Peter would celebrate all the Jewish holidays with their
friends, while their friends would join them for Easter and Christmas festivities.[94]

In general, the Boones lived quite modestly. In 1953, when Peter was born, they bought
a small house in Pacific Palisades on the G.I. Bill. Even when Boone's career took off with
Medic and he began making better money, they stayed in the small house, though they did
begin to fill it with valuable art and antiques, including some rare Japanese prints, a Ming
vase, a Benjamin West, a Turner, and two Teniers, along with some antique furniture, a collection then valued at $75,000–$100,000. But Boone's prize possession was the barber chair
Abraham Lincoln used in the White House, acquired through his friend Vincent Price.
Shockingly, much of this collection (along with their other possessions) was lost to fire in
February 1959 while they were out of town, though fortunately the Lincoln chair, which
was in Richard's den, was not damaged.[95] But the family now needed a new house. By this
time, Boone was making $250,000 a year as Paladin. Hollywood custom was for stars to
spend about a year's salary on their homes; instead, Richard and Claire chose a house in
Mandeville Canyon that cost only $45,000. Such unpretentiousness set the Boones even
further apart from the Hollywood lifestyle, though reporter Richard Gehman points out
that, having purchased a modest house, Boone added features to it (a sitting room, a double
dressing room on the master bedroom, and a swimming pool) that doubled the cost.[96] Even
so, the choice speaks volumes about Boone's priorities and values.

He had not always been so sensible about money. Having grown up relatively wealthy,
Boone tended to take money for granted, as his first two wives had learned to their dismay:
in his mind, money was for spending, with no thought to the future. When he and Claire
were first married, Boone still kept this attitude, even buying a racing stable with his brother
Bill in 1952. As Claire recounts, they had a lot of fun the next four years, traveling the California race circuit, down to Del Mar during the summer, up to San Francisco's tracks, to
Lexington, Kentucky to buy horses. But horse racing is a very expensive hobby, and with
Richard's salaries still fairly small at the beginning of his career, the stable was consuming
most of their money. At last Claire pointed out diplomatically that they really couldn't afford
to keep racing, so Richard sold out in 1956.[97] From that time on, Boone became far more
conscientious about money. By 1958, *TV Guide* reported that Boone invested any spare cash

in land, annuities, and life insurance. He also made a shrewd financial bargain with CBS. By the end of *Have Gun*'s third season, the series was so successful that the network was anxious to acquire all residual rights to Paladin, and offered the actor a million dollars to buy him out totally. But if he had taken the money in a lump sum, most of it would have gone to the government in taxes. Instead, Boone proposed that they pay him $50,000 a year for the next twenty years—an offer they accepted, setting a precedent other stars would soon follow.[98] He followed the same strategy later with his subsequent series, *Hec Ramsey* (1972–74). Although he became more careful about money, financial advantage never dictated his choices about what work he did. Though he could earn as much as $15,000 for a personal appearance, he was quite cautious about the opportunities he accepted. In particular, fearful of being typecast, he refused all the numerous rodeo appearances he was offered on the grounds that Paladin was "not a cowboy," preferring occasions where he could wear a modern tuxedo or other clothing that would remind viewers he was an actor, no more a real gunfighter than he had been a real doctor.[99]

As *Have Gun—Will Travel* grew in popularity, Boone's fans became legion. In particular, women responded to Paladin with intense fervor. His friend Peggy Rea explained that, though Boone was not handsome in any conventional sense, "he had a tremendous charisma and sex appeal that a lot of women liked."[100] By the end of the third season, Boone was receiving some 4,000 letters a month from women fans alone, more than any other Western star on TV. One woman wrote, "You know what you want, and your word is good. You make a woman feel secure. You are tender, strong and elegant." Other fans appreciated the intellectual qualities of the series and the character. After one episode in which Paladin meditated on the philosophies of Pliny and Aristotle, a San Diego columnist mused, "Where else can you see a gun fight and absorb a classical education at the same time?" while a high school teacher wrote Boone, "Yours is the only Western I recommend to my students. You speak English."[101] On the other hand, any time Boone was out in public, fans often intruded, harassing the star almost beyond endurance. All Hollywood stars got this treatment, of course; it was an accepted part of the business, but many of them managed to be more gracious with autograph seekers than Boone. In fact, he seldom signed autographs; instead he handed out copies of Paladin's card, "Have Gun—Will Travel," or had assistants hand them out for him so he would not have to deal with fans himself. Richard Gehman, accompanying Boone on a road trip from a location in Arizona back to Los Angeles, reported the actor's deep irritation when importunate fans crowded the hotel lobby, delaying their departure.

Yet on that same trip, Gehman saw a completely different side of the star, when Boone stopped in Phoenix at a labor union's rehabilitation center for handicapped children to drop off a donation he had raised for them. Boone always felt a special bond with children, focusing much of his charitable work on children's hospitals, schools, and orphanages, and programs like the Fraternal Order of Eagles' efforts to provide children with hearing aids. On this day, Boone's irritation and impatience melted away the moment he met the children, all afflicted with serious medical problems, from deafness to cerebral palsy and hydrocephaly. As Gehman observed, these children

> released the reservoir of humanity that is one of Boone's huge supply of assets as an actor. He knelt and whispered to a hopelessly gnarled six-year-old hunchback as though they were old friends. He went around passing out his cards and took his time about it, having a word with each baby. "If you ever get into any trouble around here," Boone said in his Paladin voice, "send me one of those and I'll come and straighten it out." He winked at the nurses and teachers, who laughed back. Some were fighting tears of gratitude.

Gehman points out that all stars do such personal appearances occasionally; it is part of the business of being a Hollywood star. But Boone's connection with the children seemed genuine. If it was a only a performance, it was an exceptionally skillful one, and one that no one had forced on him.[102]

Boone did not seek out publicity for this charity work, or use it to burnish his movie star reputation, but instead did it quietly, in private. Having led a life of privilege and opportunity, he was simply giving something of himself to those who had very little.

Other Work in the Paladin Years

When *Have Gun* went on hiatus for a couple of months each year, Boone was able to pursue other projects. He made a number of films in these years. When John Wayne made his film of *The Alamo* (1960), he brought Boone in to play a brief cameo as General Sam Houston. Boone never even took a salary for the job, as he was only on the set for six hours, and any pay he got would mostly have gone to taxes; instead Wayne gave him the fringed buckskin jacket he wore as his costume—and a Rolls Royce. Boone loved fancy cars, and loved driving fast in those fancy cars, so he was delighted with his "pay."[103] *A Thunder of Drums* (1961) was a cavalry picture featuring Boone as the tough-as-nails commander of a cavalry outpost in the 1870s. The role was so conventional that, with his years of experience, Boone could have handled it competently without much effort, but such a half-hearted approach was alien to his nature. Before shooting began, he requested a meeting with the screenwriter and spent two hours asking questions about the life of his character before the script picks him up.[104] He also made a number of television dramas in these years. Between April 1959 and spring of 1960, he did two productions for the *U.S. Steel Hour*, and appeared twice on *Playhouse 90*, while in January 1962, he starred in a live television presentation of Stephen Vincent Benet's narrative poem, "John Brown's Body."

But his most gratifying project came during the third season of *Have Gun—Will Travel*—not a film this time, but a return to the stage. In the fall of 1958, producer Cheryl Crawford from the Actors Studio asked him to play Abraham Lincoln in her Broadway production of *The Rivalry*, a Norman Corwin play based on the Lincoln-Douglas debates of 1858. Boone told her, "Don't torture me, please. Don't feed the animals while they're at work. They won't let me out of this cage."[105] But after reflection, he realized that if they shot the remaining third-season episodes at double speed (two episodes per week, rather than one), he could buy himself a few extra months of free time between seasons. So a spate of frantic work ensued, and by mid–December 1958, the entire season was complete. Though the series' ratings remained high, some of those involved felt that the speed had hurt the quality of the show; unit production manager Howard Joslin commented that "the scripts could have been better if we had the time to be choosy," but he acknowledged that the Broadway project was too important to Boone to be resisted.[106] In February 1959, Boone moved his family to New York. For the next four months, he happily played Lincoln on Broadway opposite Martin Gabel as Douglas, to critical acclaim.

Being back on the stage before a live audience revitalized Boone as an actor. One reason is that there was considerable improvisation involved in the production, which was not a traditional drama but a re-enactment of the original debates, inviting audience response. As Claire explained, "People would jump in and yell something out, so Dick and Marty would have to modify their dialogue somewhat to incorporate audience comments."[107] Working on the production was a delicious challenge for Boone. Everyone told him to subdue his personality in playing Lincoln—everyone but the poet Carl Sandburg, who had won a Pulitzer Prize for his biography of Lincoln. Sandburg told him, "Turn loose, boy; play Lincoln like a human being, a real salty guy." One night during the run, Sandburg came to the theatre unannounced, and took a seat in the third row.

> "Well, I knew I couldn't hide," Boone said later, "so I played every line to Sandburg." After the performance, Sandburg visited Boone in his dressing room. He looked at him silently for several minutes before he spoke. "I liked you, boy," he said finally. "I liked you very much."[108]

This simple praise from Sandburg gratified Boone more than the most effusive review ever could have.

The End of Paladin

Boone's original contract for *Have Gun—Will Travel* ran five years. By the third season, he was getting restless playing the same role over and over, and needed new challenges to keep himself fresh. After a sustained struggle with his producers, Boone began directing episodes as well as starring in them. In the end, he directed 28 episodes, more than any other director except Andy McLaglen. But even so, boredom finally caught up with him, that condition Boone seems to have dreaded above all. As he explained to a journalist in 1961, "Most actors attempt to capitalize on a success by doing more of the same. I have to go the other way. I want to do more—much more—than be a cowboy in TV."[109]

By the fifth season, then, Boone was publicly eager to leave Paladin behind him. However, CBS executives, reluctant to lose a series which was still doing relatively well, offered him $1,100,000 for another 38 episodes, one more season.[110] Surprisingly, Boone agreed. Partly, the money was too good to turn down: he always called this his "go-to-hell money," the financial stake that would allow him to do whatever he wanted at the cost of one more season. But that final year as Paladin also gave him time to build toward his long-held dream: a repertory company of his own, this one on television rather than the stage. *The Richard Boone Show* premiered on NBC in September 1963. Though Boone began the project with the highest expectations and good responses from audiences, the show was summarily cancelled halfway through the first season. It was a betrayal so bitter that Boone never got over it. He fled Hollywood to move his family to Hawaii and concentrate the next six years on being a hands-on father.

But for the six years he was Paladin, Boone controlled nearly every aspect of the series, and used it to communicate his most important concerns to the American viewing public. In the next chapter, we will go behind the scenes of *Have Gun—Will Travel* to see how he managed to place his personal stamp so thoroughly on the show, and to study the team he worked with so closely, in comparison to his show's three most popular rivals.

FOUR

Behind the Scenes: *Gunsmoke, Wagon Train, Bonanza, Have Gun—Will Travel*

Creating a successful television series requires the efforts of an extraordinary number of people, most of whom the audience never sees or thinks about. While everybody recognizes the actors who embody the continuing characters, viewers seldom give serious thought to the people behind the camera: the series creator who comes up with the original idea, the producers who give that idea a concrete form, the writers who create the specific stories that bring the characters to life, and the directors who construct the sequence of images that convey the stories to us—not to mention the army of designers, technicians and craftspeople needed to create the illusion of (for example) Dodge City, San Francisco's Hotel Carlton, or the Ponderosa as real places. Yet what we see on our television screens is shaped by all these people.

In order to understand the unique place of *Have Gun—Will Travel* among television Westerns, it is useful to carefully examine its main competitors between 1955 and 1963: *Gunsmoke, Wagon Train,* and *Bonanza*. In particular, whose vision determined the shape of each series as a whole? What priorities and values dictated the kinds of stories each series chose to tell?[1]

Gunsmoke *(1955–1975)*

Who over the age of 40 doesn't know *Gunsmoke*?—the first of the adult Westerns, and the longest-running, best-loved Western on television. Dodge City, Kansas, 1873. Marshal Matt Dillon, played by 6'7" James Arness, was the epitome of sincerity, integrity, and quiet compassion, and dedicated to maintaining civic order. Doc Adams was the town's doctor, played by veteran actor Milburn Stone. Under his grumpy exterior, Doc was fiercely devoted to his patients and their welfare, doing his best for them with the few remedies available in his little black bag. Pretty Miss Kitty Russell (Amanda Blake), bar girl and eventual owner of the Long Branch Saloon, was the marshal's friend and confidante. Though Matt and Miss Kitty often exchanged sly innuendo and lingering glances (Blake and Arness referred to such scenes as "eyeballing"),[2] their relationship remained a model of decorous affection for twenty years. Finally there was Chester Goode, Matt's loyal deputy, with a bum leg, a twang in his voice, and an endless fund of homespun stories. As played by Dennis Weaver, Chester provided his boss with unquestioning support, and his friends with a reliable source of comedy. For the first nine years of the series (until Weaver moved on in 1964), these four characters were the heart of Dodge City.

The focus of the series was not limited to the traditional "outlaw-versus-lawman" story that Matt Dillon's central role would suggest: *Gunsmoke* examined a wide range of the problems frontier people encountered. Because Dodge City in the 1870s was a crossroads, it drew all kinds of people, many passing through on their way to somewhere else, but others wanting a place to settle. Criminals and con artists came looking for a rich score; gunmen came chasing an enemy—or running from one. Many people came to Dodge to find a new start, but sometimes their pasts followed them and led to trouble. Another potent source of trouble in Dodge was prejudice—usually prejudice against Indians, but on one occasion a young Chinese man was the target of bullies, and old Civil War animosities provided another predictable source of conflict. Of course, it wasn't just newcomers or travelers that found trouble in Dodge. Like every town, Dodge had its share of those who sought prestige and power by abusing those weaker than themselves. Local residents often found themselves in violent conflict with their neighbors, or even members of their own family, over property, money, or relationships. Finally, each of the main characters, Kitty no less than the men, was exposed to frequent danger due to the demands of their professions.

When trouble arose in Dodge from any of these causes, Matt, Doc, Chester, and Kitty responded, using their best resources to solve the problem, to maintain (or restore) order and civility. As Horace Newcomb observes, together the four central characters represented a standard by which other people's behavior could be evaluated. Marshal Dillon represents "the more legalistic aspects of order," while Doc, Chester and Kitty function as observers who "will stand as the moral judges of the actions that surround them. They are ... unwilling to make simplistic condemnations of other people's actions. In short, they are the representatives of sophistication and civilization."[3]

In between the eruptions of conflict and violence, the principals could be observed in mundane daily interactions, sharing coffee and checkers in Matt's office or a beer at the Long Branch, chatting over purchases in the general store. Matt and Kitty flirted discreetly, Doc and Chester fussed at each other, Chester entertained the group with his stories, Matt teased Chester about his foibles, and Doc and Kitty periodically fretted about Matt and the dangers of his job. But whenever one of the principals was in pain or in danger (a common plot device over the years), the others mustered to assist their friend. Although many fans and critics attribute *Gunsmoke*'s popularity to its superior storytelling, others believe that the relationships among this tight-knit little group, obviously devoted to each other despite their bickering, explain more about the show's appeal than the plot of any given episode. As Dennis Weaver argued in an interview in 1986, "I think the most important thing about that show is that people identified with those characters. They became real. They became a family on television and people wanted to tune in to see what was happening to their friends."[4]

Wagon Train *(1957–1965)*

Two years after *Gunsmoke* first appeared on the small screen, *Wagon Train* made its debut, inspired by John Ford's *Wagonmaster* (1950). The setting was 1869; a wagon train was leaving St. Joseph, Missouri to travel the 2000 miles to California.[5] Week by week, the wagon train made its way across country till, at the end of the season, it reached its destination in Sacramento. The following season started over in St. Joseph with a new set of families, and the journey began again. The wagon train had a permanent staff of four characters. Ward Bond got top billing as the gruff but wise wagon master, Major Seth Adams. After almost three decades as a character actor in supporting roles (many for his good friends John Wayne and John Ford), Bond suddenly and gratifyingly found himself a star.[6] Also receiving star billing was a lean handsome young actor and expert horseman, Robert Horton, who played scout Flint McCullough, the perfect foil for Bond's crusty character. The remaining regulars, assistant wagon master Bill Hawks and cook Charlie Wooster, were played by Bond's long-time friends and associates, Terry Wilson and Frank McGrath—experienced stuntmen whose hiring Bond had insisted on as a condition of his signing for the series. Viewers soon knew exactly what to expect from the regulars: complaints and comedy from Charlie Wooster, quiet competence from Bill Hawks, and clashes between Adams' experience and McCullough's dashing exuberance.

As a series with few fixed characters and no fixed locations, *Wagon Train* had wider latitude in choosing storylines than *Gunsmoke*, though the shared Western genre insured certain common themes. The members of the wagon train, like the settlers who came to Dodge City, were generally leaving something behind in the East—failure, shame, grief—hoping to find a better life in California. Some came seeking redemption from weaknesses that had undermined their prospects in the past. But the past has a way of catching up to them, forcing a dramatic confrontation and some sort of resolution (generally positive, by the television conventions of the period). A remarkable number of the episodes feature women as central characters, most likely because of *Wagon Train*'s unique format, combining the adult Western with the popular dramatic anthology, in which the four continuing characters provided continuity while the major dramatic interest rested on the guest stars of each episode. This pattern allowed more scope for domestic stories than is typical in television Westerns with continuing characters. As a result, many episodes explored new relationships developing among the travelers in the course of the journey, a love story ending in marriage or an isolated person being welcomed into a new family.

On the other hand, some members of the wagon train, as in any human group, turn out to be selfish mischief-makers or worse, con artists with schemes up their sleeves, or villains seeking vengeance or a handy place to hide. When a person is revealed as a trouble-maker, the leaders and members of the wagon train work hard to prevent or undo the damage. Other common story lines draw on the conflicts still unresolved from the Civil War, so recently concluded, or on the Indian Wars, at their height in the 1870s—familiar Western stories about the U.S. Army in frontier outposts, and about wagon trains being attacked by marauding Indians. Although some of the stories about Indians treat them relatively sympathetically, as individuals who should be judged on their actions rather than their ethnic identity, or acknowledging that some Indian violence against settlers was prompted by white mistreatment and betrayal, more often Indians are stereotyped as marauding savages. So the series proved less enlightened about Indians than about women.[7]

The *Wagon Train* formula offered audiences a most appealing package: the pleasures of the adult Western, plus the excitement of movie stars in their living rooms, all unified by the four continuing characters into a satisfying whole. On *Wagon Train*, as on *Gunsmoke*, "The recurring cast's interrelationships, problems, and camaraderie contributed greatly to the sense of 'family' that bound disparate elements of the series together."[8]

Bonanza *(1959–1974)*

Bonanza, set in Nevada in the booming silver-strike days of the late 1850s, was another ensemble show, but this time the characters literally were a family: the Cartwrights on their 1000-square mile ranch, the Ponderosa. *Bonanza* was the first of what Ralph Brauer calls "property Westerns," series which focus on the challenges of running a large estate, and on the wealth and power of the family that owns it.[9] Widower Ben Cartwright rules the Ponderosa with his three grown sons, each by a different mother. Adam, the oldest (portrayed by Pernell Roberts), sprang from New England stock on his mother's side. The intellectual of the family, college-educated, sensitive, and serious, the hard-working Adam was clearly in training to take over the Ponderosa in due time. Dan Blocker played middle son Hoss (a Norwegian name meaning "big friendly man," given to him by his mother), a gentle giant with a gift for nurturing animals, children, and wounded things. Though Hoss could be a trifle slow on the uptake, especially compared to Adam's fierce intelligence, he combined great physical strength with an irresistible sweetness of spirit. Michael Landon was the hot-headed, impulsive youngest son, Little Joe, the romantic of the family, whose mother was a southern belle from New Orleans. Like most siblings, especially those of such dissimilar temperaments, the three Cartwright sons frequently quarreled among themselves. Hoss and Little Joe could often be found conspiring to escape work, or teasing their elder brother. Adam, as family-head-in-training, was frequently critical of his brothers' scapegrace attitudes, but in the face of outside threats, the family showed a united front.

Ben Cartwright himself, a stern but loving father, was played by Canadian actor Lorne Greene. Deep of voice, grave of manner, Ben started out as a Bible-quoting disciplinarian and environmentalist who fiercely defended the boundaries of his ranch against any intruders, however accidental. Under pressure from Greene, in later seasons Ben's character grew warmer to his sons and more reasonable about his property lines. He became the leading citizen of Virginia City by virtue not only of his wealth and power as the largest land-owner around, but also of his wisdom, exhibited in crisis after crisis. Though he was sometimes resented in Virginia City for his prominence, Ben was also respected by most of his community.

Unlike other family-focused series on television in the period, whether domestic comedies or dramas, the Cartwright sons were not (in the memorable description of series creator, David Dortort) "little brats who talk like Leonard Bernstein" but grown men. The subject of *Bonanza*, its creator maintained, was "a love affair between four strong men." Another deliberate feature of the series: there were to be no women in the Cartwright family. Dortort declared, "We do not have any Moms built into our show—or for that matter, any women. We are, as it were, anti–Momism."[10] Despite this rejection of women as continuing characters, all four Cartwrights, even Ben, take regular turns falling in love. However, all these romances are doomed to fail: by the end of the episode, the woman in question must die tragically, whether by illness, accident, or murder, or leave the territory, or marry someone else.[11] Though the romances never lead to marriage, they are dramatically useful, allowing the Cartwrights scenes of powerful joy and equally powerful suffering without disrupting the all-male family.

As strong as the bond is between father and sons, brother and brother, the Cartwrights are also bound together by devotion to their beautiful ranch. Indeed, network publicity frequently referred to the Ponderosa as the fifth member of the cast. The Cartwrights' love for the Ponderosa is marked by a profound sense of stewardship, what would soon be called environmentalism.[12] This reverent attitude to the land leads to stories in which the Cartwrights must beat back threats of environmental degradation to the Ponderosa—mining operations that would pollute its waters, invasion by grazing sheep herds that would destroy the grassland, mass logging that would strip the hillsides of the Ponderosa pines that give the ranch its name.

Other typical stories, especially in the first seasons, are drawn from historical incidents, like the discovery of the Comstock Lode, the approach of the Civil War, statehood for Nevada, and the Paiute War of 1859–60. Historical figures associated with Virginia City in this general period also make appearances in the stories, famous entertainers like Lotta Crabtree and Adah Isaacs Menken; young newspaperman Samuel Clemens, before he became Mark Twain; Virginia City madam Julia Bulette, who turned her saloon into a hospital during an influenza epidemic and was later murdered by her lover; the great Apache chief, Cochise; and Doc Holliday and Calamity Jane. But by far the most common story line (other than a Cartwright romance) concerned one or more of the Cartwrights in danger—wounded, kidnapped, or arrested and threatened with hanging—and needing rescue by the rest of the family. Another frequent threat to Cartwright well-being arose when one of the family killed someone, always either in self-defense or by accident, and found himself targeted in turn for revenge. The family relationships are so much the emotional center of the show that it attracted a large and loyal fan base, particularly among young people. By the third season (1961), a full 35 percent of *Bonanza*'s audience came from the 17-and-under demographic.[13]

Have Gun—Will Travel *(1957–1963)*

From the beginning, *Have Gun—Will Travel* offered a significant departure from the patterns of its major competitors. A key difference: unlike *Gunsmoke, Wagon Train*, and *Bonanza, Have Gun* had a single protagonist, Paladin, the sophisticated, cultured soldier of fortune, rather than an ensemble cast. This fact impacted most aspects of the series. On the level of plot, the story so common on *Gunsmoke* and *Bonanza*—the beloved continuing character needing rescue by friends or family—is simply irrelevant on *Have Gun*, creating space for other kinds of stories. Additionally, a series with an ensemble cast needs to spend some time almost every week on the relationships of the principals, separate from the plot of the episode—the jokes and complaints and flirting that binds the friends on *Gunsmoke*, Flint's cheeky irreverence and Major Adams' growling retorts on *Wagon Train*, the badinage between the Cartwright brothers on *Bonanza*. Audiences love these scenes, but they take time, leaving fewer screen minutes available to explore the issue in the plot and to develop the featured characters of the week. On *Have Gun*, by contrast, virtually all 24 minutes of the episode could be used to delve into the characters and the issues facing Paladin in greater depth and subtlety.

In another sharp contrast to the characters in the other series, Paladin leads two distinct lives, one of which is far removed from the conventional Western. At home in San Francisco, he is an elegant man-about-town, enjoying the finer things of life: dressed in silk and lace, playing a game of chess or savoring the classics of literature, history, and philosophy in the quiet of his hotel suite; attending the opera, the ballet, the theatre; indulging in the best food, wine, whiskey, and cigars the city has to offer, often in the company of a beautiful, and beautifully-dressed, woman, although he can also be found in an all-night high-stakes poker game, testing his skill and luck against the other players. Usually, the brief San Francisco scenes that frame most episodes serve to connect Paladin with the case or the client that will take him out onto the trail. A potential client seeks him out at his hotel, or a chance encounter in the Carlton's lobby piques his interest in a stranger's problems; a telegram arrives, asking for his help, or an article in one of the many newspapers he consults describes a conflict that intrigues him, or identifies a dangerous fugitive with a rich bounty on his head. More than once over the seasons, he takes on a task to repay a debt owed to a friend, or even an enemy. At other times, Paladin encounters a problem of his own—often involving a lady—best solved by removing himself from the city for awhile. Sometimes he is even driven out of San Francisco by more mundane considerations—temporary boredom with civilized life, or a need to replenish his bank account.

These San Francisco scenes also illuminate Paladin's personality and his values through his interactions with the only other recurring character in the series, Hey Boy, the Chinese porter at the Carlton Hotel, played by Kam Tong. Hey Boy performs a number of functions for Paladin: he procures the special newspapers Paladin consults regularly, and serves in turn as Paladin's factotum, social secretary, foil, verbal sparring partner, co-conspirator in romantic affairs, and liaison to San Francisco's Chinese community. But aside from these brief scenes with Hey Boy, Paladin anchors the series single-handed. So, in contrast to the ensemble shows, on *Have Gun*, the characters and the issues Paladin encounters in each new adventure get his (and our) full attention, without distractions.

Of course, once Paladin leaves San Francisco for the trail, the iconography changes dramatically. The opera cape and top hat, the lace cuffs and brocade vests, disappear; in their place, the close-fitting black trail clothes, the gun belt with the silver chess knight on the holster, the carefully-tended custom-made revolver, and the black hat. Like any good Western hero, Paladin is ready for action. Unlike the characters in the other series, however, Paladin's work offers him a remarkable degree of choice and variety, a different problem and a different locale each week. Also unlike the others, Paladin has a carefully-articulated philosophy which is an essential aspect of his character. Since he holds no official position with mandated rules and procedures, Paladin is free to construct his own ethical code. Despite the slogan on his card ("Have Gun—Will Travel") and his typical steep fee for his services, Paladin is not a "hired gun" in the traditional sense—not an employee bound to follow orders, but a consulting expert who follows his own judgment in deciding how best to solve a problem. He will not help a powerful person take advantage of weaker neighbors or relations, nor accept injustice without trying to achieve a more appropriate solution. Above all, he cannot be hired to kill anyone, even a fugitive "wanted dead or alive," no matter how high the price or how much that person may deserve killing.

Like a conventional bounty hunter, he often tracks and captures fugitives from justice, some fleeing from a trial, others escaped after having been convicted and sentenced. Unlike the normal bounty hunter, however, the reward money is generally not his primary motivation. The fugitives Paladin goes after are typically the hard cases that others do not have the skill or the legal authority to capture—those who are unusually dangerous or elusive, or who have crossed jurisdictional lines, out of reach of the proper authorities. Always his highest priority is to bring the prisoner in alive for trial or execution, despite the extra risk and trouble to himself.

This principle gets articulated most clearly in "The Outlaw" (1:2, September 21, 1957).[14] Paladin joins up with a posse chasing Manfred Holt, a deadly killer who has escaped from jail after being sentenced to hang in Laramie, Wyoming. The sheriff heading the posse matter-of-factly intends to shoot Holt instead of capturing him, to avoid the dangers of a two-week trip across country to Laramie during which Holt would be trying every trick possible to escape again. When Paladin objects to this plan, the sheriff looks surprised: "What's the difference between shooting now and hanging later?" Paladin replies sharply, "What's the difference between murder and justice?" The sheriff has a pragmatic point: Holt is dangerous and wily, has nothing to lose, and might easily kill some of the sheriff's deputies or even the sheriff himself to escape, but for Paladin, the principle takes priority. Executions should take place in public, in an institutional venue and overseen by the proper authorities.

As this exchange demonstrates, whether he is acting independently or in support of a local law officer, Paladin's default mode is to work through legal channels whenever possible, giving priority to elected officials and formal procedures. He refuses to act as the ultimate arbiter if any competent official authority is present. However, his informal status gives him certain advantages in this line of work. Where all lawmen, including Matt Dillon, have both specific responsibilities and specific limits on what they may do legally, as a freelancer, Paladin has a lot more flexibility. He can choose his clients and the challenges he is willing to tackle, and also his methods for each problem. Being unofficial, Paladin can intervene in circumstances where a lawman would have no standing, and he can even refuse a job if his client proves unreasonable, deceitful, or unjust.

Though he is expert with a variety of weapons and fighting styles, Paladin views violence both as a last resort and as evidence of failure. His preferred weapon, and the most effective, is his brain. Paladin combines a practical knowledge of tactics and strategy with a wide-ranging liberal education and a thoughtful understanding of human conflict. This makes him remarkably adaptable: depending on the needs of the case, he can function as military commander, detective, mediator, judge, mentor, or enforcer with equal effectiveness. Above all, Paladin recognizes that every dispute has more than one side. In resolving a problem, he must listen to all the different voices to determine the truth of the situation. Once he uncovers the actual issues in the dispute, he can devise a reasonable solution, and then figure out how to implement that solution.

Besides tracking fugitives, other typical assignments Paladin accepts include tracing missing persons, recovering stolen property, or mediating disputes between neighbors, business partners, or family members. He often steps in to defend victims of prejudice or those targeted for vengeance. Though he does not ordinarily hire out as a bodyguard, Paladin will agree to escort a vulnerable person or important cargo through dangerous territory and, under certain conditions, will provide temporary protection to a person being threatened. Despite his speed and accuracy with a gun, Paladin refuses to seek a reputation based on these accomplishments. His skill, combined with his lack of ego, makes him an ideal choice to confront a gunfighter threatening an individual or a community when there is no local lawman, or when the local lawman is not up to the challenge. In the reverse of these scenarios, several well-known gunmen turn to Paladin for help escaping from their reputations in order to retire safely. He is also an ideal choice as teacher on those few occasions when a client wants to improve his gun skills in order to fight his own battles. Now and then, the government calls on Paladin, because of his education, his West Point background and his distinguished Civil War service, to handle cases requiring discreet diplomacy: isolated Army posts in conflict with a local Indian tribe; senior Army officers suspected of malfeasance; or situations with foreign nationals requiring unofficial intervention. In each case, Paladin adapts his methods to the problem at hand, and devotes his skills and his energy to finding a just solution.

The Creators

Looking at the creators of each of these series reveals the source of many of the differences between them. Each creative team approached the Western with a distinct sense of what it should be, and what values they wanted their series to reflect.

Gunsmoke: *From Radio to Television*

For John Meston and Norman Macdonnell, the co-creators of *Gunsmoke,* which debuted on CBS radio in 1952 (three years before it reached TV), the highest priority was an authentic representation of the Western frontier, with all its hardships and dark, austere truths. Despising the prettified West of the "singing cowboys" like Gene Autry and Roy Rogers or the dandified Hopalong Cassidy, Meston insisted on telling the gritty truth about life on the frontier for the people who populated its isolated ranches and hard-edged, almost-ungovernable towns. He was not afraid to reveal the settlers' privations, nor the violence and cruelty that was such a common feature of their lives. In particular, Meston often wrote sympathetically about the harsh experiences of women and of Indians in the West. On the radio, Dodge City was a hard place, "an existential world of isolated beings."[15] People made mistakes, even Marshal Dillon. People died violently. Evil sometimes won. Stupidity or prejudice might defeat innocence and reason, because that's the way life really is.

However, when *Gunsmoke* transferred to television in September 1955, the tone of the series softened significantly. Though the interactions of the radio Matt, Doc, Kitty and Chester superficially resemble those of their television counterparts, the Barabases agree in their guide to the series that the radio characters were far more isolated emotionally. The Matt Dillon created on the radio by William Conrad was "more of a loner and a pessimist" than James Arness' TV marshal. In fact, Meston once observed of the radio character, "Dillon was almost as scarred as the homicidal psychopaths who drifted into Dodge from all directions."[16] Barabas explains, "On radio, Matt often makes poor value judgments and mistakes that sometimes cost men's lives. Conrad's Dillon is loud and abrasive. He has a short fuse and snaps at his friends when in a foul mood." He often seems angry and resentful at his burden of "being the law." By contrast, Arness's Dillon is slow to anger; even his occasional annoyance at Chester could be adequately conveyed by an impatient look. Though neither the radio nor the television Dillon likes killing, Arness' Matt seems much more at peace with his chosen profession than his radio counterpart.[17]

On the radio, Howard McNear's Doc is a drunk, habitually cynical, sometimes despicable, and generally motivated by greed. Death means gain to Doc, as he is paid for autopsies. Seldom does the radio Doc exhibit the gentleness so characteristic of Milburn Stone's Doc Adams, whom the town turns to for wisdom and advice. The pattern holds for Kitty's character as well. Where Amanda Blake's Kitty is a strong competent entrepreneur with only the faintest whisper of "fallen woman" in her past, the radio Kitty of Georgia Ellis is unambiguously a whore working in all of Dodge's various saloons; she is a victim who "belittles herself and feels she is unworthy to associate with the good folk of Dodge."[18] The only thing that distinguishes her from other prostitutes is that Matt has chosen her as a confidante. However, the fact that he confides in her does not mean that he loves her. Though the radio Kitty clearly loves Matt, his feelings for her are more ambivalent; their overtly sexual relationship for him seems to be mostly a matter of physical relief. Her tenuous position with him leaves the radio Kitty chronically insecure.

Alone of the four principals, Chester makes the conversion from radio to TV with little alteration. The primary difference is that the radio Chester of Parley Baer is not deputized, and shows a little less initiative than Weaver's Chester. John Peel describes the radio Chester as "a little more obsequious" than Weaver's, and also as subjected to considerably more verbal abuse. The radio Matt treated Chester with "a kind of good-natured contempt that occasionally could turn quite sharp,"[19] though he was capable of apologizing when he got too rough on Chester. And of course, the radio Chester doesn't limp. As Meston observed, "It's tough to limp on radio."[20] The limp, in fact, was a strategic choice, adopted because Dennis Weaver, at 6'4", was nearly as tall as James Arness, and had a notably athletic build. As a team, the two actors would have seemed too formidable for most of the villains who came up against them. The limp both made Chester less intimidating and justified his subordinate status.[21]

Over all, then, though *Gunsmoke* was billed as TV's first adult Western, Dodge City on television was a far less brutal place than it was on the radio. The stories had been lightened considerably, the main characters made more admirable and more nurturing of each other, their relationships softened and idealized.

Wagon Train: *An Anthology Western*

The creation story of *Wagon Train* is much simpler. NBC and Revue Productions wanted a unique entry in the popular new Western category, a series that would combine the adult western with the weekly star vehicle, like *GE Theater*. Their goal was to attract major performers known for their work in other genres, especially movies, to the small screen—and their network. The result was *Wagon Train*. A wagon train offered the ideal premise for an anthology series: each new episode could focus on a different member of the wagon train, and thus feature a different star. With the lure of an hour-long time slot and juicy starring roles, the producers were able to entice well-known movie actors to television, people like Ernest Borgnine, Ricardo Montalban, Michael Rennie, Shelley Winters, Agnes Moorehead, Keenan Wynn, James Whitmore, Cesar Romero, Linda Darnell, John Carradine, Gilbert Roland, and John Barrymore, Jr.—to name just the most famous actors from the first season.

However, NBC seemed clearer on the kinds of performers they wanted to attract to the series than on the kinds of stories they wanted to tell. The Western setting had been chosen primarily because Westerns were immensely popular in 1957, so producer Richard Lewis and his successor, Howard Christie, hired Dwight B. Newton, Western historian and novelist, to vet the scripts and stories for authenticity.[22] They also sought out directors with experience in Western films and writers who had written for other Western series, but then they asked those writers to create "strong personal stories" rather than more traditional Western plots.[23] In other words, the highest priority was creating featured roles that were substantial enough to attract established Hollywood names, thereby attracting large audiences, rather than telling authentic stories of the West. Not surprisingly with a corporate "creator," the vision for *Wagon Train* was not as consistent or coherent as some of its competitors.

Bonanza: *Dortort's Passion*

By contrast, *Bonanza* was the brainchild of writer and producer David Dortort, a native New Yorker who as a college student became fascinated with American history, particularly the period of the Old West. A stint of script-writing for film and television led Dortort to a job producing *The Restless Gun* on NBC, one of the better Westerns on television in 1957. When that show ended after two seasons due to the exit of its star, John Payne, NBC asked Dortort to come up with another Western series to meet the still-avid audience demand. In particular, they wanted a series that could be shot in color, as the network's parent company, RCA, had just begun to manufacture color TVs.[24] Dortort's proposal: *Bonanza*.

His concept was based on two priorities. First, he wanted to create something different from the familiar "one-man hero and his gun" Western, something grander. For inspiration, he turned to King Arthur and his knights. As Dortort explained in a 1962 interview, "The Ponderosa is not just a dusty, down-at-heels ranch. There's power, wealth and permanence there, and as such, it is the most important single home in television. The great house is like the castles of old, its occupants, kings, princes, knights."[25] A central element in Dortort's vision was his desire to create a father figure on television who was not a bumbler. He argued that, in the situation comedies of the 1950s, "Father always turned out to be a fool. On TV it's mother who really knows best." But his father figure would be different—strong, competent, commanding: "Ben Cartwright is not a blithering idiot, but someone his three sons can respect."[26] Those sons, by three different mothers and strikingly different from each other in temperament, were carefully designed to appeal to varied segments of the audience: the serious oldest son, Adam, to college coeds and young married couples; the romantic scapegrace, Little Joe, to teenagers; and Hoss, the gentle, good-natured giant, to children and those who loved them.

Dortort's second priority, once he had created his noble Western barons, was historical. He set his heroic family saga in a specific time and place: Nevada Territory in the late 1850s, when the Comstock Lode was discovered and Virginia City was founded, and the country was trembling on the brink of the Civil War. Such a setting, both colorful and significant in American history, provided an ideal context for the kinds of stories Dortort wanted to tell, combining education with entertainment, and all focused intensely on the relationship of a powerful, virtuous man and his three grown sons.

Have Gun—Will Travel: *When a Western Is Not a Western*

Unlike its competitors, *Have Gun—Will Travel* was, from its origins, an unconventional Western. The original concept, according to series co-creator Sam Rolfe, was a modern-day action/adventure show. His collaborator and fellow free-lance writer, Herb Meadow, had come up with the marvelous title, and together they developed the idea of a contemporary soldier of fortune living in New York City. Every morning their protagonist would descend from his penthouse at the Plaza Hotel, purchase a selection of national and international newspapers from a newsstand in Times Square, take them to Central Park, and start to read. When he found a problem that interested him, he would cut the article out with a small pair of scissors, put it in an envelope with his card: "Have Gun, Will Travel. Cable Paladin, New York City," and send it off by airmail. Receiving a reply, he'd board an airplane and head for adventure. That is the idea that Meadow and Rolfe registered with the Writer's Guild in 1956 and took to CBS. But the network wanted a Western—specifically, a companion Western as a lead-in to *Gunsmoke* on Saturday nights. If Rolfe and Meadow could convert their concept to a Western, they were told, they'd have a deal. They complied, shifting the locale to San Francisco in the 1870s, and making the requisite substitutions (horses, trains, and stage coaches for cars and airplanes, telegrams for cables, trail clothes for trench coat, and so on), and CBS bought their series.[27]

But even though it was now officially a Western, *Have Gun*'s unconventional origins continued to shape the series, through many changes in the production team over the seasons. Where the other three series experienced relative stability in the head office, *Have Gun* went through five producers in its six seasons. One reason for this comparatively high turnover is that, unlike Meston and Macdonnell of *Gunsmoke* and Dortort of *Bonanza*, who remained closely involved with their series (Macdonnell and Meston for ten years, Dortort for the entire fourteen-year run), Rolfe and Meadow had no desire to produce the series themselves. In fact, aside from co-writing the pilot and writing one other script in Season One and three in the final season, Meadow had no continuing association with *Have Gun*.[28] Rolfe wanted to be involved with the series, but did not want to produce; instead, he accepted a role as associate producer/story editor so he could supervise the choice of scripts and story material.

The second reason for the high turnover in producers is that Richard Boone, the star of the series, soon became producer in all but name: he acquired near-veto power over every aspect of the series, from scripts to casting to directors, even costuming. During his years on *Have Gun—Will Travel*, Boone gained a "Dr. Jekyll-and-Mr.-Hyde" reputation in Hollywood. On the one hand, as Richard Gehman reported in January 1961, "Few other stars are so earnestly, piously and vehemently hated. Scratch some actors who have worked on his shows and out gushes sulfuric invective." Some directors reacted the same way, while producers and network executives generally doubled down on the sentiment. At the same time, as Gehman went on to report, "Boone is genuinely loved—and admired—by the people of the *Have Gun* company. They have developed a camaraderie and an *esprit de corps*."[29]

The source of both reactions: Boone's driving ambition to get everything right, combined with his legitimate sense that the entire series rested on his shoulders. Those members of the team who did their work well and, above all, brought the right attitude to the work got Boone's generous support. Those who brought less than their best game—got lazy, or egotistic, cut corners or made decisions without thinking them through—would be scalded by his anger and contempt. Factor in Boone's lifelong resistance to authority, and it should surprise no one that his conflicts with producers, in particular, became legendary. Since few producers would be willing to tolerate so much interference for long, the turnover in the head office should be no surprise either. But until the last season, each new producer shared the vision of *Have Gun* as more than a traditional Western, and made decisions accordingly.

Have Gun's first producer was an industrious young New Yorker named Julian Claman, a veteran of CBS's prestigious *Playhouse 90*. He got *Have Gun* on its feet, found its first important writers and hired its most prolific and proficient director, Andrew V. McLaglen. Claman also successfully defended "Hey Boy's Revenge" (1:31, 4/12/58) against the network censors who wanted to block its broadcast for fear that audiences would object to its sympathetic treatment of Chinese characters.[30] However, the relationship between Claman and Boone had never been close, and at the end of first-season shooting, the two had a major blow-up, though none of the witnesses identify the cause of the fight. Recognizing that the network would side with an irreplaceable star over a producer, however capable, Claman left *Have Gun* at the end of the season. Reluctantly, Sam Rolfe had to step up into the producer's role literally overnight.[31]

As one of the series' creators, Rolfe had some definite ideas about directions for the show. In particular, he wanted to take *Have Gun* international in the second season, moving closer to the original non–Western vision of the series. As he pointed out to *Variety*, "There's no reason that the show should have to stay in a western setting, since the central character, though a gunman-for-hire, is also pictured as a literate sophisticate," and the title and character both lent themselves to a world setting.[32] Rolfe shared with the magazine his plan to film four shows in Mexico, possibly in a jungle site with some ancient ruins, then to move on to Hawaii for four to six more episodes, and, in subsequent seasons, to Japan and other parts of Asia. Though Rolfe's international plans never came to fruition, the show traveled more and more widely, doing far more location shooting than most of its competitors. Because the episodes were set in so many different kinds of outdoor settings, it was vital to the feel of the series that the show shoot as much footage as possible away from the studio. In the 1950s, numerous movie ranches and sites with varying landscapes were available within a day's travel of Los Angeles, and the *Have Gun* crew used all of them, but they also shot a number of episodes in Lone Pine, California, 200 miles north of Los Angeles in the shadow of the Sierra Nevadas, sometimes filming on site for a month at a time. Other locations in California that the company used included Squaw Valley, Bishop, Big Bear Lake, and the San Bernardino National Forest; they also traveled to Tucson, Arizona; Gallup, New Mexico; various sites in Utah; and three years in a row to Bend, Oregon, where they shot multiple episodes. Unusually, when *Have Gun* went on location, the entire episode was filmed there, interiors as well as exteriors, except for the Hotel Carlton scenes, all of which were shot on the standing set at the studio. Other series characteristically only filmed exterior scenes on site, and returned to the studio to shoot the interiors.[33] But here again, Boone's insistence on location shooting cost the network some money, but paid off in greater authenticity. Presciently, he had also argued for shooting the series in color, but the network refused, insisting that "color TV is nothing but a fad."[34]

The second season was even more successful with audiences than the first, as the character of Paladin began to be more fully established, and as new writers came on board to add depth to the issues being explored. However, by the end of that season, once again conflicts increased between star and producer. Boone wanted more and more control, and Rolfe kept resisting. As pre-production work on the third season began, Rolfe and Frank R. Pierson, his new story editor, were working together to make sure *Have Gun* remained a Western with a difference. In an interview, Pierson observed, "I was consciously trying to reach out for New York actors to bring in with fresh faces and attitudes so we could really invigorate the shows with something beyond the usual clichés of the 'Western.'"[35] But as the third season began shooting, tension between Rolfe and Boone quickly escalated. Boone kept asking to direct, and Rolfe kept refusing. Boone's problem, of course, was that he was starting to get bored, a chronic threat for such a voracious spirit. After more than 80 episodes, the character of Paladin was well-established, and Boone was eager for new challenges, new ways to grow—and also to gain more control over the final product. It led to increasingly bitter fights between producer and star.[36]

The outcome of the conflict was inevitable: once again, the producer was deemed replaceable while the star *was* the show. In Frank Pierson's version of the story, Rolfe and Boone had a fistfight on the set, and afterward Rolfe told his second-in-command, "'To hell with this shit, I don't want to do it any more. You take over.'" Later, Pierson mused, "Who knows what the argument was about? Boone ... had a temper to move and there were always little problems here and there on the set. Sam really didn't like that sort of junk and I don't think it was just one big thing that did it. He was through dealing with it, through dealing with the star's temperament any more."[37]

At that point, even though Pierson had just joined the show as story editor a few months before, he was the only one who knew "where the scripts were and who was writing them and where they were going to go," so he stepped up as de facto producer, though because he was so inexperienced, he was officially overseen by Ben Brady from CBS. And just before Rolfe left, Boone finally got his chance to direct a couple of episodes. Ben Brady also approved the star for another couple of directing opportunities, a total of six episodes by the end of the season. Once Boone got what he wanted, he became much more manageable. As director Andy McLaglen told Grams, Boone in the director's chair "was like a child at Christmas. When he got to call the shots, he enjoyed every moment. He allowed the actors to tell the story, and the camera was a conduit for the audience."[38] This observation, about allowing the actors to tell the story, is key; though part of Boone's object in directing was to increase his own control, he exercised that control unselfishly, even generously, not to make himself look better but to support the efforts of the team, and to give the audience the best possible show—attitudes strongly rooted in the values he learned at the Actors Studio.

With Pierson in the producer's seat, *Have Gun* seems to have entered a period of relative serenity; at least, there are no stories of major confrontations between Boone and Pierson in these years. Significantly, Pierson accommodated his star's desire to complete shooting the third season in a shortened period in order to perform on Broadway for four months, though it caused some stress on the entire crew to work at that speed. At the end of Season Three, Brady left to pursue his own projects, and Pierson officially took over the producer's role for Season Four, which would turn out to be both the most ambitious and the most successful season of the run. As producer, Pierson was open to all sorts of innovations, including controversial subject matter. For example, the fourth-season opener, "The Fatalist" (4:1, 9/10/60), featured Martin Gabel, Boone's Broadway co-star in *The Rivalry*, as Nathan Shotness, a tough but humorous Russian Jew who ran afoul of a local outlaw and needed Paladin's help. In 1960 there was still sufficient prejudice against Jews in American society that CBS ran a certain risk in broadcasting this episode—and tellingly, the *Variety* review of the episode describes Gabel's character as a "Russian peddler" without mentioning his Jewish identity, even though in the episode Paladin and Shotness exchange quotations from the Torah, some in the original Hebrew.[39] But the audience had been exposed to a respectful look at a cultural minority that was unfamiliar to most of them.

Pierson took other chances that season, clearly with Boone's support and approval, including some controversial casting choices. For example, he hired William Talman, best known as the district attorney on *Perry Mason*, for two episodes, to play a crippled old rodeo hand in "The Killing of Jessie May" (4:8, 10/29/60) and a hapless but well-meaning sheriff in "The Long Way Home" (4:21, 2/4/ 61). The problem was that Talman had recently lost his job on *Perry Mason* after being arrested for smoking marijuana at a wild Hollywood party, and been blacklisted.[40] Though he was not guilty of the charge and was eventually acquitted, network executives, fearful of public protest, objected to his hiring for *Have Gun*. When Boone heard the story, he snapped, "Oh, bullshit, that's all over and times are changing," and Pierson stood firm: Talman got the roles, and later, when no protest greeted his work on *Have Gun*, he got his old job back on *Perry Mason*.[41] More controversially, Pierson hired a number of black actors for the series. In 1950s television, as J. Fred MacDonald has documented in *Blacks and White TV*, black actors were exceedingly rare, and were hired "only when a script specifically called for black characters. When an 'extra' or incidental character could be of any racial background, invariably he or she was white."[42] But *Have Gun* was an exception to this pattern. Six episodes broadcast between October 1960 and

December 1962 showcased seven black actors, five of them in featured roles, only one of which was explicitly black.[43] All were hired by Pierson.

At the end of the fifth season, Pierson decided it was time for him to leave. After three seasons as producer, he was burned out on the show; additionally, Boone was pressing for still more control, so the future would hold more stress for Pierson in the producer's role, and less fun. He was also not altogether happy with the way Boone was directing himself. So near the end of the season's shooting, after an amicable conversation with his star, Pierson left the show. Robert Sparks came in as producer, while Don Ingalls, who had been story editor since the second season, became associate producer.[44]

However, new conflicts began almost immediately. Significantly, after four producers who had shared a vision of *Have Gun* as the "non–Western" Western, Sparks seems to have wanted a much more traditional series. As he told a reporter, "That final season was more like a Paladin adventure than a period western. I wanted to do western episodes with quality writing but Boone insisted on non-western locations."[45] Partly, after five years of Paladin, Boone was no doubt desperate for more variety in the stories. One episode this season took place in a warehouse, another almost entirely in a stone prison. The last episode to be filmed (though not the last broadcast), "Lady of the Fifth Moon" (6:29, 3/30/63) recounted Paladin's mission to get a Chinese princess safely from San Francisco to Monterey and onboard a ship for China, where she could fulfill her imperial destiny.[46] Boone even wanted to film episodes in Mexico, Sparks reported, but it wasn't in the budget, adding that Boone "just didn't want to do westerns any more. He struggled and we fought." Finally, the conflict became too much. Sparks left the show halfway through the final season, and Don Ingalls stepped up to produce the remaining episodes. The final season limped to a close, stopping short at only 32 episodes instead of the 38 that had been contracted for.

Have Gun: *Directors*

Andrew V. McLaglen (1920–), the son of famed British actor Victor McLaglen, was *Have Gun's* first director, and its most trusted. Andrew had started as an actor, like his father, but then shifted behind the camera and got his practical training assisting directors like John Ford, Budd Boetticher, and William Wellman before signing a long-term contract with CBS-TV.[47] By December 1956, when the *Have Gun* pilot was ready to film, McLaglen had already proven his television mettle in numerous episodes of *Gunsmoke*, so producer Julian Claman hired him to direct not just the pilot, but the first 26 episodes of the series. (By the end of Season Six, McLaglen had directed over half the episodes of *Have Gun—Will Travel*, 116 out of 225, far more than any other director for the series.)

In the 1950s, directors of episodic television had to work on a tight schedule—one day to rehearse, and three days to shoot a thirty-minute script. Under those conditions, directors could not afford the time to be fancy; as actor Rayford Barnes described it, "they had to get the best they could on the schedule. Get that footage and no retakes. They followed the script closely; there wasn't much time for improvisation or changing too much."[48] Under such conditions, Andy McLaglen had many strengths as a director. First, he was very efficient and disciplined. He told David Rothel about the time he completed eleven and a half pages of script in one day: "Well, that's a lot of pages, and they didn't expect it just to be roughshod; it had to include closeups, over-the-shoulders. You had to prepare yourself."[49] Second, even with the tight shooting schedules, he found ways to be creative, and sought to pack every shot with unexpected images. For instance, when Paladin entered a room, instead of focusing on his face, McLaglen would often show a close-up of the silver chess knight on Paladin's holster. As Richard Schickel observed admiringly, episodes of *Have Gun—Will Travel* were consistently "polished slick and trimmed tight," more dense with visual detail than any of the show's competitors.[50]

But perhaps McLaglen's most important quality as a director for *Have Gun* is that he made an ideal creative partner for Boone. As a consummate professional, McLaglen gained his star's respect and cooperation; fortunately, he envisioned the director's responsibilities in a way that avoided conflict with Boone. What McLaglen cared about was the technical choreography of the show, the camera angles, lighting, and shot composition, not the overall meaning of the script or how the actors interpreted their characters. As McLaglen explained, he left those details to his star, pointing out that, as a New York-trained actor, Boone was naturally focused on the characters and their motivations.[51] Rather than feeling challenged by Boone's interventions, McLaglen thought it made his work easier: "Richard demanded a lot [of the actors], a lot of work on scripts and everything, which I then didn't have to worry about. I never had any brush with him at all."[52] He also observed that, although Boone always had ideas about his scenes, he took direction readily.

Though by 1956 McLaglen had plenty of experience directing Westerns, both for the large and the small screen, he also had worked on other kinds of films. In choosing additional directors, the producers and Boone preferred those who were not Western specialists. Instead, they hired directors with the same extensive experience in theatre and in live television that Boone had, especially those who worked well with actors. For example, Buzz Kulik (1922–1999), who directed a total of twelve episodes between Seasons Two and Four, had experience both with stage work and live television, and was praised for his "uncanny ability to elicit strong performances from his cast."[53] Directors with this sort of background were vital in helping *Have Gun* avoid Western clichés.

The only two first-season directors other than McLaglen both had strong personal ties to Boone. Lewis Milestone (1895–1980), who brought Boone to Hollywood in 1950 for his first movie role and became one of Boone's closest friends, directed two episodes. Though Milestone's pre-war movie career had been distinguished, later the director struggled. Like Boone, he was known in Hollywood as a "difficult" person; he refused to sign contracts with any of the studios, preferring to work freelance, and he fearlessly confronted studios and producers over contractual and artistic issues. Worse, after World War II he became politically suspect, blacklisted in 1949 as a suspected Communist sympathizer. Though he salvaged his career, after a fashion, with the jingoistic *Halls of Montezuma* (1950), where he first met Boone, movie work remained scarce for him throughout the rest of the decade.[54] Boone very likely used his influence to get the director work on his series, as he so often helped those he believed in. Though Milestone disliked television, at least one of the two episodes he directed for *Have Gun*, "Hey Boy's Revenge" (1:31, 4/12/58), is among the stand-outs, even in a series whose standards are quite high.

Lamont Johnson (1922–2010), who directed six episodes in the first season plus four more in the second,[55] certainly owed his contract to Boone. A founding member with Boone of the Brentwood Marketplace group, Johnson had made his television directing debut in 1955 with a live production of *Wuthering Heights*, starring Boone and Peggy Webber, on NBC's *Matinee Theater*—broadcast one hour per day for five days.[56] When Boone landed his new series, he insisted the producers hire Johnson to direct, giving his friend and colleague the opportunity to break into filmed TV.

One of the most surprising names on the list of repeat directors for *Have Gun — Will Travel* is Ida Lupino (1918–1995). Lupino had a prestigious career as an actress from 1931 to the mid–1940s, but even as she was being acclaimed for her acting, she was carefully preparing herself to move into directing. With her second husband, Collier Young, Lupino founded an independent film company, *Filmakers* [*sic*], specializing in low-budget, issue-oriented films. Lupino initially served as producer and screenwriter for the company. But when the director of their first production suffered a mild heart attack just before shooting was to begin, Lupino stepped in to direct and proved surprisingly effective in the job. She then went on to direct numerous projects of her own. At the time, she was the only female film director in Hollywood. After four "women's films" about social issues, including one about rape (*Outrage,* 1950), Lupino directed *The Hitch-Hiker* (1953), the story of two hunters who pick up a hitch-hiker along the road, with horrifying results. It was the first film noir directed by a woman.[57] Despite this film's success, as a woman in a "man's" job, Lupino got few opportunities to direct films. Instead, she turned to episodic television, and became the most active woman working behind the cameras in the formative years of TV.[58]

In 1959, Boone offered her the opportunity to direct for *Have Gun,* in what became the first Western ever directed by a woman.[59] Like all the other directors hired for multiple episodes, Lupino was thoroughly professional and disciplined, which meant she was able to create a good working atmosphere on her set and to bring her productions in on time and on (or under) budget; but above all, she was known for her skill at handling players of both sexes and her sensitivity to the problems and needs of her cast, qualities derived from her own training and experience as an actor. As Boone explained to columnist Erskine Johnson in 1961, "Ida stimulates me as an actor because she knows acting. In a weekly show, you get into acting patterns. Ida gets you out of them."[60]

As a result of the hard-boiled style she demonstrated in *The Hitch-Hiker,* the first episode Boone gave Lupino to direct was not a stereotypical "woman's story" but a script by Harry Julian Fink, a writer famed for his graphic descriptions of physical violence. "The Man Who Lost" (2:31, 4/25/59) is a dark character study of a man accused of killing a cattle rancher and "attacking" his wife—a euphemism for *rape* (a word which could not have been spoken on TV or even in the movies in 1959, and an act which could only be suggested in the most oblique way). The suspect denies the accusation, urgently and plausibly, until confronted in the end by his victim; then, with a single word and a chilling smile, he reveals both his guilt and his utter lack of repentance. Lupino's work on this compelling episode was so good that Boone brought her in to direct seven additional episodes over the next two seasons.[61]

Although McLaglen always found Boone easy to work with, other directors had a very different experience with him; a few even cut short their contracts in frustration. For example, Don Taylor was originally contracted to direct four episodes, but left after two. As Taylor explained:

> At one point during an episode I said to him, "Why don't we do such-and-such?" Boone said, "Nope." I said, "Then how 'bout so-and-so?" He said, "Nope." About five "nopes" later, I asked, "Well, what do *you* want to do?" He said, "I'll just walk over here and sit down." And I said, "Okay!" He's directing—I'm only directing traffic, a stop-and-go director. There's no joy in that.[62]

Obviously, Taylor thought he was dealing with an arrogant star refusing to take direction. However, as Frank Pierson observed, despite Boone's reputation for ego, he never threw his weight around just because he could. Rather, he was "a reasonable man who wants to know the reasons for what you're doing. If you have them, he won't give you any trouble. But he takes the trouble to know everything about what he's doing, so you'd better not try to fool him."[63] Perhaps if Taylor had explained the effect he was trying to accomplish, Boone would have accommodated him.

For example, when Ida Lupino directed her first episode of *Have Gun*, she too made a suggestion that Boone refused. But rather than getting testy, she explained to him, "Darling, the reason I ask you—here, get behind the camera and see how lousy it is for you. You don't want me to shoot right up your nose, do you?" Boone looked, growled, "Ah, you little—," then did the scene her way.[64]

On another occasion, Andy McLaglen opted for strategy when he had difficulty with Boone during filming of "The Race" (5:7, 10/28/61), which featured Boone and Ben Johnson competing in a cross-country horse race. To complete the episode properly, McLaglen needed to shoot some running inserts—close-ups of the actors on horseback, running flat out, filmed from a camera car driving alongside. But Boone loathed horses, though he carefully concealed the true intensity of his feelings, so he sent word to his director that he was not going to do any running inserts. McLaglen thought Boone was indulging in a bit of prima-donna attitude, but instead of arguing, he played along. He rigged a saddle on a platform fastened to the camera car, and prepared to film Boone sitting on this saddle instead of on a real horse. When Boone saw the set-up, he couldn't face the embarrassment of riding the prop saddle in front of the whole crew, so he agreed to do the scene on horseback.[65] Problem solved—by indirection, and by appealing to the actor's pride in a non-confrontational way.

By the second season, and more urgently in the third, Boone began to agitate for permission to direct some episodes himself. Once he had gotten the character of Paladin well-established, the acting became less challenging, and Boone, as always, hungered to stretch and grow artistically. He explained to Dwight Whitney of *TV Guide*, "It's the director who has all the fun. Any time a camera is involved it's the director who tells the story, more than the writer, producer or anybody else. And that's what I want to do."[66] Boone ultimately got his way, though it took some major explosions and two changes of producer to achieve this goal. By the time the series ended, however, he had directed 28 episodes, second only to McLaglen. As reporter Richard Gehman observed, in directing as in everything else he did, Boone

> is on top of every detail. Sitting in a chair while he is both acting and directing a scene, the camera on him, his face bears an expression of high tension and close attentiveness. He has developed eyes in the back of his head; at the slightest sound of an actor making a wrong move, he whirls and corrects the man.[67]

Boone himself admitted, "When I direct a show, I'm pretty arbitrary. If I have a fault, it's that I see an end and go for it with all my energy; and if I'm bugged with people who don't see it or won't go for it, it looks as though I'm riding all over them." He always insisted on a closed set, because visitors were too disruptive. It was important to him that everything happening on the set was connected with the work.[68] Not surprisingly, Boone's most significant strength as a director was his ability to work with actors, a characteristic that carries over from his acting classes and his work as a director on stage. As Harry Carey, Jr., told David Rothel, Boone was "very sympathetic toward actors and he understood them. He knew how to get you pumped up for a scene."[69]

Have Gun's *Writers*

By early 1957, the pilot had been completed and approved by the network. The next step was to find scripts for the season. Julian Claman and Sam Rolfe invited a crew of about ten writers to a private screening of the pilot. A few of the men were old hands at the Western, but many were newcomers to the genre,[70] because from the beginning, the producers were determined to find fresh ideas rather than the same old stories. The most prestigious writer in the room was Malvin Wald, who had been writing screenplays and television scripts since 1941, including 25 television episodes alone since 1953. Wald was not only prolific, but distinguished and innovative; he had won an Oscar in 1948 for his screenplay for *The Naked City*, the work which invented the police procedural.[71] Another in that first group was Gene Roddenberry, engineer, former combat pilot and commercial airline pilot, veteran of the Los Angeles police, and future creator of *Star Trek*. After eight years as a police officer, Roddenberry had left the LAPD to write full time for television, and sold several television scripts starting in 1953. Ken Kolb, writer of six *Medic* episodes, was also there, probably at Boone's suggestion. After watching the pilot, the writers tossed some story ideas around as a group, then went home to generate more ideas to submit to Claman and Rolfe. If an idea was approved, then the writer would be given the go-ahead to write a script. Within a few weeks, Claman was reading scripts with his wife, the actress Marian Seldes—a fellow student of Boone's from the Neighborhood Playhouse and the Actors Studio, who would star in two first-season episodes, including one written for her by her husband.

In the first season, Sam Rolfe wrote seven scripts in addition to the pilot; Ken Kolb sold six solo efforts and contributed to another five as a "script doctor," polishing scripts submitted by others; Gene Roddenberry sold five, while series co-creator Herb Meadow had one solo script accepted, as did many of the other men who had screened the pilot. In fact, all but six of the thirty-nine scripts for the first season were created by that initial group of writers.

Writing for episodic TV in the 1950s was a hard game. Few series had a permanent stable of writers. Script writing was mostly done freelance, and writers seldom sold more than three scripts to any given series, even over multiple seasons. Under these conditions, the only way to make a living as a television writer was to write for as many different series as possible.[72] However, in the six seasons of *Have Gun*, a small stable of writers got an unprecedented number of repeat assignments, though never averaging more than four or five episodes per season. Despite Roddenberry's frequently-repeated claim to have been "head writer" for *Have Gun* (presumably because 24 of his scripts were ultimately broadcast, tying for the greatest number of scripts by a single author), there never was a head writer on the show, because there was no permanent writing staff. All the scripts and many of the story ideas came in from free-lancers. Unlike contemporary Hollywood, where producers return unsolicited scripts unopened for fear of copyright infringement lawsuits, *Have Gun*'s producers accepted scripts and stories from anywhere, including fans. Some of those fans had good ideas but were not capable of writing professional-level screenplays; in such cases, the producers would buy their proposals and then hire a screenwriter to write the script. Other submissions came from experienced writers. Albert Aley, for example, after watching several episodes of the show, submitted a number of ideas to Claman; in the end, five of his scripts filled out the first season.

The second season saw a number of changes among the writers. When Sam Rolfe stepped up as producer, Don Ingalls (a former LAPD officer recommended by Gene Roddenberry) came in to replace Rolfe as story editor—the person responsible for selecting scripts, and for generating additional story ideas and finding writers to turn them into polished scripts.[73] Albert Aley wrote another six scripts for Season Two, as did Roddenberry. From the beginning, Roddenberry's stories manifested the qualities and themes that would be so central to *Star Trek* a few years later. The roster of characters often included racial and ethnic minorities, all treated respectfully; antagonists were often portrayed as good individuals taken over by fanaticism or constrained by social patterns they could not see how to break, and stories were often built on a conflict between logic and emotion.[74] He also contributed many of the comic stories (generally, there were four to five of these per season), and wrote his fair share of scripts featuring women in important roles. In other words, Roddenberry sold so many scripts to the series, especially in the first half of the run (17 of his 24 episodes were broadcast in the first three seasons), because he was a versatile writer, and because his values and concerns matched those of the producers, and in particular matched those of Richard Boone.

In the second season, Rolfe brought in two new writers who, as regular contributors, added distinctive voices to the mix. Harry Julian Fink, Georgia-born and New York–bred, later famous as the screenwriter of *Dirty Harry* (1971), *Magnum Force* (1973), and *The Dead Pool* (1988), caught Rolfe's eye with a powerful story he wrote for the television series *Climax!*, a Western based on a brutal hanging Fink had witnessed in Palestine. On the basis of that single script, Rolfe hired Fink in January 1958, and by July of that year found him so indispensable that he brought him out to Hollywood full-time. Fink was known for his extraordinarily dark scripts. As Rolfe explained, however, the most brutal prose was usually found in Fink's stage directions.

> Harry will document every fight in great detail. He will tell us the exact position of the body, how the nostrils flared and the eyes stared sightlessly into the sun, and a small trickle of blood appeared at the corner of the mouth. It's hard, cruel writing—which, of course, we can't photograph. What we do get in a Fink script are characters so unyielding that, when they meet, there just has to be a violent explosion.[75]

Fink provided five scripts in the second season, and thirteen more in the next four, generally among the strongest and most interesting—and reliably the darkest—scripts of the series. When a *Have Gun* episode ends with no redemption or resolution of the conflict, it is almost always one of Fink's stories. Boone described Fink as "one of the best writers in the business." The star who insisted on detailed control of all aspects of the show, in particular the writing, added significantly, "I've never rejected anything in his scripts."[76]

The other new voice Rolfe brought in that season was Shimon Wincelberg, who ultimately supplied the series with 24 scripts, tying Roddenberry's total. A German-born Jew, Wincelberg moved with his family to New York in the late 1930s when he was a teenager, then served in Army Intelligence during World War II.[77] In the early 1950s, he started writing professionally, a few short stories and a screenplay; then in 1958 his teleplay, *The Sea is Boiling Hot*, was cited as one of the best plays of the year. As so often happened, it was a personal connection that brought Wincelberg into the *Have Gun* family; the wife of one of the producers was a friend who recommended him.[78] His first script, "In an Evil Time" (2:2, 9/20/58), was also his first Western, so he brought a fresh eye to the genre. Though Wincelberg provided only three scripts in the second season, in each of the subsequent seasons he typically contributed five to seven. Like Roddenberry's, Wincelberg's stories show a sensitivity to cultural minorities and to women (central themes of the series as a whole), combined with a dry sense of humor and a gift for creating intriguing characters who know how to talk.

Two new writers, the last of the major contributors for the series, joined *Have Gun* in the third season. Robert E. Thompson (known as Red for his shock of red hair) started writing for television in 1957, selling several scripts to *Matinee Theatre*, three to *Wagon Train*, and four to *Bonanza* in its first season (1959-60) before writing for *Have Gun*. Between 1959 and 1963, Thompson sold 19 scripts to the series.[79] Some of his scripts combine a light comic touch with a warm human story, but Thompson also wrote some of the most powerful stories in the series, of tormented characters facing difficult choices, trapped in hopeless situations, suffering from delusions, or struggling with misplaced loyalties. And, like many of the other frequent writers for the series, his characters often have a distinct and compelling way of speaking.

The other new member of the writing team was Frank R. Pierson, who joined the crew at the beginning of the third season as associate producer/story editor. *Have Gun—Will Travel* was Pierson's big Hollywood break. He had worked as a journalist with *Time* and *Life* for a number of years, avoiding writing for Hollywood (largely because his mother was a well-known screenwriter and he didn't want to compete with her). But as he approached thirty, he felt it was time to get serious about his writing. He quit his job, lived frugally, and sent out script after script—seventeen half-hour shows in seventeen weeks one summer, he reported—but none of them sold. Finally, he decided it was time to give up and find a real job to support his family. That very weekend, he got word that Sam Rolfe wanted to see him. Rolfe was looking for somebody "who was not trained ... who wasn't writing like all the other shows on the air." Rolfe liked what he heard from Pierson, and decided to give him a chance. He handed the young writer a number of *Have Gun* scripts that hadn't quite worked for one reason or another, and gave him two weeks to see what he could do with the rejects. By the end of the first week, the results were so satisfactory that Rolfe hired him as story editor.[80] For the next three seasons, first as story editor and then as producer, Pierson continued to play a serious role in the selection of stories and scripts for the series.

As the series progressed, some scripts by women writers began to appear—fifteen scripts out of 225, the bulk of these broadcast in Season Five. Although they represent only a small percentage of the total, in such a heavily masculine genre as the Western, even this number is worth noting. Nine of the scripts came from a mixed-gender team, including six by Peggy and Lou Shaw (notably, her name always comes first in their credits). Four more women between them produced six additional scripts.

Boone and the writers who created the scripts for him soon developed a mutual admiration society. As Pierson explained to Richard Schickel, writers loved working for the series because "Boone wants them to write real lines for a cowboy, of all people. They know they can say important things and that Boone will say them right, so they mean something."[81] In turn, Boone defended "his" writers as the equals of the best in the business, even if they were working in a disregarded genre like the Western, arguing, "I'll take Gene Roddenberry, Sam Rolfe and Harry Julian Fink and stack them against [Rod] Serling, [Paddy] Chayefsky, [Gore] Vidal, [Reginald] Rose, [Horton] Foote and Shaw any day of the week."[82]

Actors: Principles of Casting

The working conditions on a television series in the 1950s were quite challenging for the entire crew, but especially the actors. Not only did a season for a television series contain

39 episodes, two to three times as many as a modern season, each episode was significantly longer: a half-hour episode contained nearly 25 minutes of script, compared with the 18 (or even fewer) that is now customary. Typically, it took four days, ten to fourteen hours a day, to shoot a half-hour episode: one day to plan and rehearse, and three to film. Fridays were used for publicity and promotions. For an hour-long series like *Wagon Train* or *Bonanza*, the shooting schedule expanded to five or even six days per episode. For the regulars on a series, nine months of that schedule would be followed by a brief hiatus, and then the whole routine started over for the next season.

Casting for television in the 1950s differed from today's conditions in several significant respects. In those first decades of the medium, actors seldom auditioned for appearances on TV series.[83] Instead, agents sent their clients' names to the casting director or producer of a given show, while casting directors kept lists of actors whose performances they had liked. Actors could also be recommended by friends on the show, or even friends of friends. Officially, Lynn Stalmaster and Associates was responsible for casting *Have Gun* for its first four seasons, but Julian Claman also assembled his own roster of preferred actors, their agents, and their fees per half-hour episode.[84] Due to both Claman's and Boone's New York experience, this list was dominated by New York stage actors, especially those with Neighborhood Playhouse or Actors Studio connections or experience in live drama anthologies on TV. Boone also suggested members of his Brentwood workshop, students from his acting classes, or actors he had worked with on *Medic* or the many movies he had made during his early Hollywood years.[85] Production secretary Peggy Rea was invaluable to the producer in creating this list, since Claman was new not only to Hollywood but to Westerns. Rea already had two years' experience as production secretary on *Gunsmoke*, overseen by the same network executives and cast by the same company, Stalmaster. Even more vital, she had a strong working relationship with Boone as a member of his Brentwood Marketplace workshop.[86] Her casting work proved so proficient that in the final two seasons, Rea took over from Stalmaster as casting director, with Boone's enthusiastic approval.

Like any TV drama, *Have Gun* required a certain number of pretty young women and handsome young men; however, the most urgent need for a Western series, even an unconventional one, was a deep roster of character actors. By 1957, Hollywood was full of such men with decades of experience in Western movies, well-versed in all the clichés of the genre. However, since avoiding those clichés was a high priority for Boone and the production team, too much Western experience could be a handicap rather than an advantage for actors hoping to work on *Have Gun*.

Because *Have Gun*, unlike its three main competitors, had only a single protagonist, casting its featured and supporting roles required a different calculus than the other series. *Gunsmoke* and *Bonanza*, each with four stars dominating the episodes, needed solid professionals in the guest roles but not major names, actors who could play their parts without overshadowing the stars. *Wagon Train*, by contrast, put its guest stars in the center of the episodes in order to entice big Hollywood names onto the small screen. In most *Wagon Train* episodes, even Major Adams and Flint McCullough function more like supporting characters than protagonists. But on *Have Gun*, featured players shared the spotlight equally with Paladin. As a result, *Have Gun* needed actors who could stand toe to toe with Richard Boone. The producers decided against hiring major names as guest stars—no Fess Parkers or Raymond Burrs or other top TV stars of the period—partly because they might take attention away from Boone, but more importantly because such prominent actors would be too costly for the budget. What the show needed was not big names but skilled professionals with a specific kind of training. Given Boone's passionate commitment to Method acting, it was vital that the actors hired to fill the featured and supporting roles on *Have Gun* be able to improvise scenes with him, in order to help Boone keep his performance from falling into predictable patterns.[87] This meant that stage experience or work in live television was a higher priority for the featured performers on *Have Gun* than its competitors.

Although stage experience was a definite plus on *Have Gun*, the New York stage actors Boone hired did have to learn some new habits to work in television. Many would arrive on the set each day eager to talk about their role, their motivations—a standard part of the rehearsal process for a stage play. But in television, once an actor arrived on the set, there was no time for such analysis. As Rayford Barnes reported, on the first day, Boone would discuss the script and the role briefly with the featured performers for the week, but if they raised the topic after that, he would say (as Barnes paraphrased him), "Hold it, we hired you because you are a professional, and if you don't know what your motivation is and what you're doing, then you don't belong here.... That should be behind you when you get here."[88] As committed to Method acting as Boone was, he also recognized that, in television and movie work, the character analysis had to be completed before the actor arrived on the set if the shooting schedule was to be maintained.

In the same way that *Have Gun* learned to rely on a group of screenwriters, over the seasons Boone assembled a kind of informal stock company around the show, a significant number of actors who appeared in multiple episodes over the years. As Hey Boy, the only continuing character in the series besides Paladin, Kam Tong naturally leads the list with 79 episodes over six seasons, though most of these are quite brief and not all include dialogue.[89] The second name on this list is Hal Needham, with 34 credited appearances, although this number both understates and overstates his place in the series. Understates it because, as Boone's stunt double (a position he landed near the end of the second season), Needham appears in virtually every episode for the next four seasons, but stunt performances are typically uncredited. On the other hand, most of his credited appearances were in tiny roles, a line or two at most, given to him not only because he was at hand on the set, but because he was also a student in the acting class Boone ran for members of the crew. On a few occasions, he played more substantial roles, and in "Dream Girl" (5:22, 2/10/62), in which all but one of the featured roles were played by crew members, Needham starred as a young miner in love with a dance hall girl, giving quite a creditable performance. But in general, his acting was confined to bit parts.[90]

In contemporary Hollywood, the rules do not allow actors to appear more than once per season on any series unless they are playing a continuing character, but in the 1950s, the rules were more lax. For Boone's favorites, two featured appearances a season seems to have been the norm: for example, Harry Carey, Jr., did twelve episodes in six seasons, Roy Barcroft did eleven, and Hank Patterson ten in five seasons. These men proved the exception to the rule about drawing cast members from outside Western circles: by the time *Have Gun* started filming, all three were well-established character actors, each with decades of experience in Westerns. Harry Carey, Jr., called Dobe for his brick-red hair, as the son of Western star Harry Carey was virtually born into the business.[91] However, Dobe did not start his acting career till after he returned from serving in World War II, when he became a member of John Ford's stock company. In the next ten years, he made at least seven important films with Ford, many of them starring John Wayne. This background made him ideally suited to play a wide variety of characters on *Have Gun*, some of them featured roles, more often as part of an ensemble.[92]

Roy Barcroft was another of Boone's favorite featured actors. Like Carey and numerous others among the regulars, Barcroft had made a film with Boone in the early 1950s. Barcroft, fifteen years older than Boone, started working in the movies in 1937, at first just a series of mostly uncredited bit parts. However, his large size and distinctive growl soon established him as a sought-after "heavy" in Western films and serials. By 1957 his movie career had begun to stall (as the movie studios cut back dramatically on the number of B films they made), so he shifted to television, where he appeared in most of the Western series then filming.[93] On *Have Gun*, Barcroft, like Carey, played a much wider range of characters than he was accustomed to, some heavies but also several roles with more nuance. This pattern surely showed Boone's influence at work. Except for a few actors whose personal characteristics kept them confined to a narrow range—whether by age, ethnicity, or some quirk of personal appearance—Boone made sure the repeat performers were cast in a variety of roles, and often against type.[94]

Hank Patterson, the oldest of the three, did not seem to have any personal connection with Boone before being cast on *Have Gun*, but he was already well known in Hollywood as one of a handful of character actors who had "cornered the market on portraying cantankerous old coots, usually in a rural setting." By 1957, he had been in close to fifty movies in eighteen years, mostly Westerns and science fiction, and also in virtually every Western series on television, both children's series like *The Roy Rogers Show*, *The Gene Autry Show*, and *The Cisco Kid* and those for adults. He would eventually land a recurring role on *Gunsmoke* as Hank the Stableman (32 episodes from 1959 to 1975).[95] From their first episode together, Boone took delight in working with the then-seventy-year-old actor, and encouraged the producers to bring him back season after season.

A number of the "stock company" members knew Boone from having done episodes of *Medic* with him.[96] Others of the recurring actors had connections to other key production personnel. Andy McLaglen brought in quite a few actors over the years, including his close friend Ken Curtis. One of the characters Curtis portrayed, the scruffy prairie rat Monk in "The Naked Gun" (3:14, 12/19/59) and again in "Love's Young Dream" (4:2, 9/17/60), created the template for the character Curtis would later play on *Gunsmoke*, deputy Festus Hagen—a role he got through McLaglen's recommendation. Werner Klemperer, featured in two episodes, had gone to high school with McLaglen. Ed Faulkner, who appeared in minor parts in 12 episodes, also got on the show through McLaglen, who was a close friend of Faulkner's brother-in-law.

Faulkner's experience is another example of Boone's commitment to helping unknown young actors. A letter of introduction to McLaglen got the actor on the set; the director introduced him to Boone, who said, "Let's give Ed a read." Boone read with Faulkner personally, and a couple of weeks later, the young actor had a part—and, even more important, a mentor for what turned out to be a successful 18-year career in television and film.[97] Perry Cook was the son of *Have Gun*'s first-season production supervisor, Glenn Cook. When Perry joined the team as his father's assistant, Boone recognized the young man's interest in acting and took him on as a student, then got him his first role.[98]

Another young actor that Boone took under his wing during *Have Gun* was the troubled but fiercely talented Robert Blake. A child actor who had become well-known under his real name, Mickey Gubitosi, in the 1940s in Our Gang comedies and as Little Beaver in the Red Ryder serials, Blake escaped Hollywood at age 18 for a stint in the Army.[99] When he returned two years later, he began to study acting more seriously, eventually making his way successively onto TV in 1952, into Boone's acting class and three *Have Gun* episodes (although which of these came first, the episodes or the class, is unclear), and then into the repertory company of *The Richard Boone Show* (1963–64). Jeanette Nolan was recommended to Boone by one of the associate producers. Actually, his friend Peggy Webber had been telling him for years that Jeanette Nolan was one of the best actresses in America, but he had repeatedly brushed aside Webber's suggestion.[100] Once he finally had the chance to work with Nolan, Boone recognized her extraordinary gifts, especially her versatility, and she too was invited to join the company for *The Richard Boone Show*. Boone's long-time friend, Warren Stevens—his New York roommate during their Neighborhood Playhouse days, fellow Fox contract player, and co-founder with Boone of the Brentwood Marketplace group—starred in three *Have Gun* episodes, and later joined *The Richard Boone Show*, while Harry Morgan, another of Boone's close friends, did two episodes. His second appearance, as the sheriff in "American Primitive" (6:21, 2/2/63), so impressed Boone that he issued the invitation to join the repertory company. (For a chart of the "stock company" members and the number of episodes each appeared in, see Appendix.)

Over the years, a number of established, even famous, actors played roles on *Have Gun—Will Travel*. One of the biggest of those names was Vincent Price, Boone's long-time friend and neighbor, who played a Shakespearean actor touring the West in one of the great comic episodes of the series, "The Moor's Revenge" (2:15, 12/27/58). Lon Chaney, Jr.—the Wolf Man himself (also the Mummy, Dracula, and Frankenstein's Monster) made two appearances on *Have Gun* in roles that gave him scope for serious acting without monster make-up. The most touching of those roles was in "The Scorched Feather" (2:22, 2/14/59), playing Indian scout Billy Blue Sky, a tormented man whose half–Comanche son was trying to kill him. Victor McLaglen, Andrew's father, made one guest appearance on the show in "The O'Hare Story" (1:25, 3/1/58), playing a character based on William Mulholland, the man who brought water to Los Angeles at the beginning of the twentieth century. June Lockhart, a well-established stage and television actress since 1948, and soon to achieve national fame as the mother on TV's *Lassie* (1958–64), appeared in two episodes in the first season as Dr. Phyllis Thackeray, Paladin's first love interest: "No Visitors" (1:12, 11/30/57) and "The Return of Dr. Thackeray" (1:35, 5/17/58).[101] Buddy Ebsen, best known in the 1950s for his work on the Disney series, *Davy Crockett,* as Davy's fictional sidekick George Russel, played homicidal heavies in two *Have Gun* episodes: "El Paso Stage" (4:30, 4/15/61) and "The Brothers" (5:11, 11/25/61). Of course, Ebsen's greatest fame would come a year later as Jed Clampett on *The Beverly Hillbillies* (1962–1971). John Carradine, famous horror movie star, played against type as a mission priest, Father Bartholome, in "The Statue of San Sebastian" (1:39, 6/14/58). Hans Conried appeared as an old Mexican nobleman who believes himself to be Don Quixote in "A Knight to Remember" (5:13, 12/9/61).

One final list of names deserves mention: actors who became famous after appearing once or twice on *Have Gun* early in their careers, like Claude Akins, Martin Balsam, Dan Blocker, Peter Breck, James Coburn, Michael Connors, Angie Dickinson, Peter Falk, Clu Gulager, DeForest Kelley, George Kennedy, Werner Klemperer, Jack Lord, Suzanne Pleshette, Sydney Pollack (who became famous as a director rather than an actor), Pernell Roberts, Wayne Rogers, and Jack Weston.

Richard Boone, Star as Mentor

Have Gun quickly became so hot that practically everybody in Hollywood wanted to get involved. According to Rayford Barnes, some movie actors who had never done television before were telling their agents they wanted to work with Boone. But there was no room for prima donnas on *Have Gun*, Barnes declared.[102] Team play was the central value of the show. If a visiting actor tried to behave like a "star," the crew had methods of putting them in their place. But those who demonstrated the right attitudes, even in the smallest jobs, were typically noticed and rewarded. Actor Peter Breck's first appearance on *Have Gun*—in fact, his first appearance on television—was as an extra in "The Teacher" (1:27, 3/15/58), where he had no lines and only one scene, which he spent lying in a bunk. However, as a trained stage actor, Breck couldn't just lie there. So he invented a backstory for his character, a young Confederate veteran. As he told David Rothel,

> I decided to make him totally paranoiac and schizophrenic because of the fact that he had been in the war. Paladin had that seven-and-a-half-inch-barrel gun, and I never took my eyes off it. I would stare at it. And every time he moved towards me I would gather myself up and never take my eyes off the gun.

Boone saw what the young actor was doing, and pointed it out to the director: "Get the kid, get him on camera." So, thanks to Richard Boone, Breck wound up with more camera time than most of the others in the scene. Boone appreciated both the "actorliness" of the performance, and the fact that Breck was not hogging the scene, as he could have done once he realized he had Boone's attention. Impressed with his work, Boone brought the young actor back the following season for a lead role in "The Protégé" (2:6, 10/18/58). It was the start of a solid television career.[103]

Boone's generosity was occasionally repaid in unexpected ways. For example, when *Have Gun* started production, a young actor/singer/songwriter named Johnny Western had a small role on a show called *Boots and Saddles* which filmed just down the lot from *Have Gun*.[104] The glimpses Western got of Boone in costume had intrigued him, and the more he learned about the new show, the more eager he was to be a part of it. Western confided this desire to Lynn Stalmaster, casting director for *Have Gun* as well as *Gunsmoke* and *Boots and Saddles*, and mentioned that he'd been working on his fast draw. Stalmaster soon found a small role for him as a hot-headed youngster who forces a shoot-out with Paladin in "The Return of Dr. Thackeray" (1:35, 5/17/58). At this point in his career, Western had very little acting experience, so he was quite nervous. But Boone generously coached the young actor, to help him feel comfortable and look good in his big scene.[105] After the episode wrapped, a grateful Western was inspired to write a song about Paladin as "a knight without armor in a savage land."

He wasn't thinking about broadcast possibilities or about selling the song; he wrote it strictly as a way to thank Boone and Sam Rolfe for the opportunity they had given him, and to express his admiration for Paladin. He quickly made a recording of the song, just himself and his guitar, and dropped copies off at the studio for Rolfe and Boone. A few days later, Rolfe called: he and Boone had taken "The Ballad of Paladin" to the network, which now wanted to use Western's composition as the theme song for the show.[106] Starting with Season Two, though the opening retained Bernard Herrmann's evocative score, "The Ballad of Paladin" played under the closing credits of every episode from then till the end of the series. The song became an immediate hit whose royalties provided a lifetime annuity for Western.

But that was not the end of the story. The song won Western a recording contract with Columbia, including a session with Mitch Miller to record "The Ballad of Paladin" for the end credits. However, Miller decided he'd rather record the song with Jerry Vale, a pop singer from New York also under contract to Columbia, who had gone several years without a hit. A distressed Western took the news to Boone on the *Have Gun* set. Furious, Boone stopped production dead and used the set's one phone to call Mitch Miller in New York. As Western listened from two feet away, Boone announced himself to Miller and said, "What the hell is this thing about Jerry Vale doing the song?" Miller explained his reasoning, but Boone just snapped, "Listen, you sonofabitch, the kid is going to sing the song and that's all there is to it." A long pause as Miller murmured something, then Boone said, "I knew you'd see it my way, Mitch," and hung up the phone. As Western recalled gratefully, "Dick just kicked the doors open for me, and I owed him forever and ever and ever. He completely changed my life on that day."[107]

Another young man whose life Boone changed was Hal Needham. Needham was working as an extra on a Season Two episode called "The Haunted Trees" (2:38, 6/13/59), set in a lumber camp. One scene called for Paladin to climb a huge tree to rescue a lumberjack who had been shot near the top. As Boone's stunt double struggled laboriously up the tree to take his position, Needham, a former professional tree-topper, approached McLaglen and offered cheekily, "Would you like me to show you how it's done?" Getting the director's nod, he strapped on the cleats and harness and ran up the tree ("like a monkey," McLaglen recalled), then, in Needham's words, "barber poled it coming down." Boone and McLaglen were both impressed. Though Needham had been hired only for a day's work as an extra, they asked him to stick around for a few days while they finished the episode, in case they found other ways to use him. The following Monday, Boone's stunt man was fired. Hearing the news, Needham approached the star: "Mr. Boone, I'm the best stunt man in Hollywood. The problem is, I'm the only son of a bitch who knows it." Then he offered Boone a proposition: "You give me a shot at doing the things you got to do tomorrow and if you like 'em, keep me. If you don't, you don't owe me a dime." Intrigued, Boone accepted the deal.[108]

The next day's stunts both involved a stagecoach. In the first, Needham's job was to jump from the top of a rock onto a moving stagecoach. The rock he chose was about twenty feet above the coach (and thirty feet above the ground); his target was only three and a half feet wide by five feet long and moving fast, but Needham nailed the jump perfectly—though with so much momentum that he plunged completely through the top and into the body of the coach. Fortunately, he didn't hit any of the passengers inside, so no one was injured. This stunt was impressive enough, but the second really sealed the deal. This time, Needham and a stunt woman were required to jump out of a runaway coach. As the two stunt people sat inside, Needham explained, the coach was "kind of just mopin' along" so he didn't jump. When the director stopped the coach and asked him why he hadn't jumped, he replied, "Well, you were going so slow I thought it was a rehearsal." Boone exclaimed, "That's the kind of a stunt man I want. Back that thing up and bring 'em through like there's no tomorrow." They did, and Needham and the stunt woman jumped, executing the stunt perfectly.[109] Though Needham was not all that close a match to Boone physically, being a few inches shorter and thirty pounds lighter, his total dedication to the work made him Boone's choice for stunt double.

However, the transition from extra to stunt man was not accomplished instantly—and again, as he had with Western, Boone used his power to get justice for a subordinate. For several months after Needham became Boone's stunt double, the production company continued to take him on location as an extra, only bumping him up to the higher status—and pay—of stunt man on the days he actually doubled Boone. Frustrated and annoyed, Needham told the production manager that he would not work as an extra any longer. Stalking off the set, he passed Boone, who hailed him: "Hey! We're going to have a good time in New Mexico next week!" Needham told Boone he wouldn't be going to New Mexico for the next episode, explaining, "They want to take me up there as a God-damn extra and I don't want to go up there as an extra. I'm a stunt man." So Boone called the production manager and announced (as Needham told the story),

> "Me and Hal aren't going to New Mexico." The production manager said, "What?" Boone says, "Well, if Hal ain't goin', I ain't goin'. He ain't goin' because you want to take him up there as an extra." And that was the last day I worked there as an extra. He forced the whole issue right there.[110]

As he had with Johnny Western, Boone stepped in to defend the hard-working "little guy" who was being taken advantage of. Needham soon joined the acting class Boone started on the set for members of the crew, and not long after was promoted to stunt coordinator for the remainder of the series.[111]

With stories like these, no wonder his crew and many of the artists who worked regularly on the series—writers, directors, and actors alike—adored Boone. They knew they could count on him not only to make *Have Gun* something they could all be proud of, but to treat them fairly. Though he sometimes lost his temper with those who did less than their best work, it was clear to all of them that his top priority was not making Richard Boone look good, but making the show look good, making a meaningful statement about certain key values in American society. In the remainder of the book, we will focus on the values that *Have Gun—Will Travel* supported.

The Acting Company: Featured Players

ACTORS IN MULTIPLE EPISODES

79   Kam Tong (Hey Boy: recurring character)
18   Lisa Lu (two featured roles, plus 16 as Hey Girl: recurring character, Season 4)
12   Harry Carey, Jr.
11   Roy Barcroft
10   Hank Patterson
9   Perry Cook, Robert J. Stevenson
8   Richard Shannon
7   Rayford Barnes, Dorothy Dells, George Kennedy, Natalie Norwick, Denver Pyle
6   Barry Cahill
5   Charles Bronson, Ken Curtis, Robert Gist, Earle Hodgins, Wright King, Vic Perrin, Jacqueline Scott, June Vincent, Robert Wilke
4   Charles Aidman, Chris Alcaide, Anthony Caruso, Norma Crane, Jena Engstrom, Kevin Hagen, Mike Kellin, Strother Martin, Don Megawan, Fintan Meyler, Ralph Moody, Jeanette Nolan, William Schallert, Harry (Dean) Stanton, David White
3   [selected list] Rodolfo Acosta, John Anderson, Jacques Aubuchon, Parley Baer, Harry Bartell, Roxanne Berard, Whit Bissell, Robert Blake, Lillian Bronson, Crahan Denton, Lawrence Dobkin, Abel Fernandez, Ben Johnson, L. Q. Jones, Patric Knowles, Eddie Little Sky, Scott Marlowe, Michael Pate, Warren Stevens, Karl Swenson, Grant Withers
2   [selected list] Philip Ahn, Martin Balsam, Peter Breck, Lon Chaney, Jr., James Coburn, William Conrad, Buddy Ebsen, Jack Elam, Werner Klemperer, June Lockhart, Mike Mazurki, Harry Morgan, Warren Oates, Marian Seldes, William Talman, Jack Weston

BIT PLAYERS

34 Hal Needham (one featured role)
22 Stewart East
12 Ed Faulkner
11 Olan Soulé
 8 Peggy Rea
 6 Charles Couch (sometimes listed as Chuck; stuntman)
 5 Ed Nelson, Bill Wellman, Jr., Lane Chandler, Brad Weston, Ollie O'Toole
 4 Bob Hopkins, Shug Fisher

PART II: TEXTS

An Overview

Now we turn to a detailed discussion of the kinds of stories *Have Gun—Will Travel* featured in its six seasons. Though plots, settings, and character types were certainly influenced by *Have Gun*'s Western genre, the themes developed in the episodes were determined less by the standard clichés of the Western than by Richard Boone's concerns and priorities as an artist and as a thoughtful observer of American culture.

The first of those priorities was character analysis. Certainly *Have Gun* could have been a simple action-adventure series, like most TV Westerns of the time; Boone's powerful physique and athletic prowess made him an ideal action hero on screen. But action for action's sake was never Boone's focus. His passionate commitment to Method acting, which placed as much emphasis on minor roles as featured ones, gave character a much higher priority on *Have Gun* than adventure; words and ideas were valued as much as action. This intense focus on character is facilitated by *Have Gun*'s single protagonist. With no group of continuing characters whose relationships require ongoing development, each episode of *Have Gun—Will Travel* was free to explore the week's featured characters and the dilemmas they face in greater depth, even as their interactions with Paladin reveal his nature and his values.

The second priority was philosophical. Although the 225 episodes of *Have Gun* explore numerous topics, one question recurs more often than any other: how to create and sustain a healthy community on the frontier, where social institutions are only shallowly rooted and violence is endemic. Although other Westerns of the period also raised this question, they did it in more limited fashion, restricting themselves to a single community and more concerned with a group of intimates (Dillon and his friends on *Gunsmoke*, *Bonanza*'s Cartwright family) than with the community as a whole. But on *Have Gun—Will Travel*, the question of community is investigated more broadly, across a range of challenges and problems. One key approach to this question of community examines the iconic figures of the lawman and the gunfighter, those professionals of the gun. Another investigates the place of the "Other" in Western communities—racial or ethnic minorities and women, those who diverge from the cultural norm of white Anglo males. By exploring how these outsiders fare in the communities of the West in the late nineteenth century, the series promotes thoughtful reflection on the way they are treated in twentieth-century America.

The Lawman and the Gunfighter: The Problem of Violence

In contrast to the real world the audience inhabited in the 1950s and '60s, a society dominated by massive impersonal institutions, the television Western showed viewers a world where individuals solved their problems through direct action. In frontier towns, the institutions of the law were primitive and tenuous. Because the authority of the sheriff was sometimes only grudgingly accepted and judges were few and far between, men often chose to resolve their conflicts personally. But in a time and place where most men wore guns on their hips, "do-it-yourself" conflict resolution often meant violence and death. If ordinary citizens seldom turned to the sheriff for help, outlaws and gunfighters were even more likely to reject the authority of the law. If an accused criminal resisted arrest, a sheriff had no practical alternative but to use his gun.[1]

This violence was accepted by television audiences with surprising equanimity, at least until the early 1960s, when concerns about the level of violence on TV began to affect the Westerns. In the first place, the violence seemed justified, because the fragile civilization of frontier towns must be saved from the "bad guys." Besides, as John G. Cawelti pointed out, the audience knew not only that this violent frontier world belonged to the past, but that it had been relatively short-lived: within a few decades, civilization would triumph. Therefore the Western, he argued, gave audiences "a fictional justification for enjoying violent conflicts and the expression of lawless force without feeling that they threatened the values or the fabric of society."[2]

In the struggle to bring civilization to the frontier, the lawman and the gunfighter are key figures, linked in a complex, paradoxical relationship by the guns each depends on. From one point of view, they are opposites. The lawman belongs to a town, and uses his gun to maintain law and order, to support his community and advance or at least stabilize the boundaries of civilization. By contrast, the gunfighter is the classic loner, representing the old heroic libertarian West, the solitary man going his own way and resisting the demands of society. At best, the gunfighter manages to keep just on the right side of the law as he uses his gun to advance his own narrow interests, whether he is earning money as a gun-for-hire or a bounty hunter, or building a reputation in a sequence of deadly duels. At worst, the gunfighter crosses the line into open outlawry, robbing and killing freely, often as part of a gang.

Despite these significant differences, lawmen and gunfighters have more in common than we might suppose. Most importantly, because both use guns as tools of their trade, ordinary folk view them with almost equal fear and suspicion. Nor are these categories completely separate: there was frequent overlap between them. When a town was overrun with outlaws and troublemakers, only a lawman who was himself a gunfighter (like the real-life Wyatt Earp and Pat Garrett) could effectively control the violence. But, as Norm Macdonnell, the producer of *Gunsmoke*, explained, "Half the time the town-tamers were worse than the gunmen they were hired to tame. They were constantly suspect, no matter what good guys they were."[3] Being sheriff was a thankless job: dangerous work, with long hours and low pay, and often little support from the townspeople he protected. Even *Gunsmoke*'s Matt Dillon is at times a marginal figure in his own town. Though the townsfolk appreciate that he is performing an essential function, they also resent him as the enforcer of rules. So a Western lawman was often isolated—in his way, as isolated as the gunfighter who drifted from town to town, accepted nowhere.

Significantly, Paladin shares features with both the lawman and the gunfighter. Like the gunfighter, he uses his gun with professional skill to earn his living; however, unlike the gunman, his gun is the last resort for solving problems rather than the first. More important, unlike a typical gunfighter, Paladin refuses to build a reputation on his prowess with a gun. Like the lawman, Paladin serves the cause of justice. However, where a lawman's job is to maintain order in a specific community, Paladin's mission is to support the cause of civilization across the West, to reinforce the institutions and ideals of justice wherever he finds them embattled, particularly when he encounters a lawman who needs help with a difficult conflict.

In such situations, violence is always imminent, and often unavoidable. But, in *Have Gun*, this fictional violence had a more serious purpose than providing a welcome catharsis for the audience. In episode after episode, the questions are raised, both about Paladin's own actions and those of the people he encounters, especially lawmen and gunfighters: when is violence justified? What conditions must be met for killing to be legitimate? What alternatives have been tried before violence is chosen? What choices will strengthen the community? How does the community respond to the situation—by supporting, abandoning, or actively undermining the forces of law and order? Paladin's first choice, always, is to look for alternatives to the "kill-or-be-killed" finality of the gunfight. Only if these alternatives are rejected does he turn, regretfully, to violence, whether to defend himself or to protect the law-abiding. And in each case, Paladin's ethics provide the touchstone to judge the individuals and the communities he encounters across the West.

Ethnic Minorities in the Western

As J. Fred MacDonald explains in his important study, *Blacks and White TV*, in the first decade of commercial television, progressive critics saw the potential transformative power of the new medium, particularly for African Americans. By offering national exposure to talented black performers and by telling dramatic stories that explored the truth of their lives, television had the potential to undo centuries of negative stereotypes and help blacks claim an equal place in American culture. In those first years, when most TV sets were found in the large cities of the Northeast and the upper Midwest or along the West coast, the promise seemed to be fulfilled. The new medium was voracious in its need for talent; black singers, dancers, musicians, and actors were featured so often that it was easy to believe television was indeed "color blind."[4]

However, in the mid–1950s, changes in the television industry sharply curtailed the opportunities for black performers. First, as we saw in Chapter Two, television became immensely lucrative. When the visionaries who saw television as a medium for education and social progress were replaced by businessmen who saw it as the world's greatest advertising tool, avoiding controversy became the networks' highest priority. Second, by 1953 television finally spread broadly across the South, so that the region's cultural sensitivities affected every aspect of television but the news. In this era of widespread agitation for civil rights—the Montgomery bus boycott, lunch counter sit-ins, and protests over school integration—national news stories frequently revealed the South's ugly Jim Crow traditions to the rest of the country.[5] Though the Southern affiliates were required to air the news, and agreed to show certain sporting events with black participants, notably boxing, though not football (college football games with black players were not broadcast in the South until the mid–1960s), they resisted black inclusion in every other way they could. They sometimes refused to broadcast weekly variety shows when black performers were featured, and they dropped dramas or comedies with blacks in roles other than the familiar menial stereotypes—black women as housekeepers and nannies, black men as comic valets, handymen, and chauffeurs. About the only serious dramatic role a black man could play in this period was as a boxer. In addition to such direct censorship by the affiliates, Southern viewers were quick to boycott advertisers on "offensive" shows. No wonder networks and advertisers alike grew timid, unwilling to risk financial damage.[6] As if these factors did not raise sufficient barriers to black participation on television, the fervent assertion by the FBI's J. Edgar Hoover that black "agitators" for civil rights were all Communist subversives scheming to overthrow the government resulted in many black performers being blacklisted.

However, even though black actors were largely shut out of TV drama in the 1950s, television could not entirely ignore the topic of racial and ethnic prejudice. By distancing the problem of prejudice into the past, and by focusing on minorities other than blacks—less threatening groups like American Indians, Chinese immigrants, and Mexicans—the Westerns were able to address racial prejudice in a way the American public could tolerate. As timorous and hesitant as these efforts look now, they deserve acknowledgment as first steps in an important dialogue.

Before 1950, racial and ethnic minorities in Western movies were typically portrayed as villains—marauding Indians attacking innocent white settlers, or brutal Mexican bandits terrorizing a border town. The savagery of such characters was a given, no explanation needed. But then more sympathetic portraits of Indians began to appear, starting with *Broken Arrow* (1950), a film starring James Stewart as a young Indian agent who negotiates a lasting peace with Cochise, the heroic leader of the Chiricahua Apaches. The film, which presents Cochise as dignified and powerful, a complex, fully human being with justifiable motives for fighting against the whites encroaching on his territory, started a trend of films about noble (if doomed) Indians.[7] Though the pattern had run its course in the movies by 1957, its influence carried over to the television Western, where each of our series treats Indians with genuine, if limited, sympathy.

Mexicans and Chinese also played acknowledged roles on the frontier—the former as generations-long residents of California and the southwest territories acquired (stolen?) by the U.S. from Mexico, the latter imported in large numbers as miners and railroad workers; as a result, characters from both groups appear now and then on TV Westerns in this period. In fact, two of the four series, *Have Gun—Will Travel* and *Bonanza*, include a recurring, if minor, Chinese character, and an early *Gunsmoke* episode critiques anti–Chinese prejudice. However, Mexicans seem less common on television Westerns than in the movies, in either positive or negative roles. They are especially rare on *Gunsmoke* and *Wagon Train*, probably for practical reasons: there were few Mexicans in Kansas, and even fewer along the northern route the wagon trains followed to California. The first continuing Mexican character on adult Westerns was the drover Haysoos on *Rawhide,* who did not join the cast until the third season, in 1961.[8]

On the one hand, so many sympathetic stories about these less threatening minorities suggests that "tolerance and acceptance of the Other" was a message TV audiences would accept, within certain limits. On the other hand, despite sincere efforts on the part of these series to treat minority characters respectfully, by modern standards their efforts often fail. Typically, such characters are marginalized: treated as simplified stereotypes, their numbers limited, the stories told about them restricted to a narrow predictable range. Above all, minority characters are seldom the protagonists in their own stories or presented from their own point of view; instead, they feature as victims needing rescue by virtuous white people rather than as agents capable of defending themselves. And the more prominent the role, the more likely it is to be played by a white actor in dark make-up rather than by an actor of the same ethnicity as the character.[9]

Women in the Western

If racial and ethnic minorities begin to get serious attention in this period as victims of injustice, the same cannot be said for women. As incredible as it sounds to a 21st-century audience, in the pre-feminist 1950s, no one saw American women as a disadvantaged minority, not even women themselves. In fact, they had no concept of themselves as a group with common interests and problems. Instead, women were taught to see each other primarily as rivals. Since the quality of her future life was entirely dependent on which man she married, a woman's life task was to acquire the most prestigious mate possible and maintain her claim to him against other women who might be scheming to steal him for themselves. Unlike other victims of discrimination, who could easily see the source of their common problem, women lived as if in separate silos, each isolated in her own house. If a woman felt trapped and unfulfilled in her ordained role of wife and mother (as so many American women in the 1950s did), she believed her problem was personal and individual, a result of private failings, not of the limits prescribed for women—that is, a result of her gender. American women would not learn to identify their common cause with each other till about 1970, as feminist consciousness-raising groups began to develop in the wake of Betty Friedan's *The Feminine Mystique* (1963), which finally labeled the "problem that had no name."

Meanwhile, women made up half the population and at least half the television audience. As television presented the world to its viewers, what reflections of themselves did women see when they watched? What possibilities, realistic or escapist, were presented to them? The variety shows featured a certain number of glamorous singers and dancers, and some great comediennes, among them Martha Raye, who headlined her own weekly show in 1955–56. But the prestigious live drama anthologies of the early 1950s gave women their most frequent and reliable opportunities to play featured roles. Though *The Loretta Young Show* (1953–61) was filmed rather than live, its weekly dramas generally centered on important women characters, even when Miss Young did not play the lead role herself. But as filmed continuing-character series supplanted live drama in the mid–1950s, women characters became far more peripheral, the range of their roles seriously diminished. As Andrea Press observes in *Women Watching Television*,

> For the most part, on early television women are depicted primarily *as women*. Rarely, if ever, are early television women shown to be mature, independent individuals. Family women in particular are shown to be women whose existence is closely bound up with, and by, others in their family group, particularly their male partners. In addition, family women on early television are consistently pictured almost exclusively in the domestic or private realm; rarely do they legitimately venture into the male, public world of work.[10]

On 1950s television, the only female characters viewers saw working outside their own homes were domestic servants (who work in another woman's home), plus Eve Arden of *Our Miss Brooks* (1952–56), playing a high school teacher who, between classes, comically looks for a husband. They almost never saw women as protagonists, as important characters in their own right, except on the daytime soap operas; as Press points out, women in the prime-time television dramas were typically important only as they affected a male character. Women's relationships with men, whether positive or negative, were virtually all defined in either romantic or domestic terms.

Most importantly, viewers saw relatively few women of any kind. The world of drama on television, like the actual public domain of the period, was overwhelmingly, normatively, male. As Kathryn Weibel points out in *Mirror Mirror: Images of Women Reflected in Popular*

Culture, even as late as the mid–1970s, women were seriously under-represented on television dramas. Though in the daytime soaps and evening sitcoms women characters were only slightly outnumbered by men, in the prestigious nighttime dramas, among continuing characters, men outnumbered women by two to one; in the popular adventure series, the ratio was eight men for every woman.[11] If the numbers are dismaying in the 1970s, they were worse two decades earlier, especially during the years dominated by the Western.

Beyond the normal scarcity of women on TV, other factors contribute to their small numbers on the Western. First, in the actual history, white women were a relatively small percentage of those who traveled west—the pioneer wives of the wagon trains and the homesteads, on one hand, and on the other, their opposites, the prostitutes and dance hall girls who entertained the solitary men surging onto the frontier. Second, as we saw in Chapter One, the Western was a particularly masculinized genre, designed to reinforce and celebrate masculine virtues, masculine desires for freedom and adventure. So it is not surprising to find women characters not only scarce but functioning primarily as adjuncts to men, as dramatic foils—romantic objects, victims needing rescue or revenge, or, in the dance hall girl, a source of entertainment, glamour, and occasional intrigue, even danger. As a result, like racial and ethnic minorities, when women appear they are typically marginalized, stereotyped, limited to a narrow range of roles, restricted to secondary status, and rarely presented from their own point of view. Most of the time, we see women through the eyes of the men they impact, rather than in their own terms.

But on *Have Gun—Will Travel*, a very different pattern emerges, both with the ethnic minorities and with women. Women are featured characters in fully 68 percent of *Have Gun's* 225 episodes ("featured" meaning characters whose actions are vital to the story, whether as protagonists or in supporting roles); 59 of these episodes include more than one important female character, another rarity on TV dramas. Compare these numbers to *Have Gun's* competitors in their first three seasons: only 35 percent of *Gunsmoke's* episodes feature women characters, including the handful of episodes when Kitty plays a significant role in the action; 53 percent for *Wagon Train*, and 48 percent for *Bonanza*, mostly love interests for the Cartwrights, and generally only a single important woman per episode.[12] Not only are the sheer numbers significant, but the women on *Have Gun* reflect a much wider range of character types, social positions, ethnic backgrounds, and life problems than on any other Western (for that matter, on any other episodic drama) of the period. Though many of these women fill conventional domestic roles as wives, mothers, daughters, sisters, a surprising number hold responsible positions in the larger public world as managers of estates, as small-business entrepreneurs, or even public officials, while a few pursue traditionally male occupations. Significantly, the problems women face in the episodes often have little or nothing to do with the usual "women's issues"—romance or family relationships; many women engage in some non-domestic activity that impacts their communities. Quite a few single women are shown working in menial jobs as waitresses, hotel maids, and saloon girls. Not only were such characters virtually unknown on other TV shows, they were erased from the stories of women's lives in other mass media: all that sort of thing was to be left to men.

The same pattern holds true of racial and ethnic minorities, who, like women, appear on *Have Gun* in comparatively high numbers. Naturally, some of these characters are only minor figures, but many play substantial or even featured roles. Repeatedly, American Indian, Mexican, and Chinese characters are treated as complex and non-stereotyped figures, especially the sympathetic characters, but even the villains among them usually have identifiable human motives for their choices. More significantly, on *Have Gun* these characters are often seen from their own point of view, not just from a white perspective. Nor are these familiar groups the only ethnic minorities represented in *Have Gun*'s stories: three different episodes feature groups of East Indians, two include a Russian Jewish father and daughter, while other episodes feature Armenian, Gypsy, Greek, Hawaiian, and Mennonite characters or communities, in addition to episodes with characters from the more common European nations. Paladin's interactions with people from all these different cultural backgrounds reveal his familiarity with and respect for each of them, frequently including at least some knowledge of their assorted languages.

Even more unusually, *Have Gun*'s producers worked hard to match the ethnicity of the actor to the role whenever possible. Most remarkably of all, as we saw in Chapter Four, six episodes of *Have Gun* feature black actors, only a few playing explicitly black characters, something almost unknown on television in the period.[13] In a time when television was overwhelmingly, matter-of-factly white, *Have Gun — Will Travel* offered unprecedented opportunities for actors of color.

The explanation for all this inclusiveness and sensitivity to racial and ethnic minorities is simple: it was a core value for Richard Boone. Not only was he a political liberal (at least as a young man) who had grown up in multi-ethnic California, but throughout his life he despised racial prejudice, as we saw in Chapter Three in his reactions to certain controversies during *Medic*. As for women, clearly Boone was a man who genuinely liked and admired women, who enjoyed their company and appreciated women *as people*. Though sexual attractiveness was obviously not unimportant to him, Boone seemed to recognize and value women's many other qualities more than most men. Without question, he took women seriously enough to include many in his series, in roles not limited by contemporary assumptions about "women's nature."

Given Boone's virtual veto power over *Have Gun*'s scripts and casting (as described in Chapter Four), the pattern of stories and actors that appear in the show's six seasons is compelling evidence that he wanted to expose audiences to a wider range of characters, a broader variety of cultures, both American and foreign, than they were accustomed to. Judging by the patterns, he wanted to stretch their sympathies, if only a little. Though, as we will see, the other three Westerns gave some attention to the issue of tolerance, *Have Gun — Will Travel* went far beyond its competitors, in ways that link the show to the spirit beginning to roil and transform American culture, especially the civil rights movement and the new openness to other cultures signaled by developments like the creation of the Peace Corps by President John F. Kennedy. One goal of *Have Gun* was to broaden the notion of what it meant to be American, who was entitled to inclusion in the "community."

These four topics, then—lawmen and gunfighters, ethnic minorities and women—form the material of the next four chapters. Though this analytical scheme unfortunately leaves out many excellent episodes that do not fit into any of these categories, focusing on these four topics will illuminate the key ideas at the heart of the series.

FIVE

Frontier Justice

The Western has been described as "America's primary story of social authority, of the legitimate and illegitimate uses of violence in the process of creating order, making civilization."[1] As the most common figure of authority on the frontier, the lawman inevitably plays a central role in the genre.

In the raw towns of the West, the "law" typically rested on a single man, the sheriff or marshal, and the few basic rules he could enforce: you can't cheat at cards; you can't shoot a man unless he's armed and facing you; you can't steal his horse or his cattle; you can't rob at gunpoint; you can't lynch a prisoner without a trial. An honest, competent lawman laid his own life on the line every day to keep order in his town, to protect the weak and the law-abiding, and to hold the guilty accountable for their crimes. A good lawman applies the law judiciously, even humanely, with due consideration for local customs and extenuating circumstances, rather than with absolute rigidity. He must be courageous, willing and able to fight his own battles, but if a town is lucky, their lawman is also a good psychologist, able to manage troublesome people and to defuse conflicts, preferably before violence erupts. A dangerous, difficult, and poorly-paid job, it often earned the sheriff no more affection than money: as the enforcer of rules and limits, a lawman often got as much resentment from his community as support and appreciation. As Matt Dillon put it, "Some people think I'm too soft, some think I'm too tough. If a police officer does his job right, he pleases nobody."[2] Taken together, these factors make the lawman a heroic but often solitary figure.

Undoubtedly this is why so many 1950s television Westerns were centered on lawmen. Of the forty-five Western series that dominated the television landscape between 1955 and 1964, eighteen (a full 40 percent) featured a lawman of some kind,[3] although two of the four series we are examining have relatively little concern with the lawman. The characters of *Wagon Train* are almost never shown near a town, so the issue of local law seldom comes up; for the duration of their journey, the wagon master, like the captain of a ship at sea, provides what law there is. In *Bonanza*, the law's presence in the series is rather haphazard. In some episodes, Virginia City has a functioning sheriff (though never the same one twice in the first season), but often the Cartwrights seem to provide what law there is. In the second episode, "Death on Sun Mountain," when a Ponderosa ranch hand is murdered, Adam is certain he knows who is responsible, but Little Joe argues that they need proof, otherwise "we might ride into Virginia City and hang an innocent man"—as if justice lies in private hands rather than in any sort of system or official.

In contrast, both *Gunsmoke* and *Have Gun—Will Travel* are centrally concerned with the law and lawmen, and the violence that is an inevitable aspect of the job. However, the two series take very different approaches to these topics. While *Gunsmoke* explores the personal and professional challenges facing one good lawman ("good" meaning both competent and ethical), *Have Gun* is ultimately more concerned with the law as a philosophical and social institution. In 58 episodes across the seasons (nearly a quarter of the total), Paladin deals with lawmen. Some are both capable and fair-minded, while others struggle to perform their duties, either overwhelmed by external problems or handicapped by their own limitations. Collectively these episodes, along with twenty which feature a trial or some key issue of law, turn *Have Gun* into a sustained meditation on frontier justice, exploring the nature and limits of law in these thinly civilized regions, the challenges facing the men who try to enforce it, and their often uneasy relationships with the citizens they are elected or hired to serve. And when violence occurs, as it often does, *Have Gun* is far more likely to raise questions about the legitimacy or the inevitability of that violence than any of its competitors, including *Gunsmoke*.

In Dillon We Trust

Marshal Matt Dillon is clearly a good lawman. Consequently, what he does to uphold law (or at least order) in Dodge City is ultimately shown to be proper. That is, although certain characters may challenge his judgment from time to time, the audience does not; the episodes generally validate Matt's choices. Western critic Gary Yoggy, in *Riding the Video Range*, captures the public impression of the marshal throughout the years of the series:

> Dillon remained the focal point, backbone, and protector of the community. Dodge City would revert to anarchy and chaos were it not for its lawman. The town had no security in laws; its only security was its lawman, for laws could be subverted but lawmen could not.... What makes Matt Dillon unique is that he knows the people of his town, understands them, and is willing, in extenuating circumstances, to bend the law for them.[4]

As this description makes clear, the marshal's judgment determines what is allowed in Dodge City, and that is seen as a good thing. Because Dillon's integrity is a given of the series, viewers welcome his exercise of authority as not just appropriate but praiseworthy. Yet, examined more closely, Dillon's attitude toward the law and the requirements of his job reveals some troubling inconsistencies.

Sometimes there are rules the marshal has to follow, whether he likes it or not. For example, in "Hot Spell" (1:2, 9/17/55), Matt rescues the sardonic gunfighter Cope from being lynched as a horse thief. After Cope proves he purchased the horse he was accused of stealing, he lingers in Dodge, amusing himself by annoying the "good people" who had been so eager to hang him. The prominent rancher who had headed the lynch party urges Matt to run Cope out of town before he causes trouble, but Matt replies, frustrated, "I don't like his kind any better than you do, but he's done no wrong here." Later, he changes his mind and orders Cope to leave Dodge "because I don't like you." But Cope, enjoying Matt's conflict, points out mildly, "There's no law against that. There's no law that says I gotta leave, is there?" Helpless, Matt admits there isn't. As Cope continues to antagonize the residents, though always staying just the right side of the law, the lynch mob once more comes for him, and Matt is forced to interpose himself between the gunman and the good citizens of Dodge, at the risk of all their lives. Fortunately, the marshal is once more able to shame the mob's leader into abandoning violence. But the danger past, Matt again orders Cope to leave Dodge for good. This time, Cope agrees cheerfully, while making it clear both that he is *choosing* to leave, and that he might return at any time.

This episode is thoughtful, exploring the ironies and frustrations of Matt's dilemma, the contrast between what the law allows and what the marshal believes is best for his town. Though Cope is a highly disruptive force in Dodge City, he is clever enough to cause trouble in ways that leave him legally blameless. As a result, the marshal laments, he has no legitimate grounds for expelling the gunfighter from town. Yet in an episode only three months later, "General Parcley Smith" (1:11, 12/10/55), Matt orders another gunman to leave town "because I don't like your kind." Like Cope, this man has broken no laws in Dodge; in fact, he has even found an honest job there. But in this episode, unlike the earlier one, there is no claim that the man has to have violated the law in some way to justify his expulsion. This time, Matt's personal judgment, his sense of what is required to keep the peace in Dodge, is all he needs to justify his actions. This inconsistency is never even acknowledged, let alone resolved.[5]

Although the responsibilities and constraints of his job sometimes weigh heavily on Dillon, on other occasions he treats his official position as something he can lay aside when it is inconvenient. In "The Queue" (1:10, 12/3/55), a Chinese man newly arrived in Dodge is attacked by two local ruffians who cut off and steal his queue, his traditional long braid, hoping the shame of his disfigurement will drive the despised foreigner out of town.[6] When Matt confronts the ruffians in the Long Branch, they blandly deny that they have the missing queue, prompting the marshal to snarl, "You want me to *beat* the truth out of you? ... Chen's going to get his pigtail back even if I have to take this badge off to find out who's got it." The statement implies, disturbingly, that he can escape the obligation to follow the law simply by removing his badge, and then resume his office once he has achieved his end. Though Dillon does not follow through on the threat, none of the bystanders in the Long Branch seem disturbed by it. Because Matt is defending a helpless victim, whatever he does must be right—a classic case of ends justifying means. The same idea recurs in "Cow Doctor" (2:1, 9/9/56). When Doc is seriously wounded by a farmer who hates doctors, Matt threatens the attacker grimly: "If Doc doesn't come out of this, I'm going to quit being a marshal and come after you as a plain man. And so help me, I'll kill you." On a human level, we sympathize with the marshal's desire to avenge his friend, attacked so pointlessly, but no one has a right to take the law into his own hands, not even—or perhaps especially—a lawman, given his power over others. Yet again, there is no criticism, stated or implied, of Matt's violent threat.

Because Matt Dillon is the hero of the series, his choices generally work out for the best on *Gunsmoke*, but consistent, objective application of the law is not a key principle for this series. The ultimate authority here is not the code of law, but the judgment of a good man. For example, though Matt usually insists on trials for suspected criminals rather than allowing a mob to lynch them, as in "Hot Spell," on other occasions he takes the law bloodily into his own hands, even when other choices were available to him. In "No Indians" (2:11, 12/8/56), Matt and Chester use themselves as a decoy for a gang of marauders which has been robbing and murdering settlers, then scalping the victims in order to throw blame on the Pawnee. Matt is determined to stop the ruthless gang, which has already killed at least four families, including women and children. However, he turns down help from the nearby Army post, arguing that the marauders would spot the soldiers and leave the area to continue their depredation elsewhere. But because he and Chester alone cannot hope to arrest the gang and take them back for trial, Matt sees no alternative but to set up an ambush. Chester is horrified at this underhanded approach, but Matt observes, "Every man is responsible for his own actions. If I have to answer to the law, that's all right, too. Right now, I just want to see [the gang] dead." When the six gang members ride in to the trap, the lawmen start firing from cover without announcing themselves or giving warning, killing four of the six outright. The remaining two surrender, but then try to claim the moral high ground. The outraged leader charges that what Matt did was "just plain murder!" while his partner argues that Matt should hang for the killings, even if he is a marshal: "You didn't even give us a chance!" But when Matt finds irrefutable proof of their guilt in one man's pocket, both Chester's discomfort with the ambush and the survivors' outrage at Matt's refusal to "play fair" simply disappear from the audience view. The violence is quietly accepted, justified by the virtuous marshal's judgment.

In "The Round Up" (2:4, 9/29/56), Dillon faces another dangerous situation too big for one man to face alone, but here also he stubbornly refuses help, with devastating consequences. A round-up is coming to town—a huge crowd of cowboys fresh off the trail after long hard months, wild to spend their money on drink and women and to carouse through the streets of Dodge. Because Chester is laid up with two sprained ankles, the merchants want Dillon to deputize twenty of them to help head off trouble. He refuses, arguing that so many ad hoc deputies will cause more trouble than they prevent, especially when liquor is flowing freely. The marshal is determined to handle the situation himself, but when his old friend Zel shows up and offers to give him a hand, Matt accepts the offer. However, as they are patrolling opposite sides of the street, Matt is suddenly ambushed by a group of Dodge City gamblers using the chaos of the round-up as an opportunity to remove the marshal from office permanently. In self-defense, he fires rapidly, killing five men surrounding him. Unfortunately, one of the five turns out to be Zel, who had come in behind Matt to help, and now lies dying on the floor. In a frenzy of grief, rage and guilt, Matt rampages through the gambling halls and saloons of Dodge, breaking tables and glassware, confiscating guns, closing down the games, pistol whipping those few who try to resist. Even Kitty's protests about "unfairness" are disregarded: he remains implacable.

It is a strange, dark episode. The violence, much of it Matt's, is disturbing, not only to us but to Matt himself, but his reaction is opaque, the moral of the episode left indeterminable. In the end, Dillon buries his friend, but won't put up a headstone. Instead, he carves a notch on his gun handle. He explains to Chester that Zel had no respect for men who notched their guns, but this notch is Zel's headstone: "Every time I look at that [notch], I want it to remind me of what happened last night." His voice is grim, but we are left wondering what lesson he has drawn from these events: don't let friends help? Don't shoot without looking? Don't let round-ups come to Dodge? Confiscate all guns at the city limits (which, in fact, was the law in the historical Dodge City in 1879)? The dark mood is left unresolved, and unsettling.

Later in the second season, in "Bloody Hands" (2:21, 2/16/57), Matt gets so disgusted with the endless killing his job demands that he resigns, and goes out to the countryside to fish and relax. But his retirement doesn't last long. When a gunfighter named Stangler takes advantage of the marshal's absence to terrorize Dodge, an apologetic but desperate Chester begs Dillon to return, because they can't manage without him. Chester swears he would face down Stangler himself if he could, but he just isn't good enough with a gun. Only Dillon has the skill, and without him, Dodge City is at the mercy of gunfighters like Stangler. Grimly, Matt takes the gun Chester offers him and rides back to take up his burden again. It is a sympathetic portrait of a man doing an unpleasant job because somebody must, and here and now, he is the only one with the necessary qualifications. At this moment, the toll of all the killing on his spirit is made very clear. But afterward, it is seldom mentioned again, and Dillon continues to uphold the law, and to kill when necessary, for another 19 seasons.

Clearly, there is much to admire in Matt Dillon. He is a decent man, doing his best in a difficult and dangerous job, trying to keep order in Dodge so that all its residents can thrive. He is presented as fair and reasonable, a man who only brings down the weight of his authority on those who deserve it, those who are unwilling or unable to control themselves and to acknowledge the rights of others. But, examined closely, the marshal does not apply the rules of his profession consistently. Though in general he enforces the law objectively and uniformly, even when it costs him, Dillon also allows personal emotion to govern his choices more often than we would expect, sometimes bending the rules to save his friends when they find themselves in trouble with the law, as each of the principals eventually does. In each case, the conflict between friendship and duty causes problems for the marshal, but his responses under these circumstances can be disturbingly inconsistent.

In "Tap Day for Miss Kitty" (1:22, 3/24/56), when an elderly farmer insists he is going to marry Kitty despite her adamant refusal, she threatens to shoot him with a shotgun if he doesn't leave her alone. The next night, Nip is wounded in the back by a shotgun, the shooter identified as a woman by her footprints. Because Kitty has no alibi for the attack, Matt is forced to investigate her as a suspect, despite her deep bitterness at his lack of trust and even though he is certain she is innocent. Again, in "Chester's Murder" (2:27, 3/30/57), a jealous cowhand who had threatened Chester is found dead. When circumstantial evidence points to his deputy, an anguished Matt must take Chester into custody and then fight off the angry mob demanding a conviction.

By contrast, in "Doc's Reward" (3:14, 12/14/57), when Doc kills a stranger who blocks him from reaching a desperately ill patient, Matt refuses to enforce the law. In an agony of guilt, Doc confesses, "I shot that man before he even turned his gun on me. That's not what you'd call self-defense, is it?" Matt initially says, "That's not for me to decide, Doc." But when Doc insists, "You've got to arrest me," Matt reveals he has decided the issue: "The day I arrest you—that's the day I quit." Some townsfolk do grumble darkly about such a double standard. When Matt buys Doc a very public beer in the Long Branch, a gambler sneers to the crowd, "Now, if I went out and killed a man, I'd be drinking water—in *jail*—hey, Marshal?" Matt merely growls, "I'd throw a gambler in jail for almost any reason, mister." When the gambler objects to this attitude, Matt orders him to leave the Long Branch rather than dealing with the substance of his complaint. Doc himself is uncomfortable, murmuring, "Maybe I ought to be in jail," but Matt stubbornly declares, "I'll decide that." In other words, as marshal, his opinion of right and wrong outweighs that of everybody else in Dodge.

In each of these cases, the problem is ultimately resolved satisfactorily. Kitty is cleared when Nip's real attacker reveals herself—his housekeeper of twenty years, furious that he planned to marry somebody besides her. Chester is cleared of his murder charge as well, while the man Doc killed turns out to be an outlaw with a $1,000 price on his head, making the killing not only legally sanctioned but profitable. Of course, Doc refuses to profit from his violence, and gives the reward to the dead man's brother, even though the young man had tried to kill him in revenge. But instead of hating his attacker, Doc treats the wounds he got from Matt, and teaches him a quiet lesson in forgiveness and understanding. As this conclusion confirms, the focus of the episode is Doc, not Matt; the key issue is not the necessity for even-handed application of the law but the psychic effects of killing and the problem of judging character. Yet even so, the script's approval of Matt's inconsistent standards is rather startling to objective eyes.

Ultimately, the real concern of the series is the *personality* of Matt Dillon (and, to a lesser extent, his friends). Dillon is a simple man, decent and well-intentioned, with a strong sense of right and wrong, but not a deep thinker. Introspection or philosophical reflection is foreign to his nature. He does what needs to be done without asking too many questions about his own decisions. In this, the character reflects the vision of the actor who portrayed him. Though Arness began the role with good intentions, insisting he would not change the character so beloved on the radio, in fact he was never comfortable with the radio Dillon's hard edges or his fallibility. Under Arness's influence, the character became much more idealized and was seldom allowed to make mistakes.[7] And that suited the audience just fine: they wanted to admire Dillon, to identify and sympathize with him, not judge him. They cared more about Matt's emotional reactions to his situations than his philosophy about his job.

Have Gun—Will Travel: The Lawman and the Law

By contrast, *Have Gun* is concerned with the law as a philosophy and an institution, its role in creating civilized communities on the frontier. One of the key features of a civilized community is that violence is reserved to the state rather than the individual.[8] In the relatively primitive towns of the West, where often the only representative of the state was the lawman, this ideal was seldom realized (though more often in the historical West than in the mythical West of the movies and television, as discussed in Chapter One). Still, controlling and limiting violence must be one of the goals of the lawman, as we saw with Matt Dillon, however much the reality might fall short of the ideal. It is also Paladin's primary goal with each mission he undertakes, to resolve conflicts through some method other than personal violence.

Though Paladin takes many different kinds of cases over the seasons, his most characteristic adventures find him serving the needs of the justice system in one role or another, especially in his frequent encounters with a sheriff or marshal. Sometimes the lawman is only a minor character, but often he plays a significant role in the action. When Paladin's cases take him into wilderness areas with neither towns nor lawmen, or into towns that have no legally constituted authority, the man in black may temporarily function like a sheriff to resolve a specific conflict, but where local lawmen are in place, he defers to their authority. In practice, however, this principle does not always produce the justice that is Paladin's ultimate objective. Unlike *Gunsmoke*, where (in Yoggy's phrase) "laws could be subverted but lawmen could not," in *Have Gun—Will Travel*, it is the law that is paramount, particularly as represented and defended by Paladin, while individual lawmen often prove less than ideal. Every time he encounters a law officer, then, Paladin must make careful judgments about the most appropriate and effective way to work with him. The good ones earn his immediate cooperation and assistance. Those who are well-intentioned but vulnerable in some way— outnumbered or overpowered, too old, too young, inexperienced, or struggling with fear or resentment—he provides with reinforcement, instruction, or moral support in living up to the requirements of the job. Some lawmen, while not unprincipled, define their jobs more narrowly than the ideal: they will offer the law's protection to the members of their own community, but leave outsiders and passers-by to take care of themselves. These men Paladin shames, persuades, or maneuvers into extending their responsibilities a little more broadly. Other lawmen are merely venial: complacent, or lazy, more concerned with protecting their own skins than with doing the job they have been hired or elected to do, while a few are simply too stupid to understand the problem Paladin has brought to them. Such men Paladin uses like tools as best he can, or goes around them. In the worst-case scenario, if the local lawman is corrupt or a brutal bully, Paladin appeals to a higher authority to get the man overruled or replaced. In each case, he must carefully evaluate the lawman's character to determine the most appropriate response. And each time, Paladin exerts his efforts to limit and control the violence.

The Lawman's Dilemmas

Typically, the problems lawmen face in these episodes fall into predictable categories. Some problems arise from outsiders: escaped outlaws that the lawman is duty-bound to pursue, gangs invading the town, or gunfighters bringing their grandiose egos and twitchy trigger fingers into a once-peaceful community. These tend to be the most straightforward problems for a sheriff to confront, though often the most violent as well, since outlaws by definition have few qualms about bloodshed and can seldom be controlled with less than lethal methods. Therefore, except in the pursuit of fugitives, Paladin's help typically takes the simple form of additional firepower.

Other problems arise from within the community. Many small towns find themselves dominated by their most prominent citizen, the local Big Man (or, rarely, Big Woman): the largest landowner, the town banker or merchant, the owner of the stage company that carries all the town's goods, the rancher who controls access to local water; the Big Man might also be a political official, like a mayor or a magistrate. Whatever the source of his power, the Big Man typically assumes his position entitles him to dictate to the community, despite his neighbors' opinions. Such abuses of power require a different solution from the violence appropriate with outlaws. Because leading citizens play an important role in the community, they cannot simply be expelled; some sort of compromise or accommodation must be achieved in order for the community to thrive. Since the lawman is often the only town official, the only representative of the community as a whole, the responsibility for resolving the problem often falls on him. Some lawmen have enough independence and integrity to serve as a counterweight to the Big Man, enforcing justice even-handedly, but weaker or less ethical men might accede to the Big Man's wishes for fear of losing their jobs. Some of these men capitulate with reluctance, even shame, conscious of their failure, but others follow orders willingly, even eagerly, with no recognition that they owe something to their town as well. When Paladin encounters a lawman constrained by one of these powerful figures, he calibrates his assistance to their character: the ethical ones, and those who are well-intentioned but weak, get his assistance in limiting the Big Man's power. The sell-outs he ignores as long as they do not interfere with his work, but those who block his efforts at a fair solution are courting danger.

Even more serious problems arise for a lawman when his whole town, or a significant portion of it, turns on him. In the most understandable version of this pattern, citizens might abandon their lawman in time of trouble (an outlaw attack, for example), refusing to help him out of fear. Sometimes citizens reject the rules the lawman attempts to impose as too rigid or unreasonable; other towns don't respect their lawman because of a personal characteristic—a weakness, like old age or inexperience, or even (as in two different episodes of *Have Gun*) out of racial prejudice, because he is Indian.[9] In the worst cases, citizens openly attack the lawman—most often when he tries to protect an unpopular prisoner they would rather lynch themselves instead of turning him over to the law. Under these conditions, Paladin freely offers the lawman his assistance, whether that means fighting the mob at the sheriff's side, or using his powers of persuasion to break the mob's frenzy.

Whatever the problem facing the lawman—outlaw, Big Man, or mob—Paladin's principle remains the same: no one is above the law. Without law, without accepted rules, there is no civilization, no community life. For Paladin, the principle is essential—not just worth dying for but, if necessary, worth killing for, an even greater risk.

Lawmen versus Outlaws

When outlaws and gunmen invade a town, whether their goal is plunder, safe haven, the fun of bullying the populace, or freeing a captured gang member, the townsfolk often huddle in terror behind their barricaded doors, leaving the lawman to tackle the gangs alone. In that situation, the best help Paladin can offer is to join his gun to the local lawman's. In "The Five Books of Owen Deaver" (1:32, 4/26/58), "The Tender Gun" (4:7, 10/22/60), and "Fandango" (4:24, 3/4/61), the outlaws marauding through town refuse either to give up their criminal activities or to submit to arrest, so Paladin and the local lawman have no choice but to keep shooting until all the members of the outlaw gang are dead. The violence, though regrettable, is legitimate and necessary in order to preserve civic peace. When the problem is an escaped criminal with a bounty on his head—wanted "dead or alive," as in "The Outlaw" (1:2, 9/21/57), "The Long Way Home" (4:21, 2/4/61), and "American Primitive" (6:21, 2/2/63)—violence is even harder to avoid, despite Paladin's heroic efforts to bring the fugitive in alive.[10] Though these pursuits too often end in the outlaw's death, that is not Paladin's choice, or his fault.

But sometimes there are alternatives to this level of violence, if Paladin and the local lawman are clever enough to find them and determined enough to impose them, as in "Charley Red Dog" (3:13, 12/12/59). The town of Santa Maria, New Mexico has been overrun by gunfighters because it has no lawman. The town council wants to hire Paladin to restore order by killing Joe Denver, the gunfighters' "alpha dog," in order to control the rest. But Paladin rejects this proposal. He is no assassin, he asserts, and besides, "What this town needs is *law*. Law, seven days a week, twelve months a year." Fortunately, Santa Maria has an volunteer eager for the job. Unfortunately, he is a 19-year-old Navajo, Charley Red Dog, whose only apparent qualification is a certificate and badge from the "United States Marshals Correspondence Institute," plus a determination to prove himself and to do a good job for the town, even at the risk of his own life. The town fathers are skeptical of his abilities, as is Paladin: he had met Charley on the road to Santa Maria, and though Paladin had allowed Charley to confiscate his pistol (though not his concealed derringer), he could see that Charley was as naive as he was idealistic, with little practical knowledge of guns. But as inadequate a lawman as Charley might be, he is all they have, so Paladin persuades the council to let the young man try the job for a few days while Joe Denver is out of town—with secret assistance from himself to help establish Charley's authority.

Paladin's first step is to make himself conspicuous in town as a tough guy and a gunman. He starts a fistfight in the saloon, and takes his victim's pistol to replace the one Charley had taken from him, sneers at the others dismissively, and, when they respond to his insults, demonstrates his speed and accuracy with his gun by shooting up their poker game. This makes him look dangerous without any actual bloodshed. Drawn by the gunfire, Charley enters the saloon to confiscate all the weapons in the place—his first act as marshal. Though the roughnecks mock and threaten the young marshal, Paladin instantly begins to placate him. As Charley snaps impatiently, "How many times must I take your gun?" the gunfighter meekly hands over his purloined pistol As the others stare in disbelief, Paladin assures them earnestly, "I've seen this man work. Maybe *you* want to draw down on him, but not me." Following his example, the rest grumble but surrender their guns. As Paladin had told the town council, "Respect can be as contagious as measles if it's properly spread around." Round One to Charley, thanks to Paladin's masterful performance.

Charley wins Round Two on his own, fair and square. When a rabid Indian-hater storms into his office, fists and insults swinging, Charley responds with surprising toughness and skill in the battle. This defeat of his attacker impresses Paladin, and encourages him. But Round Three is a bigger challenge: six men plan to jump Charley at night, alone in his office. Although a lawman has to be able to handle some odds, six against one is a bit steep, so Paladin determines to lower the odds without letting Charley know. He lets the marshal fight alone at first, then shoots out the lamp with his derringer, plunging the office into darkness so that he can slip in unseen. After disposing of three attackers, Paladin slips out again, leaving Charley to deal with the remaining three, which he does successfully. The marshal's victory in Round Three establishes that, despite appearances, he is capable of keeping order in this obstreperous town.

But when Joe Denver rides into town the next morning, the town council and Paladin, despite their new respect for their marshal, urge Charley to let Paladin handle the gunfighter, as a task beyond his abilities. Paladin even promises not to kill Denver but to bring him in for trial for the six men he has killed, thus preserving the law's proper monopoly on violence, but he needs his gun to accomplish this. Charley refuses: "no guns in town" means no guns, not even for a friend. Facing Denver is his job, not Paladin's, though he has to knock his would-be champion unconscious to keep him from interfering. In the end, to everyone's shock, Charley defeats Denver in the gunfight—thanks to a trick Paladin had taught him on the trail.[11] Afterward, Charley reveals that he knew Paladin had helped him in the office fight with his "illegal" derringer, but points out, with new wisdom, that "a man learns to overlook things—a gun in the hands of a friend, or a worthless diploma from dishonest correspondence schools." However, the worthlessness of his certificate doesn't matter now, because he has proved he can be an effective marshal for Santa Maria. In the end, the only killing in this episode is done by the legally-appointed lawman; Paladin is just the strategist and stage manager.

Other times, however, even Paladin's support is not enough to solve a lawman's problems. In "Never Help the Devil" (3:31, 4/16/60), Sheriff Jim Toby, a lawman Paladin has long respected, has lost control of his town. The infamous gunfighter, Kramer, in shooting down his latest victim, has been wounded in his gun arm, though a sawed-off shotgun strapped to his arm makes him still too dangerous to tackle head on. The town is eager to see Kramer die in a shoot-out with his victim's young brother, hurrying home to challenge the gunfighter. But Sheriff Toby, who should have stopped the gunfight, and who should now be protecting Kramer from the mob, has gotten too old and too slow to handle this situation. As he explains grimly to Paladin, he'd take off his badge if the town could afford to hire a good man to replace him. But because they don't have the money, he stays on: "In spite of everything, for 364 days a year I'm still the best man available." When Paladin points out sorrowfully, "Time was, it was 365 days," Toby's consuming shame is palpable. Still, he refuses to risk his life to protect the wounded gunfighter from the mob, declaring defiantly,

"I got the right to choose the man I die for, and it ain't Kramer." Besides, Toby adds, those people filling the streets are his friends, and he won't kill them to defend such a worthless man. His feelings are understandable, but wrong: what he is required to defend, and if necessary kill or die for, is not Kramer as an individual but the principle of the law. But, in the face of his old friend's intense shame, Paladin refrains from pointing this out.

In the end, Paladin solves Toby's immediate problem by agreeing to escort the wounded gunman safely out of town, headed for jail sixty miles away—a job he takes not for Kramer's sake, or for the $200 the gunman has offered Paladin, but to uphold the law, and to protect the young revenge-seeker whom Kramer will kill if they meet. Most importantly he does it for "the man that Jim Toby used to be." But Toby has not yet hit bottom. Before the end, Paladin has to witness his friend's complete, very public degradation. To get Kramer out of town past the mob, Paladin has to let him keep the shotgun—with which he shoots an enemy in the crowd at point-blank range. Kramer insists the man had tried to draw on him, and demands, smirking, that Toby confirm his story. Sick at heart, obviously lying, Toby agrees, but he cannot meet Paladin's eyes. A once-decent lawman can sink no lower. Not only can he no longer prevent or punish violence in his town, now he is forced to collude at deliberate murder committed at his very feet. Paladin is torn, mourning the man Toby once was, but also appalled by his friend's moral collapse, which has left his town so vulnerable. Removing Kramer will help in the short run, but in the long run, there is nothing Paladin can do to help the sheriff or his town.

"Birds of a Feather" (1:26, 3/8/58) features another town overrun with gunmen, and a once-competent lawman (an old acquaintance of Paladin's) now too weak to keep the peace. But in this early episode, the lawman is a minor character, so minor that he is not even a significant factor in the resolution. Instead, Paladin teams up with one of the gunmen to achieve a peaceful solution. It helps that these gunmen are not outlaws but mercenaries, hired by rival railroads in a bitter dispute. Continental leased the right-of-way across Raymond Gorge from the TC&O Railroad, but TC&O is now denying the lease. The result is a standoff: Continental holds the Gorge, but TC&O holds the depot, so neither company can use the rails. But instead of taking the dispute to court, the railroads are battling it out in Big Spur with their respective armies of gunfighters, while Sheriff Dave Quinn helplessly watches his town disintegrate from the violence. As Quinn huddles in despair, Paladin steps in to do his job for him.

After conferring with agents of both companies, Paladin agrees to help Continental reclaim the depot, but he has no intention of resorting to violence to remove the little army inside the building, led by gunman Ralph Coe. Instead, Paladin convinces Sheriff Quinn to give him a legal eviction notice for the depot, despite the lawman's reluctance to get involved. But Paladin promises to take the responsibility the sheriff has abdicated; with an eviction notice, he can solve the problem peaceably. Paladin then goes to Sukey, Continental's agent, to point out how much money Continental is losing with the line shut down, $7,000 or $8,000 per day altogether. Paladin's proposal: offer Coe $10,000 to surrender the depot, with the eviction notice as cover. That would be infinitely cheaper than continuing the impasse, and no more men would die. After a moment's reflection, Sukey accepts the proposal, and so does Coe once Paladin explains to him that he doesn't have to split the money equally with his men, but could keep the lion's share for himself.

Paladin serves the eviction notice, and Coe and his men dutifully vacate the depot, much to his employer's disgust, while Sukey and his men take possession. But if Sukey's problem is solved, Paladin's is not. When Coe and Paladin ask Sukey for their money, he swears—

safely barricaded inside the depot with his army—that he gave all the money to Paladin earlier. At first Coe believes this lie, but finally Paladin is able to convince him that Sukey has cheated both of them. Then the man in black invents a stratagem to get their money. With the help of the old cannon on the square, and some handy dynamite, they force Sukey to live up to his bargain. Then Paladin makes the rival agents agree to settle the dispute in court, where it belongs, so that the town can again thrive, free of their hired guns. It is a most satisfactory outcome, and a surprising one: in this case, the gunmen are shown to be more honest than the "respectable" businessmen, and even get their due reward in the end.

Though Sheriff Quinn now has his town back, there is no final scene between him and Paladin to resolve the issues raised by the lawman's limitations, as there would be in later seasons. Quinn had attributed his failure to handle the gunmen to his advancing age, like Jim Toby. Paladin retorts, not without sympathy, "Then turn in the star." But, like Toby, Quinn resists, insisting, "A little law's better than none"—the same point Toby made, that "364 days a year" he's the best man around, as if that were good enough. But these two episodes contradict their assertions: on the frontier, a weak lawman is clearly a threat to his town, leaving it vulnerable to unrestrained violence.

Lawmen Versus Big Men

If dealing with outlaws is a relatively straightforward problem, Big Men can be more challenging to handle. But some of the lawmen Paladin encounters do a better job than others of balancing their responsibilities to all their constituents. In "Killer's Widow" (1:28, 3/22/58), Marshal Jaffey, though not an ideal lawman, is far from a failure. Responsible but pragmatic, Jaffey considers moral judgments outside his job description but is scrupulous about legalities. So he firmly resists both the local Big Men—Randolph, the banker, and Griffin, owner of the largest ranch in the neighborhood—when they want him to arrest Paladin on trumped-up charges. But he watches the gunfighter carefully to make sure he obeys the law to the letter, and he refuses to intervene when Randolph and Griffin try to take unfair, though not illegal, advantage of Lucy Morrow, a vulnerable young widow. Through each twist in the episode, Jaffey remains admirably even-handed in his application of the law. Though he will not help Paladin win justice for Lucy, he prevents the banker and the rancher from retaliating when they realize Paladin has used legal means to outsmart them. This rather limited definition of his job keeps Jaffey out of the highest ranks of lawmen, but at the same time, his independence from the Big Men who consider themselves entitled to dominate the town creates a constructive atmosphere for the other citizens, who can be sure the law will treat them equally.

Generally, however, featured lawmen in this series have a harder time with their Big Men than Marshal Jaffey. Even the ones who are successful in the end often must fight an internal battle as well as an external one. For example, in "The Campaign of Billy Banjo" (3:36, 5/28/60), Sheriff Cooley has genuine principles, but only a crisis helps him find the courage to act on them. In fact, the sheriff is confronting two problems. The immediate issue is that, on the eve of an election for state Senate, his town is a powder keg, divided between feuding groups of ranchers and miners, each with its own candidate. His long-term problem is Elise Jones, a handsome, ruthless woman who owns the mines, most of the ranch land in the area, and the saloon, and has no qualms about using her power for her own advantage. Her economic stranglehold on the town makes Elise the actual authority; despite his badge, Cooley is little more than a hired hand doing her bidding.

Subordinate as he is, the sheriff clearly cares about his town and would like to do his job more honestly if he could. To reduce the risk of violence, he confiscates all the guns in town until after the election, and he even arrests one of Elise's ranch hands who had severely beaten some miners in a pre-election brawl. But when Paladin informs Cooley that one of the miners has died of his injuries, the sheriff refuses to take any legal proceedings until after the election, when tempers have cooled: "A murder trial now would bust this town wide open!" His anxiety seems genuine concern for his community, not just an excuse to sweep an inconvenient murder under the rug. But Jansen, the miners' candidate for Senate, contemptuously assumes that Cooley is just taking Elise's side in the conflict.

However, despite Elise Jones's overwhelming economic advantages, she faces a serious challenge in this election: her ranchers and cowboys are outnumbered by the miners three to one, so in a fair election her candidate—her charming weakling of a husband, Billy "Banjo" Jones—will certainly lose. With the miners so angry and threatening, she orders Cooley to return the confiscated guns to her ranch hands, despite the danger of a bloody riot. When he objects, she reminds him that he needs her support if he is to stay in office. Shamefaced, he capitulates and hands out the guns. Meanwhile, Paladin has arranged for the miners to vote secretly the night before the election, to avoid confrontations and shenanigans at the ballot box; as a result, to Elise's complete shock, Jansen is elected by a wide margin.

When the miners combine their victory parade with a funeral procession for the dead miner, Elise orders Cooley to break up the march, arguing that they are defying his authority: "They won't let you live! They'll make you eat that badge!" As the sheriff hesitates, the cowboy who killed the miner also turns on Cooley, threatening to shoot the sheriff if he doesn't get protection from the marchers. Then Paladin quietly observes that this is the lawman's last chance to decide which side he's on. After a long tense moment, Cooley arrests the cowboy for murder. By reclaiming his authority and his pride, acting like a real lawman for the first time in a long time, the sheriff sets a more positive course for the town. Justice once again has a champion who will treat everyone equally.

Other lawmen may have to act even more directly against their powerful patrons, though they sometimes need a push from Paladin to fulfill the responsibilities of their office. For example, the marshal of Johnsonville in "The Uneasy Grave" (4:37, 6/3/61) already defines his job in a limited way. He claims he is only responsible for the "respectable" citizens of the town; the others must look after themselves. But his position is complicated by the fact that he is heavily dependent on his town's leading citizen, Leander Johnson. When Johnson kills a good-natured Irish drifter who made the mistake of falling in love with the dance hall girl Leander wanted for himself, the marshal refuses to arrest Johnson because "nobody saw what happened except *her*"—the woman they were fighting over. For the marshal, as for the rest of Johnsonville, Kathy is not a sufficiently credible witness to challenge the rich and respectable Mr. Johnson. Yet the lawman is not as blind to conscience as this behavior suggests. When Paladin urges him to do his job—to investigate, to look for evidence about the murder because "that's what you get paid for," the marshal murmurs bleakly, "But who do I get paid *by*?" Suddenly it is clear: he owes his job to the Johnsons, and must serve their interests in order to keep his badge. Significantly, once Paladin elicits Leander's public confession that he murdered Terence O'Hara, the marshal, however reluctantly, steps forward to arrest his de facto employer. As a lawman, he is neither noble nor principled, but we are shown the pragmatic reason for his choices, and by fulfilling his responsibilities against his own self-interest, in the end he partially redeems himself in the audience's eyes. The process isn't pretty, but justice does prevail, and without further violence, though it required a forceful shove from Paladin.

In "The Posse" (3:4, 10/3/59), the unnamed sheriff, like Cooley in "The Campaign of Billy Banjo," is a decent man completely overshadowed by the local Big Man—in this case, McKay, the largest ranch owner around. But unlike Cooley, this sheriff is not able to reclaim his authority: McKay is too strong for him. As the episode begins, a posse is tracking the man who brutally murdered a local couple and stole their money. Though officially the sheriff is in charge, it is McKay's orders that get obeyed, even when he directly contradicts the lawman. This becomes a serious problem for Paladin when the real murderer, a sly local man named Dobie, sets him up for the crime, lying and planting incriminating evidence. The sheriff tries valiantly to question Paladin in an appropriate manner, and wants to take him to town for a formal trial, but McKay disagrees. Quick to accept Dobie's "evidence," certain of his own judgment, and impatient with legal niceties, McKay intends to hang Paladin on the spot. This episode, then, becomes another pointed philosophical debate about the difference between lynching and execution, murder and justice. Though the sheriff is on the right side of the argument, he is outnumbered and overpowered, and eventually McKay stops even pretending the sheriff is in charge of this posse.

Curiously, McKay tries to justify himself to his prisoner even as Paladin sits on a horse with his hands tied behind his back and a noose around his neck. With passion, he recounts how hard he and his neighbors worked and how much they sacrificed to claim this beautiful land, fighting off mountain lions, Indians, and outlaws in turn. "It wasn't the law that done that," McKay declares proudly. "A lot of hard work, sweat, a few guns, a couple of ropes.... That's why we've got more faith in trees than court-houses." Then he adds, with a contemptuous look at the sheriff, "If you think we're going to turn all this over to somebody who's too weak or lazy to make a go of ranching, you're mistaken." Suddenly it is clear why these men have no respect for their sheriff; they see him as a failure, and the only causes for failure as a rancher they can imagine are character flaws—weakness, laziness. Where the sheriff worries, timidly, about rules and procedures and limits, real men aren't afraid to take the law into their own hands. McKay insists, "We're good people, doing what we gotta do! What we do is good." In reply, Paladin drily quotes Herodius's third essay: "'We can contend with the evil that men do in the name of evil, but heaven protect us from what they do in the name of good.'"[12]

In the end, Dobie overplays his hand and reveals his own guilt, and he takes Paladin's place in the noose, pleading for help—with dreadful irony—from the man he had just framed for his crime. Though McKay apologizes to Paladin, almost humbly, for his mistake, Paladin refuses to shake his hand, instead asking the sheriff what will happen to Dobie. The sheriff replies quietly, "You found out what kind of a man *I* am, Mr. Paladin"—that is, a weak one, not in command of this situation, despite his badge. "I guess it all depends on whether McKay's learned a lesson from all this." Paladin warns McKay, "What you do here today, you live with the rest of your life." But McKay doesn't get it. As Paladin rides away, he hears Dobie scream and beg, then the crack of the whip that drives the horse under Dobie into a gallop. He turns to see Dobie's pinto running free and riderless and the body swinging from the tree.

Though the sheriff is a sympathetic character, painfully aware of his own limitations, the prospects for this community are discouraging. True, this time the posse has hanged the right man, but it is still a lynching, not a legal execution. The town may have a sheriff, but it does not have law: it has McKay. Though the rancher is sincere in his beliefs, he is deeply wrong, unable to recognize that what might have been practical necessity in the earliest days of the community has become inappropriate in a town settled enough to have a sheriff. Worse, since McKay's belief in his own righteousness remains unshaken despite his mistake, he is unlikely to change his ways. The sheriff cannot control or convince McKay, though he can, and does, judge him—almost as harshly as he judges himself. It is a troubling outcome, much darker than we expect from a popular television entertainment.

The sheriff in "Bear Bait" (4:34, 5/15/61) also has a Big Man problem which makes his badge little more than a joke, though unlike his counterpart in "The Posse," this man does not seem bothered by his figurehead status. Kincaid, the owner of the Circle Y, allows his wild young cowhands to wreak havoc when they come to town, and has forced the sheriff to let him discipline his own hands. The sheriff's only strategy is to limit their numbers— no more than three in town at a time—and then to give them nearly free rein as "boys just having fun," even when their "teasing" crosses the line into harassment or even violence. When three of these young men murderously attack Paladin, he kills one in self-defense and insists that the sheriff try the other two for assault, but Kincaid demands evidence of the assault before he will "permit" a trial. The sheriff hesitates and hedges, unwilling to confront the Big Man, while the only witness to the assault—a young waitress who had sought Paladin's protection from these same hooligans—is too frightened to say what she saw. When she balks, the sheriff is able to announce, with obvious relief: "Well, no evidence, no trial." Because Paladin refuses to accept this injustice, Kincaid forces him into a bloody exchange of gunfire that leaves three men dead—both cowboys, plus Kincaid himself—and Paladin wounded. But to all of this bloodshed, the sheriff is nothing more than a disengaged observer, like any civilian in the crowd. For all the good his presence does this town, it might as well not have a sheriff, though perhaps with Kincaid removed, their situation may improve. But the sheriff gives no indication that he has any principles, however free he now is to exercise them. It is an ominous ending indeed.

Lawman Versus the Town

The most challenging problem for a lawman, however, occurs when his town, or a significant part of it, rebels against him. In "A Matter of Ethics" (1:5, 10/12/57), the sheriff is determined to protect an unpopular prisoner from a lynch mob. Though the man shot the town founder's unarmed son in cold blood, the sheriff is determined that the outlaw will be tried and hanged legally, even if he has to stand alone against his town with only Paladin to help him. Similarly, in "The Hanging of Aaron Gibbs" (5:8, 11/4/61), the marshal fulfills his painful duty by calling in the state rangers to keep his town from lynching three much-hated convicts before their execution date. Other episodes reveal how dangerous such situations can be for the lawman. In "The Prisoner" (4:14, 12/17/60), when the sheriff stands between his just-cleared prisoner and a virulent lynch mob, they nearly kick him to death in their frenzy to get to the young man. To save the lives of both sheriff and former prisoner, Paladin is forced to shoot the mob's leader. In "The Night the Town Died" (3:21, 2/6/60), a sheriff is saved from a crazed lynch mob, not by Paladin, but by his own wife. Certain that her husband would risk his life to protect the victims from the mob, she invents an arrest warrant to send him to a nearby town until the trouble is over. Though her stratagem saves her husband's life, both the town and the lawman are destroyed by the shame of their actions that night, the town for lynching a neighbor, and the sheriff for not having tried to save the victim.

The outcome of all these stories of conflict between a lawman and his town—the lawman's success or failure, and the level of violence—depends in large part on the quality of the lawman. Paladin helps as best he can, but he generally refuses to solve the problem single-handed. He insists on some kind of partnership with the legal authority.

One of the most important factors in a lawman's success is developing a good working relationship with his town. In "The Five Books of Owen Deaver" (1:32, 4/26/58), a young sheriff has all the qualities necessary for a good lawman except one: he doesn't understand his people or what they need. Owen is idealistic, but also rigid and certain of his own judgment. He is convinced that a written code of laws is preferable to the ad hoc approach to law common in western towns, which typically have no mayor, no town council, just a sheriff and maybe a judge who comes through once a month. In such circumstances, the sheriff generally decides what counts as a crime (like Matt Dillon in Dodge City). As Owen points out, "Sheriff might get up on the wrong side of the bed one morning and decide that everything is a crime. I wake up smiling, and nothing's illegal." But with a written code, what's lawful is specified, predictable, and objective.

While his theory is admirable, his application of it is misguided. Without consulting his fellow citizens, Owen has decided that the ideal law for Three Winds is the municipal code of Philadelphia, contained in the five books of the title. Within two months of his election, his attempts to impose this code on the town have completely alienated the residents. But as Paladin (an old friend of Owen's parents) points out, the laws appropriate for a major Eastern metropolis do not fit the needs of a small Western town. For example, the Philadelphia code prohibits spitting on the sidewalk. But Three Winds doesn't even have sidewalks yet. So when Owen insists that businesses must not be left unattended, that customers may only buy a limited number of drinks per day, and most controversial of all, that no one but the sheriff may carry guns within the town limits, because those are the laws of Philadelphia, Three Winds naturally resents and resists him. Worse, the economy of Three Winds has been devastated by Owen's rules. The cowboys from nearby ranches who used to come to town once a month to spend their salaries now ride 80 miles to the next town, where they can drink as much as they like and don't have to surrender their guns.[13] Worst of all, the "no guns" rule issues a challenge to every gunfighter in the territory; they will be descending on Three Winds in droves to take on the foolhardy young sheriff.

So when the gunfighters come, the alienated townspeople refuse to help Owen. He did not consult them in establishing his "laws," so they will not risk their lives to fix the problem he created. Only Paladin offers to help—and in his stubborn pride, Owen only accepts his offer when he has no other choice. In the end, the two of them manage to kill the four gang members who come to break their leader out of Owen's jail. But with the immediate crisis past, Owen is still facing a rebellious town, with no idea how to back down from his principles without losing face. Again Paladin saves the day, negotiating a deal: the citizens, he insists, have to agree to give the law some support, while Owen has to back down from his absolute positions and consider the opinions of his constituents and neighbors. "There's a basic unwritten law of jurisprudence," Paladin points out to the young sheriff; "you can't enforce a law that goes against the will of the majority." Those who try, he observes, earn an ugly name for themselves: "tyrants." After a deep internal struggle, Owen gives up his five books, and the relieved merchants agree to work with him. As a result, Three Winds will be a much happier, and more peaceful, community.

Fortunately, with Paladin's help, Owen Deaver was able to solve his problem, to recognize his mistakes and grow from them, but not all lawmen had that ability. When Paladin's old friend Tom Carey unexpectedly turns up as "The Marshal of Sweetwater" (6:11, 11/24/ 62), he too claims the right to run his town according to his own judgment, but this time Paladin cannot save his friend from his own failings. Carey had been the scout in Paladin's first command as a young cavalry lieutenant, and "just about the best friend I ever had." After the Army let the scouts go, Carey had dropped out of sight, only to re-emerge recently as the man who cleaned up Sweetwater. Now Carey is happy in his new position, confident that, even in his first time living in a town, he knows how towns ought to be run. Therefore, he intervenes in a variety of issues that ordinarily should be the responsibility of families or individuals, arguing that "it's the marshal's job to stop trouble" and "I only step in when folks decide wrong"—for example, when a mother keeps her sick child out of school, but Carey is convinced the boy is merely lazy, or when a rich rancher refuses to sell some of his land to a neighbor and Carey orders him to make the deal. Gently, Paladin tries to point out to his old friend that there are limits to his authority: "The law is very clear and specific about what a lawman can and cannot do," but Carey dismisses these concerns as Paladin's typical "fancy ideas" from books. Recognizing he cannot win this argument, Paladin lets it drop, but clearly he is disturbed by what he sees.

Like Sheriff Deaver, Carey imposes stringent and deeply unpopular rules on his town. Convinced that the greatest sources of trouble are alcohol and women—that is, loose, disreputable women—he has decreed that the saloon may sell no more than three drinks to a customer, and no drinks before 7 p.m. Under such conditions, it is impossible to run the business profitably—which is why the previous owner of the saloon sold so cheaply to an unsuspecting buyer, a handsome, clever, ambitious young woman named Marie, who arrives in town on the same stage as Paladin. Carey is initially determined to drive Marie out of town, but soon becomes mesmerized by her beauty and her spirit as she resists him, both in his tyrannical role of marshal and when he comes awkwardly courting her. Her rejection, however gentle, drives him to frenzy, especially since he believes that Paladin is the romantic rival who has displaced him. Because Paladin had already criticized his actions as marshal, this double betrayal pushes Carey over the edge into an insane fury. When Carey draws on him, a grieving Paladin has no choice but to cut down the man who was once his closest friend.

Though Carey is not intentionally evil, he causes great harm through his combination of profound ignorance and absolute confidence in his own judgment. A man who has never lived in a town before thinks he understands town life well enough to decide how people should behave; an old prairie rat with no experience of women thinks he can properly direct a young woman with far more knowledge of the world than he has. Though Carey means well, the mistakes he makes are so terrible that he cannot be allowed to continue in a position of authority. With less power, he would have been a laughingstock. Instead, his badge has turned him into a tyrant and a bully who must be stopped for the sake of the town.

Jim Buell in "The Trap" (5:25, 3/3/62) is another lawman who loses his town through abuse of power, but the dynamic is totally different from Owen Deaver and Tom Carey. For twenty-three years, Buell has served Pine Bluff as its marshal, and for twenty-two of those years, he did the job well. But recently something has snapped, and he has begun seeing himself as not just marshal but "judge, jury, and hangman." He has killed men without need, and brought overblown charges against others: for instance, he has accused his current prisoner, young Davy, of attempted murder for shooting at the jail when he was drunk. But the real reason Buell is determined to punish Davy is that, in the marshal's eyes, he had gotten away with murder the year before. He beat a man to death in a drunken brawl, his victim a newly-married man expecting his first child. The jury called it self-defense because the other man was armed with a pitchfork, but Davy's reaction to the threat was disproportionate and sickeningly brutal. Worse, Buell is certain that Davy, feckless and irresponsible, will kill again if he isn't stopped. Though the marshal may be right about this, his treatment of Davy is far from legal. Because no lawman can be allowed to take the law into his own hands, the town sends a posse to claim his prisoner and his badge. Paladin, caught in the middle and struggling to make sense of the conflicting stories, finally recognizes the truth, and with sympathy for Buell, helps him make the necessary surrender by assuring him that his neighbors do not judge him harshly, that they understand his sacrifices.

> Twenty-three years of intimacy with the misery and madness of men, wrapping bodies in ponchos and kicking dust over the blood, and telling a wife you just shot her husband, or a father that his son must hang, and telling yourself that the law will be done, no matter what the personal pain, the anguish. I understand that twenty-three years of anguish, torture, can twist a man. The ironic thing, marshal, is that only the very best survive long enough to break.

With that, Paladin gently takes Buell's badge and hands it to the posse's leader. Buell will find a new quieter life with the good woman who loves him, and Pine Bluff will find a new marshal to carry them forward. And this time, no one had to die. It is a good day's work.

The Trials of Paladin

Although sheriffs are the most common representatives of the law in a Western, they do not constitute an entire legal system by themselves. For those outlaws who survive their confrontation with the lawman, arrest must be followed by a trial for the action of the law to be complete. But in the TV Westerns of the 1950s, trials are relatively rare—only one inquest in *Gunsmoke*'s first season, and one less-than-realistic trial on *Bonanza*. This pattern suggests that the Western dramas were more interested in action, in the good guys' violent confrontation with the bad guys, than in the intellectual conflict of the courtroom. However, *Have Gun—Will Travel* is, as usual, the exception: altogether, sixteen episodes depict trials, while another four raise other significant legal issues. Half of the trials are relatively formal proceedings, with a judge, a jury, and some legitimate claim to authority, while the remainder range from kangaroo courts to a kind of tribunal of public opinion. But all of them, formal or informal, solicit testimony and attempt to determine guilt; and Paladin's role, whether he is an advocate or a defendant (several times he is both), is to champion the primacy of law, evidence, and logic in the pursuit of justice.

All these episodes display Paladin's knowledge of the law, his rhetorical skills, and his astute understanding of psychology, as he often faces a hostile individual or even a hostile crowd whom he tries to persuade with his words rather than overpower with his gun. All these trials and other legal conflicts share one more feature: in each, the process is flawed, less than impartial and fair. One or more of the participants is using the law to achieve illegitimate goals. As a result, the question in each trial is not just the guilt or innocence of the accused; the integrity of the legal system itself is at stake—the very notion of justice. These episodes, then, reinforce *Have Gun*'s characteristic concern with larger philosophical issues, with the rules that make community life possible.

The first factors to consider in evaluating the legitimacy of a trial are the judge's source of authority and the role the community plays in the proceeding. On these grounds, all the informal trials are deficient. In "The Posse" (3:4, 10/3/59), as we saw earlier, Paladin is suspected of a horrific murder, but the "judge"—the man whose orders are obeyed—has no legal authority. McKay is a private citizen whose power derives from his wealth and prominence in the community, his decisions governed not by law but only by his own sense of right and wrong. And, though Paladin speaks skillfully in his own defense, there is no independent jury weighing the evidence: a posse in the field is not a jury in the courtroom, even if it is composed of the same individuals. In two additional episodes, "The Long Night" (1:10, 11/16/57) and "Ambush" (3:32, 4/23/60), Paladin is one of a group of suspects being interrogated to determine which is guilty of murder. As with "The Posse," the suspects are being judged not by a legal representative of the community's interests, but by a private citizen looking for vengeance. In another case, "Saturday Night" (4:5, 10/8/60), the interrogator actually has legal authority, but he perverts it for his own advantage. Marshal Brock throws five men in his jail cell after a Saturday night brawl, including Paladin, an innocent bystander who had gotten swept up in the melee. But when one of the five—a wealthy young Mexican sheep rancher—is found dead in the cell with $2,000 missing, the marshal does not investigate the crime; instead he forces the four surviving prisoners to "identify" the murderer, who will be turned over to the dead man's family to be tortured and killed. So his legitimate authority is used in illegitimate ways—especially since the marshal himself is finally revealed as the murderer, his motive nothing nobler than resentment and greed.

In all these episodes, Paladin serves as lead investigator, trying to find the truth and, even more important, to head off vigilante justice. Each time, through his efforts, the guilty party is ultimately revealed. But even when those punished are genuinely guilty (in all but "Ambush"), not one of these "trials" is legitimate: lacking the authority of a community, lacking an honest and unbiased judge, lacking a jury and due process and a concern for evidence and logic, there can be no justice.

But even formal trials on the frontier often fail to meet the test of justice. In "The Trial" (3:38, 6/11/60), Paladin is hired by a wealthy man, Morgan Gibbs, to bring his fugitive son in alive to stand trial. But when another bounty hunter kills the young man under Paladin's dismayed gaze, the father accuses Paladin of murder and insists on a trial. However, this trial is more like a lynching, since Gibbs dominates the courtroom the way he dominates the town. He appoints both the five-man jury and the judge, a hapless drunk who had "read the law" thirty years earlier—not an independent thinker, but a figurehead who openly defers to Gibbs' dictates. The verdict is also a foregone conclusion, for Gibbs has ordered a gallows to be built outside the courtroom. But having stacked the deck against Paladin, Gibbs paradoxically insists on certain legal formalities, making sure that witnesses are properly sworn in, and that the correct legal terminology is used. He even allows Paladin to conduct a defense, and to cross-examine witnesses who support his story about a second bounty hunter, the actual murderer. But none of these trappings of justice affect the outcome. Without any deliberation, the jury finds Paladin guilty and he is sentenced to hang immediately. However, Paladin refuses to accept the verdict of this illegitimate proceeding, and as he struggles to disarm his guard, the gun goes off, accidentally killing Gibbs. Though the drunken old judge tries to prolong his brief moment of authority, Paladin simply walks away from the "court" in disgust. Since the trial represented no principle other than Morgan Gibbs' need to punish someone, *anyone*, for his son's death, it has no authority Paladin feels bound to honor, no connection to justice.

In "The Last Judgment" (4:25, 3/11/61), another trial combines attention to the letter of the law with total violation of its spirit, though this time Paladin is only the defense attorney, not the defendant as well. Elroy P. Greenleaf, duly appointed Justice of the Peace, has made himself the law in his community. He is determined to hang Dr. Simeon Loving, whose crime was treating a gunshot victim without realizing that the man was a wanted criminal. When the recovered patient later killed the deputy pursuing him, Greenleaf charges Dr. Loving with murder. The gallows is ready and waiting, the verdict pre-determined, but the judge insists on the forms of legality, so he cannot hold a trial until he can find a defense attorney. Paladin, passing through town, is drafted to defend the doctor. His first act as defense attorney is to send a telegram summoning a federal judge with the authority to remove Greenleaf from office. That accomplished, he turns to the trial itself with two objectives: first, to drag out the proceeding as long as possible, stalling for time till the outside judge arrives, and second, to convince the townspeople that Greenleaf's version of the law is illegitimate and should be rejected.

Though a scoundrel, Greenleaf is good-humored and shrewd, and so confident of his victory that he actually enjoys the contest of wits with a worthy opponent like Paladin. Of course, he has also stacked the deck against the defendant: he is not only the judge in the case, but also the prosecutor. Further, every member of the jury is in his power, afraid to vote against his wishes. But Paladin uses their very fear to work against the judge, reminding the jury and the other townsfolk of Greenleaf's total control over their lives. Dr. Loving, he points out, is being tried simply for doing his duty as a physician. If he can be hanged on these grounds, then any of them could be next, for any reason—or no reason. Greenleaf reinforces Paladin's point by genially intimidating two of the jurors, reminding one of the large debt he owes the judge, and another of the way Greenleaf saved him from hanging after he stole a neighbor's horse. Paladin, in turn, engages in counter–jury-fixing, offering to pay the first juror's debt so that he is free to vote against the judge, and threatening violence against the second to make him as frightened of voting against Paladin as he is of voting against Greenleaf. His object is to make them recognize how inappropriate Greenleaf's behavior is, how dangerous to all of them individually and to the community as a whole, so that they will finally rebel against his tyranny.

In the end, when the prosecutor/judge calls for a verdict, Paladin reveals that a federal judge will arrive by nightfall to take Greenleaf into custody and try Dr. Loving in a legitimate court of law. If they rush to hang his client now, he warns, they may be held legally responsible for their actions. Greenleaf, feeling his control slipping, gives up his pretense at the law and turns to violence, ordering the sheriff, his toady, to kill Paladin. Instead, in the ensuing gun battle, Paladin wounds the sheriff and kills his deputy, then captures the fleeing judge. Now that Greenleaf has been dethroned, the community has a chance to reclaim its soul, but is also required to accept responsibility for its own choices. As Paladin rides out, we see them dismantling the gallows Greenleaf had ordered built. Clearly, they have learned a lesson: even Greenleaf will not hang without a legitimate trial.

In "Trial at Tablerock" (6:14, 12/15/62), Paladin serves again as defense attorney in a trial of inadequate legality, one which forces the participants to decide what kind of justice they want. The district prosecutor, Mr. Adams, is determined to destroy the gunfighter Virge Beech, who kills with impunity by provoking men into drawing on him, then claiming self-defense. Because the prosecutor's brother was one of Beech's victims, Adams tries to hire Paladin to kill Beech in a fight, but Paladin refuses coldly. Not only does he not do such work but, he points out, the prosecutor has legal recourse: the law allows him to indict a gunfighter for deliberately provoking a fight. But Adams doesn't want justice, he wants vengeance. When Paladin turns down the job, a young man eager for fame and fortune challenges Beech in his place, but proves no match for the gunfighter. Though a saloon full of witnesses sees Haskins draw first, Adams instantly charges Beech with murder, and the town supports him. Like Adams, they are so desperate to escape Beech's bullying that, in the heat of the moment, they do not worry about the ethics of their actions or the dangerous precedent they are setting.

Deeply troubled, Paladin warns the circuit judge that the charge against Beech is fraudulent, but discovers that Judge Bryant, far from an ally, is another obstacle to justice. As the judge explains with bitter cynicism, like Paladin he had once been a believer in reason and law, "until residents of my own state impeached me for actually dispensing justice, logically and lawfully." Now, he keeps his position by giving the people what they want. Since neither the judge nor the prosecutor represents the unbiased law necessary for justice, Paladin takes matters into his own hands. Blandly pointing out that Beech's lack of a defense attorney "not only jeopardizes the legality of these entire proceedings but it makes every person in this room liable to prosecution," he manipulates Adams into appointing him to defend Beech. The trial becomes a duel between them, with the judge serving as a scornful referee. A better legal strategist than the prosecutor, Paladin takes advantage of Adams' mistakes in ways the judge is forced to uphold. For example, Paladin politely insists that the trial follow formal procedures, like swearing witnesses in before they testify. Most devastating of all, he elicits testimony that reveals some witnesses are lying and the rest are colluding—which everyone in the saloon already knew, but now it is on the record.

In the end, Paladin makes the issue explicit: what is on trial in this room is not Virge Beech, but the justice system itself. He reminds the court about the principles that system is based on, until the judge, more and more uncomfortable, chastises him: "This is not an elocution platform. The purpose of a trial is simply to determine whether or not the defendant is innocent or guilty." Paladin agrees soberly: "Yes, Your Honor, and any other reason for holding a trial would be—*hypocrisy*." His voice is mild, but his words sting, since every person in the courtroom knows that, in this instance at least, Beech is not guilty. The judge looks troubled, the jury chagrined, but a frustrated Adams protests frantically, "Virge Beech is a murderer! That's your precious truth! I've seen him take life—every man in this room has seen the same!" The Judge, his conscience stung, cuts to the heart of the matter: "If you must string him up, take him out and do it for something he's actually done! But don't ask me to run a proper court and then whine that the law casts too bright a light for a lynching."

Desperately, Adams rests his case and calls for a verdict, but to his surprise, the jury foreman hesitates. Diffidently, he explains, "Like the judge was saying, Mr. Adams, talking about lynching is one thing, but sitting in a courtroom and twisting around the law—that's something else again." Judge Bryant, faced with the last thing he expected, an honest jury, abandons his cynicism and dismisses the case for lack of evidence. However, the judge is practical as well as ethical. Though Beech is not guilty of this charge, he is still a danger to the town. So he is free—but, the judge adds, only on condition that he not use firearms in town again, and he appoints Paladin to enforce the order. Naturally, Beech's first act is to put on his gun and challenge Paladin, who sighs, takes his stance, and kills Beech on the spot—the only solution possible, since the gunman refuses either to leave or to accept the limits on his behavior necessary for life in a community. So, for a fee of $1,000—a fee not for killing Beech, the man in black explains firmly, but for defending him—Paladin helps achieve an appropriate solution. Most importantly, despite the prosecutor's lapse, and the town's genuine fear of Beech, they finally uphold the principles of justice. Because they do the right thing, Judge Bryant's faith in the law and his fellow citizens has been restored. The town is going to be all right.

On the other hand, even a virtuous and well-intentioned judge can cause significant harm if he finds himself working in an unfamiliar context. In "The Prisoner" (4:14, 12/17/ 60), a Boston judge temporarily riding circuit in the West is sent to Coffinville to hold a hearing. Eleven years earlier, Justin Groton had been arrested with his older brothers, members of a ruthless gang, and sentenced to hang along with them. But since Justin was only 13 at the time, his execution was postponed till he reached age 21. Somehow his file got lost, and at age 24, he is still in jail, so the judge is sent to hold a hearing on the matter. Unfortunately, the judge refuses to acknowledge that there is any difference between law in Boston and law in Coffinville, and in his ignorant idealism, he nearly perpetuates a grave injustice. It is only Paladin's arguments that prevent an innocent man from being hanged.

Feelings against the Groton gang and the Groton name still run high in Coffinville, even against the gentle boy who has lived in their jail for over eleven years.[14] Though the sheriff who has guarded the prisoner for all these years has come to feel a genuine affection for him, Keel, the mob's spokesman, is still eager to hang Justin, arguing that he must be killed to protect the town because "the same blood runs in his veins as in all the other Grotons." In the hearing, Paladin serves as an informal but passionate spokesman for the defense. He points out that any crime the boy could conceivably have committed at age 13 has surely been paid for by eleven years' imprisonment, but the judge refuses to consider the question. The purpose of the hearing, he declares, is merely to set a new date for Justin's long-delayed execution; he has no jurisdiction over the previous sentence. But Paladin reveals that the earlier trial was only a kangaroo court, in which Keel (a miner) had been one of the judges. Though troubled by the irregularity of the previous procedure, the judge rules that it had a "quasi-legal basis," and points out that there is no statute of limitations on murder. But Paladin forces Keel to admit that Justin never killed anyone, that he was captured before any possible murder could have taken place. At this, the Boston judge changes his mind: since no capital crime was committed, he rules, Justin Groton is free.

In a simpler kind of drama, that would be the conclusion, a classic happy ending, but not on *Have Gun.* Even as Justin rejoices in his official freedom, the town shuts itself against him in fear, and violence spreads rapidly. Keel, determined to hang the last Groton despite the judge's ruling, raises a lynch mob, which viciously attacks first the sheriff and then the judge when they try to protect the boy. Finally Keel shoots at Justin, and is prevented from killing him only because Paladin shoots faster and straighter. Using the threat of more deaths, Paladin drives the rest of the mob out of the street, and then talks the hurt and angry Justin into putting down his gun, to prove that Keel was wrong about the kind of man he is. Now the episode can end. There is no guarantee that Coffinville has learned its lesson, but the rabble-rousing Keel is dead, and Justin has not only been saved from hanging but helped to make a positive choice in his life, while an idealistic but naive judge has learned that justice is less abstract and universal than he thought, thanks to Paladin.[15]

All these stories about frontier justice, both those focused on lawmen and those focused on trials or other legal issues, suggest that what is at stake is the nature of the community itself. Where the earliest stories about the West feature conflicts between larger-than-life individuals, the "good guy" and the "bad guy," the stories on *Have Gun—Will Travel*, and to a lesser extent on *Gunsmoke*, explore the more complex challenge of creating a community whose legal and political institutions are able to maintain order. By definition, laws impose limits on individual behavior. Citizens must decide what limits they are willing to accept, how much control they will cede to authority figures—a lawman or a judge—and what standards they expect those authority figures to meet in order to earn the town's obedience and support. At a minimum, the citizens must have confidence that those who govern them are fair and competent, sensible and humane. One concern of *Have Gun* is to explore what happens when the contract between lawman and community breaks down through failings on one side or the other. Paladin's mission in his interactions with all the officers of the law he encounters is to help balance the scales of justice and hasten the arrival of a settled middle-class civilization on the Western frontier.

SIX

Gunfighters and Outlaws

In the Old West, no figure was more disruptive of community peace and order than the gunfighter—a man who used a gun with professional skill.[1] In a world where most men wore side-arms, gunfighters could be distinguished from ordinary cowhands by the way they wore their gun belts low on their hips, with the holster tied down to their thigh so the pistol wouldn't catch on the holster in a quick draw. Some of these men were outlaws, using their guns to rob banks, trains, and stage coaches, or to terrorize the citizens of a town. Others were mercenaries, hiring out for contract killings, earning "fighting wages" in a range war, or serving as bounty hunters for fugitives from justice. Occasionally, a gunfighter would even employ his guns on the right side of the law (like the real-life Pat Garrett and Bat Masterson) to help a frontier town overrun by violence, intimidating, driving out, or killing the outlaws and troublemakers. But gunfighters, even those who were not outlaws, were typically feared as much as they were admired. As one man bitterly tells Paladin, gunfighters are different from ordinary people: "People make things. Babies! Poems. Gold. Silver. What do *you* make? I'll tell you what you make—dead bodies is your business!"[2] That is, the image of the gunfighter, whether hot-headed bully or a cold professional, is a man who kills without conscience or qualm, not for worthy causes like justice or self-defense, but selfishly—to gain prestige, to protect his honor or his reputation, or to earn blood-money.

True, gunfighters' professional lives were not completely lawless (in the Western, if not in history). In order to stay marginally legal, they must abide by a code. The first rule: no shooting from ambush or without warning. A fight had to be open and fair: two men, both armed, and facing each other. Since the man who drew first could not claim self-defense, both combatants tried to wait to the last moment, making the ability to draw more quickly than your opponent essential to survival. However, legality was not the only issue in a gunfight: honor, too, was central. Like the traditional duel it grew out of, in the Western gunfight a man's reputation was at stake—not only his reputation for speed and skill with a gun, but his reputation for courage. If a man was called out, he had to face his challenger or be branded a coward.[3] Here is the male dilemma at its most paradoxical: in order to defend his manhood, a gunfighter had to risk his life repeatedly, facing any man with a gun willing to challenge him, in a fight that typically ended in death for one of them. A Westerner who refused to wear a gun might live longer, but at a cost of being seen as less than manly—a high price for any man to pay.

Though the gunfighter is ubiquitous in the Western, *Have Gun—Will Travel* characteristically tells more thoughtful, complex stories about such figures, in part because Paladin is himself a member of the brotherhood. But with all the skills of a gunfighter, Paladin chooses to use his gun not to gain power and prestige for himself, but to help other gunmen find a different way to live if they are ready to give up the deadly cycle of challenge and death. Taken together, these episodes about gunfighters explore the tangled relationship between violence and manhood on the Western frontier.

Paladin as Gunfighter

In his working life, Paladin is subjected to all the stereotypes about gunfighters. In *Have Gun*'s pilot episode, "Three Bells to Perdido" (1:1, 9/14/57), a potential client takes one look at Paladin's card with its terse motto, "Have Gun, Will Travel," and announces with contempt, "I know the breed. Can't work. Can't sleep. They've got to have action. And *money*." In "Killer's Widow" (1:28, 3/22/58), when Paladin expresses regret about a bank robber he had been forced to kill in self-defense, a rich banker reacts with disbelief: "Certainly a man like you don't care whether he ... I mean, you are *paid* for what you do; it can't really mean anything." In "Saturday Night" (4:5, 10/8/60), Paladin defends himself against a charge of murder by arguing that he had no reason to kill the dead man, a stranger to him, but the marshal merely remarks, "Money gun don't need a reason." In "The Waiting Room" (5:24, 2/24/62), a cold-blooded murderer being taken in for trial tells Paladin with mocking confidence, "You're worse than I am. I kill for pleasure, or to take power, or the love of a fight. But you—you kill for money."

But he encounters the most ferocious prejudice against gunfighters in "Everyman" (4:27, 3/25/61). Mr. Danceman hates all gunfighters, because his son was shot down by one, and tells Paladin genially, "I'm going to kill you, gunfighter." At the threat, Paladin naturally turns to face him, but Danceman just smiles contemptuously: "Always ready to go for the gun, aren't you? It's a sign of the breed"—as if Paladin's reaction indicated pathology rather than prudent self-defense. However, the unarmed Danceman announces, the fight will take place in the morning, so Paladin could save himself by leaving tonight. But, he proclaims confidently, "You won't leave. You've got gunfighters' pride. That makes you stay. It's kind of a curse, ain't it? Once you're called out, there ain't nothing you can do except kill or be killed."

But Paladin repeatedly rejects these assumptions about his nature and his profession. In "The Bostonian" (1:21, 2/1/58), his description of himself as a "businessman" is dismissed haughtily by his clients, a sophisticated Boston couple newly moved West and being bullied by neighboring ranchers. They look at his card, sniffing, "A strange kind of business.... We don't sanction killing." Paladin remarks quietly, "I don't care much for it either. I try to avoid it whenever possible, but there's always that risk." In "The O'Hare Story" (1:25, 3/1/58), Paladin is hired by a community to resolve a conflict with a neighboring community over water rights. The mayor is convinced that violence is the only solution, but one councilor offers to double Paladin's fee if he can resolve the situation without killing. A second man objects, "Don't cinch him in too tight—he's a gunfighter. What's he gonna use in case of trouble?" Paladin instantly replies, "Brains." When the man admits, "They can have *temporary* effects," Paladin points out, "But it does leave people alive, and that's an advantage when the dust settles." Even at the end of the final season ("Eve of St. Elmo," 6:28, 3/23/63), Paladin is still reinforcing this point, as he tells a potential client, "I don't hire out for hatred. I don't hire out for revenge. I've been tempted many times to use this gun as an instrument of judgment, to be judge, jury, executioner. I have thus far resisted this temptation, and I don't think I'll make an exception in this case," however much gold his client offers.

Though generally Paladin makes such declarations confidently, sure of his principles and his judgment, there are occasions when he hesitates and doubts himself. In "The Man Hunter" (2:1, 9/13/58) he tells the vengeful brothers of the young fugitive he had been forced to kill that, though he's an expert in the use of a gun, "I have killed only—*I hope*—when there was no other choice left me." That brief reservation, his acknowledgment that he might sometimes fail to live up to his own standards, humanizes Paladin, making him something more compelling than an idealized hero, too perfect to be true. In "Killer's Widow" (1:28, 3/22/58), when Lucy's home is attacked in the middle of the night, Paladin kills the invader, then apologizes to her for the bloodshed on her doorstep: "I'm sorry this had to happen here." Fiercely, Lucy exclaims, "Did it have to happen at *all*, Mr. Paladin? Or have guns and killing become your way of life?" "No," he says firmly, but then hesitates: "I hope not." When he solves her problems without further bloodshed and without taking a fee for himself, she calls him a "remarkable man," but he demurs with sorrowful self-awareness: "No. Just a man who's used a gun—perhaps too often." That humility, acknowledging that even constant vigilance is not enough to guarantee he always lives up to his own principles, sets Paladin apart among men of action.

However, Paladin faces his darkest moments of self-doubt in the only two-part episode in the series, "A Quiet Night in Town" (4:17–4:18, 1/7/61, 1/14/61). Driven nearly mad with outrage, he behaves uncomfortably like a conventional gunfighter, using his superior skills ruthlessly against others. When he stops overnight in a lonely town with a prisoner he is taking in for trial, a quartet of bored cowboys, fueled by liquor and prejudice and desperate for excitement, decide to take matters into their own hands. They smash Paladin's gun hand with a rifle butt, and then lynch his prisoner as he watches helplessly. In fury, Paladin stalks the four young men, offering them a stark choice: surrender and face trial for murder, or die. The primary instigator, Joe Culp, laughs off the choice, knowing the gunfighter's hand is useless, but a contemptuous Paladin insults and bullies Culp into drawing his gun, then shoots him dead with his left hand. The only local law officer is Remy, full-time storekeeper and part-time deputy. A solid, sensible man, Remy is appalled, both at Joe's death and at the chance Paladin took shooting left-handed, but Paladin bleakly reminds Remy that guns are his profession. Even shooting with the wrong hand, Paladin would inevitably win. Joe was a fool to accept his challenge.

When the gunfighter starts after the other three, determined they will also pay for their part in the lynching, Remy argues that, though Joe unquestionably committed murder, the others are guilty only of watching. But Paladin challenges the deputy: his prisoner died "by mistake" and "for nothing?" When Remy reluctantly agrees, Paladin insists bitterly, "Then we'll let it be the same for them—by mistake, and for *nothing*." Remy is reluctant: not only are those his friends he'll be trying to arrest, but Paladin's anger troubles him. "I'll hate to shoot, Paladin—so it's sure I'll be doing it for justice alone. What about you? Will you still be mad when you squeeze the trigger? That would be revenge, wouldn't it?" Paladin does not reply, but his face is eloquent. Despite his confident words, obviously he too is worried about his motives.

But in the end, he finds his way back to his principles. Sincerely, he offers the remaining three men the same deal he originally offered his prisoner and Joe Culp: "Live—and stand trial." Two of the trio choose to fight and die in the street. Though wounded by his friends in the crossfire, Remy is more concerned with Paladin's state of mind than his own injuries. Anxiously he asks, "Was you mad when you squeezed the trigger?" Sorrowing over the deaths but clear in his conscience, Paladin is now sure that his goal was truly justice, not revenge.

That leaves only Roy—a decent young man, but the only one of the four really Paladin's equal with a gun. Like his friends, he is reluctant to surrender, but unlike them, if Roy decides to fight, the crippled Paladin will probably not be able to beat him. Roy's girlfriend argues desperately that Paladin is worse than the men he's been hunting: they killed only one man, while he has killed three. But Paladin denies her argument: "No. I had a reason. They were just playing." In the end, a telegram reveals that Paladin's prisoner was innocent after all; another man has confessed to the murders he had been accused of. Sick with shame, Roy drops his weapon, but Paladin insists wearily, "I don't want your life. I don't want revenge. You turn yourself in to Remy, and I'm done with it." He has done what he had to do, and now the violence has burned out of him. Further, he knows he can trust Remy to handle this situation properly. It is not a happy ending, but it could have been far worse: Paladin's innocent prisoner died, along with three of his four executioners, but the fourth has accepted his guilt, and Paladin himself was able to hold to his principles, despite the overwhelming temptation to lash out in anger, abusing his power. Justice and community standards have been reaffirmed.

Paladin's Creed: The Source

In the first episode of Season Six, "Genesis" (6:1, 9/15/62), we finally learn in a flashback how Paladin became Paladin. After the Civil War, our unnamed protagonist is a dissolute playboy whose respectable family pays him an allowance to stay far away from them, in order to protect their reputation. Playing poker in San Francisco with the ruthless Norge, the young man loses $15,000 which he cannot repay, as Norge well knew when he accepted the IOUs. Now the hapless gambler faces scandal and prison unless he agrees to do Norge a small favor: kill a man named Smoke. A killer wanted in a dozen states, Smoke has driven Norge out of his own town, Delta Valley, and Norge wants him removed. If the young man—carefully chosen for his war record and his success as a duelist—will promise to fight a duel with Smoke, then Norge will tear up the IOUs. If he refuses, he faces disgrace for his family and ruin for himself. Sick with self-disgust, but helpless in Norge's trap, the gambler agrees.

But the duel with Smoke (a role also played by Richard Boone) takes a very different form than the young man expects. Arriving in Delta Valley, he is knocked unconscious from behind, and wakes to find himself penned in a compound with all his gear and his gun but no bullets, and Smoke camped above him in the rocks. Aging, gray-haired, with a mocking, courtly manner, a slight Southern accent, and an ominous cough, Smoke is dressed all in black, and sports a chess knight on his black holster. In a condescending drawl, the old gunfighter taunts his challenger: "In the books there's a name for a man like you: a paladin. A gentleman knight in shiny armor, all armed with a cause and righteousness and a fine pointed lance, and yet a mercenary—a man who hires out for gold. What was your price, my paladin? How much gold did Norge give you to slay the dragon?" Smoke is not refusing the duel, he explains, merely exercising his right as the challenged to choose the time, the place, and the weapons. He wants to be sure his opponent has the skill for a fair fight.

The next morning, Smoke appears suddenly on the rocks overhead and orders the young man to draw his gun. Frustrated, the challenger snarls, "You know my gun is empty!" But the gunfighter, amused, observes that the lack of bullets is what keeps the prisoner alive. All Smoke wants is to check out his opponent's skill: "Draw your gun and show me the speed that you think will match mine. Your life depends on it!" The prisoner does as ordered, but his draw is painfully slow and awkward, because his holster is a standard cavalry issue, made of soft leather, with a flap that snaps over the butt to keep the gun from being accidentally dislodged. Obviously, his duels have all been the old-fashioned Eastern kind, not the Western fast-draw style. Smoke tosses down a knife and tells him to cut away half his holster to get his gun in the open, and then to soak the soft leather in water and let it dry stiff. And, the gunfighter advises, he should practice his draw if he wants to beat Smoke in a duel. The young man follows these instructions, and begins to practice steadily. When he has improved his draw sufficiently that even Smoke is impressed, the next question is: how well can he shoot? Smoke places one bullet in a tree branch on the cliff, and tosses a second down to his captive—who accurately hits the target. The old gunfighter agrees that his challenger is ready; they will fight at daybreak.

In the morning Smoke appears again in the rocks overhead. "So ends the apprenticeship," he announces, tossing down two bullets. After some jockeying for strategic advantage, both men draw and fire. The younger man's arm is creased, but Smoke is mortally wounded, and he falls into the compound. With his dying breath, Smoke tells his victorious opponent,

> You think you've slain the dragon. Know what you've done? You've turned the dragon *loose*. The one decent thing I ever did in my life was to chain him away from these people. Who's going to stop Norge now? You? Oh, your armor does shine brightly and your arm is strong enough, but where is righteousness, noble paladin? Where is your cause? You remember: there's always a dragon loose somewhere.

Smoke's funeral in Delta Valley is another revelation to the young man. Smoke had first arrived in the town ill, near death, and the people had tended him generously. In gratitude for their help and acceptance, he protected them from Norge's ruthless depredations. Loving Smoke, the townspeople treat his killer with cold contempt. As the funeral cortege moves off to the cemetery, the young man weeps in shame at what he has done, and swears a fierce silent oath. And when Norge comes to Delta Valley to reclaim his kingdom, he is shocked to find the former ne'er-do-well standing in Smoke's post, wearing Smoke's black clothes and his holster with the chess knight. The nameless remittance man has become Paladin, ready to fight dragons wherever he finds them, in whatever disguise.

Smoke gave the younger man much during his days in that enclosure. First, of course, his *nom de guerre*, Paladin; then, instructions on being a gunfighter. But more important, Smoke taught his unwilling disciple a creed different from that of the typical gunman (which Smoke himself had been before Delta Valley transformed him). Where most gunfighters would have fought a challenger like our Paladin-to-be when he first offered, without concern for a fair fight, Smoke takes the time to study his opponent, to determine what kind of man he is, and to instruct him in the craft in order to give him a fighting chance. By his own example, Smoke demonstrates to his captive that, for a smart man, a gun should be the last resort, not his first. Finally, where other gunfighters use their guns for power, or prestige, or money, Smoke holds out a different model to Paladin, encouraging him to pursue a righteous cause, to seek out "dragons" like Norge, and stop them from abusing their neighbors. In short, he gives Paladin a creed—a principle to live by, and a model to live up to.

In giving Paladin a moral purpose for his gun, this creed also protects him from the temptations of the gunfighter's life, the psychological rewards some men found so addictive: the adrenaline rush of each new life-and-death contest, the feeling of power and control, and the ego-gratification of a reputation for a fast gun. Because none of these motivate him, he does not find himself trapped in the life, as so many gunfighters do. But however freely he has chosen his path, however righteous the causes he selects, it is not an easy way to live. Like all gunfighters, Paladin risks death every time he faces another man with a gun. In "The Black Handkerchief" (3:9, 11/14/59), when a young man who has unintentionally put Paladin in danger asks the gunfighter if he's afraid, Paladin replies sharply, "You think I hold my life in so little regard that I'm not afraid to lose it?" Then, recognizing that Pete is struggling with guilt as well as fear, Paladin reassures him gently, "I chose my own way of life and my own probable way of losing it. And that's *my* responsibility."

In "Fandango" (4:24, 3/4/61) Paladin articulates another disagreeable aspect of the gunfighter's profession: how fine a line separates life from death. "Twitch of a finger—a tenth of a second, one way or another," Paladin grumbles discontentedly; "that's a poor thing for a man to dedicate his life to." But when Lloyd Petty, a once-famous gunfighter who had left the life a decade earlier, insists on trying to take prisoners from the sheriff to lynch them himself, Paladin does not hesitate to confront him, and wins the shoot-out because Petty's draw had slowed—barely perceptibly, no more than a tenth of a second, but enough to enable Paladin to beat him. The encounter leaves him chilled at the fragility of life, and appalled by Petty's choice to gamble both their lives on the speed of his draw. Yet, for the good of those who cannot defend themselves, Paladin will stay at his job, whatever the personal cost, so that if his non-violent strategies fail, his gun is there as a last line of defense.

A Gunfighter's Life: Getting In

Given the obvious drawbacks, why would anyone take up a gunfighter's life in the first place? What is the appeal of the deadly violence, or the justification that makes it acceptable, or the circumstances that make chronic violence and an ever-present threat of sudden death seem preferable to other options? Some men are clearly drawn by the thrill of the fight, the adrenaline surge that accompanies such life-and-death challenges. Others pick up the gun for frankly selfish reasons—to win fortune, prestige, or power over others, or to assert their manhood. Some are driven to it in self-defense, while others want revenge against a man with a gun. But whatever a man's initial motive, gunfighting is easier to get into than out of, and the costs usually prove higher than he had imagined.

For men like Manfred Holt in "The Outlaw" (1:2, 9/21/57), fighting is an essential part of being a man. If Holt doesn't like a fellow, he has no alternative but to fight him. And he fights with a gun, because, as he admits frankly, he's no good with his fists. "What's the sense of fighting a way you're going to get licked?" he demands logically. Holt has a kind of integrity: he makes sure that his opponent has a gun and is facing him—no ambushes, no cheating—but he doesn't care whether the other man is any good with a gun. His concept of a "fair fight" doesn't extend that far. Given Holt's primitive understanding of manhood and violence, a society striving for civilization has no place for him, but he is far from the worst, especially compared to the men who lust after the violence itself, and the prestige it brings, the "notch-collectors." In "A Sense of Justice" (2:8, 11/1/58), a gunman watching from across the street immediately recognizes Paladin's profession and his quality. Viewing Paladin as if he were a trophy he wants for his wall, Tom practically salivates: "That'd be a man to cut a notch on. No need to be ashamed of *that* notch. Big man. Big target, easier to hit. But that man's got to be beat. I can beat him." Tom has all of Holt's violent competitive streak with none of his integrity. Characteristically, both Holt and Tom end up dying by the gun they live by.

Self-defense is the most justifiable reason for picking up a gun, but that doesn't make the gun easy to put down when the danger is past. Exhibit One is young Kurt Sprague in "The Protégé" (2:6, 10/18/58). Driven out of his hometown by a gunman who provokes confrontations so he can shoot men down in a "fair fight," Sprague hires Paladin to teach him how to use a gun so that he can go home and confront the bully. He turns out to be a natural, and after weeks of Paladin's coaching, Sprague easily kills his tormentor in a shoot-out. But the successful gunfight goes to Sprague's head like a deadly drug, and he becomes the very thing he had fought—a bully with a fast gun, feeding his ego by forcing weak, frightened men to face off against him. Similarly, Winston Ainslee in "Shot By Request" (3:5, 10/10/59) takes up the gun in self-defense. A professorial Easterner forced to move West for his asthma, Ainslee becomes the butt of bullies whose "games" include seeing which of them can knock him out with only a single punch. And, like Sprague, Ainslee turns out to be really good with a gun. His first duel ends the bullying, but now his reputation as a gunfighter draws an endless series of challengers eager to take him down: eleven to date, and no end in sight, as each new success increases his reputation and tempts more men to test themselves against him.

Though Sprague and Ainslee share a common motive for picking up a gun, their response to the experience of gunfighting is radically different. Sprague gets addicted to the power, the ego boost, and the adrenaline rush, and is unwilling, even unable, to put the gun down. By contrast, after eleven successful duels, Ainslee is sickened by the slaughter and eager to retire from gunfighting, but needs to do so in a way that will stop challengers calling him out. He can't change locales because of his health, and the local sheriff is no help: as long as the fights are "fair," he refuses to intervene. So Ainslee hires Paladin to cripple his gun hand in a shoot-out, to take him permanently out of competition, so he can live his life in peace.

In both of these stories, prowess with a gun is linked to manhood, but in a way that critiques standard American assumptions about manliness. The pre-gun Sprague is "one of the nicest boys in town," liked by everybody, a church-going, suit-wearing, respectable young man—qualities that, perversely, stamp him as less than manly by Western standards. In learning to fight his own fights and successfully confronting a bully, Kurt Sprague achieves power and status. For the first time, he feels like a man, "like I'm *somebody*," as he explains to an appalled Paladin. But what kind of man? With a gun on his hip and notches on its handle, Sprague has turned into a clone of the man he first killed, a travesty of manhood, angry, aggressive, and brutal. With the support of Kurt's father, a grieving Paladin faces down his protégé, killing Kurt to protect the town from the monster he has become. Only as he's dying does Kurt's madness melt away. This conclusion affirms that Kurt's understanding of manhood, and that of the culture as a whole, is profoundly wrong: Paladin, who uses violence only as a last resort, who refuses to take pride in his skills as a gunfighter, and who mourns for his protégé's fall, is the manlier man.

Like Sprague when Paladin first met him, Ainslee's manhood too is clearly deficient by frontier standards—a cultured intellectual, a man in a Van Dyke beard and a three-piece suit who can quote Latin by the hour but cannot defend himself in a fistfight. The cowboys, unable to understand or respect his accomplishments or his character, derive endless entertainment from tormenting the former schoolteacher, and Ainslee's new skills with a gun, while earning a certain level of respect, don't change their fundamental resentment and dislike of him and his elegant Eastern manners. However, although Ainslee gets no more ego gratification from killing men than Paladin does, his attitude toward gunfighting is not as detached as it seems at first. Though he is sincere in his desire to lay down his gun, he has enough pride in his skill that he can't bring himself to deliberately throw a fight, even one he himself has paid to lose. As a result, the duel with Paladin will have significant dangers for both of them, despite its pre-arranged conclusion.

Another powerful motive for taking up the gun, revenge, is likewise a declaration of manhood, asserting the right to redress wrongs personally rather than letting the law deal with guilt and punishment. Young Terry Gallagher is obsessed with killing Doggie Kramer, the brutal gunfighter of "Never Help the Devil" (3:31, 4/16/60), who shot his brother down in the streets.[4] Though Paladin is taking Kramer to jail in Santa Fe, Terry swears he will pursue his quarry there and call him out. Paladin, recognizing the dark truth—"You *want* to be known as the man who shot Kramer"—suggests, "Maybe you ought to find out first how a thing like him ever happened to get started." Matter-of-factly, Kramer says, "I shot the man that killed my father in a barroom brawl"—an exact parallel to Terry's situation. That first draw-down, however justifiable by Western standards, clearly led to more fights and a growing reputation, until Kramer has become a ruthless killer, surrounded by enemies eager for his blood. He tells the young man pointedly, "You and me are just the same, kid"— driven by the same desire for revenge, and headed for the same fate. But Terry demonstrates so much speed and accuracy with his gun that Kramer realizes he is outmatched, so he tries to assassinate his rival with a concealed derringer. His shot misses, but Paladin's doesn't, and Kramer falls dead. Standing over Kramer's body, Terry insists defensively, "We're not the same," but Paladin will not relent: "He *would* have been right." The aspiring gunfighter reflects for a moment, then offers to take Kramer's body back to town to save Paladin the trip. It sounds considerate, but Paladin wonders aloud if Terry has a hidden motive, if he still wants to be known as the man who "brought Doggie Kramer back wrapped in a poncho." Embarrassed, the young man protests that he didn't kill Kramer, but Paladin presses: "Three, four tellings—it wouldn't make any difference. Gallagher, Kramer: you'd be tied together for the rest of your life, just like brothers." Terry would have the reputation, whether he had done the killing or not, a reputation that would likely turn him into another Kramer. At last Terry recognizes the choice he's being offered, and after a moment's hard reflection, decides to walk away. "Thanks," he tells Paladin, and means it. With Paladin's help, he has realized that the best way out of a gunfighter's life is not to enter it in the first place.

Getting Out

As these stories suggest, life as a gunfighter is isolating, dangerous, and soul-deadening. After awhile, if a man doesn't get drunk on the adrenaline surge, like Kurt Sprague, he loses all moral feeling to become a killing machine, like Kramer—or worse, he gets sick of the everlasting blood and the constant vigilance, the need to sit with his back to the wall, always alert for challengers, unable to trust anyone, unable to rest. But, as several *Have Gun* episodes attest, the only thing more dangerous than gunfighting is trying to give it up once a man has earned a reputation with a gun. This is where Paladin's unique qualifications come in: with all the skills of a gunfighter, he has no trace of the addiction, and has the strategic imagination to invent non-lethal escapes for those gunfighters who want it and can bring themselves to trust him. In "Shot by Request," Ainslee is one of the lucky ones: with Paladin's help, he gets out of the profession still breathing and on his feet. In the end, Paladin doesn't even have to draw on Ainslee, or take the risky shot they had planned. As they face off, the brother of

Ainslee's most recent challenger shoots the former schoolteacher from ambush, injuring his right hand. Once Ainslee is unable to defend himself, the sheriff abandons his previous hands-off attitude and steps in to protect him from all who would challenge him, including Paladin. So Ainslee achieves his retirement without sacrificing either his life or his reputation. He is able to give up the violence he had never wanted for a scholarly, peaceful life.

Paladin's old friend Jake Trueblood, a famous gunfighter, takes a different way out in "The Mark of Cain" (5:19, 1/20/61). After years of the life, he gets sick of "too many hot-headed young gunfighters running around with their tongues hanging out for the reputation of being the man that gunned down Jake Trueblood." To protect himself from these men, he goes into seclusion in an isolated cabin, accompanied only by his woman, with periodic visits from Paladin to bring him news of the world and a bottle of whiskey. For Jake, this isolation is not a huge sacrifice. He is as much mountain man as gunfighter, and his woman is Indian, so they are relatively content living in the wilderness by themselves, except for the fear that some young gun will find Jake and take him down. But not every gunfighter who wants to retire could stand such isolation, especially if he has a family, as a surprising number of these men do on *Have Gun*. In "A Place for Abel Hix" (6:4, 10/6/62), an aging gunfighter hides his identity so he can put down his gun and move with his wife into a quiet little town. Here, she will have a community and he can succumb in peace to the disease that is slowly sapping him. For two years they live quietly until a pair of drifters recognize him. This revelation of Hix's reputation brings him trouble but, ironically, not from young guns seeking to challenge him but from the local Big Man, Judd Bowman. Hating gunfighters, Bowman harasses Hix relentlessly until he picks up his gun one last time. But in this last gunfight, held in secret, Hix dies not because he returns to the violence he had foresworn but because he refuses to do so. He easily beats Bowman to the draw, but chooses not to fire—a restraint his opponent does not reciprocate. So Hix's death is not the triumphant victory Bowman has claimed, but simple murder. From one point of view, Bowman has done Hix a favor, giving him a swift and relatively painless death compared to the lingering agony of his disease. But Bowman's hypocrisy—engaging in a gunfight to demonstrate his hatred of gunfighters—is breathtaking. However, Paladin soon ferrets out the truth of the fight, destroying Bowman's false triumph and restoring Hix's standing as a peaceful, law-abiding citizen, so Hix and his wife get the churchyard burial Bowman had denied them, while the community is freed from Bowman's dark dominance—a good ending all around.

In "Beau Geste" (6:5, 10/13/62), another aging gunfighter has an even more dangerous problem. John Dobbs, a straight-arrow sheriff known as the West's "fastest-draw lawman," has announced his retirement, thereby making himself a target for friends and relatives of the men he killed in the line of duty. These men flock to town, eager to challenge the sheriff as soon as he gives up the protection of his badge. Paladin, hired by an anonymous friend of the sheriff's, finally learns the secret behind Dobbs' retirement: he is losing his eyesight, and trying desperately to conceal the fact. If his enemies knew how little he could see, his life would be instantly forfeited. But Paladin has a scheme. Step one, he intimidates the other gunmen into giving him first crack at Dobbs. Then, Paladin explains to the sheriff, when they face off, Dobbs will win the draw, but shoot to miss—since, unlike any other opponent, Paladin will not be trying to kill him. Dobbs' victory would show the others that he is still unbeatable, so they would withdraw their challenges. In Paladin's plan, nobody has to die. In any other scenario, many men might die—most likely, Dobbs among them, since he can't see to shoot. Though the sheriff is suspicious, fearful about trusting a stranger, in the end he gambles on Paladin's scheme, and it works. The "tough guy" Paladin has impersonated slinks out of town, humiliated, and the other gunmen quickly ride away, unwilling to face Dobbs' lightning draw. The former lawman is then able to leave town peacefully with his faithful housekeeper and fiancée—Paladin's secret employer—for a new life in Oregon as a rancher, his reputation left behind. Like Winston Ainslee, thanks to Paladin, Dobbs can now safely walk away from his gun without further bloodshed.

In "Young Gun" (2:9, 1/8/58), infamous gunfighter Roy Calvert has hung up his weapon for good, after more than 20 successful duels, but as events prove, he hasn't really changed his faith in violence as a way to solve conflict. For the sake of his wife, who had suffered years of ostracism as a "killer's wife," Calvert leaves his reputation behind and moves to Wyoming to take up ranching, hoping she will finally find acceptance as a member of the community. But Calvert's neighbor, Wellman, finds out about his past and spreads the word, so Mrs. Calvert is once again shunned. As the ex-gunfighter tells Paladin bitterly, "When she took sick, nobody came to call except the doctor. Then she died. Pneumonia, he said, but she just gave up. And nobody came to her funeral." In revenge for his wife's mistreatment, Calvert is determined to destroy the town. The drought afflicting the region gives him his opportunity, as his land contains the only water in the area. Vindictively, he blocks the other ranchers from crossing his land to water their suffering cattle. With the stakes so high, the conflict is bound to turn violent. Roy won't pick up a gun himself because of his promise to his dead wife, but he doesn't hesitate to train his young son, Jeff, to take his place as a gunfighter. That's why Wellman tells Paladin, "There's only one way to break Calvert—*get that boy*."

But, unlike his father, Jeff is at best a reluctant gun. True, when Paladin first sees the young man, he's engaged in a gunfight with a man who is clearly no match for him. But not only is Jeff not the instigator, he tries very hard to persuade Casey to drop the challenge, even offering a public apology. However, when Casey refuses to back down, Jeff kills him rather than wounding. He is following his father's creed: "When you draw, you shoot to kill." Though Jeff doesn't agree with his father, either with his philosophy or his actions in this dispute with his neighbors, family feeling insures he will follow his father's orders, even if his heart is not in it. As a result, when the ranchers try to drive their thirsty cattle past Calvert's barriers to get to the water, Jeff kills two cowhands in the fight, and is prepared to kill more men if the ranchers come again. There is yet another source of Jeff's reluctance for this fight, as Paladin discovers—his Romeo-and-Juliet love affair with Meg Wellman. But as the conflict escalates, Jeff is forced to choose: follow his heart and go with Meg, or stand with his father, however unreasonable Roy may be. In the end, filial loyalty trumps love, though both young hearts are breaking.

If neither Wellman nor Roy Calvert compromises, there will be a range war in which many men will die, their families devastated by losing the man of the household. For the sake of the community as a whole, and especially for the two young lovers, Paladin searches for a nonviolent solution. Jeff, he realizes, is the key. Though he has already shot down three men, Paladin suggests Jeff may not yet have a taste for killing and he presses the young man to think carefully about his choices, about the profession his father is pushing him toward: "A man draws a gun for a reason. Every man has his own. But most men have a point at which they draw the line. I have mine. What's yours?" Anguished, Jeff exclaims, "You think I *like* it? You think I want to watch somebody coming at me? Like Casey this morning—I *had* to kill him!" Paladin asks quietly: "Did you?" But Jeff can see only what his father has taught him: "It's all I know!"

If Roy refuses to allow the cattle to water, Paladin announces, he will lead the herds and their protectors through himself—unless the Calverts would prefer to fight him one on one. Roy eagerly accepts the challenge on behalf of the Calverts, only to have Jeff claim the job himself. Paladin tells Roy with quiet scorn, "You ought to be proud of yourself. You've turned this boy into a killer. He's going to *enjoy* the same kind of life you have"—that is, a life of isolation and loneliness, ostracized by fearful neighbors. Then, without warning, Paladin quickly draws and fires at Jeff's target, putting a bullet in the heart, and adds significantly, "If he *lives* long enough." It is the first time in this episode he has drawn his gun, and the results are dramatic. The two Calverts look at each other uneasily. It is one thing for Jeff to face opponents like Casey, or the cowboys defending their herds, but a gunman of Paladin's caliber is a more serious matter. The stakes have suddenly gotten much higher.

The next morning, Roy, sensing Jeff's anxiety, urges him to back out because he isn't ready for this opponent, but his grim-faced son refuses, fatalistically: "What difference does it make now?" As Jeff and Paladin face each other in the street, the man in black insists, "It won't be self-defense this time. You'll have to draw first." As Jeff hesitates, steeling himself, a horrified Roy suddenly jumps between them, shouting, "No, Paladin! Me!" As he draws, Paladin fires, and Roy spins and falls in the street. But he's not dead—it's just a shoulder wound, a rebuke to Roy's principle of "shoot to kill." Paladin suggests getting Roy to a doctor, then looks at the two Calverts: "Unless we're not finished?" Jeff says decisively, "We're finished," and Roy smiles in triumph: "You see, Paladin? I didn't turn him into a killer." In the end, protecting his son both from death and from life as a gunfighter proved more important to Roy Calvert than his quarrel with Wellman and the town.

The next day, in a gesture of reconciliation, Meg and her mother come to the Calvert ranch where Mrs. Wellman asks permission to pay her respects at Mrs. Calvert's grave. She acknowledges that her act will not make up for past slights, but it is a start, and Calvert finally agrees, as Jeff and Meg begin to paint over the target on the barn which Jeff will no longer need. Though Wellman and Roy Calvert may need more time than the others to come around, Paladin's intervention means the future for this valley looks considerably brighter, especially for Meg and Jeff. They have all recognized that violence is more a problem than a solution.

The episode is a pointed lesson in the drawbacks of the gunfighter's life, both in the pain that Roy's profession caused his family, and in Jeff's struggles to win his father's approval without following in Roy's bloody footsteps. Paladin's conversations with Jeff about the principles of using a gun are significant as a counterbalance to his father's simple "shoot to kill" rule. Paladin insists that each man who fights with a gun must decide what his own principles are, when it is appropriate to shoot and when it is not, when it is necessary to kill and when a less-deadly option will be sufficient. Because Paladin is a man of principle and accurate aim, and because Roy Calvert loves his son enough to change his mind, this story has a happy ending.

But in "Episode in Laredo" (3:2, 9/19/59), another gunfighter with a young son makes a different choice. Unlike Roy Calvert, Sam Tuttle isn't ready to give up his profession, even after 31 successful shoot-outs, though it has cost him a normal life with his wife and son. To protect them from his fearsome reputation, Tuttle lives separately, while they hide in Laredo under the name Smith. But on the boy's ninth birthday, Tuttle has returned for an hour's visit with his son, whom he hasn't seen in three years. As a security measure, he has reserved the entire hotel for his stay. But the night before Tuttle's arrival, Paladin rides into Laredo in the middle of a raging thunderstorm, seeking a room. When Tuttle's henchman offensively denies this reasonable request and provokes a gunfight, Paladin kills Kovac in self-defense. He intends to be gone before Tuttle arrives the next morning, but Tuttle, alerted by the hotel keeper, Logan, arrives early to confront this challenge.

Tuttle is not a bully, not someone who enjoys violence for its own sake, but the scenario here is inescapable. Even though he doesn't care about Kovac, he will have to kill Paladin for defying his orders. His reputation demands it: "If I let you ride out of here, they'd say I was afraid.... And then every saddle tramp in the state would start wondering. Let one man go, and I have to fight ten." But Paladin has won his respect, so Tuttle proposes that for an hour they sit and talk, pretending it is an ordinary morning. The gunfighter is surprisingly sympathetic, his loathing for his profession equaled only by his contempt for Logan and for the crowd outside, drawn by a lust for blood—his or his opponent's, they don't really care. But the conversation makes Tuttle feel worse, not better, so in anguish he insists they fight now.

Just as they take their positions, "Mrs. Smith" appears at the door, bringing the boy for the promised visit. Chillingly, the nine-year-old is wild with excitement when he sees the two men ready to shoot it out. But the woman warns Sam she cannot leave and return later, so he breaks off the fight to spend an hour with the engaging boy, who obviously doesn't know Sam is his father. It is a touching scene which makes clear that husband and wife still feel strongly for each other, and both love their son, but at the end of the hour, the boy is sent out of earshot so his mother can confer with Tuttle. She warns him she cannot conceal his identity from the son much longer, and mentions Paladin's suggestion that she and her son move to San Francisco, where they can more easily remain anonymous. Stricken, Tuttle objects: with no forwarding address, how can he send her money? But she grimly reminds him that, given his reputation, he is not likely to live many more years. For financial security, she must look for another man—any man who will have her. Tuttle is horrified, but Paladin interjects mildly, "Of course, you could go with her, Sam." But Tuttle demurs: "What would I do? A man's got to make a living." Incredulous, Paladin exclaims, "Does it matter? If you have to dig a ditch, does that matter?" Tuttle insists stubbornly, "It matters a *lot*. You don't understand how a man is. I'm important now. People stand back for me. They tip their hats.... People point out to me as I walk down the street." As his wife looks at him in horror, he admits for the first time, "I *like* being number one. I like being Sam Tuttle. And there's nothing—*nothing*—I want bad enough to give that up." The poison has him so firmly hooked that he chooses his gunfighter's prison over his family he obviously loves, if the price is to live in humble anonymity.

Recognizing a lost battle, Mrs. Tuttle walks away from her husband with immense dignity, and the two men resume their interrupted duel. But before either can draw, Tuttle hesitates: "If you were alive—maybe you could sort of look after her in San Francisco. Give her advice." To his surprise, Paladin refuses to bargain for his life, and stays coiled in his gunfighter crouch. After a moment, Tuttle suddenly straightens and walks toward him, shouting, "Get *out*! I reserved this whole hotel!" At the last moment, Tuttle chooses to defy the rules he has lived by, relying on his power as "Sam Tuttle" to let him get away with this small rebellion. But as Paladin heads quickly for the door, Logan emerges from the kitchen, protesting violently: if there is no fight, no death, he will miss out on the publicity he had counted on to increase business in his hotel. He shoots Tuttle in the back, exulting, "Folks will ride for miles to see where you died!" But as Logan prepares to shoot Tuttle again, Paladin kills the little man in his tracks, though it is too late to save the gunfighter. All he can do is take the news to Mrs. "Smith."

This is a taut, somber episode. Tuttle is a tormented character, simultaneously despising the life he has created for himself and refusing to give up its privileges, even to gain his family, despite his longing for them. His son is a bright, eager boy whom Tuttle obviously adores, while his wife is a remarkable woman, strong and dignified, far stronger than her husband.[5] Tuttle's choice proves just how addictive it is to be "Sam Tuttle, famous gunfighter." Under these conditions, his choice to violate the rules and let Paladin walk away is an act of remarkable courage—but one that seals his fate.

Gunfighters, the rock-star celebrities of the frontier, occupied an uncomfortable position in their society—prominent and pampered, often treated with obsequious respect, but too dangerous to be fully accepted as members of the community. The crowd's respect was as much a product of fear as true admiration, and underneath the hero-worship lay the crowd's thirst for blood. As Sam Tuttle recognizes bitterly, his fans don't care about him as a man, only as a champion gladiator who entertains them with death—and whether that death is his opponent's or his own matters little to them. It is a lonely, stressful way to live, hard on the man himself, harder on his family (if he has one). His interactions with these gunmen require Paladin to judge them thoughtfully, to be sure he understands their true character. As a gunfighter himself, he knows how easy it is to slip into the life, how difficult and dangerous to give it up. Because has learned to use his weapon for a larger cause than his own prestige, he is always willing to help those who want a better alternative, but he is also prepared to do what is necessary to protect the community from those who use their guns ruthlessly and selfishly—whether these men are on the right side of the law, however marginally, or have gone to the dark side.

Outlaws

Unlike gunfighters, outlaws are by definition outcasts. They refuse to respect the rights of individuals and of private property, and reject the reciprocity that makes life in communities possible. While some of *Have Gun*'s outlaws are unrepentant, two-dimensional "bad guys" who enjoy preying on the vulnerable, others have more complicated stories to tell, a mixture of traits requiring more complex responses. Encountering such outlaws, Paladin tries to judge them not by their criminal status alone, but by the totality of their character.

More than once Paladin finds himself respecting, or at least sympathizing with, the outlaws he confronts, without condoning their criminal activities. As discussed earlier, Manfred Holt in "The Outlaw" (1:2, 9/21/57) believes he is entitled to kill men he doesn't like as long as they are armed and facing him, whether they have any skill with a gun or not. A society aspiring to civilization has no place for a man with such a primitive philosophy. However, within his own terms, Holt proves himself a man of integrity and even honor. Paladin begins their relationship by making the ethical but dangerous choice to take Holt in for legal execution rather than giving him to the sheriff who will shoot him in cold blood. In turn, Holt gives his word not to try to escape on the journey if Paladin will allow him a brief delay to visit his newborn son, in a nearby cabin. On the trail through the mountains, Paladin's horse slips and throws him into a steep rocky wash whose walls he cannot scale without help. This accident gives Holt the perfect opportunity to escape, but if he leaves, Paladin will surely die of thirst, hunger, and exposure in this natural trap. To Paladin's surprise and relief, Holt passes this test of character: against his own self-interest, he throws down a rope to help his captor climb out. Repaying the favor, Paladin draws the posse away from the Holt cabin on a wild-goose chase so the gunman can safely meet his infant son. But as much as Holt respects his captor, he finally refuses to go back with him. Though not afraid of dying,

Holt deeply fears the shame of a public hanging, and insists on his right to die "like a man," on his feet with a gun in his hand. Paladin has come to respect and even like Holt, but he knows the outlaw will keep killing helpless men if he is not stopped, so he has no choice but to fight and kill him. It is a duty he owes to the society Holt disrupts so unacceptably. But Paladin mourns even as he fires.

Pappy French, the protagonist of "In an Evil Time" (2:2, 9/20/58), is no Holt, not a killer with a code but only an aging small-time crook who earns Paladin's affection, despite himself. True, Pappy has no scruples at all: in a recent bank robbery, he betrayed his partners by taking all the loot himself and leaving them to shoot it out with the law. Now that Paladin has caught him, he alternately scams and schemes and threatens, trying to make a deal that will let him keep some of the stolen $50,000 as a final stake. Paladin isn't fooled for a minute, but he can't help admiring his prisoner's spirit. Though horseless and with a broken leg, the old scoundrel seems indomitable. But in a reflective moment, he admits he's had enough. After forty years as an outlaw, all he has in his pockets is "$42 and some small silver. That comes to about a dollar a year, don't it? You know any Chinese coolie that'd work for that?" Though Pappy isn't asking for pity, this realistic assessment of his own life earns Paladin's sympathy, and then his help. When Pappy's vicious young partners follow him into the wilderness, seeking both the money Pappy hid and a bloody revenge, Paladin chooses to help the old villain rather than abandoning him. In fact, he even gives Pappy a gun to provide covering fire. In this crisis, they function as a team, and Paladin ultimately kills both of Pappy's partners, though not before the vicious Morley wounds Pappy fatally. For Paladin, this should count as a success: he has recovered the stolen money for the bank, and the whole gang is dead or dying. But he grieves the loss of the old scallywag, a little man who had struggled hard to survive in "an evil time."

Paladin feels even greater sympathy for another outlaw in "The Long Way Home" (4:21, 9/4/61). The dangerous fugitive Isham Spruce, though wanted for murder, turns out to be a far better man than the posse of bounty-hunters chasing him. Spruce, a former slave, had left his family in the South and gone to the West looking for honest work. Though he found it, he also found prejudiced men who harassed and bullied him until he fought back, with fatal results. After Paladin captures Spruce, he tries to build a relationship with his prisoner, listening sympathetically to his story, offering to help him get a lawyer, even writing a letter so the illiterate ex-slave can send money to his wife. In short, Paladin treats Spruce humanely, though that does not diminish the prisoner's determination to escape. So when a rattlesnake bite leaves Paladin helpless and in mortal danger, Spruce doesn't hesitate to run. Yet, repaying Paladin's humanity to him, he lingers in the vicinity long enough to send a farm boy to town with news of Paladin's plight. Unfortunately, this generous gesture seals his doom. It gives the posse time to find and kill him. Though not responsible for Spruce's death, Paladin is deeply distressed by it, as he recognizes how far Spruce's character and worth exceed the men who killed him so casually.[6]

Some of Paladin's most troubling cases involve outlaws who are mentally defective, obsessed, or psychotic—in some way not fully responsible for their actions. In "Fandango" (4:24, 3/4/61), two teenage boys who slowly beat a third to death with clubs, fists, and a heavy chain have been condemned to hang. But there are mitigating factors: first, the assailants, 15 and 16, had not intended to kill their victim (himself a thief and a bully); second, both boys are fatherless, raised without any steady discipline. Third and most significant, James, the younger boy, is of "low mentality" while Bobby, the instigator, is perhaps a psychopath; at least, he clearly does not understand the seriousness of his crime. James and

Bobby's childlike responses to their impending execution make it more disturbing to Paladin and his old friend, Sheriff Ernie Backwater. Both men are uncomfortable about hanging these boys, but Ernie is equally uncomfortable about letting them go, given how violent their crime was, and how unrepentant they are.

To add to the lawmen's dilemma, the victim's brother, Lloyd Petty, an ex-gunfighter, is determined to lynch the prisoners himself, and willing to kill the sheriff and Paladin, if necessary, to do it. Though Paladin and Ernie manage to kill the attackers, the jail is dynamited in the attack, knocking down some of its brick walls, including the cell wall where Bobby's chains are fastened. Just as Bobby realizes he is free and prepares to run, Paladin appears, gun cocked and ready. Bobby freezes, but after a long moment, Paladin suddenly uncocks his gun, not able to shoot the boy in cold blood. Bobby leaps to freedom, leaving James behind, still firmly chained and screaming in terror. The sheriff tells Paladin grimly, "You made a mistake," but Paladin disagrees: "No. I made a judgment." Though Ernie is certain Bobby will kill again, Paladin is not so sure, not sure enough to kill an unarmed boy.

This is an unprecedented moment in the series. Paladin's default position has always been to uphold the law, particularly when its representative is, like Ernie Backwater, a good, responsible man. But this time, the law itself is being questioned, or at least the issue of legal culpability: clearly, Bobby's grasp of morality is so deficient that it isn't right to execute him. On the other hand, because he has no understanding of his crime, he might well kill again, so it isn't fair to the community to let him run free. And in the absence of any effective treatment for mental illness in the 1870s, there is no satisfactory answer to this dilemma. But mass-market TV was supposed to offer simple, comforting solutions for problems like juvenile delinquency. What *Have Gun* offered its audiences instead was a sympathetic treatment of the characters that revealed how complex the problems could be, how unreachable the solutions.

"The Brothers" (5:11, 11/25/61) gives us a different kind of madman. As Paladin takes the ruthless outlaw, Bram Holden, to trial for murder, captive and captor find themselves shackled together on foot, without water, and crossing an empty desert where they would have died if they had not been rescued by a strange little man in a wagon. However, this rescue is not the good news it first appears. Possum Corbin becomes convinced that Holden is his long-lost brother, Arnie, because both are left-handed—which means that the revenge Possum has urgently sought is finally in his grasp. He explains cheerfully how, nine years before, his brother stole all the gold they had mined together and ran off with Possum's woman. Then, when she got sick on the trail, Arnie abandoned her to die a lingering death alone. Possum has been hunting his brother ever since, determined to torture Arnie to death in revenge. With Holden at his mercy, he has his chance. But Holden ruins Possum's plans: he grabs at Possum's shotgun but it goes off in the struggle, and the prisoner dies, much to Possum's disappointment. However, once the object of his hatred is dead, Possum's madness subsides, and he complacently allows Paladin to take him in for trial. But as they drive along, a left-handed horseman passes them on the trail, and Possum reaches frantically for his shotgun, shouting, "That's him! That's Arnie! I've finally tracked him down!" When a bemused Paladin reminds him of the dead body in the back of the wagon, Possum only says blankly, "Who?" Dismayed, Paladin suddenly understands just how crazy Possum is: he has probably spent the last nine years finding and killing "Arnie" over and over, without achieving a lasting resolution to his grief and fury. He might well have killed as many men as Holden, but when his monomania is not on him, he is a far better man than Holden. Under these circumstances, what can the law say to such a criminal, so little responsible for his own actions? The episode does not specify what will, or should, happen to Possum, just leaves us to contemplate the irony.

But if "The Brothers" ends ambivalently, "Sweet Lady of the Moon" (6:26, 3/9/63) ends with unambiguous tragedy. Nine years before, in an insane frenzy, Carl Soddenberg had killed three members of the Trainer family, but when Carl's doctor persuades the state Supreme Court that he is cured of his homicidal mania, he is freed. Despite the court's ruling, relatives of Carl's victims are eager for revenge, so Paladin has volunteered to protect him on his journey to a new life. To Paladin's surprise, Carl is thoughtful and mild-tempered, forgiving of the suspicion and harsh treatment he receives from almost everyone, and anxious to prove that his cure is genuine. He calmly tells Paladin his story, how the feelings came to him when he was twelve: "I had to kill things. Once it was a cat, another time it was a dog, a cute woolly lamb, finally a man.... You can't understand what unhappiness is, what it is to lose hope, to despair, unless you've had what I've had. When I killed something, I felt better, I was relieved. The whole world smelled sweet again." But since the doctor cured him, those feelings have stopped.

On their journey, they pause at the farm of Carl's old friend, Ben Murdock, where the doctor will join them. But the Trainers attack there, and Paladin and Murdock are unhappily forced to kill all four attackers, one a boy of nineteen. When Carl recognizes how distressing these killings are to Paladin and Murdock—four more men dead just to save his life—he cannot bear the guilt and disapproval, and runs away into the forest. Murdock follows, certain that Carl will come back with him. But many hours later, Carl returns alone, weary and defeated, declaring he has not seen Murdock. As a concerned Paladin prepares to look for the farmer, Carl insists on being chained up for the sake of Murdock's frightened and very pregnant wife, Mary. The doctor, with faith in his cure, protests, but Carl is adamant, so Paladin chains him to the water pump in the yard, gives Mary his derringer "to keep for me," and rides out.

As the full moon rises higher in the sky, Carl gets more and more restless; horribly, the madness is coming on him again. Finally, he demands to be released, crying, "I'm no animal!" Meanwhile, Paladin finds Murdock, knifed to death—clearly Carl's work—and rides desperately for the farm. As Carl begs to be freed, the doctor explains helplessly that he doesn't have the keys to Paladin's chains. In his fury, Carl wrenches off the top of the pump and attacks the doctor viciously, then begins a slow advance toward Mary, even while he begs her over and over, "Run away, please run away," as horrified by what he is doing as she is, but helpless to stop himself. She shoots him with the derringer, but the tiny bullet only slows him down a little. Fortunately, Paladin arrives just in time to kill Carl with the rifle.

The devastation is almost total: four Trainers are dead; Carl is dead, his moment of normalcy all too fleeting; the doctor, who had worked so hopefully to cure mental illness, now must start over; and Murdock's reward for trying to help a troubled friend is death, leaving his wife to bring a new baby into the world alone. The only redeeming note is Paladin's offer to stay at the farm until Mary can get a hired man, and Mary's hope that her child will resemble its father, a brave, gentle man. So many good intentions come to such tragic ends, Carl's tragedy not least among them. It is a remarkably sympathetic portrait of the madman—indeed, of all the characters involved.[7] But, as all these episodes indicate, when the outlaw is a madman, happy endings are largely unobtainable.

Paladin encounters a different sort of challenge when the guilt of the fugitives he captures is less certain. Technically, guilt is not his concern: his job is to get wanted men into the hands of the authorities where a jury will decide the question, but given the dangers of transporting a prisoner single-handed and the life-or-death choices he might have to make, it would be more comfortable to have a clear sense of the prisoner's guilt or innocence. In "The Man Who Lost" (2:31, 4/25/59), Paladin doesn't get that certainty till the very end. Ben Coey is accused of killing a rancher and assaulting his wife ("assault" being code for "rape"). Hired by the woman's brothers, Paladin captures Coey and is bringing him in for trial when a storm delays them for days in a way station, the prisoner chained to the iron bedstead for safe-keeping. Throughout the ordeal, Coey steadfastly maintains his innocence, with a modest demeanor that makes this claim plausible. Yet he is fatalistically certain that the woman will identify him as her attacker, despite his innocence, and that her brother will kill him. At such statements, Paladin looks at the man thoughtfully, evaluating: this is not the way guilty men normally act. Of course, Coey's periodic attempts to escape throw doubt on his innocence. But, as Paladin is certainly aware, more than one innocent man has been lynched by an honest mistake. The whole encounter is deeply unsettling for him, but his doubt is not resolved until the Gages bring their sister to the way station to confront the captive. As the harrowed woman stares at the man chained to the bed, unable to speak, Coey smiles at her, not a nice smile, and says softly, tauntingly, "Hello, beauty." It's an admission, the more horrible for its quiet brazenness, for what it says about the character of this man, so plausible in his denials, so cold and cruel at heart. All doubt erased, Paladin feels a revulsion so sudden and intense that he backhands Coey with his full weight, to wipe the evil smirk off his face. But even with Coey's guilt now morally certain, Paladin insists on a legal trial rather than a lynching, though he has to kill one Gage brother and wound the other to achieve his goal.

In "The Twins" (3:35, 5/21/60), the issue is not so much the guilt of Paladin's client as his true identity. Sam and Adam Mirakian are identical twins, so alike that the only living person who can tell them apart is Adam's wife, Beth. Everyone agrees that Sam Mirakian, always a troublemaker, has shot and killed a man; the question is whether the man who hires Paladin to help clear his name is really Adam, as he claims, or Sam pretending to be Adam in order to throw blame on his brother. Paladin convinces his client to turn himself in, but when he brings Mrs. Mirakian to the jail to verify his client's identity, she insists sorrowfully that this is not her husband, Adam, but his brother. At first Paladin is grimly angry with his client for misusing him, but the prisoner steadfastly maintains his identity, and when Beth is questioned further, inconsistencies appear in her story that raise Paladin's suspicions. Those suspicions are confirmed when Beth takes Paladin to meet her "husband," and the prisoner, breaking out of jail, follows them to the hills to confront his brother and the man he'd hired to help him. In the deadly shoot-out that follows, Paladin realizes, but only too late—after he has killed his client in self-defense—that the man who hired him was indeed Adam, and that Beth has chosen the exciting bad-boy Sam over her decent, boring husband, and schemed to help him take Adam's place. Over his client's dead body, Paladin vows, "You may not be quite like your brother, but I promise you, before this day is over, he will be like you." And he keeps his word: though Sam shoots at him and leaves him for dead, Paladin makes his way back to town and kills Sam in a gunfight, leaving Mrs. Mirakian to mourn her choice, while he mourns the betrayed man he had not been able to help. Guilt is definitively established—but only at a high price.

Finally, in "The Predators" (6:8, 11/3/62), Paladin captures another fugitive who insists on his innocence, but this time the outcome is more satisfactory. John Tyree is accused of torturing and killing a U.S. marshal, so Paladin is taking him in for trial, in handcuffs because Tyree fights back and comes close to escaping. The two are natural adversaries, but, as in

"The Brothers," they also have a shared dilemma: on foot in a desert and desperate for water, they are at least temporary allies in the struggle for survival. And there are indications that Tyree might be innocent, as he claims. When they find the body of a man who has been staked out and tortured to death in the same manner as Marshal Silmser, Paladin readily admits Tyree couldn't have killed this man, which suggests a third party may have killed both victims. But that is not proof enough for Paladin to risk removing the chains from his prisoner just yet.

In a last desperate hope of water, Tyree leads Paladin to the Tymmes ranch, whose well is reputed never to run dry, but to their dismay, the bucket holds only sand. Then unexpected rifle fire from the house wounds Tyree in the foot. Working together for survival, the two men manage to break in through the back door. But inside, they find only a young woman and a teenaged boy, fiercely defending their last gallon of water. A few days before, marauders had killed the boy's father when the three tried to run to Fort Apache. Not knowing the way to the fort, the young woman and her adopted brother returned to the house, where they are waiting grimly for the gang to come and kill them. In the face of this threat, the four form a defensive alliance. She skillfully takes the bullet from Tyree's foot, and he helps to fight off the marauders when they return, while Paladin handles the negotiations and wrings a confession from the gang's leader that he had killed both the man on the trail and Marshal Silmser—thus clearing Tyree. And in using dynamite to fight off the marauders, Paladin succeeds in unblocking the well again, so the water runs freely.

The shared ordeal has created a strong connection between Tyree and the young woman. After a desperately hard life, she is determined to make a home and a family of her own in this place. Tyree, recognizing the quality of her character, decides to stay and build it with her. And, now that Tyree's character has been thoroughly tested and proved sound, Paladin finally removes the handcuffs, observing mildly, "Friend, I don't make many mistakes." Tyree snarls, "You can go to the *devil*!" but then smiles and adds, "—Friend." A new little family will form at this ranch from three lost people, and Paladin, having cleared his prisoner and dealt with the real murderer, has done his job successfully. It is an unexpectedly happy ending.

In confronting the gunfighters and outlaws that play so prominent a role in the Western, Paladin's immediate goal is to minimize violence in order to support an infant civilization. But more broadly, he studies these characters in order to understand what drives them, to determine which can be helped or changed, and which cannot—just as he did with the lawmen in Chapter Five. Although all TV Westerns feature such gun-wielding characters, *Gunsmoke*, *Wagon Train*, and *Bonanza* typically treated them more conventionally and superficially. While they are important for their impact on the continuing characters, they are seldom given the deep psychological explorations they receive on *Have Gun*. In the same way, guns and violence are endemic in all Westerns, but only *Have Gun* consistently considers the larger philosophical questions on the topic.

In the next two chapters, we'll examine the way other kinds of misfits—ethnic and racial minorities, and women characters—are treated on *Have Gun*, in comparison with its competitors.

SEVEN

The Other Americans:
Racial and Ethnic Minorities

Though most of the characters in the TV Western in this period are white and male (indeed, most characters on TV in any genre in this period are white and male), the Western has always made a certain amount of room for non-white, non–European, non-male characters. Partly this is a necessity of the historical record, as American Indians, Mexicans, and Chinese undeniably played significant roles in the story of the settlers moving west.[1] Besides, Indian war parties and Mexican bandits are as essential to Westerns as outlaw gangs and cattle rustlers, providing drama and challenge to the virtuous settlers. However, the television Western in the 1950s–1960s typically marginalized all these minority characters: the numbers of each were limited, the stories told about them were restricted to a narrow predictable range, and they were typically treated as two-dimensional stereotypes. Above all, minority characters were hardly ever portrayed as protagonists in their own stories or presented from their own point of view. They were only important for their impact on a white male hero.

But, as we saw in the introduction to Part II, Americans were also newly sensitized to prejudice against racial and ethnic minorities, and cautiously willing to entertain dramas on the subject, as long as the stories were safely distanced—for instance, set in the past—and *as long as the characters were not black*. As a consequence, all of our series periodically advocated tolerance and sympathy for minority groups. But *Have Gun—Will Travel* went far beyond the superficial approach of *Gunsmoke, Wagon Train*, and *Bonanza* to grapple seriously with the position of minorities in American culture. While the series did not always achieve 21st-century standards of cultural sensitivity, it featured minority characters more frequently and more appreciatively, in greater variety, and with more agency and psychological complexity than any of its competitors.

The Chinese

The only minority continuing characters on any of these series are Chinese, suggesting they were the least controversial for the audience. Hop Sing, the Cartwrights' Chinese cook, appeared in 14–18 episodes per season for the entire run of *Bonanza*, but almost entirely in brief inconsequential scenes, a source of easy humor delivering lines like, "Missa Cartlight, you betta come home tonight because Missa Hoss, he eat too much. He not feel good. He come in kitchen, I cut off his hand."[2] Although two episodes in the show's first season do give Chinese characters, including Hop Sing, a more prominent role, on closer examination, these episodes allow them less centrality and agency than first appears, while later seasons return to the topic only once.[3]

In "San Francisco" (1:28, 4/2/60) Hop Sing gets a moment of heroism. When Hoss, Little Joe, and Ben, vacationing in San Francisco, are shanghaied by a ruthless ship owner, Hop Sing and his local cousins come to the rescue, locating the Cartwrights and helping them escape their captors. But the episode is played primarily for laughs, while Hop Sing's activities are restricted to the final scenes. Another episode, "The Fear Merchants" (1:20, 1/30/60), is far more substantial, critiquing the anti–Chinese prejudice suddenly roiling Virginia City, but despite the topic, Hop Sing is given little more action than usual, and scarcely any more lines. The featured Chinese characters in this episode are Hop Sing's uncle, Li Cheng and his 18-year-old son, Jimmy, who has been falsely accused of murdering a pretty white girl and threatened with lynching.[4] Though the script treats both Chengs sympathetically, they are portrayed as virtuous but passive victims, needing rescue by the Cartwrights, and all of the featured white characters get more substantial speeches than the Chengs. Although the conscious intent is to encourage acceptance of the Chinese as equals, the automatic prominence of the featured white characters undercuts that message. In the end, though neither the characters nor the episode's creators seem to recognize the fact, the Cartwrights' friendship for the Chengs feels merely patronizing.

A similar pattern is revealed in *Gunsmoke*'s only episode about anti–Chinese prejudice. In "The Queue" (1:10, 12/3/55), when young Chen arrives in Dodge City looking for work, he seems a typical Chinese "coolie," bowing obsequiously and saying things like, "Me very sad. No likee bring trouble," and "Me very good cook. Ham'n'eggs. You see." However, talking later with Matt and Doc, his English miraculously improves, and Chen explains that the pidgin he used earlier "is the way you expect me to talk, isn't it?" In other words, he had conformed to cultural stereotypes, acting ignorant and subservient as a form of self-defense. Matt and Doc are impressed with Chen's dignity and intelligence, especially his desire to build a life for himself in this new country. But when two ruffians beat him savagely and cut off his queue, Chen is determined to avenge himself upon the men who stole his honor, his manhood. Though Matt sympathizes, he point out that if Chen kills these men over his queue, he is still thinking like a Chinese. In order to truly become American, he must adopt a different standard of honor. After reflecting, Chen accepts this argument, and gives Matt his severed queue as a "souvenir."[5] Clearly, the intention of the episode is to hold Chen up as superior to the ignorant white men who brutalized him so unthinkingly. But Matt's argument, and Chen's acceptance of it, implies that Chinese notions of honor are less valid than American, thus undercutting the respect for Chinese culture that has been overtly declared in the episode.

Hey Boy, Hey Girl

But *Have Gun—Will Travel* reveals a significantly different attitude toward the Chinese. Some critics insist that Hey Boy is a stereotyped character, pointing in particular to his name as offensive and demeaning, but Hey Boy himself seems to have a different opinion. In a first-season episode, when a customer calls, "Hey, you!" he snaps irritably, "My name Hey *Boy*, not Hey You." And it is surely significant that, though Paladin knows Hey Boy's true name, Kim Chang, he consistently uses the familiar work name.[6] Demeaning name or not, the character's situation is distinctly better than his counterpart's on *Bonanza*. Though Hey

Boy's scenes are brief, his actions are typically more substantial than Hop Sing's, and his character much more developed.

As porter at the Carlton Hotel, Hey Boy performs a number of menial but important functions for Paladin: he serves many of Paladin's meals (especially when he dines in his suite), procures the special newspapers Paladin consults regularly, brings his mail and telegrams, acquires the tickets Paladin orders for the opera, the theater, or the train, delivers his messages and flowers to assorted ladies, and packs his bags when he travels. On this level, their relationship is clearly hierarchical: Paladin gives orders and Hey Boy carries them out. But their relationship is more textured and complex than this outline suggests. If Hey Boy is subordinate, he is far from subservient. He often comes up with his own schemes and expresses his opinions without hesitation. He is deeply, if vicariously, involved in Paladin's activities: he not only delivers Paladin's mail, he often reads it—to practice his English, he claims, but he is obviously driven also by a lively curiosity about Paladin's plans. He also reads newspaper stories over Paladin's shoulder, pointing out possible job opportunities for his employer's consideration. On other occasions, fearful for the gunfighter's safety, he tries to persuade Paladin not to take certain cases. Such a strong concern signals something beyond a simple financial relationship.

In romantic affairs, Hey Boy is Paladin's facilitator and co-conspirator, helping him arrange cozy dinners for two, or, alternatively, managing his escapes from a lady he would rather not encounter. Occasionally, it is true, Paladin expresses mild annoyance at Hey Boy, and is not above teasing him (indeed, in a few unfortunate scripts by less-sensitive writers, Paladin even makes fun of the porter's English pronunciation), but in the majority of their encounters, Paladin treats Hey Boy with appreciation, affection, and even respect. Tellingly, the two often converse in Chinese, typically no more than ritual greetings and pleasantries, but sufficient to show Paladin's familiarity with, and respect for, Chinese language and culture.[7] But occasionally the two dig more deeply into the traditional wisdom of the sages, exchanging quotations from the philosophers and poets.

At the end of the third season, Kam Tong, the actor who played Hey Boy, was offered a larger role in a new series. When he left, Lisa Lu joined *Have Gun* as Hey Girl (with no explanation for the change). Though she performs the same sort of tasks as Hey Boy—bringing messages, packing bags, and so on—Hey Girl speaks better English than her predecessor, and is a more graceful and less comic figure. She is also more assertive. On several occasions, she scolds Paladin for avoiding work when he has bills to pay; once she lectures him at length on the advantages of marriage, and, where Hey Boy encourages and facilitates Paladin's flirtations, Hey Girl often mildly disapproves of them. But she also demonstrates skills that Paladin admires—for example, handwriting analysis, and flower arranging, plus the ability to tell the difference between diamonds and costume jewelry. In general Paladin regards her with an avuncular affection. However, despite these small details, Hey Girl remains less well-developed as a character than Hey Boy, with no family background or other history. And when Kam Tong's new series was cancelled and Hey Boy returned in Season Five, Hey Girl disappeared as mysteriously as she had come.[8]

In three different episodes over the seasons, Hey Boy plays a more substantial role than usual. In "Gun Shy" (1:29, 3/29/58), when precious items are stolen from Hey Boy's uncle—an antique jade chess set which is a family heirloom, and over $400 in cash—Paladin volunteers to track the thieves and recover the lost items. Throughout his investigation, Paladin treats Hey Boy and his uncle with dignity. Questioning Uncle Sing Wo to get a description of the thieves, Paladin even conducts some of his interview in Chinese, with Hey Boy's help to translate some complicated details. And though Sing Wo's fierce description of how he would punish the thieves makes Paladin smile at the contrast with the old man's physical frailty, there is no condescension in the smile, just a wry recognition of the ironies of aging, common to Chinese and Anglo alike.

After these opening scenes, the rest of the episode details Paladin's successful efforts to retrieve the stolen items, but the final scene finds him back at Sing Wo's laundry, deep in a chess game with Hey Boy using the heirloom set. Though the series has established Paladin as a formidable chess player, this game ends when Hey Boy quietly announces, "Checkmate." A startled Paladin does a double-take, then laughs in acknowledgment: the unassuming Chinese porter has defeated the "superior" Westerner. Suddenly we are reminded how ancient and sophisticated Chinese culture is, and what depths may lie behind a simple exterior. Between the modest winner and the gracious loser, the episode ends with an understated but resonant acknowledgment of equality.

If Uncle Sing Wo's race is incidental, racial prejudice is the heart of "Hey Boy's Revenge" (1:31, 4/12/58). Like many Chinese immigrants in the mid–19th-century, Hey Boy's brother and their beautiful young sister make the long expensive journey to America in order to escape poverty and famine at home. To earn his passage, Kim Sung signs a contract to work for a railroad company, while Kim Li's passage is paid by the rich elderly Chinese merchant she has agreed to marry. But Kim Sung soon discovers that the promises in his contract are worthless, and sends Hey Boy a letter detailing how the railroad mistreats its Chinese laborers, working them long hours, cheating them of their wages, shorting their rations, even serving them rotten food.[9] When Kim Sung protests these conditions to the construction boss, Travis, he is brutally beaten, and writes his brother and sister that he now fears for his life. As a result, when Travis's letter announces that Kim Sung has died in an "accident," Hey Boy, Kim Chang, does not believe it, and sets off on his own to confront Travis.

When Paladin returns from a trip to find Hey Boy dismissed from the Carlton for unexcused absence, he investigates with growing concern. Finally, Mr. Chung, Hey Boy's friend and owner of a small art gallery in Chinatown where Paladin is a well-regarded customer, confesses Hey Boy's mission. Mr. Chung also introduces Kim Li (played by Lisa Lu), and shows Paladin Kim Sung's letter, which, remarkably, he is able to read, though not without assistance, further confirming his serious study of Chinese culture.[10]

Fearing for Hey Boy's safety, Paladin quickly heads to the railroad camp, where he discovers that Travis is a confident, ruthless bully, contemptuous of the "China boys" who work for him and shameless in his exploitation of them. All he cares about is getting the work done as quickly and cheaply as possible, regardless of how the Chinese workers suffer, or how many of them die in the process. Then in the town jail, Paladin finds a much altered Hey Boy. No longer the genial porter, Kim Chang is a dignified somber man determined to avenge his brother's murder with his own hands, even if it costs him his life—as it nearly has. When he attacked Travis with a knife, the boss man would have killed him if the sheriff hadn't intervened and taken the prisoner to jail. Paladin urges his friend to turn to the law: two of Kim Sung's companions witnessed the murder firsthand, enough evidence to bring Travis to trial, but Hey Boy dismisses this idea, exclaiming bitterly, "Who would listen to a coolie against his boss?"[11] No argument of Paladin's moves him—not the fact that he will hang if he kills Travis, nor that his death would leave his sister completely alone. Hey Boy is bent on his revenge.

Paladin looks elsewhere for help, without success. The sheriff is not a bad man, but is more bystander than active participant, while the Chinese witnesses to the murder are too terrified of Travis to testify against him. With no other way to save his friend, Paladin hires out to protect Travis from "the China boy." So when a mob of Chinese workers breaks the prisoner out of jail, they find Paladin standing between them and their quarry. A grim Kim Chang argues, "He killed my brother; he cheated these men. He will be punished!" Paladin agrees, but insists, "Not by you. You're in the United States now. And while you're here, you'll live under our law ... you'll obey the law, you'll get its protection, and its justice." Bitterly, Hey Boy scoffs, "The law is for the *whites*, not Chinese," and asks rhetorically, "How will American justice help us?" In reply, Paladin again urges the witnesses to tell what they saw. Finally, the two point at Travis: "Him! Kill Kim Sung!" and the sheriff arrests him for murder. Thanks to Paladin, American justice does help the Chinese, at least in this instance. Travis will hang lawfully, while Hey Boy is neither killed by the ruthless boss nor executed for his murder.

He even gets his job back at the Carlton, no doubt through Paladin's influence. But there is one more loose end to clear up if all is to end well. Kim Li still faces marriage with an elderly stranger in order to pay the cost of her passage—until an "unknown personage" sends her money to repay the debt. Despite Paladin's airy denials that he is the "unknown," a pained and dignified Hey Boy tries to return the money, saying earnestly, "Excuse me—but I *know* you." At this moment, he is not Hey Boy, the subservient porter, but Kim Chang, the head of his household, speaking to his friend as an equal. Serious in his turn, Paladin replies,

> Your sister's life has value, too. It would be sinful to waste it on a marriage of convenience. Let her find some man to marry whose face she looks on with happiness, some man whose words are magic in her ears. Let her find love, Hey Boy. That's a rare thing. Money is cheap, common, and relatively plentiful.

And besides, he argues, the money is really from Travis—the money he paid Paladin to defend him. When Hey Boy still cannot accept, Paladin finds the compelling argument, the one that speaks to Chinese values. "Don't dishonor our friendship," he says sincerely, and hands the envelope of money to Kim Li. On those grounds, Hey Boy is finally able to accept.

Though Paladin obviously plays the most active role in solving the dilemma created by racial injustice, Hey Boy is far from the passive victim that the Chinese characters on *Bonanza* are. Unlike Li Cheng and Jimmy, Hey Boy takes steps to solve his own problem, risks action, and makes choices, as do the two frightened witnesses. Where, on *Gunsmoke*, American notions of justice and honor are treated as superior to Chinese versions, on *Have Gun*, American justice is forced to live up to its own highest standards—to treat all comers fairly, citizen and immigrant alike. It is a more challenging perspective, requiring genuine acceptance of the Chinese as equals under the law, an idea which is reinforced by the personal relationship between Paladin and Kim Chang.

Two other *Have Gun* episodes also feature the Chinese community.[12] "The Lady of the Fifth Moon" (6:29, 3/30/63), an atmospheric oddity from the end of the series, is ultimately unsuccessful, but "Hatchet Man" (3:25, 3/5/60), set in San Francisco's Chinatown, sensitively explores a conflict between Chinese and American cultural values. Aside from Paladin and one minor figure in the opening scene, all the significant characters are Chinese. The protagonist is Detective Joe Tsin, the police department's only expert on crime in Chinatown, who has so hampered the criminal enterprises of the Tong that they have placed a $1,000 reward on his head. However, Tsin has refused to accept help from the department: if he cannot defend himself from the Tong and their paid assassins, he will lose face, and for a proud Chinese, death is preferable to dishonor. The police hire Paladin behind Joe's back to provide discreet protection, but when Joe learns of this plan, he bitterly castigates his father and fiancée for having so little faith in him, and lectures Paladin, "Perhaps two thousand years from now, your civilization will have learned to understand ours!" To recover face, he publicly offers to fight Loo Sam, the head of the Tong—or any substitute he chooses. This is a virtual death sentence, since Joe is no match for the Tong's hatchet-wielding assassins, the "high-binders."

Though only a supporting character, Hey Boy plays a more prominent role than usual in this episode, one which again reveals the strength of his relationship with Paladin, and his courage in the face of great fear. Though describing himself, in contrast to Joe Tsin, as a "bad Oriental" who would "rather lose face than die," Hey Boy risks his life to guide Paladin to Loo Sam's gambling den, deep in Chinatown. Though Paladin is unable to help Joe openly without violating the Chinese code of honor, he improves Joe's odds by defeating the Tong leader's chief assassin, forcing Loo Sam to fight Joe in person, or concede the victory.[13] When Joe's challenge goes unanswered, the Chinese crowd cheers his victory, but Joe is uneasy, suspecting Paladin's interference. Mildly, Paladin defends the American notion of honor: "What makes this country is not its great men standing alone, trying to do the impossible. It's men of all kinds, large and small, trying to do a job together—not for their personal honor, but for the honor of their country." Then he holds out his hand, and asks, "Am I forgiven?" Joe shakes his hand, of course, and all ends well. Paladin's speech, however, comes uncomfortably close to suggesting that Chinese ideas about honor are less worthy than American, and undercuts the respect for cultural differences that had been emphasized in the rest of the episode. On the other hand, Joe's notion of honor would not only have resulted in his death but left his community with no police presence at all, a most unsatisfactory outcome. Overall, especially compared to the other series, this *Have Gun* episode treats Chinese culture and people with considerable respect.

Indians

Although Indians are almost never the protagonist of a Western episode, and only rarely appear as significant individuals, collectively Indians are the most common ethnic minorities in the Western, since their presence helps to define the genre. Not surprisingly, all the stories on TV about Indians concern their collisions with the whites flooding into their lands. On *Gunsmoke*, *Wagon Train*, and *Bonanza*, Indians generally belong to one of two categories: (1) "savages on the warpath," primitive and brutal, attacking all whites indiscriminately, or (2) helpless victims, whether as individuals subjected to prejudice and abuse by ignorant whites, or collectively, as cultures being pushed to extinction by the invading white settlers. A number of other stories examine characters who find themselves torn between Indian and white culture. Some are whites who identify more with Indians than with their own people: children kidnapped by Indians and raised with the tribe until they think of themselves as Indian, or frontiersmen who voluntarily share the life of a tribe for decades, typically marrying Indian women and having children with them. Several of these mixed-race children ("half-breeds" in the now-offensive 1950s term) get their own stories, few of them happy. Finally, a few borderline characters are Indians who have assimilated to white culture (found only on *Have Gun*). For these liminal people, the conflict between an increasingly dominant white culture and an Indian way of life that is vanishing often confronts them with painful choices.

In 1950s Hollywood, Indians are usually presented from a white perspective, as objects to be interpreted from the outside, not subjects with their own point of view. In fact, most full-blood Indian characters are stereotypes with little individuality or depth—those few that are more than members of a raiding party or a village, that have names or even a few lines of dialogue. Despite the wide variety of tribes in the West, each with its own customs and traditions, TV Indians generally all look alike.[14] Whether labeled Pawnee or Apache, Comanche, Cheyenne, or Arapaho, they live in teepees and hunt buffalo, the chiefs wear the enormous bonnets of eagle feathers characteristic of the Sioux, and the braves count coup and scalp their enemies. Conforming to these stereotypes, Indians on *Gunsmoke*, *Wagon Train*, and *Bonanza* seldom seem fully human, although *Gunsmoke* dealt well enough with Indians to earn praise from the Association of American Indian Affairs, as did *Have Gun*.[15] Given these circumstances, it is perhaps fitting that Indians are the characters least likely to be played by actors of the same ethnicity, even on *Have Gun*, which was unusually scrupulous about such casting choices. But this was more a practical necessity than the result of prejudice: most Indian characters with speaking roles were played by non–Indian actors, because Indian actors fluent in English were unfortunately rare until at least the 1980s.[16]

But close investigation of all these stories reveals a startling paradox. Although Indians on TV in the 1950s and '60s are usually marginalized in the drama, they are often presented as superior to the whites they encounter. As victims of prejudice and conquest, they have moral superiority over their abusers (always white); as dedicated stewards of the natural world (the original environmentalists, before such a concept existed), they are far more admirable than the exploitative whites who slaughtered buffalo wholesale for the hides, leaving the meat to rot. Though this superiority is seldom labeled explicitly, the implication colors many a concluding scene.

Plot #1: Savages on the Warpath

The old-fashioned vision of Indians as "savages on the warpath," a story familiar from decades of Western movies, is less common on 1950s television—except on *Wagon Train*. Indeed, six such attacks occur in the first season alone, a major reason the A. A. I. A. criticized the series for its biased portrayal of Indians.[17] On *Wagon Train*, Indians are regarded at best with wary caution and at worst with fear and hatred. Scout Flint McCullough's attitudes are the most nuanced: he knows many tribes well and often negotiates with them for the wagon train's safe passage through their territory, but his attitude more often reflects respect for worthy opponents than friendship or admiration, while the negotiations usually emphasize Flint's superiority to the Indians; he is more honest in his dealings, more reasonable in his terms, fairer in intention. By comparison, on *Gunsmoke*, *Bonanza*, and *Have Gun*, unmotivated Indian attacks are rare. When Indians turn to violence, they usually do so for good reasons, retaliating against specific whites who have wronged them, whether by stealing gold or silver from a developed mine, abducting their women, desecrating their sacred spaces, or breaking a treaty. Such attacks are typically presented as justified. On those occasions when Indians attack white people randomly, the raiders are carefully labeled "renegades"—that is, Indian outlaws, not ordinary tribesmen.[18]

Yet despite its characteristic negativity, *Wagon Train* occasionally presents a good Indian, or offers glimmers of sympathy for them. In one first-season episode, Bill Hawks, assistant wagon master, is troubled by how hard it is to think of Indians as "men, like us." Adams replies soberly, "Maybe if we did, we wouldn't fight them as much." In "The Nels Stack Story" (1:6, 10/23/57) an Indian even saves the whole train. An old Sioux left behind by his people to die is rescued by the pacifist Stack, and in gratitude shows them how to cross a treacherous river safely in order to escape an Indian attack.[19] But Adams criticizes Stack's humanitarian gesture as dangerous, warning him at least to tie up the starving old man and take his knife away, or "He'll stick it in your back before you can wink an eye, slit your throat, take your scalp, and dance off with it." Flint likewise presents Indians as prone to unmotivated violence. He believes the wagon train is in danger because the Sioux are on the warpath; though they are currently fighting the Pawnee, "The Sioux like to fight. Once they get a taste for blood, they're liable to attack anybody who gets in their way." In other words, unlike whites, Indians don't need a reason to fight and kill. Such statements, not just from crude bigots but from beloved series regulars, can be found in practically every *Wagon Train* episode about Indians.

On the other hand, in its first season *Wagon Train* offered one episode showing Indian culture as explicitly superior to white culture. Both the strengths and limitations of this episode make it worth close examination. In "A Man Called Horse" (1:26, 3/26/58), a white man captured and enslaved by a Crow chief as servant for his mother tells his story to Major Adams and Flint, almost entirely in flashback. Though initially intent on escape, the slave who calls himself Horse realizes that, if he does his work, he is treated fairly well. Slowly he makes friends among the tribe, learns to shoot with a bow, and after he kills an enemy scout, is accepted by the Crow as one of them—a powerful experience for a man scorned as a nameless foundling by the snobbish Boston society of his birth. He becomes a warrior (fighting against other Indians, not whites), wins the chief's sister in marriage, and finds a loving mother in his mother-in-law—deeply significant to an orphan boy. He tries briefly to return to white society with his beautiful Indian wife, but they encounter such violent prejudice that he turns his back on his "own" people for good. Even after his wife dies bearing a stillborn son, Horse chooses to stay with the Crow to support the old woman who loves and needs him, rather than returning to the white society that looked down on him.

Throughout the episode, Indians are shown to be far more tolerant and egalitarian than the whites of either Boston or the frontier, judging Horse by his actions and his character, not his birth or his wife. More significantly, there are four prominent Indian characters (the chief, his mother, Horse's wife, and a boy who is his first friend), all of whom behave like human beings, not stereotypes: they have strong opinions, they argue, they change their minds, they show anger and approval, curiosity and generosity in turn, and have understandable motives for their behavior.

But despite these positive aspects, there are significant problems with the episode. Artistically, it is one of the weakest in the series. The dialogue is often ham-handed, the dramatic structure weak, relying on extensive voice-over to carry the narrative, and much of the acting is inadequate, especially that of the guest star. As Horse, Ralph Meeker is uniformly wooden, showing almost no affect at all, while only Michael Pate (a white Australian actor often cast in ethnic roles) as the chief is remotely credible as an Indian.[20] More substantively, the episode's view of Crow life is a lie. First, we are never shown the Crow at war with invading whites, only with other Indians, a significant factor in creating such a positive view. The ending in particular is a historical whitewash. Horse's decision to remain with the Crow is treated as promising a good life for him and his Indian "mother": but in actual history, the year before this story's setting (1869), the Crow were already being driven onto reservations, their traditional way of life lost forever. The episode's cheerful conclusion is made possible only by erasing this fact.

Finally, from a political point of view, using a white man to convey the virtues of the Crow sends a troubling message. On the one hand, a white man's judgment might well be more credible to the TV audience, not only because of their shared race but, more justifiably, because any bias he had would be against the Indians rather than for them. As an outsider, his praise of the Crow is more objective than an Indian's could be. However, what does it say about Indians that whites are more authoritative speakers about Indian culture than Indians? Though the image of the Crow is positive, the Indians still are not allowed to speak for themselves. This pattern is common in too many of the stories about Indians, positive and negative alike.

Plot #2: Pity the Poor Indians

When Indians are not being demonized as bloodthirsty savages, they are portrayed as doomed and helpless victims, deserving of sympathy, even protection (though there is no mention of their deserving justice). Sometimes the focus is on individual Indians subjected to denigration, abuse, threats, even actual violence because of their race, leading the series regulars to treat the white abusers with disgust and contempt. In fact, this is the most common story about Indians on TV, highlighted on five episodes of *Gunsmoke* in its first two seasons, four *Wagon Trains*, two *Bonanzas*, and six episodes of *Have Gun—Will Travel*.[21] The other typical story summons sympathy for the collective fate of the Indians, irresistibly displaced by the river of white settlers overrunning their traditional lands. Such stories are poignant, even elegiac, mourning the demise of an ancient and noble way of life as the vast buffalo herds disappear and the tribes they sustained for centuries dwindle and fade—but the elegies are more often voiced by sympathetic white observers than by Indians themselves.

An early *Bonanza* episode, "The Paiute War" (1:4, 10/3/59), loosely based on actual events, offers a good example. In the actual history, two young Paiute women were abducted by three white men. When warriors rescued the women and killed their abusers, a hundred rowdy drunken whites marched on the Paiute village in retaliation, but 76 of them died in the attack, so the Army was called in to handle the "Indian trouble," permanently crushing the Paiutes. However, the *Bonanza* script makes significant changes to the history, some to allow the Cartwrights to play leading roles in the story, but others clearly designed to make the Paiutes more sympathetic. Most importantly, in the *Bonanza* version, the abducted women and their rescuers are Bannock Shoshone rather than Paiute, but the mob marches on the Paiutes because one kidnapper falsely accuses Chief Winnemucca's people of the murders. However, in making the Paiutes innocent victims instead of a proud people redressing a legitimate grievance and defending themselves from attack, the script reduces them to children dependent on right-minded whites (the Cartwrights) to save them. The change also implies that only the innocent deserve sympathy for the destruction that falls on them. The Indians cannot be permitted to fight back, even to obtain justice.

At least this time, the Indians are allowed to speak their own eulogy. Though the Paiute have done no wrong, Winnemucca knows his people are doomed. Whites have already destroyed the wildlife that the Paiute depend on, the bear and the antelope. This unwinnable battle with the Army is just the final blow. Like the other "wild things," he says, the Paiute will die: "And now the great sun of the Paiute weakens, and as it crosses the day, even today, will drop behind the mountains and be gone." The episode ends, rather remarkably, with the Cartwrights somberly witnessing the funeral of Chief Winnemucca's son killed in the battle while an Indian medicine man (judging by appearance, an actual Indian) sings what sounds like a genuine Indian chant.

Yet white sympathy, however sincere, is often mixed unpleasantly with condescension. In the *Bonanza* version, after the Bannock warriors rescue their women and kill the abductors, they rampage through the valley, burning cabins and killing white settlers. Though Adam agrees the abductors deserved their fate, this indiscriminate violence distresses him. Ben explains sadly, "They're primitive people, son—primitive and proud. And once they've tasted blood—" This is the same point made earlier on *Wagon Train*, that for Indians, bloodshed is intoxicating, addictive. But to call Indians "primitive" is to assert that their culture is less civilized, less *human* than the white culture around them—the very culture that produced the bullies and rapists who abused two helpless Indian women. Yet despite this bland, even unconscious, assertion of superiority, Ben Cartwright is presented as a sincere friend of the Indians.

In "The Gabe Carswell Story" (*Wagon Train*, 1:18, 1/15/58), with typical irony, a white man represents what is best about the Indians, while his mixed-race son embodies the worst stereotypes of Indians as treacherous, bloodthirsty, and cruel. Carswell, a legendary hunter and trapper who has been an adopted Arapaho for thirty years, decides that he and his half–Indian son, Jess/Little Elk, must leave the tribe. With the buffalo disappearing and whites invading the traditional hunting grounds, Carswell realizes that the Arapaho are doomed, and wants to save his son from their grim future—now, before Little Elk goes out on his first raiding party (its target: Major Adams' wagon train). Yet even as Carswell leaves, he eulogizes Arapaho culture, their reverence for the natural world and the buffalo that sustained them, in contrast to the rapacious wastefulness of white hunters, and sincerely laments the loss of this way of life.

But to Carswell's dismay, his son refuses to leave, denying the grim future Carswell foresees. Passionately declaring he is only Arapaho and hates all whites, especially his father, Little Elk lures Flint, his father's friend, into a trap, and stakes him out in the prairie sun to die painfully, swearing to "kill and torture and mutilate [whites] until we drive you from the Plains!" Learning of Little Elk's action, Carswell rescues Flint and disowns his son, telling him in bitter sorrow, "You've taken only the worst from the Arapaho and none of the good." In a final betrayal, Little Elk tries treacherously to shoot Flint in the back, and Carswell saves the scout the only way he can—by killing his son, now committed to savagery. Though Little Elk's suffering is genuine at losing his way of life and, even worse, losing his respect for his father, the episode affirms that the white man is unquestionably the nobler Indian.

The purpose of white praise and sympathy for the Indians, as all these examples show, is to prove the moral superiority of the series protagonists. Where ignorant whites rant about Indians as murderous savages, heap abuse on them, and threaten or inflict violence, our heroes—Matt, Doc, Kitty, and Chester; the Cartwrights; Paladin; Flint and sometimes even Major Adams—reject prejudice, defend its victims, and treat Indians according to their individual actions. But sympathy, however kindly or genuine, implies that the sympathizer is more powerful than the recipient. Between equals, like friends who take turns needing and offering sympathy, the issue of status is irrelevant. But when the inequality is permanent, as between a dominant group and a subordinated one, sympathy always carries a taint of condescension, the more so in this case since the sympathy for Indians rarely acknowledges white responsibility for their tragedy, no apology for broken treaties and ruthless exploitation, or Army massacres of helpless Indian women, children, and old men. And however sympathetic decent white people are to the Indians' plight, they generally refuse to grant the Indians a right to defend themselves. As the price of survival, Indians are expected to accept their tragic fate as inevitable, and go docilely to the reservation.

Finally, these stories soliciting sympathy for Indians allowed the audience to feel good about themselves by sharing their heroes' broad-mindedness. In a time when blacks' demands for equality and fairness were too threatening for many Americans to confront head on, the issue of racial prejudice could safely be raised in relation to American Indians, who by the 1950s were little more than relics of the past, few in number and marginalized on distant reservations. As a result, these stories allowed audiences to laud themselves for sympathizing with mistreated Indians without being obliged to sacrifice money, comfort, or advantage— indeed, to take any action at all.

Indians on Have Gun—Will Travel

On *Have Gun*, not only are there more stories about Indians than on its competitors, but those stories reflect a much wider range of characters, issues, and situations. Further, the Indians are treated with more individuality, even when, rarely, the depictions are negative.[22] In "The Prophet" (3:16, 1/2/60), a band of Apaches is preparing for war, inflamed by a deluded white man who thinks he is leading them—a former Army officer embittered by the abuse his Apache wife had received from his fellow soldiers, but also bitter because having an Indian wife has destroyed his career. Though the Indians are secondary characters in this episode, they are more than stereotypes, especially the colonel's angry wife, Serafina, who rightly charges that he doesn't love her people, as he claims, but only hates his own. Unusually for *Have Gun*, none of the Apaches are particularly sympathetic, while the Indian custom of torturing prisoners is uncomfortably highlighted, but even under these conditions, Paladin articulates serious respect for the Apaches' courage and skill as fighters, unmarred by condescending remarks about Indians as savages or "primitive" people.

In all other episodes, Indians are treated more positively, as human beings with understandable motives, their hostility to whites provoked by exploitation or assault. In "The Englishman" (1:13, 12/7/ 57), an aristocratic Briton nearly starts a war when Indians "attack" the Montana ranch he is visiting. Not realizing that the attack is only a practical joke promoted by the local storekeeper to terrify and embarrass a tenderfoot, Brunswick shoots back in self-defense, and wounds the chief, Harry. Outraged by this violent reaction to a joke, and inflamed by the whiskey the terrified storekeeper hands out to mollify them, the Indians threaten war if Brunswick does not answer for his crime. Though far less culpable than the joke's instigator, Brunswick is determined to avert the war if he can, and courageously faces the injured chief, who orders a warrior to charge his horse at Brunswick, once, twice, three times. To the chief's surprise, Brunswick accepts this punishment without flinching or protesting, even after being knocked down repeatedly. Such courage convinces Harry to accept Brunswick as an equal, and the war threat dissolves.

As usual, the Indians are secondary characters here in a story focused on Brunswick and his efforts to prove himself in the strange culture of the frontier, and they could easily have been presented as stereotyped "savages on the warpath," complete with the "firewater" that makes them so unreasonable and dangerous. But instead, the episode clearly acknowledges that the Indians, as much victims of the practical joke as Brunswick, have cause for their anger, and further shows them willing to recognize courage even dressed in unfamiliar clothes. Though this early script does not individualize the Indians as well as in many later episodes—in fact, they are never even given a tribal designation, just "Indians"—they are allowed to be more than simple stereotypes and clichés.

In other episodes as well, Indian violence against whites is not generalized "savagery," but targeted response to grievance. In both "The Yuma Treasure" (1:14, 12/14/57) and "Crowbait" (4:10, 11/19/60), Indians react fiercely against the white men trying to steal precious metals from their hidden mines. In "The Lady" (2:10, 11/15/58), as in *Bonanza*'s "The Paiute War," Apaches turn on settlers after drunken prospectors abduct one of their young women, while in "The Solid Gold Patrol" (2:13, 12/13/ 58), Indians attack a cavalry patrol to protest a delayed treaty settlement in Washington. Finally, in "Silent Death, Secret Death" (5:29, 3/31/62), the Nez Perce rise up against a white man who had forced them to build his private fort while treating them harshly. But they carefully limit their hostility to their abuser alone: the settlers in the fort are allowed to leave unmolested.[23] In each of these episodes, the Indians are treated neither as irrational savages, nor as "proud but primitive" people with a taste for blood, but as reasonable human beings responding to legitimate grievances. Such a perspective motivates Paladin to mediate an honest resolution between the parties whenever possible.

Stories mourning the death of Indian cultures occur on *Have Gun* as on the other series, but here too the Indians are treated as complex human beings rather than infantilized victims, and, significantly, are usually allowed to speak for themselves. In "The Hanging Cross" (1:15, 12/21/57), *Have Gun*'s only explicit Christmas episode, the conflict centers on a boy claimed by both whites and Indians. Years after four-year-old Robbie Beecher had been kidnapped by Sioux, his father spots a boy who might be his son in a band of Pawnee, and takes him away by force. But the boy, who speaks no English, insists he is Chiwa, the son of Chief Ca-la-te, and demands to return to his father. Though both Beecher and Ca-la-te have legitimate claims to the boy, the wealthy white rancher, hardened and embittered by his wife's death and the loss of his only child, comes off poorly compared to the chief, dignified, courteous, and tender to all the tribe's children. Paladin's respect for the Pawnee, his familiarity with their language and customs, reinforces this superiority, especially when Ca-la-te tells Paladin of his people's desperate plight. Though they have never broken a treaty, the Pawnee are now starving, their land stolen, the game gone, and winter coming on. So, Ca-la-te explains, he doesn't fear Beecher's threats to kill him if the boy is not returned: "Rifles cannot kill men already dead." Besides, the chief observes with grim satisfaction, if Beecher kills the only father the boy knows, Chiwa/Robbie will never accept this white man as his father: in death, Ca-la-te will win the contest for the boy's heart.

However, it is Christmas Eve—the night, Paladin explains to Ca-la-te, "when some people pretend there is no evil in the world ... the one night of the year when the white man honors the children of his tribe." Before Beecher can carry out his threat to hang Ca-la-te, his employees and their families (at Paladin's prompting) walk into the Indian camp singing, offering the starving Pawnee food and friendship. Moved by this gesture, Ca-la-te gives Beecher the ring that confirms Robbie's identity as his son; in turn, a softened Beecher (prodded by Paladin) grants the Pawnee 500 acres of his land and fifty head of cattle. Though Ca-la-te is losing the son of his heart, he can now provide for his whole band (if at an unarticulated cost: the Pawnee must trade their traditional nomadic lifestyle for a settled life as ranchers). The final tableau of the episode, Robbie/Chiwa smiling between his two fathers, suggests that, with the Pawnee settled nearby, the boy might even manage to keep both his families.[24]

Another episode also treats Indians as both doomed and morally superior to the whites they must deal with: "Fight at Adobe Wells" (3:26, 3/12/60), very loosely based on a historical incident involving Quanah Parker, the half-white Comanche chief.[25] In the *Have Gun* version, six white people are pinned down in the old fort at Adobe Wells by Quanah Parker and a handful of warriors. In addition to Paladin, there is Commodore Guilder, a rich ruthless businessman, and his despairing wife, Juliana, virtually his prisoner; the Maddocks, Ben and Madge, a decent but unimaginative couple looking for someplace to homestead; and Jones, a wounded buffalo hunter who has been holding off the Indians for days before the others arrive. By the end, all these whites but Paladin have revealed serious moral failings. Guilder is a conscienceless bully willing to sacrifice anyone else's life to protect his own. Juliana is both a tragic victim and a bitter vindictive drunk, eager to punish her husband for his cruelty. Jones is actually a bounty hunter, trading Indian scalps for money—a bounty paid by Guilder, his solution to "the Indian problem," which is why Guilder has hired Paladin to protect him from Parker. Even the Maddocks, who seem models of good sense and human kindness, later demonstrate a moral obtuseness that Paladin cannot overcome. By contrast, Quanah Parker shows himself a man of courage and honor, superior to any of these other whites.

At first the standoff is irresolvable. The Indians want Jones to punish him for his crimes, and they need water, found locally only in the fort. The whites want to leave safely, but even Paladin is unwilling to hand Jones over to be tortured, though he has been killing Indian women and children for a dollar a scalp. However, once the bounty hunter dies, Paladin arranges a parlay. Parker demands bitterly, "What kind of people can you be, White-Eyes, to pay for little children to die?" Though appalled by Jones' actions, Paladin replies somberly, "You are part Indian. Is that all good? And the white man in you, is that all bad?" He offers Parker water and the proof of Jones's death in exchange for the Indians' guns. Parker hesitates, anguished: how can he trust a white man? Paladin acknowledges this as a fair question, but points out that someone has to take the first step, to "start acting decently," despite the risk of betrayal—as he himself had taken a risk, coming alone to Parker's camp.

In the end, Parker decides to trust Paladin; he and his men come to the fort and lay down their weapons. But as they view Jones's body and collect their water, Parker tells the whites eloquently, "This will all be your land, White-Eyes. But it was ours. And when you walk here, even after we are dead, you will not be alone. And behind the laughing of your children will be ghosts of the laughing of ours." Though he knows this loss is inevitable, he pleads for a delay: "Only let us live out our time before you take it all away." Paladin's expression is sorrowful, knowing Parker's plea is hopeless. But as the Indians prepare to leave with their water and without their guns, Juliana vindictively unmasks her husband as the source of the bounty, and violence erupts in the fort. As Parker grabs for his gun, Guilder shoots his wife in fury at her betrayal. Paladin rushes to disarm the commodore, but in their struggle, Guilder's gun goes off against his own belly, and he too dies. Still holding the gun, Paladin turns to find Parker and his men all pointing their rifles at him, ready to punish this treachery. But when a horrified Paladin tosses the gun at Parker's feet, the Indian leader relents: "We will make a beginning of trust. Do not fear our guns—until you come back." The villains, Jones and Guilder, are both dead, along with the unhappy Juliana, but two honorable men, Paladin and Parker, have created something hopeful in the midst of evil.

The next morning, however, the Maddocks tell Paladin that they have decided to stay in this area to homestead: there's nothing for them back home, and their children will need a place. It's a hard land, they recognize, a cruel land, but Maddock says, "You gotta be tough, or else this country's going to be nothing but a desert full of naked savages with stone axes.

Right?" Appalled by this image, so unlike the wronged yet honorable Comanche chief of the night before, Paladin reminds them what they owe Quanah Parker, how well he treated them, but Maddock brushes that aside cheerfully: "Without you and that gun there, he'd have cut our throats like *that*. No—don't trust him." As they thank him again for saving them, Paladin shakes his head in despair. If decent people like the Maddocks are so blind to the qualities of an extraordinary man like Parker, how will Indians ever gain mercy, let alone justice?[26]

Plot #3: Straddling the Cultural Boundary

All four series include characters who stand on the border between the races: Indian-identified whites, assimilated Indians (found only on *Have Gun*), and mixed-race children. Despite their ambiguous status, most of these characters finally identify fully with one race or the other, their problems caused by the conflicts between their two cultures rather than internal confusion about identity. But a few figures, the most tragic, struggle with divided loyalties they find impossible to resolve.

Indian-Identified Whites: Stories about whites who prefer Indian ways to their own culture are surprisingly common. Some of these characters are children captured in raids and raised by their captors. In these stories, abducted boys typically end by identifying strongly with the Indians, like Robbie in "The Hanging Cross." Two early *Gunsmoke* episodes, "Yorky" (1:18, 2/18/56) and "Indian White" (2:6, 10/27/ 56), also feature boys who, after a brief return to white society, choose to rejoin their adopted tribes. Significantly, Matt cheerfully supports Yorky's return to the Arapaho, but in the second episode, tries to persuade the boy called Veehocan not to rejoin the Cheyenne he loves—not because Matt thinks Indians are inferior, but because Veehocan's band is being pursued by the Army to return them to the reservation they have fled. Knowing the Indians' defeat is inevitable and that most will die either from Army bullets or starvation, Matt tries to save the youngster from sharing their grim fate, but to no avail. The boy who was once Dennis is now a Cheyenne, for good or ill, and joyously insists on returning to his chosen people.

Unlike these boys, kidnapped white girls (found only on *Have Gun*) typically do not identify with the tribe, in part because their gender leaves them more vulnerable to unpleasant treatment, particularly sexual exploitation.[27] Two of these characters, both kidnapped as adolescents, are deeply traumatized by their experience: Mary Grange in "A Head of Hair" (4:3, 9/24/60), catatonic after only a few months with the Nez Perce, and Mollie Dean in "The Walking Years" (6:25, 3/2/63), held for over a year by renegade Apaches. Girls kidnapped younger fare better, however. Mrs. Ordey in "The Long Hunt" (2:25, 3/7/59) is taken by Ute Indians at eight years old. Rescued five years later by the half–Comanche Tom Ordey, she chooses to marry her rescuer and live with him as an Indian, maintaining Indian values of honor and revenge rather than going back to white society. The tough teenage orphan in "The Predators" (6:8, 11/3/ 62) who lived among the Apache until she was rescued as a child of ten does not identify herself as Indian, but has learned the hard way that there are worse fates for a young woman alone than life with the Apaches. If forced to choose, she declares she would return to the Apache village rather than support herself in the only jobs available to her in a white town, scullery maid or bar girl/prostitute. Like the boys' choices, these responses signal that, under some circumstances, Indian life is preferable to white culture.

When the association is voluntary, this sense of Indian life as superior to white culture is even stronger, as for *Wagon Train*'s Gabe Carswell and Horse, white men who choose to live among the Indians for years, even decades. One early *Bonanza* episode similarly affirms Indians' superiority. "The Last Hunt" (1:15, 12/19/59) tells of a Romeo-and-Juliet love affair in which a socially prominent young white man secretly marries a Shoshone chief's daughter. When the young woman dies in childbirth, her light-skinned child reveals their secret; and her bereaved husband joins the Indians with his newborn son, choosing life with the Shoshone rather than with his wealthy but bigoted father.[28] All these white men come to see the Indian way as superior to their own culture in some vital aspects.

Assimilated Indians: The opposite version of cultural crossover—assimilated Indians, those given Western educations who accept the teaching and seek a place in the larger American culture—also, paradoxically, emphasizes the superiority of the Indian characters, because the conflicts these characters face result primarily from white prejudice. In "Winchester Quarantine" (1:4, 10/5/57), Joseph and Martha Whitehorse, mission-raised Christian Cherokees, find themselves shunned in the white community where they bought a ranch because their most influential neighbor, McNally, has a vendetta against all Indians since his family was scalped by Sioux 35 years earlier. McNally makes no distinction between tribes: warlike Sioux or peaceful—indeed, Christianized—Cherokee, in his mind an Indian is an Indian, all equally hated. The other neighbors are too frightened of McNally to go against him, until Paladin intervenes on behalf of the Whitehorses. Once Paladin has defeated the bully with a non-violent stratagem, McNally is the one to be shunned, as the other members of the community reach out to the gentle Indian couple with gestures of friendship.

"Lady on a Stagecoach" (2:18, 1/17/59) also features an assimilated Indian, but unlike the realistic Whitehorses, Della White Cloud is a figure out of fantasy—an elegantly dressed Apache princess, a chief's daughter, just graduated from a lady's seminary in Boston and heading to San Francisco to join her fiancé, who is a West Point graduate and lieutenant in the Army. Despite her obvious intelligence, culture, and beauty, Della is scorned as a dirty Indian by the three haughty, middle-class whites sharing the stagecoach with her and Paladin, even after she risks her life to help Paladin save them all from a ruthless bandit.[29] As a character, Della tells us nothing about real Indians (or real women), but, like Quanah Parker in "Fight at Adobe Wells," she certainly reveals how ugly and unreasonable racial prejudice is, pointing up the blindness of those self-satisfied whites unable to recognize her superior qualities.

The remaining two assimilated Indians are, curiously, both lawmen. "Charley Red Dog" (3:13, 12/12/59) is a young Navajo who, with Paladin's help, becomes the marshal of the same Arizona town where, fifteen years earlier, his father had been killed with impunity for no reason except that he was Indian. However, in the present, Charley's race serves only to indicate how much the town has changed; though a few of the local rowdies are "Indian haters," the town council's only worries are Charley's youth and inexperience. Once he demonstrates he can enforce the law effectively, the town accepts him without regard for his race.[30] However, in the second story, "Brotherhood" (6:17, 1/5/63), prejudice against Indians is the very heart of the issue. As children, after surviving the massacre of their village by the Army, Jim and Abe Redrock were sent to Philadelphia to be educated. When they returned home, their white education did not prevent them from being treated as Indians—looked down on and scorned as inferior. Despite this prejudice, Jim has chosen assimilation because he wants "a house made of wood, and a chance for my boy to go to school and sleep on a bed instead of a buffalo hide," and "a way of life for me and my wife that has some meaning."[31]

The great mark of his assimilation is his election as town sheriff, though even Jim admits bitterly his election was a joke. Despite Jim's badge, all actual power belongs to the local Big Man, Stennis, who delights in humiliating the "sheriff" as often and publicly as possible. Meanwhile, Abe takes the opposite path from his brother, loudly asserting his Indian identity—a stance made less convincing because the script never identifies the brothers' tribe, and the only aspects of Indian "culture" Abe demonstrates are the negative stereotypes of Indians as drunkards and petty thieves. His main purpose seems to be to annoy and embarrass his brother, but underneath this disruptive behavior is a plea, however incoherently dramatized, for Jim not to abandon their Indian heritage which Abe celebrates so passionately in his speeches, if less positively in his actions.

The issues come to a head—both the quarrel between the brothers, and the town's humiliating treatment of their sheriff—when Abe wounds a man in a confrontation. Though Paladin testifies that the white man shot first, Big Man Stennis swears Abe's attack was unprovoked, so Jim is forced to arrest his brother. But instead of holding a trial, Stennis leads a mob that hauls Abe out of jail in order to "punish" him. When Jim learns Stennis's plans include a long stout rope and a tree limb, he finally decides to claim the power of his office and act like a real sheriff. Together he and Paladin rescue Abe, a task made easier because the other citizens refuse to go along once they recognize Stennis's deadly purpose. In the resulting gunfight, Stennis and his chief henchman both die. With Stennis's evil influence removed and Jim firmly in charge, the town at last gives their sheriff the respect and cooperation he needs, and the brothers are reconciled, though the issue of assimilation is never explicitly resolved.[32] As in all the other episodes about assimilated Indians, criticizing white prejudice is more important than celebrating, or even accurately depicting, Indian culture.

Not Easy Being Indian

The traditional view of Indians as "savages on the warpath" derives from historical fact: first, from the centrality of warfare in the culture of the Plains tribes, where a man's status was determined primarily by his prowess and courage in battle; and second, from the widespread Indian custom of torturing captured enemies, partly to revenge their own dead warriors, and partly to give the captive an opportunity to prove his own courage by "dying well."[33] But as the Indian way of life is increasingly disrupted by white encroachment, the traditional methods of proving manhood become harder and harder to accomplish. Several episodes on *Gunsmoke* and *Have Gun* sympathetically explore the challenges confronting an Indian or Indian-identified white man who wants to live like a warrior, or die like one.

In "Prairie Happy" (*Gunsmoke*, 1:33, 7/7/56), Tewkesbury, a white man who has lived with the Pawnee for decades, comes to Dodge City loudly warning of an Indian attack and spreading horrifying stories of "savages" who torture first and then kill. Despite Matt's sharp skepticism, many men in Dodge greet Tewkesbury's stories eagerly, ready to kill Indians without qualm or question. When a flaming arrow in the night sets fire to a boarding house, the crowd rallies to the old scout's side, ready to fight, until Matt proves that there are no Indians: Tewkesbury shot the arrow himself, to promote his war. Unfortunately, the fire killed two drunken cowboys, so Matt arrests Tewkesbury for murder. But when the old scout's dignified Pawnee daughter visits him in jail, Matt finally learns the whole story.

Quiet One explains that her father, growing old, craved a warrior's death in battle; but the tribe is at peace, and the young men refused to listen to his war talk. So he turned to the whites of Dodge to obtain his battle, the "civilized" whites who, ironically, prove far more eager for war than the "savage" Indians. In the end, Tewkesbury uses the traditional medicine bundle his daughter brings him to die with dignity at his own hand, rather than shamefully on the gallows.[34] An episode that begins with hysterical anti–Indian prejudice ends with surprising sympathy for Indian culture, as Tewkesbury sings a Pawnee death chant in his cell, and his daughter grieves in quiet dignity. Though nothing justifies his actions, the desire that motivated those actions—to live and die in a way that earns the approval of your own people—is very understandable.

Similarly, in *Have Gun*'s "A Head of Hair" (4:3, 9/24/60), another Indian-identified white man risks everything to reclaim a warrior's status. The plot of the episode is simple: Paladin hires expert tracker John Anderson to help him find the Nez Perce who kidnapped pretty blond Mary Grange, kills three warriors on the trail in self-defense, then successfully negotiates with the Nez Perce chief, trading gifts for the captive. On the way home, Anderson tries to kill Paladin and dies in the attempt. But such an outline reveals nothing of the dynamics that make this episode such riveting drama. The title seems to point us toward Mary's beautiful blond hair, but in the end, the relevant hair is Paladin's, the white woman's rescue secondary to the dark uneasy relationship between these two men, and Paladin's conundrum: having placed his life in Anderson's hands, he is not certain whether he is dealing with a white man or an Indian.

Anderson lived among the Sioux for ten years, married among them, considered himself a Sioux. Then for some unspecified reason, he left the tribe to work as a scout for the Army—coming "home," as a young lieutenant says, implying Anderson has chosen the culture of his birth over the Sioux. But we soon realize that, even though he is using his Sioux-taught skills to help the Army "exterminat[e] the Indian nation," Anderson remains more Indian than white. In fact, like many Indians, the scout has become a demoralized drunk, so poor he has neither a gun nor money for alcohol—which is why he accepts Paladin's job offer.

Once on the trail with his employer, Anderson reveals how much he still thinks like a Sioux. When they meet the three Nez Perce warriors, Paladin offers the weaponless scout a rifle to defend himself, but Anderson refuses, explaining that, for an Indian, stealing a weapon from an enemy is a feat to boast of, but accepting one as a gift indicates weakness, a cause for shame. Once Paladin has killed the three young Nez Perce, Anderson starts to take their scalps as trophies, but Paladin stops him, arguing not from white morality, but on Indian grounds: because the scout did not kill them, he is not entitled to claim their scalps. Anderson accepts the justice of this, but complains, "You leave them their scalps, they'll die and go to heaven and act like heroes. They'll lie and say that their enemies didn't kill them—they died in bed, old men. They would have taken yours." Then he adds admiringly, "You got a *fine* head of hair." Though this remark obviously disconcerts Paladin, he chooses not to respond to it.

In the course of their mission, Anderson comes to respect Paladin—for his skill with a gun in the fight against the three warriors, for his steadfastness in the test of courage set by the Nez Perce before the talks begin, and for his skill in negotiating with the chief for Mary Grange's ransom, but most of all for his spirit: "It comes to me that you'd be worth killing. You hold on to life. It will have to be torn away from you. To do so would be a fine coup for a warrior." But despite these ominous hints, the gunfighter chooses to protect Anderson from serious danger. The Nez Perce chief quietly advises Paladin to leave the "false Sioux" behind when he takes Mary Grange away, warning that Anderson will surely slit his throat on the trail. But given the traditional enmity between the Sioux and the Nez Perce, the unarmed scout would inevitably face a prolonged death by torture if Paladin abandoned him. Knowing this, Paladin rejects the chief's advice, claiming (perhaps truthfully) that he needs Anderson's help to find his way back.

Yet the chief's warning was prophetic. Along the trail, Anderson suddenly demands his pay and announces he's "going home"—that is, home to the Sioux. Somberly, Paladin warns him, "In ten years the Sioux nation will be gone," but Anderson denies history, just like young Veehocan from "Indian White" and Little Elk from "The Gabe Carswell Story." He proudly declares, "We will make a fight that the white man will remember for one hundred generations of men. Where we ride, not even the tears of God will make things grow again. We will be known as the Sioux—the enemy, the most savage, as long as the ground we walk on exists. I will go to my people!" He disappears, only to leap on Paladin from ambush a short time later. In the desperate struggle, Paladin wounds Anderson fatally, then demands in baffled anguish, "*Why?*"—wanting to understand why the scout would try to kill him, a man who had saved his life, a man he clearly respected. Did he want to steal the girl? A horse? But the dying Anderson gasps, "A Sioux warrior, going home, must take a coup," and again reaches up to touch Paladin's hair, whispering his final words: "What a truly fine head of hair you have." Paladin must wonder: if he had let the scout take scalps from the dead Nez Perce, this attack might never have happened, nor Anderson's own wasted death, but he gives no hint of such thoughts. The unexpected outcome reduces Paladin to appalled silence.

This episode is remarkable on many levels. First, the script by Harry Julian Fink is taut, packed with telling detail, and not without humor; it is directed with Andrew McLaglen's usual thick texture, and anchored by two compelling performances, Boone's as Paladin and Ben Johnson's as Anderson. More important in the context of this chapter is the treatment of the Indian characters. First, consider the young Nez Perce warrior who confronts Paladin in a lengthy scene, much of it conducted in Nez Perce with Anderson as translator. Though the warrior misjudges Paladin badly, assuming a single white man could be no threat to three Nez Perce—an arrogance which ultimately costs their lives—he is no cartoon Indian, no stereotyped humorless savage. Next is Chagra, the Nez Perce chief, a strong authoritative man, not friendly but without the arrogance of the young warriors. Unlike what too often happens in a Western when a white protagonist confronts an Indian chief, the two men are presented as equally competent and deserving of respect. Finally, there is Anderson himself, an Indian in every way that matters. As with Tewkesbury, though his murderous attack on Paladin cannot be justified, it can be understood within the framework of Indian values. His tragedy is that he cannot simply go home, but must pay a steep price; he needs to earn the badge of a warrior in order to be accepted by the people he claims as his own.

In "Return to Fort Benjamin" (3:20, 1/30/60), this story repeats with an actual Indian at the center, the most tragic of these warriors manqué. Yellow Star, the son of the Sioux chief Dark Leaf, was once a highly respected warrior, first in battle and first in his people's council, but he has fallen on hard times. He lost his place of honor among his own people after he shamefully counseled surrender to the whites, then became a scout for the white Army, which gave him a medal for bravery. But a crippling injury turns him from a respected scout into "Gimp the Indian," the butt of coarse jokes and endless abuse, given all the dirtiest, most menial jobs around the post, given whiskey that makes him a broken-down drunk. His need to reclaim his honor, to take a coup, becomes so desperate that when Lt. Pearson is murdered (by his own sergeant, we later learn), the murderer easily persuades him to claim the scalp and the "credit" for the kill. The Indian thinks his execution will allow him to die with honor as a brave warrior. But instead he will be hanged, shamefully. Worse, as Paladin learns, because Major Blake bitterly hates the Sioux, he intends to throw Yellow Star's body into the fort's lime pit for disposal, as if he were a dead animal, rather than allowing him the proper Sioux funeral pyre Yellow Star's father had hired Paladin to provide for his son.

When Paladin's investigation indicates that Yellow Star is not the real murderer, he tries to arrange a new trial, but Lt. Graham, who had been blackmailed by the murderer into supporting Yellow Star's false confession, helps the prisoner escape—partly from compassion, and partly to protect his own secret complicity in the crime: as an escaped prisoner, the former scout will be killed on sight, giving him no time to recant his confession. But Yellow Star would never renounce his coup: without it, he cannot go to the afterlife as a warrior. Cornered by the soldiers, he makes his desperate last stand, one warrior against an Army patrol, saber against rifles, until a reluctant Paladin finally shoots him. In the end, Yellow Star achieves the death he wished, as a warrior in battle, an honorable finish to a life which had become degraded and intolerable, and he receives the Sioux funeral pyre his father had wished, though attended only by a somber Paladin.

This is one of those episodes, found almost alone on *Have Gun*, where the Indian is genuinely the protagonist. Even in his pitifully degraded state, Yellow Star is considerably more sympathetic than any of the whites in this episode: Major Blake, pursuing his bitter vendetta against the Sioux even against a corpse; Lt. Graham, a man of good education and breeding fighting his own losing battle with alcohol, and lying to protect his career; Sgt. Kern, an unscrupulous bully who takes advantage of his enemies and enjoys brutalizing the helpless, especially Gimp the Indian. Yet none of these men are cartoon villains, either. Major Blake had once believed in honor, until the Sioux violated a flag of truce and tortured him into revealing military secrets; even now, his bitterness is as much at his own failure as at Sioux perfidy. If Lt. Graham is perilously weak and selfish, he is also compassionate and capable of charm. Even Kern, the murderer, killed for a reason: Lt. Pearson had routinely used the privilege of rank to brutalize his men. But these mitigating factors cannot absolve them of culpability for hounding an innocent man to death. It is a grim ending: as Paladin realizes, even with the truth revealed and the worst offenders (Pearson and Kern) dead, nothing much will improve at Fort Benjamin. The survivors are too weak, too trapped in their errors, to change. Only Yellow Star has any dignity, and that is the sad dignity of death.

Finally, *Gunsmoke*'s "Indian Scout" (1:23, 3/31/56) tells the story of an even more tragically conflicted character, ultimately rejected by both Indians and whites. In the familiar story, Amos Cartwright is a white man who lived among the Comanche for many years, but after his Indian wife died in childbirth, he left the tribe to scout for the Army. When Cartwright arrives in Dodge as the sole survivor of a cavalry patrol ambushed by Comanches, he is accused of deliberately leading his men into the ambush. Bailey, whose brother died in the fight, threatens Cartwright relentlessly until the scout kills his persecutor and flees for Indian Territory. Tracking him, Matt and Chester find him pinned down by a Comanche war party, and learn the painful truth. Though Amos had not led the patrol into the ambush, he hadn't warned them about it, either—because the attackers were his Comanche friends and family, and he didn't want the soldiers to kill them. But some Comanches were killed in the attack anyway, so Cartwright's neutrality only turns both whites and Indians against him. As a result, when he walks out alone to face the war party's leader, his late wife's brother, the warrior kills him wordlessly without even counting coup, in the ultimate sign of contempt for an unworthy enemy. Amos's desperate effort not to take sides leaves him shunned by both whites and Comanches, dying alone in a cultural no-man's-land.

Though no explanation is offered for the attack on the patrol, the episode does not treat the Comanches as motiveless "savages on the warpath." The only condemnation of the Indians comes from disreputable men like Bailey, whose prejudice is so indiscriminate that he wants to kill any Indians he can find, not just the specific Comanches who killed his brother, while the Comanche war leader who kills Amos targets an individual who could justly be said to have injured him. However, undercutting this respectful treatment, the Indian point of view is (as usual) articulated not by an Indian, but by a white man—Amos.

The Mixed-Race Children

Three of the four series tell stories about young people of mixed Indian-white parentage, eight episodes altogether. Four such characters occur in the first season of *Gunsmoke*: "Night Incident" (1:6, 10/29/55), "The Hunter" (1:9, 11/26/55), "Tap Day for Miss Kitty" (1:22, 3/24/56) and "Prairie Happy" (1:33, 7/7/56, discussed earlier), but only one of these characters plays an important role in the episode, and none of the four views their blended heritage as a problem—perhaps because three are daughters, one of them still a child. True, Golden Calf in "The Hunter," son of a Blackfoot woman and a white man—the famous buffalo hunter, Murdock—deliberately kills his father. But Murdock dies not because he is white, but because the man who had lived among the Blackfoot for decades, who had brought them the great gift of guns to make their hunt easier, has turned vicious and contemptuous of the tribe, bringing "bad medicine." Like the three young women in the other episodes, Golden Calf feels no ambiguity about his identity. When Matt calls him a "breed" (that is, a half-breed—a term whites did not see as pejorative in the 1950s), the boy replies firmly, "I am an *Indian*." Not knowing then that the brutal hunter is the young man's father, Matt urges him to leave Murdock, and lectures him at length about the evils of white buffalo hunters' methods compared to the Indian way. It's the same familiar pattern, white characters praising Indians while an Indian sits by, mostly silent. Though Golden Calf is given substantial screen time in the episode, he has only a handful of lines. In killing his father to save the tribe from his evil influence, Golden Calf performs the crucial act in the drama, but is not allowed to articulate his own story.

Little Elk in *Wagon Train*'s "Gabe Carswell Story," discussed above, is a truly tormented figure, but not because he feels torn between his Indian and white identities. Raised exclusively among the Arapaho, he thinks of himself as wholly Indian, and adamantly denies his white heritage, despite his father's arguments. Little Elk's agony, then, is not caused by an internal conflict, but by losing his father to the hated whites, which destroys his pride in being his father's son. We don't have to agree with him or approve of his actions to understand his pain. And aesthetically, this episode is quite powerful. James Whitmore plays Gabe Carswell appealingly, with warmth and sincerity, while Scott Marlowe (the young white actor who plays Little Elk) effectively embodies the son's passions and confusions. And unlike Golden Calf, Little Elk is permitted to make his own case, at considerable length. (In fact, the biggest problem with the episode is that filling 52 minutes of screen time requires padding the script in a way that often feels repetitive—a common occurrence both with this series and *Bonanza*.)

Two more episodes tell startlingly similar stories about mixed-race characters. Both *Wagon Train*'s "The Mark Hanford Story" (1:23, 2/26/58) and *Have Gun*'s "The Trial" (3:38, 6/11/60) explore a bitter dispute between a white father and his half–Indian son that arises when the father sets aside his Indian wife in order to marry a young white woman. Both older men, Jack Hanford and Morgan Gibbs, had married a chief's daughter and used their wife's connections to build a profitable trading post. Both sent their sons away to be educated as white gentlemen, denying the boys any connection to their mothers' people. When each mother kills herself out of shame for her husband's rejection, the sons defiantly reclaim their Indian heritage and turn violently against their fathers and the new brides.

Then the stories diverge. In the *Wagon Train* tale, Mark Hanford steals the new bride, Anne, from the wagon train and takes her to his Cheyenne mother's village, intending to degrade and despoil her before handing her over to his father. Instead, he falls in love with her, and she with him. But because the elder Hanford will reclaim his bride by force if necessary, the young couple's commitment to each other would bring war down on the Cheyenne, a war that the Indians would inevitably lose. Despite Flint's efforts to mediate a peaceful settlement, neither Hanford will yield. In the end, the conflict is resolved Cheyenne style, by single combat to the death between the Hanfords for possession of Anne. However, seeing Jack on the verge of killing his son, Jack's friend shoots the older man in order to save Mark. By now it is clear to all that, despite Mark's fervent claims to be Cheyenne, he really belongs in the white world. He and Anne marry and happily take over the trading post.

Have Gun's "The Trial" is far darker, and told more obliquely. Where Mark Hanford is clearly the protagonist of his episode, David Gibbs has only one rather short scene; his story emerges through the testimony of others. On the wedding night, David had confronted Morgan and the new bride, intending to kill his father, but in the crossfire the bride died instead. The bitter father, determined to hang his son for murder, hires Paladin to bring him in for trial alive, but David has other ideas. He has gone to the Indian hut where his mother killed herself, intending to complete the same Pima death rite in her honor, but he is interrupted not only by Paladin but by an old bounty hunter who shoots the young man in the back before Paladin can prevent it. Even as he is dying, David tries to complete the rite (disemboweling himself with a special bone knife, or perhaps just stabbing himself in the belly), but can't go through with it, and dies, despairing at his failure, in Paladin's arms.[35] By the end of the episode, Morgan Gibbs is also dead of a random bullet, still denying any responsibility for the deaths of his son and both wives.

Another vital difference between the episodes is the amount of detail about Indian life and the number of Indian characters. In the *Wagon Train* story, a number of significant scenes are set in the Cheyenne village, notably Mark's bloody initiation test to prove he is worthy of his Cheyenne blood (accompanied by some embarrassingly inauthentic Indian drumming). Chief Running Bear, Mark's uncle, is a featured character in Flint's many negotiations seeking a peaceful solution to the standoff. These scenes also introduce viewers to a variety of Cheyenne customs, not all convincing or plausible. In the end, however, Mark's connection to his mother's tribe reveals itself as part vengeful rejection of his father and part romantic fantasy rather than any authentic expression of identity; once his father is dead, he easily returns to white culture to run the trading post with Anne—though doubtless both will remain sympathetic to the Indians that trade with them. By contrast, in *Have Gun*'s "The Trial," David is the only Indian character we see, and him only briefly, while Pima customs and beliefs are barely hinted at. But David's commitment to his Indian heritage, despite his white education, seems far more genuine than Mark's. However, David is not the central figure of this episode; that place belongs to his father, Morgan, a self-indulgent autocrat who tries to punish others for his mistakes, and dies without having learned anything.

Like both of these episodes, *Have Gun*'s "The Scorched Feather" (2:22, 2/14/59) also concerns a deadly conflict between a white father and his white-educated half–Indian son, but at a significantly higher artistic level than the previous examples. The drama is concentrated and intensified, with only three characters involved—Paladin and the two Cielbleus, William and Robert. Father and son share the center ring, equally important to the story and equally tormented by their history—a tangle of love, hate, guilt, and anger so hopelessly entwined that it cannot be resolved, only ended by death. Unlike any other story on these series about mixed-race children, here the son's internal conflict is as devastating to him as the external struggle with his father. As Paladin comes to understand, Robert Cielbleu is "two people—and that's a madness that'll never give him any peace."

Paladin first meets Robert in San Francisco, a cultured, elegantly-dressed young man who hires him to protect his father against "the finest soldier in the world: Hotan Itan, the youngest war chief of the Shoshone Comanches." Despite his gentlemanly appearance, Robert demonstrates significant fighting skills during an attempted street robbery, so Paladin wonders why Robert chooses not to fight Hotan Itan himself. The client explains grimly, "I've fought him. He's stronger than I am." Robert also refuses to explain why Hotan Itan wants to kill his father, but when Paladin locates the old man in his isolated cabin, he understands all too clearly. William Cielbleu is Billy Blue Sky, "scout for the Army during the Indian campaigns,"[36] who, in the now-familiar pattern, lived with the Comanche for years and fought them for years afterward. Because of the reputation he earned in those wars, he now hides himself away deep in the forest, seeking safety in secrecy and isolation. But when Paladin explains why he's come, Billy angrily denies that he's in danger from Hotan Itan—until a flaming arrow streaks into the cabin, narrowly missing his head. Then Paladin learns the secret: Hotan Itan and Robert Cielbleu are the same man, or two halves of the same man, Billy's son by his Comanche wife, who died when the Army raided the village of Ashiwara—a raid led by Billy Blue Sky.

Billy, portrayed with subtlety and depth by Lon Chaney, Jr., is strikingly different from his son: a shortish barrel of a man, gruff and scruffy, shabbily dressed, with a permanent limp from a wound Hotan Itan gave him on the Ashiwara raid. Though uneducated, Billy is far from a fool, as Paladin quickly realizes. He also realizes that, however indefensible Billy's acts in the Indian wars, the scout is not a man who hates or demonizes Indians. He had loved Robert's mother, claiming her openly as his wife, not some sort of convenient concubine, and swears convincingly that he didn't know she was at Ashiwara until he saw her dead body. Further, his actions toward Robert have all been motivated by love. Billy has spent every penny he earned to give his son advantages he never had himself—money, a good education, nice clothes, so Robert could be accepted anywhere in the world. But because none of those things were possible if the boy remained an Indian, Billy grabbed his son out of the Comanche camp, out of his grieving mother's arms, and sent him away to turn him into a white man. But, as Billy laments, Robert rejected all of it; his mother "had him too long. Crammed him full of Comanche nonsense. I got him too late." Yet Billy's assessment is only partially correct: there is more white man left in Robert than he sees, since Robert tries as hard to protect his father as Hotan Itan tries to kill him, even seeking out the most skillful man he can find and paying him $2,000 to stand between Billy Blue Sky and the Comanche war chief.

As Paladin confronts the vengeful young man, his identity shifts uncannily between Robert and Hotan Itan, each with his own voice, his own vocabulary and diction, like a split personality. It is Robert who agrees to the parlay but Hotan Itan who speaks to Paladin, explaining that Robert fought hard, but he lost. When Paladin asks, "Why did you hire me?" Hotan Itan replies, "I didn't hire you, he did." Paladin then asks Robert to explain why, but Hotan Itan snaps, "He cannot tell you either. He is dead!" Paladin insists, "Dying, perhaps, but not dead," and tries to persuade Hotan Itan to abandon his revenge. He offers to refund Robert's money, but the Comanche war chief refuses, and instead offers him safe passage if he leaves now. But Paladin can't leave: "I made a bargain." Hotan Itan declares the bargain off, but Paladin says, "I did not make the bargain with you. I made it with Robert Cielbleu." The impasse unresolvable, Paladin agrees to fight Hotan Itan for his father's life according to Comanche custom. The terms: they will fight with knives, starting at daybreak, and—at Hotan Itan's insistence—to the death.

As Paladin grimly prepares for the fight—changing boots for moccasins, removing his shirt and coating his body with suet to make it harder to grasp—Billy tries to convince him to leave before Hotan Itan kills him. Paladin is willing to consider it, but only if he gets the right answers to two questions: "Is there any chance your son won't kill you?" No, Billy admits. "If you had the chance, would you kill your son?" Again, without hesitating, Billy says no. But now he has questions for Paladin: "Do you think you can kill my son?" Maybe. "Will you?" Heavily, Paladin says, "If I can." In anguish, Billy cries, "*Why*? It ain't for what you been paid. It ain't for me. Now, why?" Paladin explains grimly, "Because Hotan Itan won't give me any choice—and I think he wants to die."

The fight proves Paladin's perception true. The two evenly-matched contestants fight fiercely and wordlessly through the trees and rocks, neither able to gain the upper hand, but Paladin, older by a decade or more, is visibly beginning to tire, looking winded. He makes one last appeal to end the fight, which Hotan Itan rejects contemptuously. In despair, Paladin pleads, "Is there any way I can stop you?" His opponent replies, this time in Robert's cultivated voice, "One way, my friend: kill me!" and launches himself from above, deliberately, onto Paladin's upturned knife blade.

As the young man lies dying in Paladin's arms, his two halves seem—if not reconciled, at least both present and at peace, one man finally, not two. In quick sequence, Robert thanks Paladin for earning his fee, quietly asserts his Comanche heritage, absolves both his parents of guilt for his situation, and delivers his own epitaph, Cervantes' words for Don Quixote: "'For if he lived like a madman, at least he died like a wise one.'" A grieving Paladin buries him under a cairn of rocks, then returns to the cabin where a stone-faced, silent Billy waits. When Paladin says brutally that, with Hotan Itan dead, "Billy Blue Sky is safe from his fellow man," Billy replies numbly, "So long as he stays away from them." Still angry at the solution Robert chose, and at the part he has been forced to play in the tragedy, Paladin has no sympathy for Billy's agony. However, as the gunfighter rides away with a brief stop at Robert's solitary grave, the viewers can spare some pity for the devastated father, sitting bleak and hopeless in his cabin, guilt slumping his shoulders, his eyes full of unshed tears. If Billy has done monstrous things, he has certainly paid a high price for them—almost as high as his son's.

"The Scorched Feather" demonstrates many of the qualities that make so many *Have Gun* episodes superior to anything its competitors had to offer. Without scanting dramatic opportunities for the series protagonist, both of the featured roles are rich and rewarding for the actors, with dialogue that is pungent and precise. The issues are serious, and examined thoughtfully, simple answers and tidy endings rejected in favor of more ambivalent, more honest conclusions. The episode is not without its flaws, especially in the staging of Hotan Itan's death plunge: the editing is clumsy, giving us far too much advance notice of the deadly knife blade waiting for him, and other special effects are too transparent to fool experienced modern viewers. Perhaps the greatest flaw is Hotan Itan's death, the final line. In his stilted English, he says calmly, "Paladin: I die now," and instantly his head rolls to the side. A death so abrupt and timely is almost comic, and undercuts the genuine pathos of the preceding lines. Younger viewers, unused to black and white photography, and not understanding the technological limits of a medium still in its adolescence, typically are unimpressed. But in the context of its time, both in aesthetic and politico-philosophical terms, *Have Gun—Will Travel* was far ahead of its competitors in examining American Indians and what their treatment revealed about the state of the country, in the 1870s, and the 1950s alike.

Mexicans on TV Westerns

Where our four series are concerned, almost all of the stories about Mexican characters are found on *Have Gun—Will Travel*. *Wagon Train* offered only one such tale, "The Bernal Sierra Story" (1:24, 3/12/58), starring Mexican-born actor Gilbert Roland, in a story about a Mexican undercover operative trying to recover stolen gold that was intended to purchase guns for Benito Juarez, the leader of the Mexican Revolution.[37] On *Bonanza*, one early episode included a brief scene with a Mexican ranch hand on the Ponderosa (never seen again), and two other episodes featured Hispanic characters, but these characters are stereotyped and unconvincing. "El Toro Grande" (1:16, 1/2/60) is comic: Little Joe and Hoss go to Monterrey to buy a magnificent bull for the Ponderosa herd from Don Xavier Losaro, but the bull disappears overnight, kidnapped by the small Mexican boy who loves it as a pet. The kindly Cartwrights agree to let the boy come with the bull to the Ponderosa, along with his parents. Then they discover a stowaway on the expedition—Don Xavier's daughter, Cayatena, determined to marry Little Joe. To the show's credit, all of the actors in these lead roles have at least some Hispanic heritage; however, this touch of authenticity cannot compensate for the wooden writing and the cartoon plot. In the second *Bonanza* episode, "The Spanish Grant" (1:21, 2/6/60), a beautiful woman claims to be Isabella de la Cuesta, heir to the ancient family's land grants from Spain, in order to take legal possession of a large section of Nevada, including parts of the Ponderosa. She turns out to be Rosita, a cantina girl from San Francisco, but she is a pawn in the fraud rather than its instigator. After a relationship with Adam awakens her nobler nature, she walks away from the scheme. Rosita/Isabella is played by Patricia Medina, of Spanish/English heritage, but the other prominent Hispanic characters are played by the very non–Hispanic Sebastian Cabot and Celia Lovsky. This story is more serious than "El Toro Grande," but no more genuine a treatment of Hispanic characters or culture, and full of implausibilities, like a Mexican cantina in Virginia City with a guitarist and a male flamenco dancer performing regularly, but not a single Mexican patron in the place.

By contrast, *Have Gun* included significant Mexican characters in twenty episodes over its six seasons. Looking at these episodes collectively, several features stand out. First, a full 40 percent of the roles are played by actors of Hispanic heritage, including some lead roles, though Hispanic actors are more common in the smaller parts. Second, there are two distinct patterns to the stories: nine episodes involve one or two Mexican characters in an American setting, while eleven take place partially or entirely in a Mexican setting, exploring the characters in the context of their own culture, where Paladin is the stranger coping with foreign ways.[38] The Mexican characters in American settings play quite varied roles: a pair of brothers struggling to establish their own ranch, an expert tracker, the young scion of a wealthy sheep

ranching family, a gunfighter trying to lay down his guns, a respected ranch foreman, a dedicated housekeeper, a loyal young shepherd, and (in two different episodes) mischievous
mission boys who cause trouble and solve problems with equal skill.[39] For all these characters,
their ethnicity is not an issue, merely a detail, adding texture and background.

But for stories in Mexican cultural settings, a different dynamic emerges. First, there is
an increased likelihood of stereotyped characters, like the jealous Mexican spitfire, Chita,
in "The Black Sheep" (3:33, 4/30/60, one of the weaker episodes), or the corrupt bandit-
turned-general of the Mexican Army in "The Duke of Texas" (4:31, 4/22/61). Second, most
of these episodes highlight the pervasive class conflict in Mexico between aristocrats and
peasants. Unlike the stories of American Indians, where pity for their suffering is common
but claims for justice totally silenced, in these Mexican episodes, social justice between classes,
between the powerful and the powerless, is a central concern—as it so often is on *Have Gun*
in other contexts.

Generally speaking, Mexican aristocrats and other men of wealth and power come off
badly in these episodes: arrogant, condescending, and selfish, confidently claiming their enti-
tlements without regard for the reasonable claims of others. Some are willfully cruel, some
just blind to the humanity of the "lesser mortals" who make their luxurious lives possible.
A few are frankly criminals, like the ruthless Don Miguel Rojas of "Strange Vendetta" (1:7,
10/26/57), who steals a payroll of $230,000 in San Francisco, then fakes his own death to
manipulate an unsuspecting Paladin not only into escorting the stolen money safely home
to Mexico in his coffin, but also into eliminating Rojas's too-trusting co-conspirators, so the
thief doesn't have to share the loot. Don Francisco Reyes of "The Silver Convoy" (1:37,
5/31/58) is another brutal, arrogant aristocrat who routinely breaks the law for his own
financial benefit. Hiring convict labor to work his Sonoran silver mine, he not only abuses
the men with long hours, poor food, and intolerable working conditions, but holds them
long past the end of their sentences, or arranges fatal "accidents" for those who protest, to
prevent them from collecting the pay they have earned. Then there's the cold-blooded young
Don Alejandro of "A Knight to Remember" (5:13, 12/9/61). Infuriated by his sweetly-
demented elderly father who thinks himself Don Quixote, Alejandro hires Paladin to bring
the old man home. But since this mad "Don Quixote" will attack any stranger, Alejandro
hopes Paladin will be forced to kill the old man in self-defense, thus clearing the way for the
son to claim his inheritance.[40] On a slightly lower social level, and with better cause, another
powerful Mexican, this one in America, takes the law into his own hands. In "Saturday
Night" (4:5, 10/8/60), Francisco Begara, the patriarch of a wealthy sheep ranching family,
instead of turning to the law when his son is killed, ruthlessly looses his ferocious dogs on
his son's murderer—the corrupt local marshal.

Other aristocrats are not so much ruthless or criminal as set in the old traditions they
have always lived by, unable to see peasants as human beings rather than slaves, like Don
Luis Ortega of "Pancho" (3:6, 10/24/59). Confronting a rebellion of his peons led by the
charismatic young Doroteo (known to history as Pancho Villa),[41] Don Luis is outraged, but
also frightened and disoriented. Believing that people are born to their proper sphere, peon
and aristocrat alike, for Don Luis their rebellion challenges not just the law of the land, but
the law of nature. Though his belief in his entitlement is abhorrent, Don Luis is humanized
by his struggle to make sense of this rebellion, and especially by fear for his pretty 15-year-
old daughter. Having learned her father's attitudes toward peasants, Soledad has no com-
punction about flirting with young Doroteo as a game for her own amusement. But Doroteo
pays a high price for her smiles: Don Luis punishes him brutally for daring to look at the

patrón's daughter, first with a flogging, and when that does not dissuade the young peasant, by having him buried alive in an anthill—a slow painful death that Paladin prevents.

However, Soledad also pays a price for her action: she is kidnapped by the passionate young guerrilla leader. Mistaking her flirtation for genuine affection, Doroteo intends to marry her before he executes her father—neither of which intention she had understood until Paladin explained them. Soledad is largely a comic figure, naive rather than vicious, her failings the result of youth and ignorance and being raised in a sick social system she does not yet bear personal responsibility for. But the time is coming soon when she will no longer be able to use youth and ignorance as an excuse. By the end of the episode, with Paladin's help, she has begun to see Doroteo as a real human being, not just a pet she is entitled to play with, thus offering a little hope for the future.

By contrast to these aristocrats, the peasant Doroteo (played by a 22-year-old Hispanic actor, Rafael Campos) is an appealing figure: warm, generous, brave, idealistic, and no more violent than he needs to be. If he is as naive as Soledad herself where love is concerned, as a revolutionary he is hard-headed and practical, a gifted tactician, and committed to improving the lot of all Don Luis's peasants, not just gaining wealth and power for himself. The moral is unmistakable: in discipline, drive, and intelligence, Doroteo is far superior to Don Luis, with all his inherited privilege and power, and deserves the victories we know Pancho Villa will achieve.

Another episode examines the conflict between aristocrats and peasants in revolutionary Mexico even more thoughtfully. Unlike previous episodes, where the aristocrats are unredeemable and the peasants brave and noble, both parties in "The Exiles" (5:20, 1/27/62) are fundamentally decent, but view each other with deep suspicion, not to say contempt and hatred. However, by the end—with Paladin's help—these people achieve a mutual respect and find common cause in the welfare of the country they all love. Peasant-born Largo Ortega, provisional general of the Revolutionary Army and Minister of External Finance for the Republic of Mexico, is hunting Count Casares, former treasurer to the executed Emperor Maximilian. When the imperial government was defeated, the Count and Countess fled to California with the royal treasury, not to spend on themselves but to preserve for the day when the old regime is restored. But, as Gen. Ortega explains to Paladin, that day will never come, and meanwhile, Mexico is suffering a terrible famine: the money is needed to feed the poor. Assured that the $18 million will indeed go to the poor and not into the pockets of corrupt generals, Paladin agrees to help recover the money.

Ortega is a plain-spoken honest man, unpretentious and engaging. As Paladin learns the general's story, he finds much to admire. A peon of Indian heritage, Ortega found that the Revolution gave him opportunities to redress some of the injustices he had suffered in his pre-war condition of near-slavery. But he also learned to admire some of his enemies— like his own *patrón*, who died so bravely that Ortega determined to study the books in the *patrón*'s library to find the source of that courage, study which earned him a promotion to colonel. Open-minded enough to learn from the despised aristocrats, Ortega also proves honest enough to punish malfeasance among his own: when he found a general stealing money from aristocrats to line his own pockets, Col. Ortega personally executed the man and took his place as general. In short, Ortega is that rarest of creatures, a high public official possessing both scrupulous integrity and a commitment to impartial justice.

The Count and Countess are no less unlike their stereotype. Paladin discovers the former aristocrats cheerfully running an open-air traveling kitchen and dreaming of adding kitchens in other locations. The food, tasty and beautifully seasoned, has been prepared by the Count himself, a master chef at heart, while the Countess collects the money from their rough American clients. So these aristocrats are not afraid to work with their own hands, or to live on what they can earn by their own efforts. The treasury has been honorably held in trust for the Empress Carlotta, whom they view as the legitimate government of Mexico. When Paladin explains his mission, they are terrified, certain that Ortega, "the Butcher of San Pietro," is there to kill them, but at Paladin's promise to protect them, they agree to hear what the general has to say.

However, the interview does not go well. These three people, each so admirable, so selflessly loyal to their own cause, cannot see past their prejudices and resentments of each other's class. In Ortega, the aristocrats see only a bloodthirsty peasant contemptuous of tradition and beauty, while in the Cesares, the general sees only the arrogance of privilege and the sensual priorities of an elite who use precious land to plant vineyards for wine rather than grow corn that would feed the starving masses. They reach a deadly impasse, Ortega convinced the only way to reclaim the treasury is to kill its guardians, the Cesares bravely determined to die rather than betray their trust.

In Paladin's objective judgment, there is a fair solution: Ortega deserves the treasury funds, while the aristocrats deserve to live. But neither side will yield; so, despite his admiration for Ortega, Paladin grimly prepares to use his gun against the general in order to protect the Cesareses. At the last moment, the horrified aristocrats, recognizing that one of these two good men is going to die over the money they have hidden, finally capitulate. As the former Count and Countess hand over the funds to the general of the Revolution, an impressed Ortega salutes them respectfully: "We are not of the same government, but we are of the same people, and that will always be." They return his salute and his respect, giving up their old life and committing to the new: their traveling kitchens. Thanks to Paladin's mediation, both parties come out of this conflict with honor and with a new appreciation for their former enemy, breaking down old attitudes, and offering hope for the future of the country they all love.

Mexican Bandits

The bandit is another common Mexican stereotype, but those found on *Have Gun* are far less likely to be simple stereotyped villains. As we saw in "Pancho," Doroteo/Pancho Villa is a bandit with a cause, a guerrilla warrior who steals from the wealthy and destroys their property not to enrich himself but to undermine an unjust social system. Sancho Fernandez in "The Statue of San Sebastian" (1:39, 6/14/58) is another bandit with a cause, though a much more personal one, and one specific victim—Ian Crown, the wealthy Anglo rancher whom Sancho blames, with legitimate cause, for his brother's death. Sancho harasses Crown mercilessly, stealing his payrolls and inflicting other depredations that hit his one vulnerable spot—his bank book. Crown is a grasping arrogant bully who has earned his troubles, but this mutual vendetta, pursued with equal determination by both men, is making life difficult for the entire community, and since neither will negotiate or yield, Paladin uses his strategic gifts to find a solution—one that actually favors Sancho while making Crown believe he has won. Convincingly faking the bandit's death, Paladin gets him safely away, while charging Crown a steep fee for the death he so desired: he must return the beloved statue of San Sebastian to the local mission, its rightful owner. Far from a stereotyped bandit—or a typical resolution to a bandit story.

However, a couple of other bandits are more problematic, more textured characters. Solomon in "The Revenger" (5:3, 9/30/61), despite his lack of education, reveals a philosophical bent that Paladin comes to admire during their negotiations to solve a standoff. In fact, these two men who live by the gun find a real connection based on their shared "bad dreams," their mutual recognition that, when violence is the solution, only the buzzards win. Solomon is something more than a bandit; he is also a dispenser of justice, the only source of justice available for poor peons like Miguel. A month before, an Anglo man had come to Miguel's village in Mexico and killed Miguel's wife in a drunken attack. When Miguel observes that same man among the passengers of the stagecoach Paladin is traveling in, he appeals to Solomon for the justice no legal authority would give a peasant, so the bandit and his men stop the coach to punish the murderer. Unfortunately, before Miguel can point out the criminal among the five men on the stage, he is killed by one of them, a trigger-happy sheriff whom Solomon quickly shoots in retaliation. So far, Paladin has supported Solomon's decisions, even admitting that the sheriff deserved what he got. But then the bandit chief makes a choice Paladin cannot accept. Only the dead Miguel knew the identity of the criminal, but even with no way to determine the guilty party, Solomon still insists that one of these men must pay for the crime to give Miguel the justice he promised. The bandit cheerfully orders Paladin, whom he trusts, to select one of the passengers to be shot, giving his word that the rest will go free.

But killing a random scapegoat isn't justice in Paladin's eyes, even though none of the other passengers is truly innocent—a convicted killer headed to his execution, an alcoholic former Army officer forced to resign his commission for killing his wife's lover in a duel, and a traveling salesman who has stolen $90,000 in bearer bonds from his company. Nor does Paladin claim to be innocent himself. Even the one woman passenger, the major's adulterous wife, though obviously not a suspect in this crime, cannot be called innocent. Yet no man confesses to the murder, all have plausible alibis, and no one will volunteer to be the sacrifice, despite having nothing much left to lose. Finally, Paladin himself goes out to face Solomon. The bandit is distressed at the idea of killing a man he admires, but this is the only choice Paladin can make: "You forced me to choose, and I have to choose the one man over whom I *do* have the power of life and death." Solomon doesn't like it, but doesn't want to break his promise to Miguel. But when Solomon apologizes for this unfortunate dilemma, Paladin refuses to accept it, refuses to validate Solomon's judgment, insisting grimly, "One of us will die, and justice will *not* be served."

In the end, it is Solomon who falls in the road, mortally wounded, but he keeps his promise, ordering his men not to shoot any of the passengers, especially Paladin. A complicated man, Solomon, trying hard to obtain justice for the weak and abused against the powerful of this world—the wealthy, the racially and culturally privileged, those who can get away with murder when the victim is as insignificant as the wife of a Mexican peasant. If Solomon the bandit fails to achieve the wisdom of his namesake, still, his intent was noble, and Paladin sincerely laments the loss of this brother under the skin, with his honor, his humor, and his clear-eyed recognition of the world as a dark place where the buzzards are the only winners. It is another of the somber endings found so much more often on this series than its competitors, refusing us comfortable, tidy conclusions.

In "Heritage of Anger" (2:37, 6/6/59), Paladin once again finds himself dealing with two stubborn men unwilling to compromise; this time, one of them is a Mexican bandit. Manuel Garcia and wealthy San Diego merchant Charles Avery each claim the twelve-year-old boy one calls José and the other Joe. The boy is Garcia's godson, son of his best friend;

but eight years earlier, when Garcia's friend died, his poverty-stricken young widow gave her 4-year-old son to the childless Averys (her employers) to raise as their own, while she went back to Mexico with her infant daughter. Now Garcia is threatening to kill the merchant unless José is returned, but Avery refuses to give up the boy he loves as his son. That death threat brings Paladin into the case.

Meeting Joe, Paladin finds a well-mannered, thoughtful, intelligent boy, in all aspects of behavior and language an Anglo, but with facial features, skin tones, and a very faint accent that reveal his Mexican heritage. Before Joe came into his life, Avery admits, he used to judge people by such superficial features, so he was initially reluctant to adopt a Mexican child. But now, he tells Paladin, he doesn't care whether Joe "came from Mexico or the moon; he's my son." Despite this new enlightened attitude, he still judges Garcia in stereotyped terms, dismissing him as "a dirty bandit lining his own pockets." But Paladin mildly corrects him: Garcia, "the Robin Hood of San Ysidro," is a legend among his own people for charity and generosity. He preys on Californians not out of greed but out of hatred, born when a couple of drunken prospectors killed his wife and son. Despite Garcia's ominous reputation with Anglos, Paladin rides to Mexico, hoping to negotiate a peaceful settlement with him on behalf of all three Averys.

From Garcia, however, Paladin learns the other side of the story, why the bandit has come for his godson after all these years. Contrary to what the Averys had told Joe, his natural mother is not dead, and with the little hill farm Garcia has given her, Nita is now able to provide for her son herself, so she wants him back. Though Joe is happy with the Averys, that happiness is based on a lie, and Paladin agrees the boy should know the truth. Further, if Joe is to choose between not just two different parents but two different worlds, two lives, he has a right to see the second one for himself. So Paladin offers to bring José to meet his mother, as long as Nita promises she will allow the boy to leave if he chooses. She agrees joyfully, confident her son will want to stay with her, and Garcia seconds the promise without hesitation.

Reluctantly admitting the justice of this plan, the Averys give their permission, and Paladin escorts Joe to meet his natural mother and his younger sister—carefully arranging the initial encounter to occur without Garcia's complicating presence. But the meeting is awkward: Joe speaks no Spanish, and has no desire to live on a small hill farm in Mexico, where the only education available is at a primitive mission school. He wants to be an engineer, he tells Nita thoughtfully, and has to explain, "A man who builds bridges." At last she accepts, sorrowfully, that her son will go back to the Averys, though he promises he will see her again. But Garcia has other ideas. Despite his promise, despite Nita's decision and the boy's own wishes, the bandit violently blocks Paladin and Joe on the road, shouting, "One of my people will not be raised by those who spit on me!" But Avery is no longer a man who spits on Mexicans (however he feels about bandits); Garcia is the prejudiced one, consumed by unreasoning anger against an entire race, blind to every other consideration. He leaves Paladin no choice: in order to take Joe back to the home he has chosen, the gunfighter must kill the bandit.

When Paladin arrives at the Averys with Joe and Nita, the two mothers gingerly reach for a new relationship, with Joe in the middle. As Nita acknowledges her failure, that her son has chosen his white parents over her, Mrs. Avery, with breathtaking courage, invites Nita to live with them—an offer Nita gently refuses. Not only can she not leave her daughter or her farm, but she doesn't want her son to think of her as a servant, an inevitable result of such an arrangement despite Mrs. Avery's best intentions. But Nita does plan to be part of

Joe's life from now on, visiting him in San Diego and having him visit her at the farm in Baja: "I want him to know me. He may come to have some affection for me. *Quien sabe?*"— an arrangement Mrs. Avery quietly affirms as her right. However, after Nita leaves, Mr. Avery expresses some anxiety: he had wanted everything settled once and for all, a tidy ending with Joe entirely theirs. Paladin points out, "There's no end to this, no cut-and-dried solution. That boy will grow up with a double heritage—one he'll get from you, and the other from Nita. Between the two of you, you could destroy him." (Like the tormented Robert Cielbleu in "The Scorched Feather.") "Or," Paladin suggests, thoughtfully, "you could turn him into an exceptional human being. I wonder what you'll do?" His departure leaves that question hanging, but the omens for this unusual family are good.

"Heritage of Anger" is a remarkable drama for television in 1959. Although many Americans at the time openly considered Mexicans inferior, this story presents the two cultures as equally deserving of respect. All the characters, Mexican and Anglo alike, are complex human beings with both strengths and weaknesses. Garcia is generous to his own people and justified in his hatred of Anglos, but his anger and prejudice are so extreme that they blind his judgment, and make him a tyrant to those who disagree with him, even those he loves. Avery, once no less prejudiced than Garcia, in coming to accept and love Joe, has grown: he now judges people as individuals instead of stereotypes. Even more strikingly, the two mothers are impressive moral figures. Nita perhaps made a mistake in giving up her son, and might be considered to have made a greater one in trying to reclaim him after so many years. But when she realizes Joe would never be happy on a farm, she sacrifices her own desires in favor of his, no matter the pain it causes her. She also chooses not to walk away entirely, but to remain a genuine presence in his life, even if that means living with the kind of emotional indeterminacy Avery fears. Mrs. Avery, in her turn, should not have lied to Joe about his natural mother's death, but she makes up for it by permitting him to go meet Nita alone, despite the risk that he might prefer that other mother to her. Like Nita, she places Joe's rights and desires above her own, even generously offering to share her son with Nita rather than forcing him to choose between them. Finally Joe himself, with a foot in each culture, is astoundingly mature and responsible for his age, treating all three of his parents with honesty and compassion. He is a young man who knows what he wants for himself, and is willing to maintain the ambiguity of his status rather than make an irrevocable decision prematurely. Given the nature of this episode, it is particularly significant and fitting that this young character be played by a Hispanic actor, Ricky Vera.[42]

At a time when Mexicans in America were distinctly regarded as second-class citizens, the overall impact of these episodes—the number of them, the respect with which the culture is generally treated, the fact that Mexican characters are so often allowed a wide range of human qualities, far beyond simple stereotypes—is a testament to the values *Have Gun—Will Travel* consistently promulgated to its mass-media audience.

Blacks on TV Westerns

If Mexicans were second-class citizens in the mid–1950s, blacks were almost invisible, kept separate in their own communities, and entering the white world only in the most menial and subordinate roles. Serving their white employers, blacks were required to hide behind a humble ingratiating manner, careful not to make eye contact with white people, or to claim any human dignity or pride. In drama, the same rules applied. On television, movies, and advertising in this period, blacks were seldom found even among the crowds in urban street scenes, let alone as significant individuals. Situation comedies showed them in the same menial roles they played in real life, as housekeepers, janitors, nannies, chauffeurs, but black actors were seldom found in serious drama (and never in the professional positions they held in their own communities, doctors and dentists, ministers, teachers, lawyers, business owners, and so on). As J. Fred MacDonald points out in *Blacks and White TV*, by the 1960s, black actors began appearing occasionally on detective shows, but mostly as "local color" characters or in supporting roles in individual episodes. The first dramatic series with continuing black characters did not appear till 1965, the year Bill Cosby started his groundbreaking role as the co-star of *I Spy* and Raymond St. Jacques joined *Rawhide* in its last season as the first black cowboy on television.

As for the earlier Westerns, Macdonald observes, "Although blacks played a crucial part in the history of the actual West, only rarely did they appear in the television West created in Hollywood," and lists Sammy Davis, Jr.'s featured appearances on episodes of *Zane Grey Theater* (1959), *Lawman* (1961), *The Rifleman* (1962), and *Frontier Circus* (1962), Rex Ingram's one guest role on *Black Saddle* (1959), and Frank Silvera's on *Johnny Ringo* (1960) as his sole examples.[43] Understandably, Macdonald misses the minor roles played by black actors on *Gunsmoke* and *Wagon Train*, one first-season episode each. *Gunsmoke*'s "Professor Lute Bone" (1:14, 1/7/56) cast Jester Hairston as assistant to the quack medicine man of the title, a role with virtually no lines, the actor relegated to the background playing his fiddle—seriously underutilizing this distinguished composer, songwriter, arranger, choral director, and actor, a graduate of Tufts College and the Juilliard School of Music. After Hairston's bit part, it would be over thirteen years before another black actor appeared on *Gunsmoke*: "The Good Samaritans" (3/10/69), in which an ambushed Matt is helped by a band of former slaves traveling West to a new home, with Brock Peters as their leader.

Similarly, *Wagon Train*'s "Charles Maury Story" (1:32, 5/7/58) cast the then-prominent but now-unknown black actress, Suzette Harbin, as the maid of a dispossessed young Southern belle traveling West with an older female relative. Harbin even speaks a few lines in the episode, and her strikingly beautiful face is visible in several scenes, but her character (inevitably a former slave, though the word remains discreetly unspoken) adds little to the action.[44] On *Bonanza*, the first black actors do not appear till April 1964, in "Enter Thomas Bowers," an episode based on the historical figure of a black opera singer in the early 1860s who was suspected of being a runaway slave. Even in 1964, that episode seriously disturbed the show's sponsor, General Motors. Fearing a boycott of their car dealers by outraged Southern viewers, the company threatened to withdraw its sponsorship if the episode aired. Substantial negative publicity about this decision, coupled with resistance from NBC and the NAACP, and capped by the promised resignation of all four stars, caused GM to reverse its decision. Despite all this very public controversy, the episode ultimately aired without incident.[45]

But MacDonald seems curiously unaware that, as we saw in Chapter Four, *Have Gun—Will Travel* dramatically outpaced its competitors in featuring black actors. Between October 1960 and December 1962, six *Have Gun* episodes showcased seven black actors, mostly in featured roles. One of the characters is explicitly black—former slave Isham Spruce in "The Long Way Home" (4:21, 2/4/61); two others, minor roles played by Jester Hairston, are implicitly so.[46] However, the four characters in the remaining three episodes are not racially specific, which makes the casting of black actors even more unprecedented. Realistically for the 1870s, all the characters played by black actors belong to a lower economic class; but the more prominent roles have complex, well-developed personalities, and all, minor and featured characters alike, are treated with the respect due a human being, irrespective of race. In all these episodes, whether the character is black or only the actor playing him/her, audiences watched black people interacting with whites without any of the ingratiating subservience mandated by the racist customs of the period. These black men and women stand erect, heads up, and look Paladin in the eye.

Jester Hairston's two episodes, both in minor roles, occur late in the series. Though neither character's race is made explicit, certain suggestive details add up to a probability. In "The Waiting Room" (5:24, 2/24/62), Hairston plays a poor old man named Moses (a typical slave-style name) waiting for a train. Paladin, escorting a sociopathic killer to his execution, has chained his prisoner's hands. Noticing the old man's troubled glances in his direction, Paladin confronts Moses sharply: "Old man—[do] I bother you? Why?" Moses quietly replies, "Well, meaning no disrespect, sir, but only a devil would keep another man in chains." From a black man, this dignified statement suggests a personal experience of chains, like that of a slave (though explicit mention of the issue would have been too indelicate for 1950s television). More remarkably, Moses's response, however politely spoken, violates all the rules: a black man—poor, old, and weak—keeps his seat before a powerful, angry white man, looks that man in the eye, and dares to criticize him like an equal. Though this exchange is only a minor digression in a larger story, in 1962 it represented a small revolution to anyone paying attention.

In "Penelope" (6:13, 12/8/62), Hairston plays a more substantial role as Col. Lacey's manservant, Euclid, a dignified elderly black man who offers Paladin's own card to him as introduction, and asks the gunfighter for a favor—not for himself, but for his employer. Having spent the last year in Mexico seeking treasures for his wife, Col. Lacey is planning to ride home tonight to surprise her. Euclid insists the colonel is a good man, but if Penelope is not forewarned of his arrival, there will be bloodshed. "Understand?" Euclid asks quietly, and Paladin nods: there's a man involved.

Given Euclid's name and his long loyal association with a Southern courtesy-title colonel, he is likely a former slave, though (as in "The Waiting Room") the point is never raised explicitly. However, he shows none of the servility that custom demands of black men: he carries himself with great dignity, very erect; he speaks proper English, though with a definite Southern accent, and announces his ability to read with no more than appropriate pride. Though respectful to Paladin, saying "sir," he is far from obsequious, and he meets Paladin's eyes frankly. Nor is he afraid to assert himself with this white man. When Paladin asks why Euclid doesn't deliver the warning himself, he instantly replies, "I'm an old man, and what life I have left is precious." Paladin gets it: the servant has too much good sense to be caught interfering between his master and mistress. Then, his business concluded, Euclid walks away—not rudely, but without waiting to be dismissed, nor hesitating to turn his back on a white man. But when Paladin calls after him to inquire how Euclid got his card, the old man grins engagingly: "From the Chinese gentleman, sir. He's *most* understanding!" And it reveals Euclid as smart enough to know that his best source of advice is another servant, another invisible man.

This short scene contains all of Euclid's lines. Twice more in the episode we see his face, though—once waiting anxiously for Paladin's arrival and watching him ride up to the ranch, and again at the end, when Paladin leaves the house with peace restored between the colonel and his faithful, long-suffering Penelope. As Euclid waits patiently outside the door, Paladin nods once to him, a wordless sign—"all's well that ends well"—and the old servant smiles radiantly, nearly the last image in the episode. Though he remains invisible, officially subordinate, he can feel proud: through his efforts, his foolish master has been preserved.

"Odds for Big Red" (6:4, 10/7/61) casts a black actress in a legitimately race-neutral role. In this *Have Gun* episode, singer/stage actress Virginia Capers makes her television debut as Ada, dance hall girl and best friend of the episode's heroine, Big Red.[47] The episode is unredeemably weak: the script is incoherent, sentimental, and full of logical gaps, while the directing is leaden-paced, but Capers stands out in her small role. An imposing figure, Ada fiercely defies Paladin in order to protect Big Red, who was dangerously wounded by a stray bullet (not Paladin's) when he was forced to shoot his quarry in Big Red's saloon. Though Ada has only a handful of lines, her expressive face is often on screen in reaction shots; even in the absence of dialogue for her, she is a significant presence in the scenes. Finally, though the actress is unmistakably black, nothing indicates that the character is— a clear example of color-blind casting, long before the term was invented.

These three are all minor, if vivid, characters, but the other three episodes offer black actors substantial roles. The earliest, "The Killing of Jessie May" (4:8, 10/29/60), features Hari Rhodes in a strong supporting role.[48] As Paladin hunts Jessie May Turnbow, a young killer who has murdered eleven people to avenge his father's death, he encounters a pair of companions—George Jondill, a gregarious middle-aged white man, and Ansel James, a quiet, powerfully-built black man in his early 30s. Nothing about James' character marks him as explicitly black. His speech is relatively uneducated but contains no trace of black dialect, while his manner with Paladin is direct, neither confrontational nor ingratiating: man to man, equal to equal. As Paladin shares a convivial meal with his hosts, we realize the white man and the black are not quite equals: Jondill calls his companion by his first name, while Ansel says "Mr. Jondill." This difference might signal nothing more than the respect of a younger man for an older, or it could reflect the traditional racial hierarchies in which a white person of any age and position is superior to any black person.[49] But clearly the hierarchical imbalance does not diminish the deep affection and trust these two men share.

Only one incident even hints that the character might be black like the actor. When Jessie May arrives at the camp after dinner, clearly a close friend of the other men, Paladin forces a resentful Ansel to place chains on the prisoner's wrists, as he cautiously keeps his gun on them. When the gunfighter takes Jessie May outside to remove him from his friends, Ansel tells Jondill in cold fury, "I hate chains on a man. I hate chains worse than death." As spoken by Hari Rhodes, the line resonates powerfully. In 1876, a black man of Ansel's age would almost inevitably have been a slave, with painful personal experience of chains. On the other hand, slaves were not the only people who wore chains: a man of any race who had been in prison in this period might have similar responses. Whatever Ansel's story, former slave or former convict, his repugnance for captivity is profound.

As Ansel and Paladin confront each other in scene after scene, these two characters stand toe to toe, creating an impressive image of a black man for television in 1960. When Paladin first arrests Jessie May, Ansel confronts him sharply, testing his character: "You gonna take him back for trial, mister? I mean, *really* take him back for trial?" Paladin affirms, "I am": he won't just shoot his prisoner to collect the bounty the easy way. But Ansel pushes, not satisfied: "A *fair* trial?" Disturbed, Paladin admits, "I won't say that. I can't guarantee it." After a moment, the gunfighter confesses bitterly, "I don't believe it!" Jessie May's crime is so sensational, community feeling has risen so high against him, that nobody can promise the trial will be fair as it should be. It isn't right, and he's clearly disturbed by it, but Paladin can't fix the system. He can only do his own job as honestly and humanely as possible. But significantly, he respects Ansel enough not to lie to him, or make promises he can't keep.

Though circumstances have put them on opposite sides of this situation, the two men consistently treat each other honorably. When Ansel uses subterfuge to disarm Paladin and free Jessie May, he manages the job in a competent professional manner, without anger or haste, saving the friend he and Jondill believe in without killing or even insulting his captor. Later still, once he and Jondill realize that Paladin chose to let Jessie May escape rather than turning his gun on them, as he easily could have with his hidden derringer, Ansel admits, shamefaced, that he might have misjudged the gunfighter. So it is appropriate that, when Jessie May turns his lethal homemade machine gun on his friends' camp, killing Jondill and nearly killing Ansel and Paladin, it is Ansel who finally takes out the charming young sociopath. Having allowed Jessie May to escape, thus causing Jondill's death, Ansel accepts the guilt and the responsibility, and acts to resolve the situation himself instead of leaving it to the bounty hunter. It is a dark ending, redeemed only by the comforting hand on the shoulder Paladin offers the grieving Ansel, and the equality and respect shared between these two survivors. In no sense is Ansel less of a man than Paladin. If anything, he had the harder task—killing a friend.

The following season, "The Hanging of Aaron Gibbs" (5:8, 11/4/61) featured not one but two remarkable black performers in the same episode. The great folk singer, Odetta, "the Voice of the Civil Rights Movement" and a powerful influence on most of the major American folk singers of the 1960s, starred as Sarah Gibbs, who journeys sorrowfully to bring home her husband's body after his hanging.[50] Aaron, played with stark dignity by Rupert Crosse, is condemned along with his two white partners for stealing the mine payroll, a crime exacerbated when the small explosion the thieves set to cover their escape accidentally collapsed a tunnel, killing fourteen miners. When Paladin encounters Sarah on the trail, helplessly comforting her dying mule, he hitches his horse to her wagon and drives her to Dunbar to complete her tragic mission. As played by Odetta, Sarah is remarkable: neither educated nor young, not shapely or pretty, she is nonetheless a woman of great character, accepting her misfortunes stoically, without protest or despair. Under devastating burdens, she preserves a gentle grace of spirit and a capacity for sympathy that earns Paladin's admiration along with his help. With genuine sensitivity, he even accepts the fee she offers: a $10 gold piece, her only wealth in the world. While $10 means nothing to him, his taking the money shows his true courtesy: instead of shaming her by offering charity, he allows her to feel she has paid her way.

As with Ansel James, nothing specifies that this couple is black; they are poor and rural and down on their luck, but after the Civil War, such terms described many Southern whites as well as blacks. The only element in Sarah's character hinting at racial identity is her diffidence: she speaks to no one but Paladin and her husband, and around authority figures, she keeps her eyes downcast. But a poor uneducated woman of any race in such overwhelming circumstances might well react similarly.

In the town's hysterical atmosphere just before the execution, Sarah and Aaron stand out in their dignity and restraint. Aaron quietly accepts his guilt and his fate while expressing remorse for the deaths of the miners, which had been unintentional. In their last two minutes on earth together, husband and wife clasp hands, share one last gentle kiss, and exchange a few simple phrases conveying a lifetime of love without ever uttering the word. He gives her a keepsake, a little figure of feathers and wood he's been making, and, like a thoughtful husband, takes care for her future: "You say about this to Mr. Peters, and he'll see to it that you get work in the sorting shed." And then it's time for the long walk to the gallows. They lock eyes for one last heartfelt exchange, then Aaron turns and heads steadily toward the gallows, reciting the twenty-third psalm aloud, his dignity and self-control a striking contrast to the hysterical terror of his younger white partners. At the last minute, he looks back at his wife, appealing: "Put me in the earth next to my boy, Sarah?" She nods acknowledgment, then gently speaks Aaron's epitaph to a sympathetic Paladin, summing up her husband's hard life of trials and suffering, of work and love and loss, yet with his spirit still reaching out for beauty:

> Man runs from trouble, only finds trouble waiting around the corner. It's hard for a man to go to field-working after he's known better. Used to drag home at nights with his hands cracked open to the blood. But when the boy come sick, he'd pick him up in his arms just as gentle as any woman could. He loved the boy, just like a man loves to poke his head up and smell the sun.

As her face fills the screen, a man shouts, a whip cracks, we hear some sickening thuds, and it is over. Sarah covers her head with her shawl and says, "I think I'm going to be burying him where he asked to be." Especially in an episode that is occasionally overwrought and melodramatic, Sarah and Aaron's scenes stand out for their quiet power and genuine emotion—both evidence of the actors' skill, and a remarkable opportunity for black people to transcend the usual demeaning stereotypes.[51]

Finally, in "The Long Way Home" (4:21, 2/4/61), Ivan Dixon stars as Isham Spruce, an ex-slave wanted for murder with a $5,000 bounty on his head—the first time a black actor was featured on TV as a psychologically realistic villain.[52] Chapter Six analyzed Spruce as an outlaw, but here we'll consider him as a black man. Like other characters with no formal education, Sam speaks a non-standard form of English: he says "ain't" and "I seen it" and "them Yankees" and "I ain't got no food." But Sam's speech contains one feature that is found nowhere else in the series. Soon after capturing his prisoner, Paladin realizes, "You haven't been free very long, have you?" Sam looks at him sardonically:

> Free? Now, *what you mean* by that? Oh, yeah. One day a government man come around with a big book and say, "Sam, this is your Day of Jubilo, *you free now*—free as I am. And no more hard times now. *You free* as a toad frog." And if you ain't got no food to eat, *you free* to go without. (Emphasis added.)

Where Standard English would read, "What do you mean?" "You are free now," Sam omits the copula, the linking or helping verb: "What _ you mean?" "You _ free." Though all of Sam's other grammatical errors are common with uneducated speakers of any race, this pattern of the "missing copula" was unique to black speakers of English. The languages the slaves brought with them from West Africa have no copula. Denied formal study of English, the slaves created their own dialect by inserting English words and phrases into the grammatical structures of their native languages. A similar problem explains the confusion among many less-educated black speakers about when to use a final -s on verbs: in this passage, Sam says *come* and *say* where correct grammar would require *comes* and *says*.[53] Even in Sam's dialogue, these features are not emphasized or used consistently, but not one other *Have Gun* character played by a black actor speaks this way, making Isham Spruce the most explicitly black of all.[54]

In other ways, too, Isham's options and experiences are explicitly defined by his race and his history as a slave in a way that is either totally absent or only hinted at for the other six characters. After the war, he left the south because all he knew how to do was farm, and there was no land for ex-slaves. He found a good job in a Western lumber camp, but trouble came again: one man in the camp, Sam explains to Paladin, "just couldn't leave me alone." He doesn't specify, but it must have been his race that the other man objected to. When Isham finally couldn't take the abuse any longer, he fought back, but when his tormentor died, Sam found himself a wanted man. Clearly, he had never considered appealing to the law: whatever the circumstances of the fight, a black man was not likely to get a fair trial.

But Isham Spruce is like no other black character seen on television at the time. Knowing he is a victim of injustice rather than morally guilty of a crime, he refuses to accept his defeat but strenuously fights to get free. Paladin has to beat Spruce down three times in order to subdue him enough to tie his hands. But Isham fights not just with all his considerable physical strength, but with every other weapon he has: courage, determination, and a shrewd ability to read character. When Paladin offers to find a lawyer to defend him at his trial, Spruce just laughs, grimly amused at the idea that any justice waits for him, and then, recognizing his captor's vulnerable point—his ideal of fair play—turns it against him: "Oh, no. You ain't going to buy off your conscience as easily as that." Later, Paladin suggests untying his prisoner's hands for the night so he can sleep more comfortably, in exchange for Spruce's promise not to escape, but Isham is defiant: the only promise he will make is that "you ain't taking me back alive—not if I can help it." As a disappointed Paladin prepares for a long watchful night, the prisoner surreptitiously picks up a sharp rock and begins to saw stealthily at the ropes behind his back.

On the other hand, Isham eventually notices that his captor is different from the men he is used to. Instead of abusing him physically and verbally, Paladin treats him with consideration and speaks to him like a rational human being, not an animal—to such a degree that Isham decides to risk trusting the gunfighter. In order to send some much-needed financial support back home to his wife and daughter, the illiterate ex-slave needs Paladin's help, first to write the letter he dictates to accompany the small bundle of money, and then to mail it after Isham's fate is settled—help that the gunfighter willingly provides. And if Paladin refuses to let Spruce go free, he also refuses to surrender him to the team of four bounty hunters likewise on Spruce's trail. Isham is astonished when Paladin not only passes up an easy $1,000, but is willing to fight at four-to-one odds rather than hand his prisoner over to be murdered. Isham doesn't admit as much out loud, but he adds it to Paladin's account.

None of this makes him any less determined to escape, but it does affect his behavior when the crisis arrives—and, with terrible irony, settles his fate. Paladin is face down in a river, drinking, when Isham's bonds finally sever. He jumps from his horse to attack Paladin just as the gunfighter turns with his gun at the ready, but they are interrupted by an ominous rattle. Isham shouts a warning, but too late: the snake launches from the brush and punches its fangs deep into Paladin's right forearm. Though he quickly kills the rattler, the bite is a bad one; already he is reeling from shock and the effects of the venom. Though Isham tosses him a scarf for a tourniquet, he is rushing for his horse when Paladin calls after him. He needs help, yes, but he also wants to give Isham back the letter and the money for his wife, in case he doesn't get the chance to mail it. Picking it up cautiously, Isham asks, "How do I know you wrote what I said?" Speaking with difficulty, Paladin says, "You don't. You don't know unless you get somebody to read it for you, somebody you can trust." But, he adds sadly, "You don't trust anybody, do you?" As Isham rides away, Paladin at last fixes the tourniquet around his arm, using the barrel of his gun to tighten it, and waits for help, despairing.

But against all odds, help does come: the sheriff and his posse. Instead of riding away as fast as he could, Isham lingered long enough to find a boy on a nearby ranch who delivered the message about Paladin's plight. Hearing the story, Paladin smiles with a dual relief, for himself and for his former prisoner: "Well, I can't really say I'm sorry that Isham Spruce got away." But Isham didn't get away; the sheriff wordlessly indicates the tarp-covered body hanging over the saddle as his deputy boasts, "We didn't have no trouble at all tracking him. Seems like he didn't have no more sense than an old hound dog. Instead of heading out right straight for them hills over there, he just kind of, I don't know, hung around, like he was waiting for us to get going." Suddenly sounding less cocky than puzzled, the deputy confesses, "Blame if I know *why* he did that." But Paladin knows why. Far from a foolish old hound dog, Isham was a man with a sense of honor and obligation, repaying a debt to a man who had earned his trust. Laying his hand briefly and tenderly on the dead man's back in benediction, Paladin retrieves the letter and places it in his own shirt, as the sheriff promises him that Isham Spruce will get a decent burial. It is a somber ending, but one that affirms the black man was far better and more manly than those who had owned, hunted, and killed him, as decent people should acknowledge—including the television viewers.

Other Minorities

Over the years, other ethnic minorities appeared on the series from time to time, sometimes a single individual, others a community within the larger American culture. As we have seen with the earlier groups, sometimes the characters' ethnicity is a simple fact, not the point of the episode. For example, three episodes feature East Indians, but in no case is racial or cultural prejudice an issue. In "Foggbound" (4:12, 12/3/60), Paladin helps Phileas Fogg, hero of Jules Verne's *Around the World in 80 Days*, catch up to the train he missed in San Francisco. Aouda, the young woman Fogg rescued in India, is a prominent and appealing character in the episode, but her race is thematically irrelevant. In "Tiger" (3:11, 11/28/59), a young East Indian couple is being psychologically abused by their master at his Texas estate, but their race is not the cause; the man is a sadist who enjoys tormenting those in his power. In "Caravan" (6:24, 2/23/63), Paladin helps a dispossessed young maharani escape her political rivals to seek refuge in a colony of her people in the American desert.[55] The threat comes not from outside the maharani's race, but inside it. Armenians take center place in a comic episode in the first season, "Helen of Abajinian" (1:16, 12/28/57), but prejudice is not on the agenda, only marriage: a beautiful young woman is eager for a husband, while the mate she has chosen, a skittish young American cowboy, wants to be the pursuer instead of the pursued. Paladin, knowing and admiring Armenian culture well, steps in to negotiate a fair marriage contract for the initially reluctant but later eager bridegroom.[56]

But other episodes do examine prejudice against outsider groups. In "24 Hours at North Fork" (1:36, 5/24/58), a group of Mennonite farmers is harassed and shunned by their neighbors who resent their pacifist convictions, while in "Face of a Shadow" (6:32, 4/20/63), the very last episode to be broadcast, a group of gypsies become convenient scapegoats for a local murder, until Paladin proves their innocence by identifying the real murderer.

But the most significant remaining racial/ethnic groups featured on *Have Gun* were two that Richard Boone had strong personal feelings about: the Jews, and the Japanese. In Chapter Three, we learned that Boone himself, as the child of a Jewish mother, was technically a Jew. Though he was never a religious man, his heritage gave him a lifelong interest in Jewish traditions and history. In later years, he even devoted considerable effort and money to helping the state of Israel develop its film industry.[57] So it is not surprising to find a few

Jewish characters on *Have Gun*. In "The Fatalist" (4:1, 9/10/60), Paladin is summoned to help Nathan Shotness, a tough but humorous Russian Jew who fled the Czar's pogroms for a better life in America with his daughter, Rivka.[58] But their town is under the thumb of a local outlaw, Billy Buckstone, who gets away with murder because frightened witnesses routinely "forget" what they saw, or leave town to avoid testifying. But, after surviving the Cossacks, Nathan cannot be bribed or intimidated, and intends to testify in court about Billy's latest cold-blooded murder. Worried for her father, Rivka hires Paladin to help them. A man of peace who refuses to carry a gun, Nathan initially resists the aid of a "hired killer," but when Rivka is kidnapped and threatened with death if he testifies, Nathan changes his mind and accepts Paladin's good offices. In the end, Nathan testifies and Billy Blackstone is convicted, even as Paladin safely rescues Rivka, and all ends with a peaceful dinner for three and a strong new friendship.

Paradoxically, this episode is at once very Jewish and not explicitly Jewish at all. Shimon Wincelberg's script is full of delectable self-deprecating jokes and turns of phrase translated from the Yiddish; Nathan and Rivka, both engaging characters, have all the linguistic and cultural markers of their heritage. Certain expressions reveal that Nathan is a religious man— a reference to the Almighty and another to the wisdom of praying, a habit of drawing his illustrations from the Old Testament—while at their first meeting, he and Paladin carry on a philosophical debate that starts, "As the Mishnah says..." But "Mishnah" is not explained, and if audiences don't recognize the name for the commentaries on the Torah, the Jewish Bible, they might not understand its place in Jewish religion. True, Buckstone's chief henchman, Smolett (incandescently played by Robert Blake), threatens to kill Rivka using the special method of butchering animals he had seen Nathan use, but does not mention the name of the custom ("kosher"), let alone understand its significance. The most easily-recognized markers of Jewish culture are the menorah on Nathan's table, and his blessing the wine in Hebrew at dinner. But the word *Jew* is never spoken. In fact, the *Variety* review of the episode describes Shotness as a "Russian peddler" with-out mentioning his Jewish identity.[59] To those familiar with Judaism and with Jewish culture, Nathan and Rivka's identity is overt, but audiences with less exposure to the traditions might not recognize how Jewish they are.

Obviously, this is a deliberate choice. In 1960 there was still sufficient (if covert) prejudice against Jews in American society that their presence in a drama could be controversial,[60] and the first rule of television programming was "no controversy." So, just as "The Long Way Home" discusses slavery without ever mentioning the word *slave*, "The Fatalist" gives us Jewish characters without the word *Jew*, but—perhaps more surprising—without anti–Semitism, either. Nathan's troubles all derive from his defiance of Billy Buckstone, nothing to do his religion or his culture, which are simply facts. And apparently, the strategy worked: television audiences responded enthusiastically to this engaging father and daughter. In fact, Nathan was such a popular character that Wincelberg was commissioned to write a sequel. In "A Drop of Blood" (5:12, 12/2/61), Nathan invites Paladin to attend Rivka's wedding as best man because her groom, Faivel, has no family. As in "The Fatalist," Nathan's problem is not religious persecution but his old nemesis, Billy Buckstone. Instead of hanging for murder, Billy bought a judge and his freedom, and is now determined to take his revenge on Nathan by disrupting the wedding.

But, unlike "The Fatalist," in this episode the Jewish elements are far more overt and culturally specific. Nathan's telegram summoning Paladin to the wedding begins with the date according to the Hebrew calendar, while his dialogue is shot through with Yiddish words unlike anything heard in the earlier script: *golem* (a fool), *schlemiel* (a habitual bungler, an awkward or unlucky person whose plans always go wrong), *Mazel tov* ("good luck" in both Hebrew and Yiddish). Where Nathan dresses like his neighbors (not even a visible prayer shawl, which, as an observant Jewish man, he certainly would have worn), Faivel wears the traditional black gabardine of an Orthodox Jew, complete with distinctive hat and side-locks, emphasizing his foreignness. In "The Fatalist," when Nathan and Paladin exchange texts from the Mishnah, the issue is universal: the threat to society when the law breaks down, as it has in this town under Billy Buckstone's influence. Paladin wonders why Nathan doesn't just leave, observing, "Doesn't your Mishnah say, 'Where there is no law, there is no bread?'" (Implausibly, he first quotes this in the original Hebrew, and then translates it.) Impressed that an American gunfighter is familiar with his own holy texts, Nathan replies: "It also says, 'Where there is no bread, there is no law.'" The phrasing is pithy, but there is nothing uniquely Jewish about these concerns. By contrast, in "A Drop of Blood," when Faivel brings up the Jewish holy texts, it is to complain about a passage in the Midrash commenting on a narrow doctrinal matter which is relevant only to the most Orthodox Jews, or to a future rabbi.

Most strikingly, Rivka and Faivel's wedding, a traditional Jewish ceremony complete with chupa (the canopy), Hebrew prayers, and all the trimmings, is enacted in astounding detail.[61] True, the wedding serves a dramatic purpose: tension builds by cross-cutting between the ceremony taking place inside the house and events out in the yard where the neighbors are partying, especially after Billy Buckstone and his gang arrive, threatening to burn down the house if Nathan doesn't come out to face him. Eventually, Nathan, Paladin, and Faivel suspend the ceremony and charge out to confront the vandals, successfully driving Buckstone and his gang away. Then they return to complete the ceremony, which ends with a joyful dance, a wedding hora. But the length and detail of this ceremony is unprecedented, and unmistakably in-your-face Jewish. Unsurprisingly, the network was very unhappy about this sequel. In reporting the story years later, Wincelberg had forgotten the details, but remembered that the broadcasters "didn't like the subject matter or something, and they told the producer [Frank Pierson] not to film any more episodes like that one."[62] If there was no anti–Semitism in the episode itself, there surely was in the network's reaction—if not in their own attitudes, then in their assumption about the audience's attitudes. In their minds, at least, the country was not yet ready for Jews in prime time.

If Boone included these Jewish stories in *Have Gun* out of personal interest, he had to put some powerful personal feelings aside to work on "The Coming of the Tiger" (5:31, 4/14/62), which sympathetically examines the challenges facing a young Nisei, a first-generation Japanese-American. Minoru, son of Paladin's old friend, Mr. Takara, chafes painfully at the prejudice that limits his opportunities and poisons his soul. Proud of his Japanese heritage, yet fully committed to the country of his birth, Minoru longs to be judged on his own merits, not looked down on as inferior because of his race, yet he fears this will never happen. His conflict is brought to a head by the problem his father brings to Paladin. Fearfully, Mr. Takara says, "The sleeping tiger of war is never far from us. It waits only to be awakened," and explains that the new Japanese government, taking a more aggressive stance in the world, has sent two emissaries to Mexico to be smuggled across the border into the United States—a priest and a samurai warrior, seeking "converts" to support this new militarism.[63] Takara cannot bring himself to betray these fellow countrymen to the authorities, but he urgently wants them sent back to Japan, so he asks his friend to take on this task unofficially, with Minoru as his guide to the place where the invaders will cross the border.

Minoru is tested in two different ways on this mission. First, he is reminded painfully of the contempt so many whites feel for him and his people, and his powerlessness to stop the abuse. When he and Paladin stop along the trail to visit family friends at their general store, he must watch as two hulking white men insult and threaten the Osatas—especially Mr. Osata and his daughter, Tikara, the young woman Minoru loves. Sam and Billy don't even bother to distinguish between Chinese and Japanese, using the two terms as if they were interchangeable, and calling Mr. Osata "Wong." When Billy grabs Tikara roughly and tries to kiss her despite her screams and struggles, only Minoru's fists and Paladin's gun save her from serious harm. Conciliatory under Paladin's drawn weapon, Sam insists that Billy "didn't mean no harm; just fooling. You want to live around here, you got to learn to take a joke. Ain't that right, Wong?" Humiliated, Mr. Osata manages to say, "Humor is gold to the poor": in other words, a poor man must accept what the rich or powerful offer. In the family quarters, Minoru confronts the gunfighter: "You've traveled around. Is it different?" That is, are there places where such outrages do not occur? The best Paladin can offer is, "It *will* be," which the young man finds bitterly insufficient.

When they locate the samurai and the priest, abandoned in the desert by their escorts and out of water, Minoru encounters his second test. The samurai is just the muscle on this team, but the priest is cold and clever, confident of his own innate superiority, and he skillfully plays on Minoru's resentments and confusion. Because the samurai scattered the horses, all four are on foot, near exhaustion and almost out of water, so the trek to the border becomes an endurance contest, not just physically but psychologically as well—a contest Minoru is losing. The priest works steadily on him, trying to drive a wedge between him and Paladin, dismissing the young Nisei as "a slave that pretends to walk like a man" because he allows the white man to lead him. Instead of rebutting the priest's words, Minoru tells Paladin bitterly, "I used to have a number of good answers to that. I guess I must have forgotten them all." Patiently, Paladin replies, "When a change comes, sometimes it comes slowly—but it *will* come." The priest demands, how long till Minoru will be equal? Twenty years? As Paladin refuses to offer a date, the priest muses aloud, pointedly: if it takes twenty years to be equal, in twenty more years, might Minoru be superior? Impatiently, Paladin snaps, "His *opportunity* will be equal. What he does with it is up to him."

But Minoru is weakening, losing heart, losing faith. The priest, speaking privately to the young man, praises the great honor attached to the Takara family name in Japan, holds up an illustrious samurai ancestor of that name, and urgently tells him, "There is a divine destiny to be fulfilled with us, but the spirit must be strong!" In the end, drowning in his bitterness and resentment, Minoru changes sides and forces Paladin to throw down his gun, accepting the priest's aggressive teachings over his father's caution: "'Speak soft, speak low, and wait.' For *what*? A life in the shadows, hoping for one day to be equal? *Equal!* Just for a moment, think, Paladin! Think about the possibility that I might be *better* than you!" But Minoru's longed-for "better" does not seem to be based on individual achievement, but on his group identity: Minoru *as Japanese* might have higher status than Paladin as American— nakedly racist thinking. Paladin calls him on it, with calm distaste: "I think, under the proper circumstances, you might be just about equal to those two back in the store. You might be just as superior, just as bigoted, and just as frightened." As a shocked Minoru considers this comparison, the priest quietly orders him to kill Paladin. Though Minoru argues, the priest is adamant; however, when the young man still hesitates, the samurai is released to fight in his place. But Paladin defeats the highly-trained Japanese warrior, as Minoru watches dumbfounded and the priest stares in disbelief at what this "inferior" Westerner has accomplished. Groaning, the young man admits that he's been "very foolish." Paladin says gently, "Well, some day the idea of equality will be a fact. Until then, we're all a little bit foolish." The priest murmurs with quiet respect, "When I return to Japan, I will speak of a man named Paladin."

So all's well that ends well. No one dies, the invaders are sent home with a new respect for the "inferior" Americans, Minoru and Tikara marry and she happily adopts his Western ways. Mr. Takara concludes: "And so the tiger returns to his lair." But Paladin hedges: "For now." Takara asks heavily, "Then, like I, you think it will not pass? There will be more?" A somber Paladin agrees: "Much more." But, he adds, smiling, the world still contains satisfactions—the happy young lovers looking forward to their lives, books to read, lovely art to contemplate, even an interrupted Go game between friends to complete. However, as soon as Takara turns back to their game, Paladin's smile quietly dissolves into a frown. Despite the peace of this moment, the threat lingers, with worrisome portents for the future.

This ending must have made viewers in 1962 think inevitably of Pearl Harbor, barely twenty years in the past, and of the staggering cost paid by the world—and by the Japanese themselves—for their belief in their own innate superiority. Making this episode, Richard Boone, too, must have been thinking of all these things, and of his own grim history in the Pacific during the war. How many people would willingly revisit a subject so personally painful, or treat former enemies with such generosity, such sympathy? True, the priest and the samurai are strongly criticized for the attitudes that would, sixty or so years later, precipitate a catastrophe across the entire Pacific region. But the Takaras and the Osatas, also Japanese, are treated with courtesy and respect, shown as complex, conflicted characters, with their torn loyalties and their moments of weakness as well as their virtues, while many aspects of Japanese culture are celebrated and appreciated. A substantial portion of the dialogue in this episode is in Japanese, including a number of Paladin's lines; clearly, this is another of the many cultures he knows well and admires.[64] In a strong support of authenticity, all the Japanese roles are played by Asian actors, five Japanese and two Chinese-Americans. "The Coming of the Tiger" suggests strongly that Richard Boone is no less a champion of justice and understanding than the man he plays.

In the next chapter, we will turn to a different kind of minority: women. Since women constitute just over half the population, they are obviously not minorities in any numerical sense, but certainly women are under-represented both in public life and in artistic representations of that life. Their roles are more limited not only in number, but in scope, usually secondary to a man, and often subordinate. If this is still true in the second decade of the twenty-first century, despite some genuine improvements (especially on television), in the 1950s and '60s the pattern was so much the norm as to be invisible. Yet, like the racial and ethnic minority groups just examined, on *Have Gun—Will Travel*, women received a very different sort of treatment, through the influence of Richard Boone.

EIGHT

The Other Americans: Women

One central task of popular culture is to define what "normal life" looks like, so it's no wonder American women in the 1950s did not think of themselves as an oppressed minority. As Chapter One showed, everything they read, heard or saw in the popular culture—books, magazines, movies, and television—told them that their secondary status in society, their subordinate status in the home, was not only normal but necessary and appropriate. Especially on prime-time television, most women were happy, fulfilled housewives and mothers, like Harriet Nelson on *The Adventures of Ozzie and Harriet*, June Cleaver of *Leave It to Beaver*, and Donna Stone on *The Donna Reed Show*. The ubiquity of these images made it difficult even to dream about alternative ways of life. As Kathryn Weibel points out in *Mirror Mirror: Images of Women Reflected in Popular Culture*, "It is hard for a girl growing up with a Donna Reed image of womanhood to consider a career as a doctor."[1]

Yet during these same years, and on that most improbable of vehicles, a Western, *Have Gun—Will Travel* repeatedly showed images of women leading lives different from that narrow domestic model, actively engaging the world in their own right rather than leaving all the risk and the achievement to men. True, a majority of the women on *Have Gun* defined their existence and purpose in relation to men: as wives or widows (46), as mothers (14), as young dependents—daughters, sisters, nieces (30). Another 25 women were defined by that other conventional relationship with men, the romantic/sexual. Some have caught their man (the fiancées and brides) while others are still on the hunt, but their stories are centered on achieving love and/or marriage. Most of these characters, like the other women on TV, deal with the public realm only indirectly, mediated through a man (father, lover, husband, son). But over *Have Gun*'s six seasons, a remarkable number of women confront the public world directly, pursuing activities or even professions outside their families, entering the world of work and business and politics usually reserved for men. Some of them have no choice— women without men, or women whose male family members are incapable, or mistreat rather than protect them. Others are moved to public action for a specific, limited cause and return to their original domestic role when their task is complete. But a few make unconventional, even scandalous, choices to step away from the prescribed roles for women, responding to their own deepest desires as human beings, regardless of their gender.

To evaluate the representation of women on these four Westerns, I focus on two criteria. First, how often do women characters escape the limits of traditional female roles to play an active part in the public arena? Second: how many women characters, whether in traditional or non-traditional roles, function as *centers of consciousness*? That is, how often do we see women through their own eyes, with access to their point of view, their perception of the action, rather than from the outside, through the eyes of the men they impact? By both these standards, *Have Gun—Will Travel* easily surpasses all of its competitors.

But in order to ask questions about how many women meet these criteria, we first need to track the number of featured women characters appearing on these series ("featured": important to the action of the episode, whether as protagonist or supporting character). Comparing the first three seasons of *Gunsmoke* (117 half-hour episodes), *Wagon Train* (117 hour-long episodes), and *Bonanza* (100 hour-long episodes) to the full six seasons of *Have Gun—Will Travel* (225 half-hour episodes) yields a reasonable sample of the trends in the years when all four series were being broadcast.[2] Unlike any other popular Western series of the period, *Gunsmoke* includes a female continuing character, Miss Kitty, queen of the Long Branch Saloon. But despite being one of the series stars, in these early seasons Kitty routinely has fewer, shorter, and less substantial scenes per episode than her three male co-stars. Including the rare occasions when Kitty plays a significant role in the action, women are featured in only 42 of *Gunsmoke*'s first 117 episodes (35 percent); only 13 of these episodes contain two or more featured women, including Kitty.[3] On *Bonanza*, significant women characters appear in 48 of the first 100 episodes, with 14 episodes including more than one featured woman, while *Wagon Train*, with its emphasis on substantial roles for guest stars, averaged 12 episodes a season named for women characters, with significant roles for women in 10 or so additional episodes per season, for a rate of about 53 percent, though episodes with more than one important woman are less common, only five or six per season. By contrast, on *Have Gun*, women characters are featured in 154 of the 225 episodes (68 percent), while 59 episodes, fully 26 percent of the total, include more than one important female character.[4] That's almost double the rate on *Gunsmoke*, despite Kitty's regular participation.

In the previous chapters in Part II, serious attention was devoted to analyzing the events of the episodes, because it is not enough to know that a character is a lawman or a gunfighter: it is necessary to ask what kind of lawman or gunfighter, how a man behaves in that role. But given the far narrower parameters women are typically allowed in the popular culture of the 1950s, it is more important to catalog the kinds of social roles these women characters are allowed to play, the nature of their engagements in the public world beyond the doors of their own homes, than to examine in great detail their actions in the stories.

I: Women Out in the World

On *Gunsmoke*, *Wagon Train*, and *Bonanza*, women generally occupy an even narrower range of social positions and identities than were available to the women in the audience. Despite the propaganda that defined women solely as wives and mothers, in the 1950s, many American women worked outside the home for much-needed pay—poor women, both single and married, and single women of the lower middle classes. Poor women worked as domestic servants in other women's homes, or labored long hours in textile factories and other light industrial settings. One rung up the social ladder, women worked not only to earn money, but also as a way to meet potential husbands. Some worked in menial service jobs like store clerks, waitresses and hairdressers, but young single women with a little education might find work as secretaries and stenographers. With more education still, they found jobs as nurses and elementary school teachers: not only was caring for the sick or for young children obviously "feminine" work, but such women would be under the careful supervision of male doctors and principals, thus maintaining the proper social order. (However, as soon as a woman married she was expected, or forced, to leave her job to devote herself to her domestic responsibilities.) But 1950s television never showed women working in these sorts of jobs, aside from the Eve Arden comedy, *Our Miss Brooks*, about a school teacher, yes, looking for a husband.

However, *Gunsmoke* was an exception to this rule. From the beginning, the series distinguished itself from the other Westerns of the time by including a woman among its continuing cast members—moreover, a woman in a distinctly non-domestic role.[5] As a saloon hostess, Kitty is an independent working woman, beholden to no man, so she can meet Matt, Doc, and Chester on equal terms. And by the end of the second season, she is no longer just an employee at the Long Branch, but a co-owner, a responsible public position with genuine power. Kitty Russell quickly became a touchstone for many women viewers, a woman whose accomplishments they could regard with pride. On the other hand, aside from the rarely-seen Ma Smalley, owner of the boarding house, or an occasional dressmaker, the only working women in Dodge are Kitty and the other ladies of the Long Branch. In real life these women would have been prostitutes, but 1950s TV routinely censored any hints of sexuality, so the saloon girls, including Kitty, get a discreet cover of respectability. Though they flirt and drink with lots of different men, though they wear glamorous make-up and jewels, short skirts and tight low-cut bodices covered in sequins and feathers, sex is never quite overt. Yet even so, the saloon girls clearly make a living by manipulating and seducing men into spending money, selling their company and attention if not their bodies. This limits their desirability as role models for independent women, especially during the first two years of the series, before Kitty buys half the Long Branch.

Wagon Train does much better in terms of numbers, including far more women in featured roles than *Gunsmoke*, but the roles are virtually all domestic. However, this fact not only reflects cultural norms for women, but grows naturally from the series premise. A wagon train is a collection of *families* in transit from east to west, from one life to another. In this liminal space, this in-between time, everyone is found in their domestic roles, men as well as women. The normal worldly activities have been left behind, except the daily chores of feeding and caring for the family and the animals as they travel. In the absence of normal economic activities, character is highlighted, character tested by the incidents along the trail and revealed in the interpersonal conflicts that inevitably crop up in a group of strangers thrown together under stressful conditions for the three or four months of the journey to California. This intense focus on character and on past history, often history that the pioneers are trying to forget or leave behind, often gives the featured women characters on *Wagon Train* far richer dramatic opportunities than the similarly domestic women on *Gunsmoke* or *Bonanza*. But even so, none stray beyond the domestic realm. On *Bonanza*, virtually all the women are limited to domestic functions in the ranch or farm families found near Virginia City. Despite a town setting that would allow opportunities for women to fill a wider variety of social roles, the only working women on the series are saloon girls, and even they are far scarcer than on *Gunsmoke*. True, *Bonanza*'s first season included three stories about women with significant economic and social power, but all three were based on historical figures with a connection to Virginia City. The real-life actresses Lotta Crabtree ("A Rose for Lotta," 1:1, 9/12/59) and Adah Menken ("The Magnificent Adah," 1:10, 11/14/59) each feature in an episode, while another early episode tells the story of Julia Bulette ("The Julia Bulette Story," 1:6, 10/7/59), glamorous real-life owner of a saloon in Virginia City who turned her establishment into a hospital during an influenza epidemic, and was later murdered by a jealous lover. But rather than highlighting these women's professional accomplishments, the episodes place each woman in an invented romance with one of the Cartwrights: every time, the love plot dominates the other aspects of the woman's story. The only other working woman to appear in the first three seasons of *Bonanza* is a schoolteacher, the most respectable female occupation on the frontier. However, on *Bonanza*, the teacher's story concerns not her professional role but her attempts to land a husband. As we saw in Chapter Four, *Bonanza* creator and producer David Dortort lavished all his attention on the four Cartwright men, declaring outright war on women and "Momism." Given his attitude, it is no surprise that women on this series are so consistently reduced to expendable love-interests.

On *Have Gun*, by contrast, women appear not only in greater numbers but in a much wider range and variety of roles. This observation, however, does not apply to the women in the introductory scenes in San Francisco, who are, frankly, playmates for Paladin—attractive and entertaining, perfect companions for an elegant dinner, an evening at the opera or ballet, or an intimate tête-à-tête on the settee in his suite, but interchangeable, none of them important in his life as individuals, and most not even named. In other words, on one level they reinforce the conventional 1950s views of women, their nature and their proper place in a man's life—on the margins, restricted to his leisure hours. On the other hand, these San Francisco ladies are always women of Paladin's own class; that is, they are free to reject his attentions, because he has no economic or social power over them. To win favor, he must woo them with charm, wit, and appreciation. Though sex is implied as a desired outcome in most of these encounters (quite remarkably for a period in which married couples on TV were shown sleeping demurely in twin beds), there is no double standard at play. Paladin never treats these women as trophies or conquests, never manipulates or tricks them, and reveals no trace of the condescension, even contempt, that so many men in sexist cultures express for the women who sleep with them.[6]

However, the women Paladin meets in his work are quite different, and so is his attitude toward them. For him, the gender of his women clients is just a fact, and not necessarily the most important fact about them. Where most men evaluate women primarily on their appearance, Paladin routinely *listens* to women as carefully as he looks. Whether the women are centrally involved in his cases or bystanders who get pulled in, old friends or new acquaintances, rich or poor, old or young, beautiful or plain, respectable or socially marginal, he takes them seriously as human beings with specific problems, desires, and motives that he must understand if he is to do his job successfully. Though a number of women try to attract Paladin—sometimes out of genuine appreciation for his qualities, more often to gain some practical advantage for themselves—Paladin almost never finds himself romantically involved with the women he meets in his work. Only twice in the series does he genuinely fall in love, and on two more occasions, he deliberately pulls back from a woman he feels drawn to, once for her sake and once for his own.[7] On the trail, Paladin is focused on the work, on the problem at hand, rather than considering women as potential romantic or sexual partners.

Though many women are found in domestic roles on *Have Gun*, others play a wide variety of roles in the public realm, and in significant numbers. Fourteen women are entrepreneurs or property owners in their own right, whether they are running a large ranch, a small boarding house, or a saloon. Another eight find meaningful lives, though seldom fortunes, in traditionally male professions. Perhaps only a few of the women in these first categories would have chosen such public engagement if they'd had husbands to support them, but all work hard to make a success of their business or occupation, and take pride in their efforts. A privileged few find (or aspire to) fame and fortune as entertainers—singers, actors, trick shooters in Wild West shows—public roles which they can retain even if they marry. Then at the bottom of the social and economic scale, women supporting themselves in more menial jobs as saloon girls and as domestic servants are featured characters in at least twelve episodes—something not found on any of the other series, aside from a handful of featured saloon girls on *Gunsmoke*. Finally, there are two additional categories of women characters that appear regularly on *Have Gun*: first, single women struggling with the need to create economic security for themselves, and to gain control over their own lives in a society which expects women to rely on men for these tasks; and second, stories about women stepping temporarily outside their ordinary domestic roles to engage in public activities. All of these different kinds of women almost never appear on the other Westerns, and seldom appear in any other kind of popular media at the time. Every day, American media nonverbally affirmed it: women's place was in the home. In telling these stories about women, *Have Gun—Will Travel* consistently violated that code.

Businesswomen

The first group of women, the owners of large ranches, all have considerable influence in their communities, not for their wealth alone but because they run substantial enterprises with skill and toughness. In "The Englishman" (1:13, 12/7/57), Felicia Carson single-handedly manages the Montana ranch she co-owns with her aristocratic cousin James, an absentee partner. The ranch is a large place, 12,000 acres and 6,000 head of cattle, but despite her gender, Felicia has obviously done an excellent job running the place. Moreover, when trouble with the local Indians arises, she is instrumental in resolving the issue peacefully. No wonder she has earned her neighbors' respect. Only her well-meaning but clueless cousin thinks she would be happier if he manfully "took over" running the ranch and allowed her to "sit back and be the lady of the manor."[8] In "The Golden Toad" (3:10, 11/21/59), Doris Gallman manages the ranch that her family has owned since 1832. A tough-minded widow, Doris is older than Felicia and much less elegant, but her hands-on competence is equally impressive. As she tells Paladin proudly, "I branded the first steer that walked this range. Built the first line of barb wire. And I buried two husbands." The way she says this suggests she did the first two tasks, if not the third, with her own hands. The character, like the episode itself, is comic but far from laughable: Doris is a strong, effective woman at home in a man's world. Yet all this does not make her unwomanly: at the end of the story, she cheerfully agrees to marry the neighbor she has been feuding with. Cynthia Palmer, another confident, nononsense woman rancher, appears in "The Day of the Bad Man" (3:17, 1/9/60). Her civic exertions stretch beyond her own ranch to the town of Cedar Wells, the railhead where she ships her cattle. The town is totally lawless: though her hands are often cheated at faro or killed by Amos Saint's gang, no sheriff will stay in the job because the frightened citizens won't support him against the outlaws. So Cynthia has hired Paladin to keep the latest sheriff in place, at least until her herd arrives. Though providing law and order is not her job, she has accepted the responsibility, out of self-interest but also for the good of the community— the kind of public work that, generally, only men are supposed to take on.

However, because women are no more "naturally" virtuous and good than men, those with real power sometimes abuse it, or use it inappropriately. In "The Campaign of Billy Banjo" (3:36, 5/28/60), Elise Jones dominates her town completely because she owns all of its economic engines—the mine, most of the ranch land in the vicinity, and the saloon. She also "owns" the local sheriff, not to mention her husband, Billy "Banjo" Jones, whom she has put forward as a candidate for state senate. Elise is a handsome, shrewd, dominating woman of unrestrained appetites, little education, and crude manners who clearly enjoys exercising power for its own sake, unlike the other women ranchers discussed. She orders people around with no pretense of politeness and with blatant disregard for anyone else's concerns or feelings. But Elise's ambitions have hit a glass ceiling, long before such a concept existed (either in the 1870s of the series or the 1960s of the script). In local issues, Elise's economic dominance gives her sway over the community. But, being a woman, she cannot run for political office in her own right.[9] In order to exercise power at the state level, she must work through a proxy—for example, a senator who happens to be her compliant husband. Unfortunately, Elise's plan is running into unexpected opposition. One of the local miners, Martin Jansen, has had the temerity to challenge her authority by running against Billy. Since miners outnumber cowboys in the district three to one, Elise recognizes that in a fair election Billy (that is, she) would lose. To avoid losing power, she will to do whatever it takes to win the election, even cheat or, if necessary, resort to violence.

Nor is Elise the only woman to abuse her public power, nor ambition and greed the only motives for such abuse. In "A Sense of Justice" (2:8, 11/1/58), the Widow Briggs, owner of the largest ranch around, is bitterly determined to have revenge, though she calls it justice. After her only child, Jim, is murdered, she insists on punishing the murderer herself, even though the accused is a gentle local man with the mind of a child, and the evidence against him is far from conclusive. Mrs. Briggs is adamant: she's prepared to give Andy a "trial" before she hangs him, but refuses to wait for the circuit judge, due in a few days. If the sheriff won't hand the prisoner over, she's ready to storm the jail with her mob of ranch hands to take Andy by force. Though she is the only one who really mourns her dead son, whose behavior in life was marked by the same exaggerated sense of entitlement as his mother, Mrs. Briggs' grief is genuine, and both Paladin and the sheriff sympathize with her loss. But neither her grief nor her economic clout can justify a private citizen taking the law into her own hands.[10]

For all these women, their gender does not diminish their ability to meet their responsibilities. However, the same is not true for the woman at the center of "Love's Young Dream" (4:2, 9/17/60). Augusta, a beautiful, confident, mature woman, is half-owner of Bordelli's, one of the most elegant supper clubs in San Francisco. Though her recently-deceased partner gave his name to the place, Augusta is the one who actually runs Bordelli's, but as a woman in a man's business, she faces many challenges. As she explains to a sympathetic Paladin, "A woman alone—every muscle-bound clown with ambition thinks he can swindle, bully, or just plain cheat her.... I *clawed* my way into this place. I made it into something I'm proud of." She grumbles that Mort, her late partner, far from being helpful, was "like an extra mortgage on this place." Given how hard she has worked, how much success she has achieved through her own efforts, she is not about to surrender half the business to Mort's crude, bedraggled trail-rat nephew and heir, Monk, no matter what Mort's will says. In the end, however, Augusta is able to keep control of both her club and her life, because Monk is smitten at first sight, devoting his generous heart to her service. And, though Monk is initially unprepossessing, with help from Paladin's expert ministrations he cleans up surprisingly well. In a conventional 1950s script, this would be Monk's story: he would find his "inner executive" and become the dominant partner in Bordelli's, while Augusta gratefully subsided into a wifely support role. But on *Have Gun*, this is Augusta's story. Though the unlikely pair is headed for the altar by the end of the episode, she will clearly remain the dominant partner in this enterprise, with Monk's cheerful acquiescence. Unlike many women in the 1870s and the 1950s alike, Augusta is allowed both worldly success and domestic happiness.

All these women play public roles as not just owners but managers of substantial property. They supervise workers, meet payrolls, and make decisions on day-to-day affairs in large-scale business enterprises. But smaller businesses, too, offer women opportunities for achievement and self-sufficiency. In "Alice" (5:27, 3/17/62), when the woman known as Blue Dollar Alice opened her saloon in Codyville, Arizona, twenty years earlier, there wasn't another white woman for 500 miles. In a territory that held "nothing but mud and men and aching backs and loneliness," her saloon offered those hard, dirty men someplace to get a drink, to play cards, to talk to a woman, and to play roulette on the only honest wheel in the entire territory. Alice prospered because she filled a community need, and did so decently, treating her customers with affection and compassion. If there were occasional fights, some spilled blood, or a number of "over-painted women" in the saloon willing to extend intimacy and comfort to those men, well, standards of behavior reflect the circumstances of time and place. What is appropriate for a settled, established, respectable town is very different than what was vital to survival on the frontier. Alice provided what her community needed at the time, and was handsomely rewarded for it.

In "The Marshal of Sweetwater" (6:11, 11/24/ 62), young Marie Ellis, a shrewd, ambitious dance hall girl, is working her way up from the bottom. She has scrimped and saved for years to buy a saloon of her own, explaining, "I'd had a lot of time to see how they was run, and I figured I could run me one too, and be a lady at the same time." Given the courageous and direct way she confronts her first challenges as owner, Marie is likely to be successful in her venture, like Alice. By contrast, Hanna of "Pandora's Box" (5:36, 5/19/62) struggles at the very bottom of this career ladder as the proprietor of a "clapboard and canvas saloon"— one old covered wagon that travels from little town to little town, selling cheap drinks, setting out a few tables for gambling, with a single aging bar girl to entertain the customers. At first glance, Hanna seems a handsome middle-aged woman, but a closer look reveals the hard edges, the heavy toll taken on her by this marginal life, one bare step ahead of failure. Though she fights ruthlessly to survive, the only real power she has comes from abusing her tiny staff. Under these conditions, the future for Hanna's enterprise looks ominous.

More respectably, other women run boarding houses or hotels, an acceptable business for women in the period because it drew on ordinary domestic skills—cooking, cleaning, managing households, taking care of people's daily domestic needs. Some of these women are minor figures, like the hotel keeper in "The Cream of the Jest" (5:34, 5/5/62), and Mrs. Madison, the proprietor of Madison's Boarding House in "Blind Circle" (5:14, 12/6/ 61), but several play featured roles: Ma Warren in "Gun Shy" (1:29, 3/29/ 58), Jeri Marcus in "The Trap" (5:25, 3/3/62), and Pegine in "The Knight" (5:38, 6/2/ 62). Featured player or minor character alike, these hotel managers and boarding house operators are all strongly individualized. Some of the characters are warm and friendly and treat their boarders like family (Pegine), while others strictly enforce house rules and prefer an impersonal atmosphere (Mrs. Madison). Some are quite successful, like Ma Warren, whose customers come miles out of their way for her home cooking, but others struggle on with few customers and less help, like Jeri Marcus. But all work hard to turn their housekeeping skills into a livelihood by meeting a public need for food and shelter, and, as business owners, all play a public role in the larger community.

Entertainers

Some women on *Have Gun* earn a living more glamorously as entertainers. Annette Vargas, in "The Silver Queen" (1:33, 5/3/58), is a beautiful young music hall singer of considerable fame and accomplishment; in "The Moor's Revenge" (2:15, 12/27/58), Victoria Vestris is a famous actress on tour around the West with her husband, Charles Matthews (played zestfully by Vincent Price), performing scenes from Shakespeare. Both of these women are confident, masterful professionals, sure of their abilities and comfortable in their very public roles, which allow them to be quite feminine and yet in control of their own destinies. Faye Hollister—that is, Mrs. Pete Hollister, the young bride of a rich older rancher in "The Singer" (1:22, 2/8/58)—can only aspire to such a position, a woman of moderate abilities who yet dreams so ardently of a career as an opera singer that she neglects her husband and all her domestic duties to work on her singing. Fortunately for her, she has an indulgent husband who loves her enough to support her dream and forgive her dereliction of duty.

Lastly, *Have Gun* features two different women who star in Wild West shows as trick shooters. Though both women are (or were) professional entertainers, their problems are as much personal as professional, with gender a significant factor. In "The Cure" (4:35, 5/20/61), the famous Calamity Jane has dwindled from star performer to hopeless drunk, eaten up with jealousy and rage at Ned Blackstock, her former employer and lover. Blackstock has not only kept most of the money Jane earned, but has replaced her with a young pretty new shooter he headlines, with cruel insult to his former star, as "the real Calamity Jane." Paladin tries to help Jane reclaim her name and the money Blackstock owes her, but to his dismay, the fading star chooses alcohol and her faithless lover over her money, independence, and self-respect. Fortunately, "Ella West" (1:17, 1/4/58) ends more satisfactorily. Ella too is a trick shooter in a Wild West show; unlike Jane, Ella is at the beginning of her career, a rising star. But like Jane, Ella needs Paladin's help: her employer and her fans will turn against her unless she changes her crude tomboy behavior and learns to dress, talk and behave in a more feminine manner. Worse, the man she loves, a co-star in the show, has walked away from her, disgusted by her dirty, crude persona. But her behavior is not a deliberate choice: having grown up motherless, Ella simply has no clue how to act like a woman. Too insecure to admit her fear, she lashes out instead, ranting to a saloon full of cowboys, "I ain't no lady! I can outride, out-shoot, and out-cuss any of y'all here! I can out-spit ya, out-chew ya, and out-*drink* ya!" So Paladin is called in to serve as Ella's Pygmalion. In teaching her the skills she needs, he comes to respect the real strengths of the woman hiding beneath the tomboy exterior, her courage, her honesty, and a genuine sweetness—until he finds himself so attracted to Ella that he must step back to prevent her from falling in love with him. However, once she accepts the more genteel dress, demeanor, and speech that Paladin teaches her, Ella's lover finally sees her as a desirable woman, and their relationship is healed. Ella is another of the lucky ones, like Augusta in "Love's Young Dream" and Victoria Vestris in "The Moor's Revenge," a woman who gets to have both marriage and a career, without sacrificing her independence or the qualities that make her so admirable.

The Professionals

Where these entertainers make their public impact as glamorous stars, another group of women impacts the public more quietly, in professional roles. Two are teachers (one of the most respectable professions for women), both of whom face serious challenges in their classrooms. In "The Teacher" (1:27, 3/15/58), Mollie Stanton bravely risks death to stand up to bullies who want to dictate what she teaches about the Civil War, while in "The Day of the Bad Man" (3:17, 1/9/60), Ruth not only fights back against an outlaw but inspires a young male teacher to take pride in his work after he had begun to see teaching as an unmanly profession.[11] While these teachers hold jobs deemed appropriate for women, the other characters in this group challenge contemporary thinking by pursuing professions traditionally restricted to men (not only during the 1870s of the series setting, but equally in the modern era of the audience). The most explicit of these is Phyllis Thackeray, M.D., whom Paladin meets in "No Visitors" (1:12, 11/30/57). As played by June Lockhart, Dr. Thackeray is an appealing figure: competent, caring, and practical, past the first bloom of girlhood but attractive in a clean wholesome way, with a nice sense of humor that helps her cope with the challenges of her position. Despite her skills, the tiny western town where she has opened her practice treats her with hostility, on the grounds that "Any woman sees fit to take up doctorin' ain't fit to be a woman." Though Paladin admires her obvious strength and courage, and her dedication to her profession, he probes gently for her story, observing that he would expect to find an attractive cultured woman like her "sitting on a velvet settee, fluttering your eyelashes over a fan." She just laughs: "I've tried that. It's too easy." Clearly, Phyllis Thackeray is unwilling to accept the limitations of the traditional female gender role. Instead, she demands for herself a life of accomplishment and purpose, of service to her community, the kind of life which convention restricts to men. In order to get what she wants, she is willing to work hard, to sacrifice comfort and prosperity, and to fight the prejudice of her stubborn neighbors so that she can treat their illnesses and injuries.

Through shared danger in a worthy cause, Paladin and Dr. Thackeray develop a warm relationship which blossoms into serious romance in "The Return of Dr. Thackeray" (1:35, 5/17/58). Despite their strong attraction and mutual respect, the two conclude that a marriage between them is impossible since, for each of them, their work comes first.[12] Remarkably for 1958, her need for independence is taken as seriously as his; Paladin acknowledges her right to choose her profession, with its responsibilities and rewards, over a traditional domestic life with husband and children. On the other hand, the scene confirms certain limits on a woman's options: in the 1870s, as in the 1950s, as hard as it is to imagine a woman doctor, it is even harder to imagine a woman doctor with a family.

Another woman, nurse Adella Liggett in "The Vigil" (5:1, 9/16/61), also chooses a medical profession, and equally struggles for acceptance. In the 1870s, nursing was considered inappropriate for respectable women because it required intimate contact with the bodies of men who were not relatives; as a result, Adella faces great resistance and displeasure from her own family, as well as from potential patients.[13] Unlike Phyllis Thackeray, she has not decided that medicine is preferable to marriage, but when marriage and family prove unattainable for her, as for so many women in these years whose husbands and potential husbands had died in the Civil War, Adella bravely accepts reality. Rather than whining about her fate or settling for an empty life as a spinster dependent on her brother, she finds another way to fulfill her need to nurture, to create a meaningful life for herself.

More dramatically still, in "The Tender Gun" (4:7, 10/22/60), a woman violates all expectations of gender roles to function as a law officer, but, like Adella, this role was not her first choice. When Sheriff Smugly is murdered by unscrupulous railroad agents, his widow, Maude, is elected to continue the fight against the gang. Though the episode is played for comedy, there is nothing foolish about Maude Smugly, especially as played by Jeanette Nolan. She is not outsmarted by the gang, only outnumbered; put to the test, Maude proves she is tough and shrewd enough to defeat the villains, and to manipulate Paladin into helping her against his better judgment. In fact, she turns out to be a quite satisfactory sheriff once the gang has been disposed of. Yet, despite her competence in this masculine role, she has no quarrel with a woman's lot. As she tells Paladin with a grin, she has buried five husbands, but "they was all smiling," and she has enough remaining zest for life and enough appreciation for handsome competent men to propose making him her sixth—an offer he turns down with flowery courtesy and a heroically straight face.

Like Maude Smugly, Lucy Kellaway in "The Taffeta Mayor" (2:17, 1/10/59) does not set out to challenge the limits of women's roles; she just acts responsibly in a crisis after her young husband, the reform candidate for mayor of a Wyoming town, is murdered by the corrupt administration he is running against. When no man is brave enough to replace him as candidate, Paladin convinces Lucy to run in her husband's place—which is possible because Wyoming gave women the vote in 1869. With the votes of all the town's women as well as reform-minded men, Lucy wins the election, but then, shockingly, refuses the office. She ran to honor her husband's ideals but, having destroyed the power of the corrupt mayor and sheriff who killed him, she will make no further sacrifice for these people who left him to fight such men on his own. Having no desire for political power, no ambitions beyond the domestic role she has lost through violence, Lucy is going back East to start her life over, leaving the town to solve its own problems. Paradoxically, while affirming her commitment to traditional domestic roles, Lucy violates one of the key commandments for women: she chooses to meet her own needs rather than sacrifice herself to fulfill the needs of her neighbors. Such self-determination from a woman is rarely depicted in the 1950s, and usually criticized as selfish when it occurs; but on *Have Gun*, Lucy Kellaway's choice clearly earns Paladin's respect, and ours.

Another woman active in the world chooses a more traditional path as a religious missionary. But young idealistic Sister Melissa's mission in the misleadingly-named "The Gospel Singer" (5:6, 10/21/61) is to get men in a rough town to give up their guns, and take a pledge never to use them again. Though Paladin understands that, in the current conditions on the Western frontier, her mission is doomed to failure in the long run, he respects her idealism, and admires her courage, her determination, and her sincere faith.[14] And without doubt, she is a woman who aspires to have a profound public impact on her community. However, some women, lacking a constructive way to make a mark on the world, choose a darker path. Sandy in "Bandit" (5:35, 5/12/62), bitter from a lifetime of mistreatment as a woman, becomes a vicious outlaw, robbing and killing in an effort to claim power for herself. When Paladin captures her to turn her over to the law, she fights him ruthlessly with all her strength and every dirty trick she can devise. But Paladin, despite being her captor, treats her differently from any other man she has known. For the first time in her life, Sandy recognizes there might be some value in the womanhood that had earlier seemed only to make her a victim, and she asks Paladin to teach her "how to act like a woman." But the softening comes too late. The violence she suffered, and inflicted on others in her turn, leaves her no positive solution. Paladin can neither approve of what she has done nor save her from the hanging she has earned for herself. All he can do is mourn the wasted potential of her life.[15]

Ironically, the woman who is born into the most prestigious and powerful public role of all is as desperate for escape as Sandy, longing for domestic happiness, to live and love like any ordinary woman. In "The Princess and the Gunfighter" (4:19, 1/21/61), Serafina, heir-apparent to the throne of Montenegro and unifying symbol to her people, runs away during a tour of the United States, eager for a little freedom and the chance to experience life outside the strait-jacket of duty and propriety that has constrained every moment of her life. Hired to bring the truant discreetly back to San Francisco, Paladin pretends he has no idea who she is, treating her like an ordinary woman whom he expects to do her share of the work. After a lifetime of not being allowed to do anything for herself, Serafina rises to the challenge with surprising sweetness and grace, taking pride in the meals she manages to prepare over a campfire, and (under Paladin's gentle, patient instruction) learning to relate to another human being not as an absolute superior but as an equal. Without quite admitting her royal status, she confesses the pain and frustration of her past, a childhood with no playmates, no freedom, no honest feelings, "told what to think and how to think and what to wear, what not to wear—how to walk, how to *rise,* how to sit—oh yes, how to sit. You see, it takes *years* of practice to learn how to sit like a wax dummy," she laments, and openly envies his freedom. Though sympathetic, Paladin denies her assessment of his condition: "We're none of us truly free. Once in awhile," he admits, taking her hand tenderly, "we can reach through the bars of our dungeon, and *touch*; but we're not free." Then he quotes Marcus Aurelius: "The noble acceptance of the prison of oneself is the ultimate, and only, duty of man."[16] But she is not consoled by Stoic philosophy: "Duty? Duty!" she cries, fighting off tears; "And what of happiness? What of wishes? Desires? What of *needs*?" He understands her plight better than she knows, but there is no answer to her anguish, so wisely he offers none.

In the course of three short days alone together on the trail, they fall deeply, painfully— because, as Paladin is all too aware, hopelessly—in love. They never say the word, but on their last night, as Serafina sits by the fire cradled in his arms, she pleads urgently, "Must we go back? Could we not—could we not be free, here? Together?" They kiss passionately— extraordinarily so by the standards of 1950s television. Then Paladin pulls back from her, with profound sorrow: "If there were no such thing as duty—if there were *only* wishes, I would wish away every kingdom in the world but this one, and I would never go back." Though he had truly admired and cared for Phyllis Thackeray, what Paladin feels for Serafina seems far more like the real thing, the irrational intoxication of romantic love. But he knows that even the sweetest kisses in the world cannot change what must happen. In San Francisco, when she realizes that he had known all along who she was, had been paid to bring her back, Serafina is mortified, certain that all his "pretty speeches" were paid for, too, simply part of the job. But Paladin affirms with a heartbreaking smile that every word he said to her, he meant—so much so that, if she chooses to run away again, he will take her anywhere she wants to go, provided she fully accepts the consequences of her decision. True, Serafina has been born into her obligations, rather than choosing them; however, he reminds her, if she abandons her responsibilities, many people will suffer for her freedom. In the end, as we expect, Serafina sacrifices her private happiness to fulfill her public duty, but there is one small consolation to sustain the lovers. Though each of them is locked in their own duty, they know that, for a brief moment, they managed to reach beyond the bars of their prisons and touch. Seated on her lonely throne, Serafina is the ultimate example of a woman accepting a public role, and paying the price as heroically as any man.[17]

The Woman Alone

While some of these women have partners, others are required, and some choose, to make their way in the world through their own efforts, alone. We first considered those women with considerable resources, whether a great ranch, a profitable business, or a profession to sustain them economically. But other women have none of those advantages. With no inheritance, no property, no skills, no man willing to support them or family able to help, the lucky ones might get jobs as housekeepers, but more likely they have to work in less desirable positions as hotel or kitchen maids or, less respectably, saloon girls. Obviously, such women are plentifully represented in the real world, and are likewise common on *Have Gun—Will Travel*, though they are notably scarce in the other three series, except for saloon girls on *Gunsmoke*. Although some of these characters on *Have Gun* are only background figures, a surprising number of them play vital roles in the episodes, and virtually all of them, featured and minor characters alike, are fully realized personalities (a point to be developed further in Part II.)

Housekeepers, the most prestigious of household servants, show up in several episodes. Most develop significant relationships with their employers, as in "Taylor's Woman" (6:2, 9/22/62); when Lydia convinces her boss to marry her, they both have to live with the consequences. In "Beau Geste" (6:5, 10/13/62), Sheriff Dobbs' Mexican housekeeper, Ria, secretly hires Paladin to protect him against gunfighters because he's losing his eyesight. Though Dobbs would be furious if he knew she had revealed his secret, Ria loves him enough to risk losing his love in order to save his life, and in the end, when they go off to be married, she is rewarded for her courage and faithfulness.[18] Another Mexican housekeeper also loves her master, despite the fact that he is a fool and a blowhard. In "The Return of the Lady" (2:23, 2/21/59), wealthy ambitious BG is determined to marry an English aristocrat so he can found his own Texas dynasty, but his fiancée has no real intention of going through with the wedding. Maria, his long-time housekeeper, is the one woman who truly understands and cares about BG—a fact she manages to convey without a single word of dialogue, merely through her actions and her eloquent facial expressions. When the wedding is broken decisively off, it is Maria who comforts and supports her humiliated employer.

In contrast to these relatively secure working women, Paladin encounters numerous young hotel maids and kitchen servers, most of whom seem trapped in their jobs or their towns. Mary in "First, Catch a Tiger" (3:1, 9/12/59), the pretty kitchen maid at Droggan's hotel, is literally trapped. The work itself, which she does conscientiously, is not bad, but she is not free to leave the hotel. The smooth-talking salesman who promised to take her away with him instead sold her to Droggan for $50, and Droggan insists she has to repay him in order to leave the hotel—a sum she will never be able to save. Worse, Droggan also requires her to provide certain "extra services" to his male customers, beyond serving their meals, cleaning their rooms, and bringing them hot water and fresh towels. Without a donation from some kind stranger like Paladin, Mary will never escape her trap. In "A Quiet Night in Town" (4:17–18, 1/7–14/61), another young woman longs to be something more than a waitress and somewhere better than Jody, Texas. Though Dottie is not literally enslaved like Mary, she too has no resources to escape her narrow life except through some man. Once she thought that better life was in her grasp, when a traveling salesman promised to take her to San Francisco, but it was all a lie. Now Dottie has pinned her hopes for a decent life on the handsome young cowboy who wants to marry her. Though still in Jody, she would have a home of her own, and children—surely a better life. When that hope is destroyed, her devastation is complete.[19] In "Bear Bait" (4:34, 5/13/61), though Sally works in the hotel-saloon in a somewhat larger town, she is even worse off than Dot. Even if she could afford stage fare to San Francisco (the only money she ever sees, she tells Paladin, is "what I can steal from the cash box when the old man is drunk"), the bullying young cowhands who dominate the town will never allow her to leave. When Paladin suggests she could manage stage fare to another town nearby, she sneers: "Sure. Maybe I can get a job as a dance hall hostess. I could get pawed over for a nickel a dance by the same bunch as down here, just different names." Out of pity, and against his better judgment, Paladin agrees to help her get to San Francisco. But Sally proves a much less sympathetic character than Mary and Dot. She not only lacks their work ethic, she also lacks their integrity and courage. Sally cares for nothing but Sally, which is why she fails in the crisis. When Paladin needs her to testify about the cowboys' attack on him, she is too afraid to tell the truth. Because she lies, three men die and Paladin is wounded. Though he still gives her the money to leave town, he forces it on her like a curse. Since she will still be the same weak selfish woman wherever she goes, changing towns will not change her life.[20]

Some women manage to find contentment even in these modest jobs, however. Maggie in "Saturday Night" (4:5, 10/8/60) is Sally's polar opposite, a cheerful, good-natured, virtuous young Irishwoman who enjoys her work as a waitress in the saloon's dining room. Arriving in town with nothing but "a broken heart and an empty purse," she faced bleak odds: about the only work for women was in the saloons. But the town's marshal took pity on her and found her a decent position. Far from feeling trapped or resentful in her work, Maggie rejoices to have a clean, respectable way to support herself. Young Tuolomme in "The Colonel and the Lady" (1:11, 11/23/57) is even happier in her work as a housemaid to Mrs. Lathrop—first, because she is utterly devoted to her mistress, the woman who took her out of the saloons at age 14 to give her both a home and a respectable job, and second, because she is treated more like a family member than a servant. Despite their inequality of status, these two women are bound together by strong affection and mutual loyalty. But perhaps the most touching of these women is little Miss Felton from "The Lady on the Wall" (3:23, 3/20/60), an elderly bird-like woman who is the housekeeper at the single remaining hotel in Bonanza, once a booming mine town but now a ghost town. The remaining inhabitants are four old men and the hotel's middle-aged owner, plus the nearly-invisible Miss Felton, and the only treasure in town is the luminous portrait of a young woman that hangs over the bar: "Annie," painted decades ago by the famous painter Henry Soutelle during Bonanza's heyday. When the painting mysteriously disappears, Paladin not only recovers it but learns Miss Felton's incredible secret: she is Annie, the long-ago model for the portrait, the painter's adored mistress and the rightful owner of the painting. As the old woman tells her story, basking in the memories of her golden time of youth and beauty and love, the old men are astounded, but as soon as she finishes, they quickly turn away to offer their nightly toast to their beloved portrait. Paladin alone turns to Miss Felton and sweetly toasts the living woman, the only man in the room who can recognize the young beauty lingering in the old woman's eyes.

The Indirect Road to Power

For poor single women on their own, jobs allow them to make a life for themselves, though, as we have seen, some of those lives are more satisfactory than others. However, women raised with wealth and high social status who find themselves alone are caught in a terrible paradox. Being women, they often have no legal right to act in their own behalf; being from the privileged classes, taking any job for pay would lose them status and all their friends. Their only serious option is to find some man to take care of them. Despite the unfairness of these rules, some women try their best to live within them—for example, The Honorable Diana Coulter in "The Lady" (2:10, 11/15/58). When she hires Paladin to guide her to her brother's ranch near Shiprock, Arizona, Paladin wonders why an English aristocrat is going to such an isolated spot. She explains calmly that her brother is her only immediate family, and "in England, a spinster of my station doesn't have much choice."[21] That is, if she does not or cannot marry, her only option is to throw herself on the mercy of any relative that will take her in, under whatever conditions that relative imposes. Diana earns our sympathy, and Paladin's, by the courageous and unselfpitying way she confronts her situation, doing what needs to be done with classic British stoicism.

Where Diana Coulter bravely accepts her fate, another English aristocrat bitterly resists the constraints of her gender. In "Champagne Safari" (3:12, 12/5/59), Charity, the beautiful, intelligent sister of the virtuous but foolish Lord Trevington, seethes with resentment: though she has twice the brains and discipline of her brother, as a woman she is last in the line of succession to the family title and estates. But Lord Trevington's buffalo-hunting expedition to America has given her an ideal opportunity to remove the other heirs permanently—cousin Roddy, and then brother Charles himself, before he can marry and sire a son who would cut her out of the succession for good.[22] First Roddy is killed, officially by Indians though actually by Charity's hired assassin; later Charles is saved only by Paladin's timely intervention. Charity's facility with poisons might threaten Paladin's life, as well, if he were foolish enough to underestimate his opponent merely because she is a woman. Though Charity's situation is certainly unjust—refused position and power not on her merits, but simply because she is a woman—her solution is unconscionable, and in the end, she will be punished for it.

Unlike Charity, Mrs. Sara Howard in "The Haunted Trees" (2:38, 6/13/59), a handsome new widow, has no ambition to manage her own business affairs. Though fully as ruthless and selfish as the English aristocrat, Sara's only ambitions are to live luxuriously and comfortably on some man's hard work. But with her husband dead, she needs a new man to run the lucrative lumber business she inherited. Taking full advantage of men's weaknesses, Sara has learned to get her own way by indirect, dishonest methods; she uses her beauty and her seductive wiles to manipulate men into doing what she wants. First, she avoids having to share the estate by telling her husband a shameful lie so he will disinherit his only son, Ben. Then when Ben goes into hiding around the camp rather than leaving, she stages some minor sabotages against her own operations and throws the blame on Ben, hoping to turn the lumbermen against him. When that doesn't work, she hires Paladin to remove Ben permanently. The gunfighter so impresses her that she tries to seduce him with a double bribe, marriage to her, plus control of the valuable lumber business. Luckily, Paladin has no trouble seeing through this offer. He recognizes easily that Sara's regard for him is purely selfish: her only interest is in what she can entice him to do for her.

Another woman makes Paladin and several other men an even more brazen version of this offer. In "Love of a Bad Woman" (3:28, 3/26/60), a "young, attractive widow of means" publishes a personals ad seeking a new husband. Unfortunately, as Paladin's client informs him, the woman is not, in fact, a widow: she is his wife. When Paladin answers the ad on instructions from his client, he finds a house full of elegant art works, the most elegant of which is Mrs. Sommers herself, but she complains that her husband has locked her away with his other treasures as "one of the prize objects of his collection." No longer willing to be an object in anyone's collection, she has adopted a simple plan: she has chosen six gunmen out of all her suitors, and promises to marry whichever of them kills her husband. She smiles serenely as she discusses all this death (and not just her husband's, because some of the six men hunting him will certainly die) and flirts charmingly with Paladin—or it would be charming if she were not so calculating. It becomes clear that she is very like her husband, both "collectors" with no concern for other people's lives or feelings. Though Paladin is forced to accompany Sommers as he kills all the other gunmen, and finally has to kill his client on Sommers' own doorstep in self-defense, he refuses the prize he has "won"—the widow—and walks away with barely-concealed disgust and a little fear. Significantly, the episode ends not with his exit, but with a close-up on her face, somber and puzzled: clearly, she does not understand why he refused her generous offer, does not understand how like her husband she has become, and how unattractive the result is, for all her wealth and beauty.

Domestic Women in Non-Domestic Roles

Finally, a number of conventionally domestic women feature in stories where they temporarily step outside their normal household activities to participate in the larger world. For example, in "A Matter of Ethics" (1:5, 10/12/57), a passionate young woman stirs up a lynch mob against the man awaiting trial for murdering her brother. Though it is clear both that the accused is guilty and that he will likely be convicted at trial, Amy craves a more immediate and personal vengeance. When her father rejects her arguments and prepares to stand guard at the jail to protect the prisoner, the mob she has raised attacks him violently, an act that shocks and horrifies her. She had not understood until too late that lynch mobs, once aroused, are very hard to control. Although Amy is driven to action by her feelings as daughter and sister, here those domestic ties are secondary to the philosophical issues: the difference between justice and vengeance, and the necessity of rules for a community to function, issues which are as relevant for a woman as for a man, and which Amy must accept if she is going to be a good citizen.[23]

Surely no more conventional domestic role for a woman exists than a bride—unless she is a mail-order bride, risking everything to travel alone, 2000 miles across country, to marry a man she has met only in letters. Yet that is exactly what shy, plain Christie Smith does in "The Bride" (1:6, 10/19/57). Though her marriage will see her placed firmly and contentedly in her own household, what she had to do to achieve that position is anything but conventionally domestic. In "A Sense of Justice" (2:8, 11/1/58), Sheriff Grayson's young daughter, Julia, reaches far outside her usual domestic realm in order to protect her friend Andy, a simple young man with the mind of a child. When Jim Briggs sexually assaults Julia in a lonely barn, Andy reacts with ferocious strength, pulling Briggs off her and slamming his body against the barn wall—right where a long iron spike protrudes, unintentionally killing the attacker. But when Andy is threatened with hanging for the crime, Julia confesses to the murder in order to save him—a brave step indeed when the dead man is the only son of the town's most powerful landowner.[24] In "The Monster of Moon Ridge" (2:24, 2/28/59), a clever schoolteacher uses her wit, imagination, and a tame bear cub to create a "monster" that scares her superstitious neighbors away from her isolated farm, trying to shelter her mentally handicapped son against teasing and abuse for being different. In "The Education of Sarah Jane" (5:2, 9/12/61), a young woman who is part of a generations-long feud has to decide whether to demand revenge, or let it go—a difficult choice with real-world repercussions. When Sarah Jane Darrow's father becomes the latest victim of the feud, she vows to kill a Tyler, *any* Tyler, in revenge. But when she and Paladin capture the murderer, the boy-man Whit Tyler, Whit points out that he too had killed within the feud, because Sarah Jane's father had killed his father. Though neither of the young people know the cause of the feud, both can cite the line of reciprocal murders, like an obscene parody of Biblical *begats*, a chain of victims and killers back into the dim past. To keep Sarah Jane and Whit from killing each other, Paladin ties them both up, but as they converse for the first time with a member of the other family, they begin to recognize each other as human beings, not just *"a Darrow"* and *"a Tyler."* In the end, both conclude there has been enough killing. Whit makes the first move, protecting Sarah Jane and Paladin from his brothers by swearing there are no Darrows with him. That leaves Sarah Jane with a big decision to make—one which affects not just her and Whit, but both their extended families, their whole community. Since a Darrow was the last to die, she is entitled to revenge; further, Whit is not just a random Tyler, but the actual killer of her father, so Paladin offers to take him in for trial if Sarah Jane wishes. But she announces suddenly that she wants Whit to go free; she even loans him her father's horse so he can get home. In the end, Whit and Sarah Jane may not be friends, but they are no longer enemies—due in large part to Sarah Jane's courage in making a very adult decision.

II. *Women as Centers of Consciousness*

As has been said before, because of Richard Boone's commitment to Method acting and ensemble approaches to theatre, virtually all of the characters on *Have Gun—Will Travel*, women and men, featured characters and minor background figures alike, exhibit consistent interiority, even in the absence of dialogue. The episodes and characters described so far in the chapter should make abundantly clear how vividly characterized the women are. But how do the women characters on the other series compare?

Bonanza can be easily dismissed, as almost none of their women characters were allowed much interiority, largely due to the producer's dismissive attitude toward women. (Of course, to be fair, few of the male characters had much depth and complexity either—not even the Cartwrights, at least in the early seasons.) *Wagon Train* did considerably better by its featured women characters, as by its men, since rich textured roles were what drew popular movie stars to the series. Further, with its four continuing characters often relegated to supporting roles, and with an hour-long time slot, the featured players had unusual scope to develop their characters. Though most of the stories about women stick predictably to conventional domestic issues—love, courtship, jealousy, and marriages good and bad—some of these women tell stories far different from television norms at the time, with full insight into the characters at their center.

For example, "The Ruth Owens Story" (1:4, 10/9/57) stars Shelley Winters as a woman with a young daughter, a new husband, and a secret: a scandalous past as a dance hall girl. Ruth is desperate for a fresh start in the West, but her teenaged brother nearly destroys her chance. Coming to join her after long years of separation, Jimmy fights a man who insults her, killing his attacker in self-defense. But when he learns the man told the truth about Ruth, he scornfully rejects his sister and refuses to defend himself, preferring hanging to living with her shame. Ruth must make a painful choice: will she reveal her secret to the whole train, including her husband, or allow her brother to hang for murder? Though the dance hall work is indeed scandalous—there are even covert hints that she may have been "kept" by the dance hall's owner—the script allows Ruth to appeal for understanding, if not forgiveness. Disowned by her brutal father for marrying a man he disliked, widowed almost immediately with an infant daughter to raise, nowhere to live, no money, and no family to help, she had no option but the dance hall. When she explains her story with passionate and humble repentance, publicly taking the blame for Jimmy's action, he is finally able to forgive her, while her husband accepts and loves her unconditionally. For 1957, this sympathetic treatment of Ruth's tainted past is surprising, and always Ruth's point of view is central.

"The Mary Halstead Story" (1:10, 11/20/57) also examines a woman with a shameful past. Twelve years earlier, Halstead (Agnes Moorehead) had walked out on her husband and six-year-old son, Earl. Now terminally ill, she is going west on the wagon train, trying to find her son to make amends so that he won't hate her. Like Ruth Owens, Mary suffers guilt and shame for her action. But Mary's repentance and her refusal to justify her actions creates compassion for her suffering and softens the judgment. The plot reveals that Earl is the Laramie Kid, leader of a ruthless band of outlaws, recently shot and killed by young Tom not far from the wagon train's path. Though the outlaws try to hang Tom for killing their leader, their vengeance is interrupted, and the young man is rescued by the wagon train, where Mrs. Halstead takes him in as a surrogate son. The lonely orphan boy and the dying widow build a warm relationship that survives even after she learns the painful truth about Earl's outlaw life and Tom's role in his death. When the outlaw gang kidnaps Tom to complete their revenge, she risks her life to persuade them, on her authority as Earl's mother, to let Tom go. She succeeds in her quest, but the physical and emotional stress cause her weakened heart to stop. But she has clearly made amends, if not to her own damaged son, then to Tom in his place. Like Ruth Owens, Mary Halstead has not lived a blameless life, but she is allowed to tell her own story in detail, and, because she is repentant and suffers, she is treated with compassion and even respect. Her perspective undeniably governs the episode.

Other atypical stories about women include "The Clara Beauchamp Story" (1:13, 12/11/57), in which the alcoholic wife (Nina Foch) of an Army colonel nearly starts an Indian war by insulting the local chief, and then risks her life to undo the damage she caused; "The Dora Gray Story" (1:20, 1/29/58), about an unscrupulous con woman (Linda Darnell) helping to sell guns to the Indians; and "The Sarah Drummond Story" (1:27, 4/2/58), about a settler's wife (June Lockhart) who is pregnant with her first child, and locked in bitter conflict with her husband Jeb because the child's father is probably the Indian brave who raped her while Jeb was away on a raid to harass the local tribe. If the baby is half–Indian, Jeb Drummond insists it should be taken to the reservation to raise, while Sarah is determined to keep and love her child, no matter what. Curiously, unlike Ruth and Mary, Sarah Drummond, who should be the center of the episode, is unusually passive. In the opening scenes, the very pregnant Sarah is luminous and serene, but even when the tension builds, Lockhart never conveys much powerful emotion. All the long dramatic speeches belong to Jeb and to his best friend, the rabidly anti–Indian Walt Archer, who will shun the Drummonds if they try to raise a "half-breed" baby.[25] In the end, Walt is miraculously cured of his prejudice, Sarah is allowed to keep her baby, and all ends happily. And even though Lockhart's performance is never as intense as we would like, we understand her point of view about all these events. Even with the limitations of "The Sarah Drummond Story," all of these unusual women characters are more textured and compelling, their adventures more varied, than most of those on either *Gunsmoke* or *Bonanza*.

Though *Gunsmoke* uniquely includes a woman as a series regular, one of four co-stars, that position does not guarantee Miss Kitty a high degree of interiority. For a number of seasons, she is less a real three-dimensional character than a collection of attributes. The prettiest girl at the Long Branch, she flirts cheerfully with Matt Dillon (though clearly she is more serious about their relationship than he is), and often functions as a source of saloon gossip and a sounding board when Matt needs to confide in someone, especially a detail that reveals his vulnerability. She is also useful as a liaison when a woman character needs assistance or advice, or one of her male co-stars needs nursing or comforting. But Kitty herself gets no backstory, no details about family or her life before Dodge, until the end of Season 2. In "Daddy-O" (2:36, 6/1/57), just as she purchases her half-share in the Long Branch, Kitty's charming, long-absent gambler father appears in Dodge and tries to reclaim his daughter. At first his motives seem pure: he wants to make up for lost time with her, to take her back to New Orleans where he can enjoy her company and take care of her properly. She is tempted by this idea, until he insists that she must first sell the Long Branch and turn her money over to him. At last, Kitty recognizes his selfish intent: he is less interested in her companionship than in her assets, so she rejects him, affirming her own worth as a strong, proud, competent woman able to take care of herself. It is an episode in which the character comes into her own as a fully-realized person.

But only a handful of scenes in the 74 preceding episodes give the audience much insight into her true feelings. Even when she is at the center of the plot, as happens three times in Season 1, some other character holds the dramatic center of the scene, stepping forward to save a relatively passive Kitty. In "Magnus" (1:12, 12/24/55), Kitty is threatened with death by a crazed preacher who condemns her as "wicked" because she works in a saloon, but Chester's visiting brother, Magnus, saves the day with a clever intervention, while in "Helping Hands" (1:20, 3/17/56), Kitty is initially in danger when she saves a young man from a lynch mob, but after that precipitating action, she is relegated to the sidelines, more witness than participant. In "Tap Day for Kitty" (1:22, 3/24/56), the plot synopsis indicates she should be a central character: an elderly farmer insists he is going to marry Kitty, despite her threat to go after him with a shotgun if he doesn't leave her alone. When old Nip is later shot in the back by a woman using a shotgun, Matt is forced to treat Kitty as a suspect, a circumstance she bitterly resents. Although their confrontation does allow Kitty to reveal more personality than we have ever seen from her before, ultimately the most potent scenes in the episode belong not to Kitty but to Nettie, the actual culprit—old Nip's housekeeper of twenty years, who had shot him out of hurt and jealousy because he intended to marry someone besides her. In one more episode from the first season, "Cara" (1:36, 7/28/56), though Kitty is peripheral to the plot, she gets another opportunity to reveal strong personal feeling. When an old girlfriend out of Matt's past appears suddenly in Dodge, his reaction to this woman puzzles and worries Kitty, because he conceals so completely from her what he is thinking. Does he still love Cara? Does he trust her, as Kitty definitely does not? Because she doesn't know the answers to these questions, Kitty struggles with her own feelings—concern for Matt, fear about the clarity of his judgment, but also a strong surge of jealousy. But aside from these few moments, and another handful of episodes in Seasons 2 and 3, her scenes in these early seasons are minor and largely functional.

If a continuing woman character on the series receives such short shrift, what can we expect of featured women characters? The pattern is marked: gender significantly affects the way featured characters are treated. Male characters, whether hero, villain, or fool, usually have psychologically plausible reasons for their actions, and we are allowed to understand their point of view even when we do not approve of their behavior. But female characters seldom get the same treatment. As we saw with Kitty, even when women are important to the plot, we seldom have much access to their perspective on events.

True, there are moments in some of the episodes, a scene here or there when a featured woman gets a powerful speech or an emotional moment. In fact, in "Tap Day for Miss Kitty," Nip's jealous housekeeper nearly steals the end of the episode. Confessing her guilt to Matt,

Nettie explains bitterly, "Twenty years I've been with him—cleaning his house, cooking his food, raising his kids [after his wife's death], nursing his crippled old ma. And all them years, he kept saying he'd get married when his ma died." Naturally, she heard this as a promise to marry *her* when that time came, not another woman. When he announces his intention to marry Kitty instead, she shoots him—not to kill, but to wound, to "hurt him some," as he had hurt her. In twenty years, she laments, "He never looked at me!" But now he's looking, and he finally recognizes the wife that has been waiting for him patiently all these years. It's a satisfying end to the episode, partly because Nettie, even in her brief scenes, is one of the best-developed female characters in the entire season.

An even stronger example is "Legal Revenge" (2:8, 11/17/56), which gives us one of the most compelling female characters in *Gunsmoke*'s early seasons. In an isolated cabin, a strange woman (played with chilling power by Cloris Leachman) and her wounded husband are locked in a tense but covert struggle, both rejecting interference from Doc, Matt, and Chester. The atmosphere is ominous and mysterious: as Matt investigates, he realizes that both husband and wife are armed, and neither has apparently slept in days. Matt and Doc are convinced this is a story of a marriage gone desperately wrong, a belief the outcome reinforces: as soon as the man can no longer keep himself awake, Flory kills him in cold blood. But when Matt arrests her for murder, she finally reveals the secret: the man was not her husband, but an outlaw who had killed her husband a few days earlier, though her husband had managed to wound his attacker before he died. Rather than letting Matt hang the criminal, Flory was determined to take revenge in her own hands, for her husband's sake. But since the dead man is a wanted criminal with a reward on his head, her revenge turns out to be "legal."

This is a chilling, suspenseful episode, with all the elements first-rate: a story by John Meston, taut script by Sam Peckinpah, and skillful direction by Andy McLaglen, while the character of Flory Tibbs is compelling—a striking exception to the general treatment of women on the series. But we get no access to Flory's consciousness, seeing her exclusively from the outside, through Matt, Doc and Chester's eyes. That obscurity is necessary to preserve the initial puzzle and the tension, but in the end, this lack of interiority undermines the power of the episode. Worse, Flory's character loses its coherence once the truth is revealed. She suddenly turns diffident, not only refusing the bounty she has earned but asking Matt to articulate her reasons for this choice. When he proposes, it's so she can feel "cleaner" about what she has done, she agrees gratefully. As a result, a powerful performance suddenly dissipates at the last moment in a conventional but psychologically incoherent conclusion.

Two other examples from the first season of *Gunsmoke* show the same pattern of featured women being seen only from the outside. In both "Obie Tater" (1:5, 10/15/55) and "Reed Survives" (1:13, 12/31/55), pretty young saloon girls marry rich old men, and then scheme against them. Obie Tater, being no fool, knows exactly why Ella is willing to marry him: he is rumored to have brought back a fortune from the California gold fields. But he doesn't care: he is so delighted by her warm attentions that he enters the marriage eagerly, with no feeling but gratitude. However, his bride immediately begins scheming with her two male partners to get Obie's money. Though Ella initially agrees to the plot, when her partners start torturing Obie to make him reveal his treasure, she changes her mind; horrified, she tries to defend her husband, but is killed by her partners in the struggle.

By contrast, in "Reed Survives," Lucy's motives for marrying the elderly Ephram Hunt are described as mysterious, though later developments indicate that, as with Ella and Obie Tater, the old farmer's money was an important motive. However, Lucy soon reveals herself as a classic femme fatale. She begs Matt for help, claiming her husband has threatened to kill her because of her "sinful" past as a dance hall girl—though when Matt talks to Ephram, he finds a reasonable man, if rather strict in his religious ideas, who is very much in love with his young pretty wife, and determined to treat her gently, if firmly. Meanwhile, Lucy has calculatedly seduced their handsome young ranch hand, Booth, then urges him to kill her elderly husband before Ephram learns of their affair. Unlike Matt, the naive Booth falls for her lie and shoots the old farmer, but when he comes to claim Lucy as his reward, she laughs in his face and dismisses him brutally. In agony and fury at such betrayal, he strangles her. As a result, a grim and sorrowful Matt will now be forced to hang the hapless young man. Three people dead, all because of Lucy's greed and selfishness.

Both Ella and Lucy are flat, conventional characters, following all the clichés of gold-diggers: both use their sexual allure to take advantage of an elderly, wealthy man, and both turn to male accomplices when violence is needed. Neither has any backstory: questioned by Matt about the women in turn, Kitty can only say of each that they were "mysterious" and "hard to know." Nor is either woman granted any significant interiority: they remain unknowable, of less interest than the men whose lives they have affected so dramatically. The mirror-image endings—Ella's last-minute repentance and Lucy's unrepentant arrogance—are equally clichéd, as is the death that punishes each woman for her sins.

In each episode, the individualized, three-dimensional characters are the men: the besotted husbands (played respectively by leading character actors Royal Dano and John Carradine), and the infatuated young cowhand (played by James Drury).[26] Each husband is allowed to speak revealingly to Matt of his dreams and desires, and of his love for his beautiful young wife, and each in the end accepts the blame for the outcome. Obie Tater genuinely mourns Ella, forgetting her greed and remembering only that she was "so purty," while Ephram Hunt tells Matt with his dying breath that "there's no law to cover an old man being a fool"—in effect, absolving Lucy of responsibility for betraying him because he should have known better. The ends of both episodes further confirm the men's centrality. Although Ella gets a brief line explaining her change of heart—because Obie treated her more kindly than her partners ever did—the episode ends with Obie, grieving over her corpse. Similarly, young Booth gets a moving speech to explain why and how he killed Lucy, revealing her perfidy and the depth of his despair, while Lucy's murder happens only in his narrative: no dramatic death scene for her. Despite their instrumental function in the plots, clearly these two women are not real people, with real motives or perspectives of their own to make their actions psychologically plausible. They are cardboard cutouts, easily digested stereotypes.

But compare these *Gunsmoke* characters to women of a similar social status from *Have Gun—Will Travel*. There are a number of significant saloon girls in *Have Gun* episodes, and each of them is a distinct character, with her own personality and story—and every one has motives and desires we clearly grasp. In "High Wire" (1:8, 11/2/57), Rena is a good-hearted bar girl; though she doesn't like the way Marquette runs his town, the only way she can earn enough to leave is by doing the underhanded things Marquette pays her to do. Given the chance to escape through Paladin's help, she gratefully does the right thing for once. In "The Road to Wickenberg" (2:7, 10/25/58), another bar girl eager to leave her town saves Paladin's life after the corrupt local sheriff drugs, robs, and tries to kill him. But unlike Rena in "High Wire," who is sweet but rather soft, Sue is shrewd and savvy, and always conscious of the main chance: helping Paladin seems like the surest way to get herself out of this town. Once they're away, however, she reveals larger schemes; she tries very hard, and with no little skill, to seduce Paladin, willing to trade her body for a ticket to San Francisco—and perhaps a room in the city at his expense. Though she is beautiful and clever, Sue is also selfish and thoroughly manipulative; everything she does or says is clearly an act, so her attempts to con him are doomed to failure. But her perspective is always clear as she plots her next move.

Unlike Sue, Lily in "Full Circle" (3:34, 5/14/60) has lost all of her youth and much of what beauty she once had, along with most of the confidence needed to keep fighting. All she has left is her love for a charming but ruthless confidence man, Simon Quill, who has betrayed her repeatedly and will inevitably do so again. Though Lily has no illusions about her man, she is willing to sacrifice what little she has for his sake, begging Paladin to save Simon from his enemies. She offers the gunfighter money, her body, anything he wants, in exchange for helping this worthless man. When Paladin refuses angrily, unwilling to watch Simon hurt her again, she snarls bitterly, "Where were you before? Watching over me? You care so much about what happens to me now, why didn't you see I got a good, hard-working man, instead of someone full of nothing but liquor and hard luck?" Obviously, Lily knows she deserves better, but she also knows that deserving has nothing to do with life, and that "little" is better than "nothing." With no pride left, she begs: "Simon wanted me—he *did*. Why can't I have him now?" Defeated, disgusted, Paladin agrees to help, but it ends—as it must where Simon is involved—in a blood-bath. At least this time Simon is among the dead instead of skating free while others pay for his perfidies, though that will not comfort the woman who has lost the little she had. Through each step of this dreadful journey, it is Lily's point of view we follow, never Simon's.

Where Lily is a classic victim, Topaz, the saloon girl in "Brother's Keeper" (4:33, 5/6/61) is unquestionably the sharpest person in this town, cool and forthright, with a clear eye on the goal. When Paladin stumbles into town, having been left for dead on the trail after being attacked by a mountain lion, he's looking for the two men who robbed him in his helpless state. The entire town, fearing his anger, unites to conceal the guilty parties behind a fantastic scrim of lies, but Topaz has a better idea: she frankly negotiates a deal to return Paladin's belongings if he promises to leave town without shooting anyone. And when the true villain tries to kill Paladin in a rigged gunfight, she is the most shocked and apologetic of all.[27] Another impressive saloon girl is strong in a very different way from Topaz. Kate in "The Uneasy Grave" (4:37, 6/3/61) is honest, independent, stubborn, far more courageous than any of the respectable people of Johnsonville, and determined to win justice for her fiancé, a poor cheerful Irishman murdered by the town's First Citizen. Leander Johnson, obsessed with Kate and feeling entitled to keep her for himself, kills his rival out of jealousy, but Johnson's prominence, plus the social marginality of both the victim and the only witness (Kate), convinces the marshal to rule Terence's death "accidental." Kate's story persuades Paladin to help her get justice for Terence, but as he is methodically pursuing his investigation, Kate solves the problem her own way. When Paladin prevents her from shooting Johnson, she proceeds to seduce him in an open hotel parlor, revealing his crazed obsession with a "disreputable" saloon girl to the horrified eyes of the marshal, many of the town's citizens, and his snobbish elderly mother. At this crucial moment, Paladin deftly elicits Johnson's confession about the murder, which gives the marshal no choice but to arrest the town's leading citizen.[28] But with her vengeance complete, Kate finds herself at a loss. When Paladin sympathetically asks about her plans, she answers with a melancholy smile, "I'll go where the wind blows. Someday, someplace, there'll be someone with a laugh and a loneliness that matches mine," as Terence's had done. These final moments of the episode confirm that Kate is the one who matters.

Lucy, in "Ben Jalisco" (5:10, 11/18/61) has a different kind of sad story. Her husband, an uncompromising bounty hunter (the kind that never brings a man in alive), has just escaped from prison. Blaming Lucy for his capture, he is coming to kill her, a threat which brings Paladin to her side to offer protection. Lucy is a remarkable woman: she's afraid of her husband, but calmly refuses to run because, despite her fears, she still loves him. In his absence, she works in a saloon to support herself—not a fancy place like the Long Branch, just a bare wooden shack. She doesn't wear low-cut blouses and short skirts and spangles, just a demure cotton skirt and blouse, but she hustles drinks as well as waiting tables, and she sits on the customers' laps, when required, to drink with them. That is what wounds Ben the most, as he holds her hostage: "I would rather see you dead than see you work in a saloon! Why, Lucy? To *spite* me?" In despair, she replies, "To *eat*, Ben. Just to eat. I don't sew good, and I'm not free to marry, am I?" Unmoved, Jalisco tells Paladin drily, "Did you ever notice what sad stories these saloon girls tell?" Yet Lucy has told the simple truth. Like men, women do what they must to survive; it is not their fault that they are allowed few ways to earn money, and even fewer that are respectable. And though Ben is no cartoon villain but a complex, psychologically plausible character, so too is Lucy, a woman whose motives and feelings matter deeply.

Earlier, when we looked at "Pandora's Box" (5:36, 5/19/62), we saw that the owner of a clap-board-and-canvas saloon walks a tough road, but that saloon's solitary bar girl is even worse off. Hanna at least manages to collect the money and run the show, but Decora can only do what she is told. She is still pretty, but won't be much longer. Unlike anyone else connected with this pitiful establishment, she still has a heart, still tries to show kindness to those in need, but her efforts are often sabotaged or effectively shut down; we can see she will soon stop fighting. As a spectator rather than a central participant in this mysterious revenge tragedy, Decora survives the killing, but there is no way to know if she will find someplace better to go now that Hanna's has been destroyed. Under the best of conditions, women who work in saloons don't have many options, a point *Have Gun—Will Travel* makes repeatedly and sympathetically, in part by making sure that these women's point of view is accessible to viewers.

As a hostess in a gambling operation, Sarah in "The Poker Fiend" (4:9, 11/12/60) is, socially speaking, a cut above the ordinary saloon girl, but she is also older and harder. Like Lily in "Full Circle," Sarah has unfortunately fallen in love with a worthless man—in her case, the wealthy John Paul Neal, a weak self-pitying lump of a man, perhaps the worst poker player in the world, who has been trapped for five months in a losing poker game with Sarah's employer, the ruthless Waller. As Sarah confesses to Paladin with shamed self-awareness, "Silly, isn't it? [Neal]'s forty; he looks fifty. *Over*. But I love him. I *need* him," adding despairingly, "It's the same thing, isn't it?" That equation of love and need reveals worlds about Sarah's past life, probably a bleak succession of exploitative men and broken promises. Though John Paul is rich, money is not Sarah's goal: in fact, she tells Paladin how to beat Neal at poker, explaining, "I haven't got a chance against his wife as long as he has his money." But if he is broke, Neal's wife will let him go, and Sarah will get her chance.

Unfortunately for Sarah, Paladin has been hired by Mrs. Neal precisely to save her husband's money (which she values far more than her husband) by extracting him from the game. As Paladin discovers, however, Neal is a weakling: though he desperately wants out of the game, he is too afraid of Waller to leave. But when Paladin's offer of help threatens to give Neal something resembling a spine, Sarah turns on both men fiercely, fighting for Neal with every weapon at her disposal: charm, contempt, earnest pleading, anger, in rapid succession—anything that might drive Paladin away and keep Neal by her side. She is determined and desperate, bitter and fearful, and full of self-contempt at her need for this hapless pudding of a man, all at once, and we are privy to it all.

Yet she is not the protagonist of the episode, just a significant member of an ensemble cast. During the climactic poker game in which Paladin and Waller battle for Neal's soul, Sarah is a restless, agonized observer rather than a part of the action; yet, despite having few lines, she is a compelling presence, her face often on screen in reaction shots. When Paladin ultimately wins Neal away from his tormentor, Sarah is bereft, though she heroically pretends confidence, declaring that she expects Neal back soon: "Yes, John Paul, we'll be waiting." But once Neal and Paladin are out of sight, her effortful smile collapses. The final image is not Neal's relief and joy at his escape, but Sarah's blank despair. The effect is to make this woman, with few illusions about herself and even fewer options, the focus of our sympathy. Though Neal may be the protagonist, the woman he had neither valued nor deserved gets far more of our attention. It is a quietly moving conclusion, and characteristic of the way the entire series treats women.

Finally, in "Dream Girl" (5:22, 2/10/62), another saloon girl is treated in even more unexpected ways. An innocent young miner, having collected a fortune in gold dust during five years' solitary work, asks Paladin's help to claim the girl he had fallen in love with at a single meeting years before. Buddy is so certain that Ginger will be waiting for him that he has not bothered to see her or even to send a letter in five years. Paladin's investigation reveals that Ginger is a saloon girl—just as she had been five years earlier, though Buddy believes he had met her on her way to church. As Buddy enthusiastically greets Ginger, it is clear she has no memory of him, though she plays along with his fantasy to see what she can get out of it. When he gives her the diamond ring he has just bought as her wedding ring, she grabs Buddy's hands and declares earnestly, "Well, I can't tell you how happy I am that we're gonna be married at last!" Then, strategically, she adds, "What's my name, honey? My *married* name. Go on, say it, so I can hear how wonderful it sounds." Though Paladin tries to make Buddy realize that she has no idea who he is, the sweet gullible fellow tells her all she needs to know to continue the charade.

Then Buddy asks her to meet him in private, so they can be alone together. A desperate Paladin dreams up one last ploy to reveal Ginger for the fraud she is, reminding Buddy he had intended to hold his reunion with her on the site of their first meeting, five years earlier. Buddy starts to tell her where to meet him, but Paladin interrupts: "You don't have to remind a woman of the place where she fell in love. You *do* remember, don't you, Miss Adams?" She glares at Paladin, knowing him for her enemy, but then smiles gamely at Buddy: "Sure. Sure I remember." But as she hesitates, Buddy cries, "Virginia—you couldn't have forgotten." At this name, her face changes, her smile turns soft, genuine: "*Virginia. Yeah.* I remember you calling me Virginia. And I remember telling you how it was my mother's name, and how my pa could never bring himself round to calling *me* that because he hated her so much for leaving him." Softly, she murmurs his name, from memory this time: "Buddy Webster. There was a new moon. Yeah. There was a moon shining on the water and—there were willow trees." Paladin's face is a study as he listens to her: this is a very different woman than the opportunistic saloon girl who had been playing Buddy moments before. These are genuine memories, and genuine feelings. She is not quite—not entirely —what he thought, and he is forced to reevaluate his judgment.

The young couple go off to their meeting, though Paladin cautiously keeps custody of Buddy's fortune for the moment. When Buddy returns, glowing with happiness, to announce their marriage plans, Paladin tells him the truth about Ginger's past—a truth he angrily rejects, rushing off to meet his bride. Secretly following Buddy to the rendezvous, Paladin is able to save the young man from the ambush staged by Ginger's partners. In her favor, it is clear that Ginger herself thought they were only going to steal Buddy's hard-earned money; when she realizes her two partners plan to kill the young miner in cold blood, she is horrified, and seems more relieved than distressed when Paladin shoots them both in self-defense.

But even Buddy now understands that she had never intended to marry him. Humiliated and disillusioned, the young miner follows Ginger back to the saloon, where he lashes out viciously at her. Without the dream he has worked for all these years, he declares, what good is his half-million dollars? Nearly weeping, he shouts, "That was for *you*, saloon girl! I was gonna buy you the world. I could have given you a new life!" Ginger replies, with hard-headed practicality, "Thanks, Buddy—but you'd have had to start me over from a newborn baby to do that. I gotta get to work." But Buddy can't let it go. She isn't suffering enough to soothe his wounded feelings. In a frenzy, he buys the saloon and drives all the customers out of it—but he won't let her leave with the others: he needs to punish her more. Surprisingly, Ginger stands up to him, snarling, "You ain't got enough money to buy me, you whining rabbit!" Buddy begins to break everything in the place, glassware, mirrors, furniture, and when even that doesn't satisfy the primal fury in him, he prepares to burn down the saloon in order to "ruin" Ginger.

At that point, Paladin intervenes. He too has been watching Ginger's reactions, evaluating her character—and he understands things about her that Buddy doesn't. Ruin Ginger? he says.

> Why? Because you're young and inexperienced? Because you imagined a girl to be something she isn't? She was a saloon girl when you met her, Buddy. And she's still a saloon girl. She hasn't changed a bit. You want her to pay for your lack of reality? She didn't ask you to pin this dream on her. She didn't even remember you.

Buddy wails, "But I loved her!" Paladin replies, "You loved a picture in your mind. Look at her. Go on, look at her. Now what kind of a life do you suppose *she's* had? Do you think a woman chooses this line of work if she doesn't have to? I've got an idea this world's hurt her just about enough." After a long moment's thought, Buddy apologizes to Ginger and, with humble sincerity, offers to "try and forget it and still make an honest woman of you." Ginger replies firmly, "I don't have to be married to be honest." Buddy is puzzled: if she doesn't want marriage, what does she want? She looks around at the wrecked saloon: "Well, it's not in much shape now, but...." Buddy laughs and instantly hands over the deed. As he and Paladin leave, she begins to clean up the mess, invigorated with new purpose and dignity.

This is a remarkable conclusion to this story. In 1962, to suggest that for a young woman, owning her own business would be preferable to an honest marriage—and marriage, at that, to a sweet, thoughtful, handsome, *rich* young man—runs counter to all the conventional notions of what makes an appropriate life for women. It could be argued that, like the saloon girls in the *Gunsmoke* episodes, Ginger doesn't deserve to marry a respectable man like Buddy, but that isn't the tone of the episode. Paladin, the voice of moral authority who points out Ginger's legitimate claims on Buddy's sympathy, judges her not on her profession alone but on her character. He recognizes the genuine woman underneath the less-savory behavior required by her job—and further understands the kind of life history that would lead a woman into such an occupation. He sees her strength, her pragmatism, and even a kind of integrity that is difficult to maintain in a profession that obliges her to play on men's weaknesses. More important, like all the other women (indeed, like all the other characters of either gender) on *Have Gun—Will Travel*, virtuous or wicked, strong or weak, or anywhere in between, Ginger is a textured, three-dimensional character with a point of view that we are allowed to see.

In an era when American women were restricted by law and custom to a narrow range of life choices, *Have Gun—Will Travel* challenged conventional assumptions about women's nature and abilities. Some of the challenges were overt, like Dr. Phyllis Thackeray and the other explicitly feminist characters and themes. Many were more subtle—the long parade of women characters in all their rich variety, with their own points of view, granted the dignity of full personhood, in contrast to the cardboard women on other series like *Gunsmoke* and *Bonanza*. No contemporary critic ever commented on the roles of women on the show; however, the popularity of the series suggests that audiences liked what they saw, whether or not they were conscious of everything it tried to accomplish. As Kathryn Weibel observes, the images in popular culture have a profound impact on viewers, "the subtle images endlessly depicting men and women leading 'normal' lives." In the passage quoted at the beginning of this chapter, she reminded us, "It is hard for a girl growing up with a Donna Reed image of womanhood to consider a career as a doctor." But a girl who grew up watching *Have Gun—Will Travel* would have seen women leading many different kinds of lives, and being taken seriously as human beings in their own right—a remarkable achievement for a 1950s Western.

Epilogue:
The Man Who Was Paladin

I still find time to be very grateful for my good luck. I'm not playing humble;
I've worked like hell and I do have a talent. But I know a lot of people who
work like hell and have a talent but never get a chance to click.
—Richard Boone, 1971[1]

Despite Boone's two nominations for an Emmy as Paladin (1958-59 and 1959-60), *Have Gun — Will Travel* was not the work he was proudest of. That honor belonged to *The Richard Boone Show* (NBC, 1963-64), his idealistic and doomed attempt to bring repertory theater to television.[2] Later, he often dismissed Paladin as a shallow cardboard character, a part he could play "in his sleep"[3]; yet it was as Paladin that audiences loved and remembered him best. The series continued to please viewers year after year, and would have stayed on television longer if he had been willing to continue in the role. Virtually every obituary of Richard Boone identified him first and foremost as the star of *Have Gun — Will Travel*. But a deeper irony is that, despite the actor's later feelings about the character who made his career, those who knew him best insisted that Richard Boone *was* Paladin. Claire, his wife of thirty years, declared, "I can't begin to tell you how wonderful he was. He was a true renaissance man and very much like Paladin from *Have Gun — Will Travel*. He had a wonderful sense of humor. He was always laughing. He was interested in everything, and there wasn't a subject that anyone could bring up that he couldn't talk about intelligently." Boone's son, Peter, agrees: every time he sees one of the *Have Gun* episodes, he says, "I'm seeing my dad up there." Richard's sister, B'Lou, described other traits her brother shared with Paladin, like his strong personal sense of responsibility and a deep commitment to justice: "He would not let up when he believed in something, particularly if he believed that someone who couldn't protect himself was being treated unfairly."[4]

Many of Paladin's virtues appear in the lessons Richard Boone taught his son. "My father always told me that I should be able to speak comfortably with anyone, no matter who it was—whether it be some very wealthy person or just a regular soul like myself or someone who's down on his luck. He taught me that you deal with people as people and not fall into that trap." And, Peter emphasized, his father did not just preach this doctrine, but practiced it.

Most significantly, unlike many famous fathers, Boone let his son "not try to be Richard Boone II. He wanted me to be who I am and to be very comfortable with that. He wanted me to achieve in my own way.... He always said, 'I want you to do the best that you can. I don't want you to let down or lie down on the job, but just do what you can, work hard, and everything will be all right.'"[5]

Though Richard Boone, long years later, may have looked down on Paladin, the public who watched his show week after week for six years knew better. After the last episode of *Have Gun—Will Travel* was broadcast in May 1963, Jack Smith of the *Los Angeles Times* wrote an appreciation that described the weekly episodes as sermons delivered to the American television audience: "Paladin played no less a role than redeemer. He staked his skin to deliver the weak and punish the wicked." What he admired most, Smith explained, was Paladin's devotion to duty, the way he would walk away from a magnificent meal, tickets to the opera, or an exquisite lady with a philosophical shrug and ride out into the wilderness to deliver the assistance that only he could provide. As Smith concluded admiringly, "I always knew I wasn't that much of a man."[6]

That was really what we learned from Paladin, and from Richard Boone, the man who created him: what it meant to be a man. Paladin seemed to resolve the contraries about manhood that were so troubling to Americans in the 1950s and '60s. He was strong and confident—so confident in his strength that he could be compassionate and nurturing without fear of looking weak. Undeniably a man of action, skilled in a wide repertory of violence, he also valued, music, poetry—all those products of the high culture which Americans had learned to associate with women. But when Paladin quoted Keats or Shakespeare, there was nothing remotely effeminate about it. A man of principle and conviction, he was still a careful listener, who knew there was another side to each story that needed to be heard, a perceptive judge who was open to persuasion and capable of questioning, and revising, his own judgments. Paladin was a powerful man who accepted the responsibility that came with power, and the limits: he used his power to serve the larger community rather than his own private ends. Most significantly, in a culture that valued conformity so highly, Paladin (like Boone) insisted on the rights of minorities to be respected and judged as human beings, in the context of their history and on their own terms, not for how well they resembled—or failed to resemble—the majority.

To have conveyed these values to a broad audience, through a highly commercialized medium and in a form that so many found compelling: that is an achievement that anyone could be proud of, even Richard Boone himself.

Appendix:
Recommended Episodes

The "best episodes" of a television show are always a subjective choice, but, after repeated watching, these are the episodes I return to with pleasure and satisfaction.

Season 1

1:2—"The Outlaw" (9/21/57) ★ ★ ★
Charles Bronson as a psychologically complex outlaw; script by Sam Rolfe, series creator.

1:6—"The Bride" (10/19/57) ★ ★ ★
Marian Seldes as a mail-order bride; script co-written by series producer (and Seldes' husband) Julian Claman.

1:8—"High Wire" (11/2/57) ★ ★
Strother Martin as a washed-up tightrope walker; John Dehner is deliciously villainous.

1:11—"The Colonel and the Lady" (11/23/57) ★ ★
June Vincent as a virtuous wife whose husband mistrusts her. Several strong women characters.

1:25—"The O'Hare Story" (3/1/58) ★ ★
Great character actor Victor McLaglen (father of director Andy McLaglen) in one of his last roles, in a sanitized version of William Mulholland's story.

1:26—"Birds of a Feather" (3/8/58) ★ ★
Paladin teams with another gunfighter to solve a problem. Considerable humor.

1:27—"The Teacher" (3/15/58) ★ ★ ★
Marian Seldes as a teacher being threatened for teaching both sides of the Civil War. Script by Sam Rolfe.

1:28—"Killer's Widow" (3/22/58) ★ ★ ★
Barbara Baxley as the widow of an outlaw Paladin killed. Important for Paladin's meditations on his life as a gunman.

1:31—"Hey Boy's Revenge" (4/12/58) ★ ★ ★
Hey Boy is the protagonist; Pernell Roberts is beautifully dastardly as the villain. One of the first stories on TV about the exploitation of Chinese immigrants. Script by Albert Aley.

1:32—"The Five Books of Owen Deaver" (4/26/58) ★ ★ ★
Early treatment of key ideas about law and justice, the relationship of lawman to town. Vivid characters, strong performances. Script by Sam Rolfe.

Season 2

2:1—"The Man Hunter" (9/13/58) ★ ★
Paladin becomes the hunted. Strong performances by Joseph Calleia as the sheriff and Martin Balsam as the villain. First script by Harry Julian Fink.

2:2—"In an Evil Time" (9/20/58) ★ ★ ★
Hank Patterson's first appearance, playing

Pappy French, small-time outlaw. First script by Shimon Wincelberg. Ending is a bit over-the-top (both the writing and the performance), but that is a small flaw in a strong entry.

2:5—"Duel at Florence" (10/11/58) ★ ★
Interesting analysis of a man who prefers not to fight, and why his fiancee wants him to be stronger. What does courage look like?

2:6—"The Protégé" (10/18/58) ★ ★ ★
Peter Breck stars as a young man who pays Paladin to teach him how to use a gun, and then turns into the kind of bully he picked up a gun to fight.

2:9—"Young Gun" (11/8/58) ★ ★
The cost of being a gunfighter—to the man himself, and his family. Strong script by Albert Aley.

2:11—"A Snare for Murder" (11/22/58) ★ ★ ★
Harry Morgan and Harry Bartell star in taut story of schemes and paranoia between old partners.

2:15—"The Moor's Revenge" (12/27/58) ★ ★ ★
Vincent Price and Patricia Morison play husband-and-wife Shakespearean actors in the Wild West. Comic episode, but the Shakespeare is really good. Morey Amsterdam co-stars.

2:22—"The Scorched Feather" (2/14/59) ★ ★ ★
Lon Chaney, Jr., as an old Indian scout being hunted by a Comanche war chief—his son.

2:27—"Incident at Borrasca Bend"— 3/21/59 ★ ★
Jacques Aubuchon in a great turn as judge in a kangaroo court.

2:31—"The Man Who Lost" (4/25/59) ★ ★ ★
Mort Mills and Jack Elam featured. Script by Harry Julian Fink. Ida Lupino's first directorial outing for the series.

2:37—"Heritage of Anger" (6/6/59) ★ ★ ★
A young boy is caught between the Mexican heritage of his birth and the Anglo heritage of his adoptive parents. Joseph (José) is played by Ricky Vera.

Season 3

3:1—"First, Catch a Tiger" (9/12/59) ★ ★ ★
Paladin being stalked. Strong performances from John Anderson and Harry Bartell. Thoughtful script by Harry Julian Fink, directed by Ida Lupino.

3:2—"Episode in Laredo" (9/19/59) ★ ★ ★
Famous gunfighter Sam Tuttle has to kill Paladin to preserve his reputation, but dreads the confrontation—especially because it is his son's 10th birthday. One of Gene Roddenberry's best scripts.

3:4—"The Posse" (10/3/59) ★ ★ ★
Paladin is framed for murder. Strong performances by Perry Cook, Harry Carey, Jr., Denver Pyle, and Ken Curtis, almost unrecognizable in a dark role. Another strong script from Gene Roddenberry.

3:17—"The Day of the Bad Man" (1/9/60) ★ ★
Just for fun. Mild Eastern schoolteacher pretends to be a gunfighter out of the dime novels, and fights off a real gunfighter. Robert E. Thompson's first script for the series; directed by Ida Lupino.

3:20—"Return to Fort Benjamin" (1/30/60) ★ ★ ★
Strong performances by Anthony Caruso as Yellow Star (Gimp the Indian); Robert Wilke as the major and Charles Aidman as the lieutenant. The non-speaking role of the Sioux chief is played by Chief White Horse. Strong script by Robert E. Thompson.

3:21—"The Night the Town Died" (2/6/60) ★ ★ ★
Powerful script about a lynching that destroys a town. Strong performances by Robert J. Stevenson and Mary Gregory as the sheriff and his wife. Boone's first directorial outing in the series.

3:23—"Lady on the Wall" (2/2/60) ★ ★ ★
Delicate comedy. Great performances by a quartet of old character actors, especially Ralph Moody and Hank Patterson, plus Lillian Bronson as Miss Felton. Ida Lupino directs.

3:26—"Fight at Adobe Wells" (3/12/60) ★ ★ ★
Quanah Parker, the half-white Comanche war chief, has a party of whites trapped in an old fort. Parker and Paladin both take a risk to trust each other. Sympathetic handling of the Indian themes.

3:28—"Love of a Bad Woman" (3/26/60) ★ ★
Strong performances by Larry Dobkin and Geraldine Brooks as a married couple in deadly combat. Paladin is caught in the middle.

3:30—"Lady with a Gun" (4/9/60) ★ ★ ★
The limits of revenge, the power of forgiveness, and two strong women. Directed by Ida Lupino.

3:31—"Never Help the Devil" (4/16/60) ★ ★ ★
A cold-blooded gunfighter, a once-good sheriff who has gotten too old—and only Paladin can help them both.

3:34—"Full Circle" (5/14/60) ★ ★ ★
A con man who once left Paladin to die in his place needs help again. Paladin would refuse, except that poor sad Lily begs for this worthless man's life.

3:35—"The Twins" (5/21/60) ★ ★
Adam and Sam Mirakian are identical twins, but one of them is a cold-blooded killer and one is Paladin's client; only Adam's wife can tell the men apart.

3:36—"The Campaign of Billy Banjo" (5/28/60) ★ ★ ★
Strong performances from Jacques Aubuchon as Billy, Rita Lynn as his wife Elise, and Victor Perrin as Sheriff Cooley. Directed by Richard Boone.

Season 4

4:1—"The Fatalist" (9/10/60) ★ ★ ★
The first appearance of Nathan Shotness, played by Martin Gabel. Strong performance also from Robert Blake as a baby outlaw. Script by Shimon Wincelberg.

4:3—"A Head of Hair" (9/24/60) ★ ★ ★
Powerful performance by Ben Johnson as an Indian scout more Sioux than white. Excellent script by Harry Julian Fink.

4:6—"The Calf" (10/15/60) ★ ★
Strong performances by Parker Fennelly, Denver Pyle as the heavy, and teenaged Don Grady (just starting 11 seasons on *My Three Sons* as middle son Robbie).

4:7—"The Tender Gun" (10/22/60) ★ ★
For fun: Jeanette Nolan as Sheriff Maude Smugly cons Paladin into helping her drive off a gang. A lovely two-hander.

4:8—"The Killing of Jessie May" (10/29/60) ★ ★ ★
Strong performances by Robert Blake as Jessie May, William Talman and Hari Rhodes as Jessie's friends, and a potent script by Harry Julian Fink. First appearance of a black actor on the series.

4:9—"The Poker Fiend" (11/12/60) ★ ★ ★
Great performances by Jack Weston as Neal, Brett Somers as Sarah, and Peter Falk as Waller, in one of his first appearances on filmed television.

4:15—"The Puppeteer" (12/24/60) ★ ★ ★
Powerful performances by Denver Pyle as the general, Natalie Norwick as his wife, and above all, Crahan Denton as Burnaby, the puppeteer. Script by Shimon Wincelberg. Peter Boone has a bit part.

4:17–4:18—"A Quiet Night in Town" 1 & 2 (1/7–14/61) ★ ★ ★
The only two-part episode. Strong script by Harry Julian Fink, good performances. Sydney Pollack as the villain.

4:19—"The Princess and the Gunfighter" (1/21/61) ★ ★ ★
Paladin falls in love. Lovely performance by Arline Sax. Solid script by Robert E. Thompson.

4:21—"The Long Way Home" (2/4/61) ★ ★ ★
Ivan Dixon stars as a former slave and wanted man. Script by Shimon Wincelberg.

4:23—"The Fatal Flaw" (2/25/61) ★ ★ ★
Royal Dano as the villain; Jena Engstrom as the girl he tries to win over. Strong story.

4:37—"The Uneasy Grave" (6/3/61) ★ ★ ★
Strong performances by Pippa Scott as Kate, and Werner Klemperer as the heavy.

Season 5

5:2—"The Education of Sarah Jane" (9/23/61) ★ ★ ★
Jena Engstrom as Sarah Jane, Duane Eddy as Whit, inheritors of a deadly feud. Script by Betty Andrews.

5:5—"A Proof of Love" (10/14/61) ★ ★
Charles Bronson gets a comic outing as a timid man whose neighbor has stolen his Greek mail-order bride. Fun—and Greek dancing.

5:8—"The Hanging of Aaron Gibbs" (11/4/61) ★ ★ ★
Odetta as Sarah Gibbs; Rupert Crosse as Aaron; Roy Barcroft as the marshal. Script by Robert E. Thompson. Powerful and quiet, except for some melodramatic excess in the final scene by Ed Faulkner.

5:10—"Ben Jalisco" (11/18/61) ★ ★ ★
Charles Bronson as a deadly bounty hunter; Coleen Gray as his wife, Lucy. Script by Harry Julian Fink. Dark, dark, dark, but well done.

5:11—"The Brothers" (11/25/61) ★ ★ ★
Buddy Ebsen as the villain; Paul Hartman as Possum. Only which one is crazy? Darkly funny script by Robert E. Thompson.

5:14—"Blind Circle" (12/16/61) ★ ★
Hank Patterson as an old bounty hunter trying to cope with a changing world.

5:15—"The Kid" (12/23/61) ★ ★ ★
Jacques Aubuchon as Moriarty puts up his young son as collateral in a poker game. Paladin wins. Script by Joanne Court.

5:17—"Lazarus" (1/20/62) ★ ★ ★
Strother Martin's tour de force as a drunk who gets brave when he thinks he's dying, with disastrous results. Comic with a point.

5:20—"The Exiles" (1/27/62) ★ ★ ★
Mexican general and former aristocrats in conflict learn to respect each other. Script by Robert E. Thompson.

5:22—"Dream Girl" (2/10/62) ★ ★ ★
Hal Needham stars as Buddy; Peggy Ann Garner is Ginger. Most parts in the episode played by crew members who were members of Boone's acting class.

5:25—"The Trap" (3/3/62) ★ ★ ★
Crahan Denton as an embattled marshal, reaching the end of the line; Jeanette Nolan as the woman he loves.

5:29—"Silent Death, Secret Death" (3/31/62) ★ ★
A suspenseful two-hander with Robert Emhardt as a megalomaniac trying to stay alive through cunning and deceit.

5:36—"Pandora's Box" (5/19/62) ★ ★ ★
Taking a young killer to justice, Paladin stops overnight at a traveling saloon where the kid had grown up. Strong performances from Martin West as Billy Joe, plus Robert J. Stevenson, Ken Curtis, and Lorna Thayer.

Season 6

6:1—"Genesis" (9/15/62) ★
Paladin's origin story. Not a good episode, but essential to the series, and Boone's own favorite.

6:3—"The Fifth Bullet" (9/29/62) ★ ★ ★
Ben Johnson as a man just released from prison, after being convicted unjustly. Dorothy Dells as his wife, and Peter Boone as his son. Script by Harry Julian Fink.

6:4—"A Place for Abel Hix" (10/6/62) ★ ★
Lovely performance by Robert Blake as a young Mexican shepherd.

6:5—"Beau Geste" (10/13/62) ★ ★
Sheriff plans to retire but is not sure how to stay alive afterward. Good guy wins in the end.

6:8—"The Predators" (11/3/62) ★ ★ ★
Paladin gets the wrong man, for a change. Good performances by Richard Jaeckel and Elen Willard. Another great script by Harry Julian Fink.

6:14—"Trial at Tablerock" (12/15/62) ★ ★
When District Attorney tries to subvert the law for personal vengeance, Paladin fights against him in court. Script by Gene Roddenberry.

6:16—"The Treasure" (12/19/62) ★ ★
Where is the treasure Jess Hardin hid before he went to prison? DeForest Kelley and Lee Van Cleef play great villains. Script by Herb Meadow (series co-creator) and Robert E. Thompson.

6:19—"The Debutante" (1/19/63) ★ ★
Comic episode with feminist twist. Gale Garnett as Prudence; Wayne Rogers as Daniel; Robert Emhardt as Amos. Script by Gwen Bagni Gielgud.

6:21—"American Primitive" (2/2/63) ★ ★ ★
Harry Morgan as Sheriff Ernie Backwater; Robert Wilke as Will Tybee, a mountain of a man who kills the wrong men. Script by Harry Julian Fink.

6:26—"Sweet Lady of the Moon" (3/9/63) ★ ★ ★
Crahan Denton in another mesmerizing performance as a homicidal maniac who was thought cured. Harry Carey, Jr., Dorothy Dells, and Robert J. Stevenson do solid work. Script by Harry Julian Fink. Boone directed.

Chapter Notes

Introduction

1. All the data on Westerns on TV in these years is drawn from Brooks and Marsh, *Complete Directory to Prime Time Television*.

2. Brooks and Marsh, 380.

3. However, because one-hour Westerns were difficult to produce on a weekly basis in that period, *Cheyenne* appeared only every second or third week, alternating with two other non–Western series under the umbrella title *Warner Brothers Presents*.

4. In 2010, the original *Law and Order* series tied the twenty-season milestone, but its twenty seasons produced only 456 episodes to *Gunsmoke*'s total of 635.

Death Valley Days ran 23 seasons on television after an initial 22-season run on the radio; but as both a syndicated show and an anthology show, it belongs to a different category than a series with continuing characters.

5. Brooks and Marsh, xvii.

6. This dramatic collapse in popularity is the reason I have drawn my deadline in 1963, the year *Have Gun—Will Travel* left the air. By doing so, I necessarily omit discussion of such later Westerns as *The Virginian* (1962–1971), based on the 1902 novel by Owen Wister; *The Big Valley* (1965–69), starring Barbara Stanwyck as the matriarch of a ranching family; the comic science-fiction Western *The Wild, Wild West* (1965–69); *Hec Ramsey* (1972–74), about a scientific young lawman in 1900; *Kung Fu* (1972–1975), the "Eastern Western"; *Little House on the Prairie* (1974–1983), based on the stories of Laura Ingalls Wilder; *The Young Riders* (1989–92), about the Pony Express; *Dr. Quinn, Medicine Woman* (1993–1998), and *Deadwood* (2004–2006). There were also a number of popular miniseries, especially *Lonesome Dove* (1989) and four follow-up miniseries, plus two spin-off series.

7. For *Gunsmoke*, see guides by Suzanne and Gabor Barabas and John Peel; for *Wagon Train*, se Rosin; for *Have Gun—Will Travel*, see Grams and Rothel; for *Bonanza*, see Leiby and Shapiro.

Part I: An Overview

1. "Preface," p. x.

2. During the first television season, producer-director Charles Marquis Warren was officially in command, but his stars began to resist his influence more and more adamantly until he left at the end of the first season, to the mutual satisfaction of all concerned (Barabas, 110).

3. Barabas, 32–33. For the way the radio show was softened for television, see Barabas, 106–107.

4. Barabas, 99.

5. Barabas, 85–86.

6. Rosin, 30.

7. Yoggy, 266.

8. Whitney, "Bonanza," 16.

9. Leiby, 15.

10. Leiby, 17.

11. Leiby, 196.

Chapter One

1. Hendrik Ruitenbeek, *The Male Myth* (New York: Dell, 1967), 17. Cited in Pleck, 131. As with all cultural generalizations, there would have been individual men who did not experience this uncertainty about their masculinity, especially independent businessmen and professionals with their own firms, and to a large degree, blue-collar workers as well, whose labor tended to be much more physical and therefore stereotypically masculine. But what is striking in the contemporary critics is how sweeping their statements are, how little qualified by phrases like "many men" or "most men" or "typical men." The statements about masculine uncertainty tend to be categorical and sweeping, with few reservations—additional evidence of the level of anxiety on this subject across the culture.

2. The gap between theory and reality meant that many individuals suffered considerably because their actual temperament did not match their official role. Indeed, that is the subject of a good many Victorian novels.

3. This history and description is summarized from Pleck's ground-breaking work in *The Myth of Masculinity*, which examines in detail the "male sex role identity" and the decades of research done to test its hypotheses, demonstrating conclusively that the research results universally fail to support the hypotheses. He describes the mechanisms by which the researchers misinterpret their own results to reach their conclusions, and ends by offering an alternate hypothesis for the source and nature of gender roles. Pleck's insight into the entire debate proved invaluable to my argument.

4. Pleck, 158–9.

5. Pleck, 3.

6. Numerous studies and surveys from 1959 through 1980 reveal that large proportions of American men believed they lack certain "desirable masculine traits" like "self-confidence, independence, competitiveness" (Pleck, 144).

7. Pleck, 3–4.

8. Skolnick, 52.

9. Within two months after the end of the war, 800,000 women had been fired from jobs in the aircraft industry; a similar circumstance happened in the auto industry and other parts of the industrial economy. By 1947, 2 million women had lost their jobs. Mary P. Ryan, *Womanhood in America: From Colonial Times to the Present* (Danbury, CT: Franklin Watts, 1975), p. 188. Cited in Halberstam, 589.

10. Skolnick, 67.

11. Marilyn Yalom, *A History of the Wife* (New York: HarperCollins, 2001), 350.

12. Hewlett, 243.

13. Skolnick, 68.

14. Skolnick, 69.

15. Halberstam, 588, 590.

16. See Maureen Honey, *Creating Rosie the Riveter: Class, Gender, and Propaganda During World War II* (Amherst: University of Massachusetts Press, 1984), 55. Cited by Skolnick, 66. See also Elaine Taylor May, *Homeward Bound: American Families in the Cold War Era* (New York: Basic Books, 1988), and Pleck, 6–106.

17. Kimmel, 245.

18. *McCall's*, May 1954, 207. Cited by Skolnick, 69.

19. For this discussion about the relationship between parents and children in pre-industrial society, see Hewlett, 256–264.

20. May, 11. Cited by Coontz, 27.

21. Cited in Betty Friedan, *The Feminine Mystique* (New York: W.W. Norton, 1963), 43.

22. Skolnick, 71.

23. Skolnick, 65.

24. Halberstam, 526–7.

25. This being the 1950s when the "generic 'he'" was still the unquestioned norm, the studies were unselfconsciously focused on men, with attention to women largely in their domestic roles as wives of "organization men." It was also a given that women—at least, married white women—in this period did not work outside the home.

26. Kimmel, 240.

27. Nussbaum, 27.

28. Mills, ix.

29. The situation of working-class men differed in some important ways. Because their work was typically manual labor and therefore more traditionally masculine, their self-image as men was often more secure, at least on the job. See Kimmel 248–50, and Coontz 29ff.

30. Kimmel, 238.

31. Kimmel, 251.

32. Kimmel, 251–2. Emphasis added.

33. "The Marlboro Man," *Wikipedia*.

34. For the story of Marlboro's rebranding, see Halberstam, 505. The quote about the Marlboro Man as the ultimate symbol of masculinity comes from Vance Packard's *The Hidden Persuaders* (New York: Pocket Books, 1981), 21, and is cited by Halberstam.

One of the crowning ironies of the Marlboro campaign is that three of the men who were featured in these ads later died of lung cancer: Wayne McLaren, David McLean, and Dick Hammer. In 1992, McLaren even testified before Congress in favor of anti-smoking legislation. He died less than a year later of lung cancer, at age 51 (*Wikipedia*, "The Marlboro Man").

35. Cigarette makers were among the heaviest advertisers on television in this period. Erik Barnouw explains that, in response to the American Cancer Society reports about the deleterious effects of smoking, cigarette makers sponsored more and more Westerns, "with their aura of fresh air, health, and vigor" (*Image Empire*, p. 66).

36. *Broadcasting* (Sept. 2, 1957). Cited by Barnouw, *Image Empire*, 81.

37. Barnouw, *Image Empire*, 81–2.

38. Brauer, 12. Other scholars make the same point, with minor variations in language: MacDonald, *Sheriff*, 78 ff., 111–113; Nachbar, 4–5; Mitchell, 5; Homans, 89.

39. Frederick Jackson Turner, "Significance of the Frontier in American History," Chicago, 1893. For decades, Turner's model dominated American history as a discipline, though later generations of scholars came to challenge it as based on insufficient data. Still later, however, Turner's model was partially restored to credibility. For a brief overview of the model and the attendant controversy, see Flagg, Jeffrey B. "Frederick Jackson Turner 1861–1932." http://www.BGSU.edu/departments/acs/1890s/turner/turner.html.1997.

40. *Sheriff*, 113.

41. MacDonald, *Sheriff*, 107. The language and symbols of the Western also shaped the perceptions of most American G.I.s in Vietnam, virtually all of whom had grown up on television Westerns. According to Loren Baritz's book on the war, *Backfire*, John Wayne was "a model and a standard" for astounding numbers of American G.I.s, while dangerous areas in the jungle were known universally as "Indian country," and Vietnamese scouts were called "Kit Carsons."

42. *Playboy* Panel, "The Womanization of America," *Playboy* (June 1962), 142. Mailer went on to observe, "Because there is very little honor left in American life, there is a certain built-in tendency to destroy masculinity in American men." He did not place all

the blame for this situation on women, admitting that men had collaborated with them in the process; but he believed that, among other catastrophic consequences, the incidence of homosexuality in the nation had increased dramatically, a circumstance he attributed to "a loss of faith in the country, faith in the meaning of one's work, faith in the notion of one's self as a man."

43. Mitchell, 4; emphasis added.

44. In the late nineteenth century, the "dime novels" of Ned Buntline and the Wild West shows of Buffalo Bill Cody were enormously popular; the first true classic of modern Western literature, Owen Wister's *The Virginian*, was published in 1902. Inspired by Wister and by his own first-hand encounters with Western characters and landscape, Zane Grey soon after began publishing a series of novels that dramatically popularized the genre, including *Riders of the Purple Sage* in 1912, one of the best-selling Western novels of all time, and *The Lone Star Ranger* (source of the Lone Ranger films and TV series). In this same time period, Westerns were some of early Hollywood's most popular products and its most reliable money-makers (in the 1920s and '30s, over one hundred films were made based on Grey's Western novels). See Mitchell for the most detailed analysis of Western fiction and film in this early period.

45. Warshow, 46.

46. "Forward" to "Meanwhile Back at the Ranch," *Who's Who in Television and Radio* 1.6 (1955). Cited in MacDonald, *Sheriff*, 51.

47. Nussbaum, 26–7.

48. Pumphrey, "Games," 150.

49. Warshow, 48.

50. "Frontier," 296. Newcomb adds that the on-screen dangers faced by the settlers bear a striking resemblance to the real-life threats haunting the viewers—an interesting observation that puts the anxieties of the 1950s in a more compelling light.

51. Morhaim, 9–10. In making this statement, Arness clearly does not imagine that any of the "people" watching westerns are women. Women might have been shocked, but also pleased to see the marshal help his wife with domestic chores.

52. Mitchell, 26–7.

53. Warshow, 46.

54. Mitchell, 27.

55. MacDonald, *Sheriff*, 73.

56. Hollon, 195. Cited by Winkler, 165.

57. "Our Lawless Heritage," *Atlantic Monthly* (December 1928), 732. Cited by Winkler, 162.

58. Winkler, 162.

59. Hollon, 29; cited by Winkler, 165.

60. Robert Dykstra, *The Cattle Towns* (1968), 121–2. Cited by Winkler, 165.

61. Winkler, 163–4.

62. Dykstra, 137, cited by Winkler, 171.

63. Winkler, 164–5.

64. MacDonald, *Sheriff*, 73.

65. *The Producers' Medium: Conversations with Creators of American TV* (New York: Oxford U. Press, 1983). Cited by MacDonald, *Sheriff*, 102.

66. For a good overview of the history of this doctrine, see Bobo 1–6.

67. "No Duty to Retreat," *Violence and Values in American History and Society* 20 (1991). Cited in Bobo, 3. William S. Morriss, the attorney who advised me in this research, pointed out that in the twenty-first century, "self defense" is a very complicated legal subject, with many degrees and conditions which vary from state to state. However, I am concerned only with the simpler nineteenth-century version of the doctrine which is relevant to the Western.

68. For the habit of shooting first, see Clayton Cramer, *Concealed Weapon Laws, 7*, cited in Winkler, 166–7, though the website that contained this material is no longer active. For the quotation about Southern attitudes, see Pieter Spierenburg, "Introduction," *Men and Violence: Gender, Honor and Rituals in Modern Europe and American* (Ohio State Univ. Press, 1998), 24–25.

69. It would be logical to assume that these laws banning concealed weapons were intended to limit gun access for African Americans, but Cramer's research indicates that these laws were all written in racially-neutral language, applying equally to whites and blacks. Other laws, both before and after the Civil War, did indeed ban gun ownership for slaves and former slaves, but the "concealed carry" laws were not part of that pattern. See Winkler, 167.

70. Mead, *And Keep Your Powder Dry* (New York: Morrow, 1942), 142. Cited in Kimmel, 230.

71. Mitchell, 183.

72. Cawelti, 83–84.

73. "Modern Man and Cowboy," *Television Quarterly* I (May 1962), 36. Cited in Brauer, 67.

74. A startling revelation, especially to those of us who assumed Americans have always owned handguns in large numbers.

75. MacDonald, *Sheriff*, 73–74. The gun manufacturer's quote is found in *Variety* (Oct. 8, 1958), 29.

76. Cawelti, 38–39.

77. *Sheriff*, 102–3.

78. Newcomb, "Frontier," 301–2.

Chapter Two

1. The most comprehensive sources for the history of television in the 1950s include Boddy, *Fifties Television*; Barnouw, *The Image Empire*; and MacDonald, *One Nation Under Television*. More specialized information can be found in Kisseloff, Wilk, Becker, Marill, Winick, and Brooks and Marsh.

2. On the coaxial cable, see Brooks and Marsh, xiii. For the late enrollment of Southern stations, see MacDonald, *Blacks*, 74.

3. Halberstam, 184.

4. Doherty, 4–5.

5. MacDonald, *Blacks*, 75.

6. Doherty, 4.

7. Wilk, 114–15. For the most thorough discussion of Weaver's influence, see Barnouw, *Image Empire*. A highly educated man with a degree in philosophy,

an advertising man with Young and Rubicam who started with their radio programming and later moved to the fledgling television industry, Weaver was one of the most innovative figures in early network television.

8. Al Morgan, "Revelations of Former Network Presidents," *TV Guide* (April 29, 1972). Cited in MacDonald, *Television*, 68.

9. This pattern was somewhat ameliorated by the creation of public television in the 1960s. Actually, the Educational Television and Radio Center began late in 1952, sponsored by the Ford Foundation, but it produced no programming of its own, merely served as a clearing house to provide locally-produced shows to other stations. In 1954 the Center moved to Ann Arbor, Michigan and began operating as a "network," providing five hours of programming a day, mostly on kinescope sent through the mails. Known as the "University of the Air," the Center created shows that treated serious subjects in depth, but mostly in a dry academic style, with no concern for entertainment values. In 1958 the Center moved again to New York City and got more ambitious, aiming to become the "fourth network." Now it began to import shows from the BBC and increased its output to ten hours per week. In November 1963, it was renamed National Educational Television (spinning off its radio programming), and began to produce its own shows, controversial hard-hitting documentaries on issues like racism and poverty, which drew the first accusations of liberal bias. At this point, the Ford Foundation began to withdraw its funding. Finally, in 1967 the U.S. Government created the Corporation for Public Broadcasting to provide a steady source of funding for the network.

10. For Hollywood's view of television in the 1940s, see Boddy, 67. In fact, when networks did begin to broadcast reruns of filmed episodes in the summers, they discovered that the re-runs often drew higher ratings than the original broadcasts, since few viewers saw every new episode of a series during the season. Reported in *Sponsor* (July 12, 1954), p. 186. Cited by Boddy, 141.

11. A development which has finally come to pass in the last decade, with live simulcasts of productions from the Metropolitan Opera shown in movie theaters across the country, and more lately still, with simulcasts of live stage productions from Britain's National Theatre.

12. Boddy, 68.

13. Morleen Gets Rouse, "A History of the F. W. Ziv Radio and Television Syndication Companies, 1930–1960." Ph.D. Diss., University of Michigan (1976), 79.

14. For more details on the process of syndication, see Boddy, 69–70.

15. Boddy, 72.

16. William I. Kaufman, ed., *Best Television Plays* (New York: Merlin Press, 1950), 94. Cited in Becker, 193.

17. The downturn resulted from the 1948 Supreme Court case that broke up the studios' monopoly on distribution. In the 1930s and '40s, the Big Eight Hollywood studios had turned out 400–500 films a year, which they were able to sell to theatres through a process known as block booking: if theatre owners wanted access to the studios' "A" films, they had to agree to take a substantial number of "B" films as well. When the Supreme Court banned block booking in 1948 as anti-competitive, the studios drastically reduced the number of films they made per year, and immediately cancelled most of the long-term contracts they had with the people required to create all those films: producers, writers, actors, directors, and technicians. Barnouw, *Tube of Plenty*, 116. See also Becker, *It's the Pictures That Got Small*, 22–23.

18. For a thorough examination of the complex relationship between Hollywood and television in the 1950s, see Becker, especially pp. 189–220.

19. Boone appeared in a number of these productions between 1955 and 1960: "Love is Eternal" on *General Electric Theatre* (1955), an adaptation of the Irving Stone novel in which Boone played Abraham Lincoln; "Little Tin Drum" on *United States Steel Hour* (April 1959); "The Tunnel" on *Playhouse 90* (February 21, 1960); "The Charlie and the Kid" on *United States Steel Hour* (March 1960); and "Tomorrow" on *Playhouse 90* (March 7, 1960), from a story by William Faulkner.

20. Penn, interviewed by Kisseloff, 268–69.

21. For the best background on the challenges of producing live drama, see Barnouw, *Image Empire*, 22–37; Kisseloff, *The Box*, 260; Wilk, *Golden Age* 128, 259–61.

22. Wilk, 125.

23. "Men" is indeed the proper term here. Marill (p. 21) observes that women writers were "scarce" on live TV drama, but he does not name any names. He does identify two women directors in the early days of television; Lela Swift was the first, joined by Ida Lupino, who started directing for *Four Star Playhouse* in 1953, then for *Alfred Hitchcock Presents*, and went on to a significant directing career on TV, but exclusively in filmed TV. Kisseloff interviewed one woman, Anne Howard Bailey, whose scripts were featured on such shows as "Robert Montgomery Presents," "U.S. Steel Hour," "Armstrong Circle Theater," and "Kraft Television Theatre," among others.

24. For the statistics on members of the Writers Guild working in TV in 1951, see Boddy, 87. On Coe's work with writers, see Becker 193; Kisseloff 250–51; Wilk 126–131.

25. MacDonald, *Television*, 84.

26. Barnouw, *Image Empire*, 32.

27. Mosel, interviewed by Kisseloff, 267.

28. Barnouw, *Image Empire*, 22.

29. Barnouw, *Image Empire*, 31.

30. Barnouw, *Image Empire*, 31.

31. Cited in Boddy, 86.

32. Chayefsky, *Television Plays* (New York: Simon & Schuster, 1953), 178.

33. Barnouw, *Image Empire*, 29–30.

34. The name "kitchen drama" derived from the fact that so many scenes were set in kitchens. But, as

Tad Mosel explains, that was a choice dictated by the domestic settings of many of these plays. If you're writing about a family, the kitchen is the easiest room in the house to draw people together in (interview with Kisseloff, 236). In fact, so common was the setting that actress Eileen Heckart, who did several plays with Mosel, finally begged him to create a play for her that would get her out of the kitchen: "I'm so sick of making the cocoa for Mama and the eggs for Dad." Mosel pondered the problem, and came up with a play set in a hotel lobby, "The Out-of-Towners" (interview with Kisseloff, 259).

35. Wilk, 136.
36. Wilk, 131.
37. Kisseloff, 256.
38. Boddy, 90.
39. Kisseloff, 251.
40. Becker, 194.
41. Kraszewski, no page number.
42. Boddy, 89.
43. Boddy, 190–91. The reasons for such responses were not hard to find. The continuing-character filmed series were so formulaic and repetitive that they provided nothing of substance for the critics to analyze. Critic John Crosby lamented in 1958, "After the first show, I don't know what to say about a western or quiz show, and I don't know anybody else who does either." *Detroit Free Press* (August 21, 1958), 33, cited by Boddy, 192.
44. Mann, interview in Kisseloff, 260.
45. Barnouw, *Image Empire*, 33.
46. Elmer Rice, "The Biography of a Play," *Theatre Arts* (Nov. 1959). Cited in Barnouw, *Image Empire*, 33.
47. Boddy, 199.
48. "TV Writer Sizes Up His Craft," *Broadcasting* (January 4, 1960), 42. Cited in Boddy, 201.
49. Barnouw, *Tube of Plenty*, 112.
50. Erickson, interview in Kisseloff, 513.
51. Boddy, 200.
52. Winick, 18.
53. J. Edward Dean, director of advertising for DuPont. FCC, *Second Interim Report: Television Network Program Procurement*, part 2, Docket no. 12782 (Washington, D.C.: U.S. Government Printing Office, 1965), 376–77. Cited in Boddy, 201–2.
54. Boddy, 199.
55. For details about the level of censorship writers for the live dramas experienced from 1954–1959, see Boddy, Chapter 11: "'The Honeymoon is Over': The End of Live Drama" (187–213).
56. MacDonald, *Television*, 118.
57. Brooks and Marsh, 1105.
58. Barnouw, *Image Empire*, 62.
59. *Television*, 119. As MacDonald explains, the Great Programming Shift started with ABC, but it soon spread, as executives responsible for the changes at ABC migrated to leadership positions at the other two networks. Robert Kintner left ABC to become president of NBC in 1957, while James T. Aubrey went from CBS to ABC and then back to CBS in 1960. These men carried the ABC approach to filmed

continuing-character series for the mass market into their new networks. When Oliver Treyz took over as president of ABC in 1956, he consolidated the doctrine.
60. Boddy, 187–8.
61. See Boddy 93–98 for a more detailed description of this process. Early television station owners and network executives, he points out, learned important lessons from the conflicts between station owners and sponsors in the early days of radio.
62. Kisseloff, 546.
63. MacDonald, *Television*, 123.
64. *Television*, 133.
65. Brooks and Marsh, 1259.
66. Winick, 33.
67. Rose, interview in Kisseloff, 248.
68. Barnouw, *Image Empire*, 79–80.
69. Barnouw, *Image Empire*, 81–82.
70. Interview in Kisseloff, 546.
71. MacDonald, *Television*, 128.
72. *Image Empire*, 37.
73. Todd Gitlin, *Inside Prime Time* (New York: Pantheon Books, 1983). Cited by MacDonald, *Television*, 124.
74. This phenomenon, MacDonald argues, is not restricted to television, but is common to most forms of popular culture. However, because television is so voracious, needing so much material to fill the daily hours of broadcast time, the pattern is intensified.
75. Oliver Treyz, president of ABC television, deluged with advertisers wanting to get in on the newest trend, asked Warner Brothers for another detective series, this time set in Bermuda. As Bill Orr tells the story, he rejected Bermuda as a locale: "There are mostly blacks over there. Let's go to Hawaii where there's a polyglot of people" (Kisseloff 294).
76. Brooks and Marsh, 444, 921, 1001.
77. Orr, interview in Kisseloff, 292.
78. Stan Optowsky, *TV—The Big Picture* (New York: Collier Books, 1962), 132–33. Cited in MacDonald, *Television*, 126.
79. MacDonald, *Television*, 128. He concluded by stating that no Western series since the 1960s had received high ratings. However, he wrote these words in 1990, before *Dr. Quinn, Medicine Woman* (1993–1998), a CBS series that drew large ratings despite its Saturday evening time slot, a night notorious for low viewership. However, the show was abruptly cancelled after its sixth season because its primary viewership was women over 40, not the more desirable demographic of men and women 18–40 that the networks sought. Viewers reacted to that decision with an outrage not seen since the cancellation of *Star Trek* a generation earlier. In 1990, MacDonald also could not have known about the much-honored HBO Western series *Deadwood* (2004–2006).
80. Orr, interview in Kisseloff, 297.
81. Orr, interview in Kisseloff, 295.
82. Steiger, interview in Kisseloff, 268.
83. Leslie, interview in Kisseloff, 268.
84. Bailey, interview in Kisseloff, 295.
85. Parks, 152, drawing on her 1972 interview with

Irwin R. Blacker, Western historian and consultant to TV Westerns.

86. Boddy, 193.

87. Ross Davidson, "The New Television Playwright and His Markets," *Writer* (April 1962), 61. Emphasis in original. Cited by Boddy, 197.

88. Daniel Melnich, "Disillusion Between the Lines," *Television* (June 6, 1961), 92. Cited by Boddy, 197.

89. Barnouw, *Image Empire*, 110.

90. Hargrove, interview in Kisseloff, 296.

91. Bailey, interview in Kisseloff, 295.

92. Manny Rubin, "The Beginning Writer in Television," in *The Best Television Plays*, vol. 3, ed. William I. Kaufman (New York: Merlin Press, 1954), 357. Cited in Boddy, 192.

Chapter Three

A Note on Sources. The two main sources of biographical information about Boone, and about details of his career, are Martin Grams' *The Have Gun—Will Travel Companion* (2000), and David Rothel's *Richard Boone: A Knight Without Armor in a Savage Land* (2000). Both books draw their information from a combination of published articles and personal interviews with Boone's friends, family and coworkers. Unfortunately, neither book follows scholarly conventions in documenting sources.

Rothel is careful to identify the time and place of each of his interviews, and when he quotes from published sources, he usually provides basic details—the author, the name of the publication, and sometimes an approximate date (like "the Saturday before the premiere"), though never the exact date or the page number. From this information, and from subject searches in relevant databases, I was able to obtain the articles about Boone that appeared in national publications like *TV Guide, Newsweek,* and *The New York Times.* However, many of the articles about Boone that Rothel quotes appeared in smaller regional or local publications, and often he does not identify the place of publication, so I have been unable to consult the originals. When I quote such articles, I cite Rothel as my source.

Similarly, Grams based his statements about Boone and *Have Gun* on a combination of interviews (including those by David Rothel) and published articles, many of the articles supplied by fellow fans who had collected them over the years. But he is much less clear about which quotations come from interviews he conducted personally and which from published articles, and he offers no bibliographical information at all about any of the articles he quotes from. He does provide a list of the people he interviewed, which helps. For example, he quotes fairly extensively from Sam Rolfe, one of the creators and early producers of *Have Gun—Will Travel*; but since Sam Rolfe died in 1993, and his name is not included in the list of interviews, all of Rolfe's quotes must come from published sources—none of which are identified. As reference to the original articles makes clear, Grams also has a

habit of quoting extensively and verbatim from these articles without the use of quotation marks except to identify the words of Boone's friends or co-workers which had been quoted in the original. Again, whenever possible I cite the original source; when I cannot identify what it is, I cite Grams, though with some hesitation because, in addition to other difficulties, Grams' book is abysmally copy-edited: page numbers are omitted on numerous pages throughout the book, especially the second half, and typos and misspellings are rampant. Some of these are simple and easily corrected ("Jerimiah" instead of "Jeremiah"), but others indicate genuine misunderstanding: for example, the consistent use of "Calvary" instead of "Cavalry" to refer to horse soldiers. Character names or even actors' names get recorded inaccurately: what should be "Coey" becomes "Cory," "DeVries" becomes "DeRives," Bert is listed as Ben). Sometimes the character name and the actor's name get reversed in the credits. Other errors indicate an unfamiliarity with foreign languages, as when Pancho Villa appears in the credits or the plot summary as "Pancho Via," or San Ysidro becomes "Santa Sidro," or the very Italian "Signor Bottellini" is given the title of "Senior."

The quotations I have taken from both Grams and Rothel are almost entirely direct quotes from Boone himself, or direct quotations about him by relatives, friends, and co-workers.

1. Edson, 23.

2. Schickel, 54.

3. Peter Boone: Rothel, 66.

4. Edson, 83.

5. These details of the Boone family history come from B'Lou Boone Brown, in interview with Rothel, 35–36.

6. Edson, 83.

7. Edson, 83.

8. Gehman, "Paradox" part 1, 11.

9. Claire Boone: Rothel, 39.

10. Grams, 12.

11. The Stanford incident is reported in a number of different places, but most fully in Edson, 83. Peter's quote is found on Rothel, 68.

12. B'Lou Boone Brown: Rothel, 38.

13. "Richard Boone: Evolution of an Actor," 18.

14. For details of Boone's life in Carmel before the war, the major sources are B'Lou Boone Brown: Rothel 38, 40; Edson, 83; Grams 12–13 (drawing on published articles); and Gehman, "Paradox" part 2, 23.

15. Claire Boone: Rothel, 40.

16. For Boone's wartime experiences, the best sources are Gehman, "Paradox" part 2, and Rothel's interviews with Claire and Peter Boone, though on the details of wartime service, some caution is necessary. For example, in her interview with Rothel, B'Lou says Richard was stationed on the *Hornet* when it was sunk in October 1942 (38), while Claire identifies his ship as the *Enterprise* and the *Franklin*, and says that his ships were "nearly sunk twice. Both times most of the men drowned" (40). Rothel himself lists the ships that Gehman mentioned, without citing Gehman's ar-

ticle as his source. Since Gehman's information comes directly from Boone himself, his list is probably the most authoritative, given that B'Lou, Claire, and Peter Boone all agree that Richard spoke very seldom about the war, so their remembered details may be less reliable.

17. Gehman, "Paradox" part 2, 22.

18. Claire Boone: Rothel, 40.

19. Peter Boone: Rothel, 70.

20. Actually, Boone seriously considered pursuing a career in boxing—until he saw a young Joe Louis sparring in a gym. Grams, quoting the story from Boone himself, places it in Los Angeles before the war, when Louis had come to the West coast to fight Jack Roper in April 1939. Boone reported, "I'd never seen [Louis] before, but after watching him spar for just a few minutes, there wasn't a doubt in my mind that this guy would dominate boxing for the next ten years or more. I was now a heavyweight, I thought. Sooner or later, if I were good enough, I'd have to meet up with Louis. There was no point in starting" (Grams 240). As with several stories in Boone's life, there are two versions of this one, too. Peter Boone places the story after the war, in New York (Rothel 69).

21. Claire Boone: Rothel, 40.

22. Claire Boone: Rothel, 40.

23. B'Lou Boone Brown: Rothel, 38.

24. Grams, 13.

25. Hirsch, 21. I drew on Hirsch for these details on Sanford Meisner, the Group Theatre, and the Neighborhood Playhouse School.

26. Garfield, *A Player's Place*, 44.

27. More information about Graham can be found on the website for the Neighborhood Playhouse School of the Arts, where she is still listed under "Faculty." This site explains that she started teaching at the Neighborhood Playhouse in 1921, when it was a producing theatre. The production group folded, however, and when it was replaced by the Neighborhood Playhouse School of Theatre Arts in 1928, Graham simply shifted her classes to the school.

28. Peter Boone: Rothel, 70. The Martha Graham quote is found in "Richard Boone: Has Gun and Ideas," *New York Times* (Feb. 1, 1959), Sec. II, 13:8.

29. In fact, for a brief period in late 1948, Boone and his fellow student and war vet, Jan Merlin, used dance to supplement their meager G.I. Bill income. They joined a dance troupe headed by Graham's assistant, Nina Fonaroff—with whom Boone had a "big fling" during his fleeting dance career (Merlin: Rothel 82–83). In later years, because of his own experience, Boone routinely encouraged his acting students to study dance.

30. Edson, 84.

31. For background on Elia Kazan and the Actors Studio, see Garfield, 44.

32. Kazan quote is found in Garfield, 54. When I contacted the Actors Studio to consult their archives about Richard Boone's earliest involvement with the organization, I was informed that they no longer have archives before 1982. When Lee Strasberg died that year, his widow Anna removed all the archives to her home. For details of those early years, the Actors Studio referred me to Garfield's book (published in 1980, when Strasberg was still alive), as the nearest thing to an official history they have.

33. Stanislavski was the starting place for all Method acting, though his own ideas changed over time, and each of the teachers who adopted his basic insights modified his approach to reflect their own individual emphases.

34. Garfield, ix.

35. The key principles of the Group Theatre come from Hirsch, 24.

36. The controversies, which mostly concern the use, or misuse, of the exercise Stanislavski called "affective memory," are too complex to explore here. For details, consult Hirsch and Garfield.

37. Garfield, 75–76.

38. Edson, 84.

39. This story is found in Rothel, 14, citing an article from *The Sunday Bulletin* of Philadelphia, PA, published early in 1960.

40. Quotations from Davidson, 28; Edson, 84; and Jan Merlin's interview with David Rothel, 83.

41. Schickel, 54. There are anecdotes about these incidents in Rothel and Grams as well.

42. Grams, 13.

43. Edson, 23. Grams and Rothel also cite versions of the story.

44. For Boone's quote, see Rothel, 9. For his seven-page perfect scene, see Schickel, 54.

45. "Richard Boone: Evolution of an Actor," 18.

46. Edson, 84.

47. Biographies and autobiographies of important actors who started as contract players in this period of Hollywood—major stars like Shelley Winters and Ida Lupino and Marilyn Monroe—have provided these details, along with other information about the old days of the Studio system.

48. Among other roles, Webber played Jack Webb's mother on the show, despite the fact that he was older than she was—an irony that always tickled Webb.

49. Grams, 15.

50. Peggy Webber's stories and quotations all come from Rothel's interview, 87–91.

51. No one else mentions this story of Boone having killed a man by hitting him too hard, and Webber cites no details, though she says it might have been when he was at Stanford (Rothel, 87). Certainly the story is plausible, given Boone's background as a boxer, but he could also have told her this in order to shock and impress this innocent young woman. All the friends and co-workers who talk about Boone mention his delight in jokes, shenanigans, and wild tales (Rothel, 88). On the other hand, since he shared other private, even shameful, details of his life with Webber that he told no one else except Claire, it is possible this story is true.

52. For Lamont Johnson's membership in the group, see Grams, 16. Other lesser-known members included Peggy Rea, later production assistant on *Have Gun—Will Travel*, Joe Sergeant, Russell Conway, and Mary Welch (Rothel, 107). Harry Carey, Jr. also

mentions this group, which he attended three or four times, and he adds the names of Alex Nichol and Barbara Baxley (Rothel, 111). According to Peggy Webber, a few years later Gary Cooper came to the Brentwood Marketplace workshop, "hat in hand," and said humbly, "I want to learn how to do the Method." After Marlon Brando had taken the town by storm, followed by other notable Method actors like Paul Newman, James Dean, Dennis Hopper, and Montgomery Clift, suddenly the Method was hot in Hollywood, and Cooper wanted to keep up. Another attraction for Cooper, Webber mentions, was Patricia Neal's participation in the group (Rothel 88–89).

On the other hand, Neal's autobiography, *As I Am*, makes no mention of this group, only her work in acting classes with George Shdanoff and Michael Chekhov, in which, she says, Cooper joined her (along with Anthony Quinn, Shelley Winters, Robert Stack and Arthur Kennedy). But this would have been in 1950, which is before the Brentwood Marketplace group had been established. The next few years of Neal's life—or at least, of her autobiography—are completely consumed with her relationship with Cooper, so perhaps she merely neglected to mention her association with the Brentwood group. That is more likely than that both Stevens and Webber were mistaken about the association.

53. For the details of Richard and Claire's early relationship, see Claire Boone: Rothel, 44–45.

54. Webber: Rothel, 90.

55. On the origins of *Medic*, see Webber: Rothel, 90.

56. Webber told Rothel this party was Christmas of 1953 (Rothel, 90); however, this must have been a misstatement, since Boone started shooting *Medic* in the summer of 1953.

57. For the overview of *Medic*, see Grams, 20–33, and Rothel, 180–91. Grams includes detailed synopses of several key episodes, while Rothel provides an episode guide to the complete series. Episodes of the series can be viewed on-line at http://matineeclassics.com/tv/1955/medic/details/.

58. Grams, 29.

59. In fact, after the first show was broadcast, a physician in the Midwest even offered Boone a job heading his clinic—an offer the actor diplomatically turned down on the grounds that he was "too busy" with the show (Grams, 21).

60. Grams, 26.

61. Gehman, "Paradox" part 2, 23.

62. Claire Boone: Rothel, 46.

63. Edson, 84.

64. Grams, 20.

65. Not a bad film, but one overshadowed by the release that same year of *The Three Faces of Eve*, which won Joanne Woodward a Best Actress Oscar for her performance as a woman suffering from the same disorder.

66. For Fuller's discussion of Boone's acting class, see Rothel 91–93. After many small film roles, Fuller's big breakthrough came as the star of *Laramie* (1959–1963). When that series folded, he joined *Wagon Train* as one of the scouts who replaced Robert Horton, then

went on to play Dr. Kelly Brackett in the NBC series by Jack Webb, *Emergency*.

67. Webber also mentions this incident, though in much less detail (Rothel, 89). Neither Webber nor Fuller makes it clear whether she did this scene as a paying member of Boone's acting class, or as a favor to Boone, coming in from outside the class as an experienced actress who could support Fuller in a difficult scene in a way no student could have done.

68. "Richard Boone Has Gun, Will Travel," *TV Guide* (Oct. 12, 1957), 14.

69. Rothel, 181–82.

70. "Richard Boone: Has Gun, Will Travel," 14.

71. Edson, 82.

72. Schickel, 54. The mistake that transforms an ordinary man into Paladin is the subject of "Genesis" (6:1, Sept 15, 1962), the first episode of the final season.

73. "Richard Boone: Has Gun, Will Travel," 14.

74. Gehman, "Paradox" part 2, 22.

75. Rayford Barnes: Rothel, 119. The film producer was Robert Enders, producer of *A Thunder of Drums* (1961), quoted by Schickel, 55.

76. McLaglen: Rothel, 97.

77. Edson, 82–83.

78. Gehman, "Paradox" part 2, 23. This, despite the fact that the Boone family had been involved in horse racing for three generations. Not only had Richard's grandfather, Bower Boone, owned a stable of twenty-seven race horses in San Francisco, his father Kirk Boone and his partners owned race horses, and Richard even got into the business briefly in the 1950s as joint owner with his brother Bill of Black and Blue Stables (Rothel 39).

79. Herrmann was the composer and conductor of original scores for such major films as *Citizen Kane* (1941), *Jane Eyre* (1944), *The Ghost and Mrs. Muir* (1947), *The Day the Earth Stood Still* (1951), and Hitchcock's *The Man Who Knew Too Much* (1956).

80. In the 1960s, the opening visuals changed, when television was under pressure to reduce the level of violence. In the revised version, episodes opened with a full shot of Paladin in silhouette rather than a close-up of the gun. In the distance he draws, then the camera zooms in on the gun and the chess piece. As Ralph Brauer argues, this change emphasizes the man over the gun (61).

81. Though the television series never specifies until the opening episode of Season Six, "Genesis," we eventually realize that "Paladin" is not our hero's real name but is instead a *nom de guerre* which simultaneously conceals his real identity and reveals his calling.

82. March 28, 1958, p. 27.

83. Boone's work schedule on *Have Gun*: Claire Boone: Rothel, 50. Peter's report about his father's exhaustion on weekends: Rothel, 71. Families on location: Claire Boone: Rothel, 49.

84. Claire Boone: Rothel, 55.

85. Barnes: Rothel, 121. Kinnett is quoted in Gehman, "Paradox," part 3, 27.

86. Grams, 77.

87. Carey: Rothel, 112.

88. Carey: Rothel, 112.

89. Carey: Rothel, 110.

90. No "star table": Claire Boone: Rothel, 48. Quotes from Fintan Meyler and Johnny Western: Grams, 77. The dinners at Kam Tong's family restaurant: Grams, 60.

91. McLaglen: Rothel, 95. Frank Pierson's story is in Grams, 420.

92. Carey: Rothel, 111. Barnes: Rothel, 121.

93. Peter Boone: Rothel, 79.

94. Claire Boone: Rothel, 61.

95. For the value of the Boones' art collection, see Rothel, 19–20. The Lincoln barber chair, Claire Boone: Rothel, 53–54. At the time of the fire, the three Boones were living in New York for four months where Richard was playing Lincoln on Broadway, so they were never in danger. The police suspected arson, but were never able to resolve the issue.

96. Gehman, "Paradox," part 1, 10.

97. Claire Boone: Rothel, 48.

98. *TV Guide* (May 10, 1958), 11. Boone's arrangement with CBS: Claire Boone: Rothel, 54.

99. Edson, 82.

100. Peggy Rea: Rothel, 109.

101. Edson, 82.

102. Gehman, "Paradox," part 1, 11.

103. Boone spent six hours on the set: Adler, 18. For the "fee" of a Rolls Royce, see Claire Boone: Rothel, 54. There is more to the story, however. Boone was not Wayne's first choice for this role. Andy McLaglen, who had worked for years with Wayne, tells the rest of the story. Wayne had originally intended to offer the role to James Arness, who, in his pre–*Gunsmoke* days, had been under contract to Wayne. At Wayne's request, McLaglen set up a meeting between the two men at the end of shooting on a *Gunsmoke* episode McLaglen was directing. Wayne arrived with his whole entourage, but Arness failed to show up— for reasons McLaglen never learned. Annoyed, Wayne snapped, "The hell with him. Who's that other guy you work with?" McLaglen asked, "You mean Boone?" "Yeah, I want to meet with Boone." And that is how Boone got the role (Rothel, 99). He went on to make two more films with Wayne, *Big Jake* in 1971, and *The Shootist* in 1976, Wayne's last film.

104. Compare Boone's attitude with that of his unnamed young co-star (probably Richard Chamberlain). As Boone told Richard Schickel contemptuously, though the part was a real opportunity, this young man "didn't even know his lines when he came on the set. His idea of a clever bit of acting was to try to upstage somebody. He's the kind of actor who gets parts by being very big on the cocktail circuit" (Schickel, 55).

105. "Richard Boone: Evolution of an Actor," 19.

106. Grams, 84.

107. Claire Boone: Rothel, 50.

108. Edson, 84.

109. Mac Step, *The Desert Sun* (March 21, 1961), cited in Rothel, 139.

110. The money was spread over a three-year period, to reduce the tax bite. In the end, the season was cut short at 32 episodes.

Chapter Four

1. The primary sources for background material on these four series are episode guides designed for a fan audience: for *Gunsmoke*, SuzAnne and Gabor Barabas, and John Peel; for *Wagon Train,* James Rosin; for *Bonanza*, Bruce and Linda Leiby, and Melany Shapiro; and for *Have Gun—Will Travel*, David Rothel, and Martin Grams, Jr.

2. Barabas, 98.

3. Newcomb, *TV*, 74.

4. Barabas, 207.

5. Actually, in the real West, the heyday of the wagon trains occurred a couple of decades earlier than this, from the mid–1840s through the 1860s. By 1869, the transcontinental railroad had been completed, following roughly the same route the wagon trains had used, so wagon trains soon began to disappear.

6. In Ford's *Wagonmaster*, a film about Mormons moving west, Bond had played not the wagon master of the title (a role filled by Ben Johnson), but Elder Wiggs, the leader of the Mormons, "a man with great faith in God and himself" (Yoggy 264). There may be some carryover from Elder Wiggs to the character of Major Adams, who also has a strong, if nondenominational, faith that often colors his language and behavior.

In many ways, Bond's career was remarkable. He got into movies as an extra while playing football for the University of Southern California in the late 1920s, through his teammate Marion Michael Morrison— later to be much better known as John Wayne. Bond appeared in 200–250 movies during his career, usually playing cops, thugs, working class stiffs, and noncommissioned officers because of his size (6'2", 200 pounds). Sixteen of those movies were with Wayne, and 25 or 26 were directed by John Ford, whom Bond and Wayne first met in 1929 on a football film, *Salute*. One astounding statistic: on the American Film Institute's lists of the 100 best films of all time, both the original list and the tenth anniversary edition, Bond appeared in a record seven films, more than any other actor—though always in minor roles: *It Happened One Night* (1934), *Bringing Up Baby* (1938), *Gone with the Wind* (1939), *The Grapes of Wrath* (1940), *The Maltese Falcon* (1941), *It's a Wonderful Life* (1946), and *The Searchers* (1956). He also appeared in a near-record eleven films nominated for Best Picture Oscars.

7. In 1960, the series was criticized by the Association on American Indian Affairs for its habit of portraying Indians as "drunken, cowardly outlaws" and "usually attacking wagon trains" (MacDonald, *Sheriff*, 114). For more detailed discussions of Indians on all four series, see Chapter 7.

8. "Wagon Train," Museum of Broadcast Communications website.

9. Brauer, 1975. Other popular examples of property Westerns include *The Virginian* (1962–1971) and *The Big Valley* (1965–69).

10. "Togetherness—Western Style," 18.

11. When Adam gets engaged in a three-episode story arc in 1964, fan response was so vehemently neg-

ative that the story line was revised so that the young woman married a Cartwright cousin instead (Shapiro 14). In 1972, Michael Landon wrote an episode in which Hoss marries, but characteristically, his bride is dead by the end of the episode. Dan Blocker died before the episode was shot, however, and the script was rewritten to make Joe the bereft bridegroom.

12. According to the Oxford English Dictionary, the first use of "environmentalism" in this sense occurred on May 20, 1966, in the *Washington Post*.

13. MacDonald, *Sheriff*, 67.

14. In this formula, "1:2" before the date indicates the season (the first) and the episode's broadcast order (the second). This form of annotation offers more detailed information that the traditional sequential numbering of episodes from the beginning of a series to the end, without identifying seasons.

Note: all quotations from the episodes are drawn from my personal transcriptions.

15. Barabas, 106.

16. Dunning, 304.

17. Norm Macdonnell later claimed that the radio Dillon was significantly influenced by William Conrad's own personality, according to GunsmokeNet. com.

18. Barabas, 107.

19. Peel, 14.

20. Barabas, 107.

21. Ironically, Arness was the one with an actual limp. Wounded by machine-gun bullets in the landing at Anzio, he had trouble with his leg the rest of his life. Toward the end of the series, the limp got so noticeable that many viewers wrote in to ask about it. Producer John Mantley created several scenes to explain the character's limp (for example, having Matt attacked by a bear), but none of them were ever broadcast. Finally, he just got a double for Arness so the letters about his limp would stop (Peel 34).

22. Yoggy, 264.

23. Interview with Frederick Shorr, associate producer of *Wagon Train*, 1958–1965, in 2008 (Rosin, 30).

24. According to Melany Shapiro, this is the main reason the series was initially broadcast at 7:30 p.m. on Saturday nights, so people who were out shopping could catch the show on color TVs in the stores (5). It also bought the series some necessary time to improve. Even though *Bonanza*'s first-season ratings were fairly dismal, the network maintained its commitment to the series to serve its larger corporate interests.

25. Whitney, "What a Bonanza!," 16.

26. Quoted in Shapiro, 5, though Dortort also made similar comments to John Poppy, 87. Dortort's description of the sitcom family seems based on selective memory. Certainly it does not accurately reflect the fathers on *Ozzie and Harriet* or *Leave it to Beaver*, who are generally wise and calm.

27. Rothel, 18. See also Grams, 34.

28. In addition to the pilot, "Three Bells for Perdido," Meadow wrote "Winchester Quarantine" (1:4, 10/5/57) and "Shootout at Hogtooth" (6:9, 4/10/62), and co-wrote "The Treasure" with Robert E. Thomp-

son (6:16, 12/29/62) and "Brotherhood" with story editor Albert Ruben (6:17, 1/5/63).

29. "Paradox," part 3, 26–7.

30. Grams, 46.

31. Grams tells the story, 57–58.

32. *Variety*, April 29, 1958.

33. Rothel, 96.

34. On his dedication page, Grams quotes Richard Boone to this effect, five or six years after the series went off the air, but does not identify the source of the quote.

35. Grams, 69.

36. See Grams, 73.

37. Grams reports the story of this conflict, 73–75. The fistfight seems like an implausible story, given Boone's history as a boxer; still, Pierson is normally a credible source.

38. Grams, 75.

39. *Variety* review cited in Grams, 344. For detailed analysis of this episode and its sequel, "A Drop of Blood" (5:12, 12/2/61), see Chapter 7.

40. See "William Talman," IMDb, for the story.

41. Rayford Barnes, who had a small part in "The Long Way Home," tells the story to David Rothel, 120.

42. MacDonald, *Blacks and White TV*, 48.

43. For details about these episodes, see Chapter 7.

44. Grams, 102.

45. Cited by Grams, 104.

46. Grams, or perhaps Sparks, mistakenly describes the setting of this episode as the "far east," even though Paladin never goes further from home than Monterey.

47. For details of McLaglen's career, see IMDb.

48. Barnes: Rothel, 120.

49. McLaglen: Rothel, 97.

50. Schickel, 55.

51. Grams, 65.

52. McLaglen: Rothel, 95. This hands-off attitude didn't mean that McLaglen was oblivious of actors and their problems. An anecdote from the second season is typical. Don Keefer (a New York actor who had worked with Boone at the Actors Studio in 1947 and been in *Away All Boats* with him) was cast in a role that required him to ride a horse. Keefer carefully refrained from telling the producers that he didn't know how to ride, and on the set concealed his nerves as best he could: "I just got on [the horse] and did it," he said. But McLaglen picked up on his anxiety, and quietly told the actor, "You don't have to ride on it, I'll cut around you." That is, Keefer was able shoot his scene just sitting on a stationary horse—a typical act of kindness from McLaglen (Grams 267).

53. Kulik's obituary, *Los Angeles Times*, January 16, 1999.

54. For details of Milestone's career, see IMDb.

55. There is some ambiguity about discussions of episodes and seasons, as episodes were not necessarily broadcast in production order. More than once, an episode was shot in one season but not broadcast until a later season. Thus, the most accurate way to state Johnson's involvement is to say that he directed six episodes that were broadcast in the first season, and four more that were broadcast in the second.

56. Webber: Rothel, 91.

57. The biography of Lupino by William Donati, based both on substantial research and on extensive interviews with Lupino in the last several years of her life, emphasizes her active pursuit of a directing career, carefully planned and developed. Most of the interviews she gave to the press during her life instead emphasize her anxieties and fears about directing. Certainly she had contradictory ideas about her role as a woman, subordinating her own career to that of her husband, so in some of these interviews she may have been presenting herself in that appropriate feminine light. Resolving the contradiction will take more research into Lupino than is proper for my project.

58. Between 1955 and 1969, even while starring with her third husband, Howard Duff, in a largely autobiographical sitcom called *Mr. Adams and Eve*, Lupino also directed fifty episodes of other shows in a wide range of styles and genres, from *Twilight Zone* and *Alfred Hitchcock Presents* to *Gilligan's Island*. In fact, she directed the pilot of *Gilligan's Island*. The cast had been struggling and the series was near cancellation before it even began, but her soothing and supportive presence pulled the cast out of their tailspin and sent them on to success (Donati 231).

59. Grams includes an amusing description of Lupino directing this episode, violating all the Hollywood cliches by wearing velvet pants instead of the classic director's puttees, and brandishing a lipstick instead of a riding crop. "When she wanted a wrangler to keep a tight rein on his horse, she said, 'Dahling, please hold the poodle-dog's leash.' In the climactic scene where she wanted a horse to shy, Miss Lupino told the assistant director, 'Baby, let's bring in a nervous poodle here.' She referred to the barn as a 'garage,' to star Richard Boone as 'Dicky Bird' and to the villain as 'Lovely.'" (Grams 288).

60. Quotation found in Lupino, IMDb.

61. Those episodes included the season opener for the third season, "First, Catch a Tiger" (3:1, 9/12/59)—always a prestigious position, followed by "Charley Red Dog" (3:13, 12/12/59); "Day of the Bad Man" (3:17, 1/9/60); "Lady on the Wall" (3:23, 2/20/60); "Lady with a Gun" (3:30, 4/9/60); "The Trial" (3:38, 6/11/60); and "The Gold Bar" (4:26, 3/18/61). Four of these ("Charley Red Dog," "Day of the Bad Man," "Lady on the Wall," and "The Gold Bar") include significant comedy, but the others are relatively dark and intense. These eight episodes together demonstrate her wide range as a director.

Donati's biography of Lupino lists only the last three of these episodes, and talks about "The Trial" as the first *Have Gun* episode she directed, quoting an anecdote from Lupino about her anxiety directing Boone the first time. In Donati's defense, since Columbia House only began releasing *Have Gun* episodes on video in 1995, about the time he would have been finishing his manuscript, it would have been difficult for him to get accurate information about individual episodes from sources other than Lupino. In addition, by the time Donati came to know Lupino, her memories were very imprecise, so perhaps she herself did not remember the five episodes that preceded "The Trial."

62. The story is quoted in Grams, on a page which has no number—a common occurrence in this volume. Generally it is possible to determine a page number by referring backward or forward; but in this case, even that system breaks down. There is a page numbered 310, followed by four pages without numbers, then a page numbered 313 (instead of 315). The quote is found on the second page following 310.

63. Schickel, 55.

64. Donati, 226. However, Donati does not include Boone's reaction in the anecdote. For his response, see Toni Myrup Frank, "Ida Lupino to Get 'Heart of Hollywood,'" *Santa Monica Evening Outlook* (Nov. 13, 1975), 27–28.

65. See Grams, 397.

66. Whitney, February 6, 1960, 19.

67. "Paradox," part 3, 27.

68. Gehman, "Paradox," part 3, 27.

69. Carey: Rothel, 111.

70. In the beginning, the writers were all men—a circumstance taken for granted as "normal," though by the end of the series fifteen scripts by women had been produced.

71. He would go on to produce the TV series of *The Naked City* from 1958 to 1963. For career details, see Wald, IMDb.

72. See Kisseloff, and also Kraszewski, for details about the process.

73. Ingalls would remain with the series to the very end, as story editor, then associate producer and in Season Six as producer.

74. Roddenberry, IMDb.

75. Whitney, "Fink," 23.

76. Quoted in Grams, 70.

77. For Wincelberg's biography, see Answers.com.

78. Grams, 255.

79. His work for *Have Gun* also gave him his big career break by introducing him to Sydney Pollack, at the time an actor, who would go on to become a director, and would hire Thompson to write the screenplay for his first movie, *They Shoot Horses, Don't They?* (1969). The screenplay won Thompson an Academy Award nomination.

80. Pierson tells the story in Grams, 68. This job was the beginning of Pierson's distinguished career i n television and film. When Sam Rolfe finally left *Have Gun* early in the third season, Pierson took his place as producer for three seasons, before going on to write for other series. He also wrote the screenplays for such classic films as *Cat Ballou* (1965), *Cool Hand Luke* (1967), and *Dog Day Afternoon* (1975), all three of which were nominated for Oscars, and the third of which won. When he turned to directing for both film and television, he won awards in those fields as well.

Pierson was also active in professional organizations as President of the Writers Guild of America-West, 1981–83 and 1993–95, and President of the Academy of Motion Picture Arts and Sciences, 2001–2005. In

2003, he won the Austin Film Festival's Distinguished Screenwriter Award. Later he taught at the Sundance Institute and was the Artistic Director of the American Film Institute, as well as a consulting producer on AMC's acclaimed series, *Mad Men*. ("Frank R. Pierson," Wikipedia.) Pierson died July 22, 2012, at the age of 87.

81. Schickel, 55.

82. Quoted in Grams, 63–64.

83. For example, see Rothel, 100, for Johnny Western's story of how he got his small role on *Have Gun*. This apparently was typical of the period.

84. Grams, 41.

85. Of course, the fact that two actors' names appear in the cast list of a film does not guarantee that they met during filming, unless they shared a scene. However, the overlap is certainly suggestive of contact. Featured players on *Have Gun* with whom Boone had previously shared a movie included Harry Carey, Jr., Roy Barcroft, Philip Ahn, Charles Bronson, Parley Baer, Claude Akins, Jack Elam, Harry Morgan, Vic Perrin, Rodolfo Acosta, John Anderson, and Harold J. Stone.

86. Actually, thanks to Boone, Rea herself played small parts on *Have Gun* at least once a season in order to keep up her Screen Actors Guild membership. (Rothel, 107.)

87. This is one reason why *Have Gun* was one of the few series that actually used the official rehearsal day, Monday, to rehearse, instead of giving the actors an extra day of rest. See Schickel, 55.

88. Barnes: Rothel, 119.

89. In Season Four, while Kam Tong was away working on *The Garlund Touch*, Lisa Lu filled in for 16 episodes as Hey Girl, in addition to the two episodes she had already done as a featured actor.

90. Another bit player with an astounding number of credits is Stewart East, with 22 episodes over the six years (IMDb says 26, some uncredited)—always in tiny roles, as the waiter in the Hotel Carlton, a bartender, a cowboy, a barber, or some other background character with a line or two at most. East seems to have been a member of Boone's acting class for the crew; aside from bit parts in two movies in 1958, and a small role in *Blazing Saddles* (1974), his appearances on *Have Gun—Will Travel* constituted the bulk of his acting career.

91. Dobe's mother, Olive Carey, was also an actress. She played his mother in Ford's *The Searchers*, and also played a small role on *Have Gun—Will Travel*, "The Mark of Cain" (5:19, 1/20/62)—an episode in which Dobe did not appear.

92. Carey also had two personal connections that made him a natural for the show: he met Boone in 1953 on the set of a "bad movie," *Beneath the Twelve-Mile Reef*, and he "practically grew up" with Andy McLaglen, presumably on the sets of John Ford movies when McLaglen was serving as assistant director. Carey: Rothel, 112.

93. For details of Barcroft's career, see IMDb.

94. The exceptions included people like Robert J. Wilke—one of those actors whose name no one remembers, but whose sharp-featured face is instantly recognizable—who played grim sardonic heavies in each of his five episodes on *Have Gun*, just as in most of the films and television he did. June Vincent, a cool elegant woman of enormous dignity, likewise played a fairly narrow range of characters.

95. Later, he would be even better known as farmer Fred Ziffel, the proud owner of Arnold the Pig, on the rural comedy *Green Acres* (1965–71). For details of Patterson's career, see IMDb. The quote about "cantankerous old coots" comes from Answers.com.

96. Including Robert J. Stevenson, Denver Pyle, Natalie Norwick, Charles Bronson, June Vincent, Anthony Caruso, and Lorna Thayer.

97. Faulkner, IMDb.

98. Grams, 341.

99. Blake: IMDb.

100. Webber: Rothel, 91.

101. Interestingly, both Grant Withers and John Anderson appear in supporting roles in both Dr. Thackeray episodes—but playing strikingly different characters. Dr. Thackeray is the only repeating role in the two episodes.

102. Barnes: Rothel, 121.

103. Breck: Rothel, 116. Following his *Have Gun* work, Breck got important roles in two Western series, *Black Saddle* (1959–60) and *The Big Valley* (1965–69).

104. *Boots and Saddles* (1957–58) was set in the fictional Ft. Lowell, near Tucson, Arizona, in the late 1800s. It was available only in syndication.

105. In the actual shoot-out, Western beat Paladin to the draw—but McLaglen was able to cut in a way that concealed that inconvenient fact. (Rothel 100). See the entire interview (99–107) for more details about Western's involvement with the show and "The Ballad of Paladin." Grams also tells the story in an interview between Johnny Western and Les Rayburn (48–56).

106. Though CBS initially tried to buy the song outright for $500, Western's shrewd agent finally negotiated a much better deal: Western would get screen credit, plus SAG royalties for his performance of the song, and BMI royalties on the song itself. In the end, Western gave Boone and Rolfe a small percentage of the deal (8⅓ percent each), partly because each man had suggested a small but significant improvement to the original song, and also in acknowledgment that the deal would never have happened without their championing of his song (Rothel, 102; Grams, 53).

107. Western: Rothel, 106–7.

108. Grams, 297.

109. Grams, 276.

110. Grams, 90.

111. In fact, after *Have Gun* went off the air, Needham stayed on with McLaglen as his stunt coordinator for a total of twelve years before branching out on his own, eventually going on to become a director of popular action films like *Smokey and the Bandit* (1977), *Hooper* (1978), *Smokey and the Bandit 2* (1980), *Cannonball Run* (1981) and *Stroker Ace* (1983), all starring Burt Reynolds and a rotating stock company.

Part II: An Overview

1. Of course, this description applies not so much to the historical West as to the mythical West of the Western.

2. Cawelti, 38–39.

3. Whitney, "Gunsmoke," p. 10.

4. *Blacks and White TV*, p. 3. Much of the material in these paragraphs is drawn from MacDonald's book, the first detailed study of African Americans and television.

5. However, the nightly network news programs were only fifteen minutes long, not reaching their half-hour format till 1963.

6. MacDonald, 78–80.

7. For a thoughtful analysis of *Broken Arrow* and its many less successful imitators, see Stedman, *Shadows of the Indian*, 206–215.

8. The character's name is actually Jesús, of course; "Haysoos," the phonetic spelling, was used in the credits to avoid audience outrage at having a character named for Christ, although the name is quite common in Mexico.

Earlier, children's westerns from the late 1940s and early 1950s did include featured minority characters, like Tonto on *The Lone Ranger*, and Hispanic characters in Disney productions like *Zorro* (1957–1959) and *Elfago Baca*, a six-episode miniseries broadcast between October 1958 and February 1959, based on the historical Mexican lawman, but such characters were absent in adult Westerns until the mid–1960s. All these minority characters were treated sympathetically, but except for Jay Silverheels, the Mohawk Indian who played Tonto, none of the actors playing ethnic characters in the two Disney series were actually ethnic themselves. Guy Williams played Zorro, while Italian-American Robert Loggia played Baca.

9. The primary exception to this rule: Chinese characters were mostly played by actors of Asian heritage, though Hollywood used Chinese-, Japanese-, Korean-, or Filipino-American actors interchangeably.

10. Press, 29.

11. Weibel, 47. Discouragingly, though the numbers have improved on television, thanks to all the female forensic pathologists, district attorneys, detectives, police captains, and neurosurgeons, the numbers in the movies are getting worse. Maureen Dowd reported that a new study by Martha Lauzen, professor in the Center for the Study of Women in Television and Film at San Diego State University, shows women making up only 15 percent of protagonists and only 30 percent of speaking characters in the top 100 grossing domestic films of 2013 (*New York Times*, March 3, 2014), A23. Even when a movie has female protagonists, according to Kevin B. Lee, they get significantly less screen time than their male counterparts. The lead actors in this year's Oscar contenders average 85 minutes on screen, while the lead actresses average only 57 minutes (*New York Times*, March 2, 2014; Art and Leisure, 12).

12. The first three seasons of the other series consist of 117 half-hour episodes of *Gunsmoke*, 117 hour-long episodes for *Wagon Train*, and 100 hour-long episodes for *Bonanza,* a sufficiently large sample, from the same years *Have Gun—Will Travel* was broadcast, to give a representative idea of the patterns. *Wagon Train* included rather more women than *Bonanza* and *Gunsmoke* due to the producers' goal to create juicy roles to attract prominent movie actors, including women.

13. An additional two episodes, late in the season, include a couple of black extras, something that was also sadly uncommon in the period.

Chapter Five

1. Horace Newcomb and Robert S. Alley in *The Producers' Medium: Conversations with the Creators of American TV* (New York: Oxford University Press, 1983). Cited by MacDonald, *Sheriff,* 102.

2. In "The Round Up," 2:4, September 29, 1956.

3. A few series also offered a more specialized official, like the Wells Fargo agent in *Tales of Wells Fargo* or the insurance investigator of *The Man From Blackhawk*.

4. Yoggy, *Riding the Video Range*, 97.

5. One major source of the inconsistency is the fact that many different writers created the scripts for the series. The producer could have mandated more consistency, or appointed a staff member to keep track of such issues, but clearly this was not a priority for Charles Marquis Warren, producer and director of the first season. His associate producer, Norm McDonnell, one of the creators of the radio *Gunsmoke*, would probably have been happy to address such issues, except that Warren, disliking and resenting McDonnell, blocked his access to the set (Barabas, 75–77). In later seasons, the actors paid considerable attention to the consistency of their own characters, but here in the first television season, it was no one's job.

6. In the original radio version of this script, the ruffians kill Chen by strangling him with his queue. On television, however, such a conclusion was apparently too grim to be acceptable. See Barabas, 105–6.

7. Barabas, 83.

8. An ideal our own culture seems to be moving away from, with the current emphasis on gun rights and "Stand Your Ground" laws.

9. These two episodes, "Charley Red Dog" (3:13, 12/12/59), and "Brotherhood" (6:17, 1/5/63), will be discussed in greater detail in Chapter Seven.

10. These three episodes, plus "Fandango," are discussed in greater detail in the next chapter. Other episodes also deal centrally with the high cost of a hunt for fugitives: "The Man Who Lost" (2:31, 4/25/ 59; see Chapter 6) "The Killing of Jessie May" (4:8, 10/ 29/60; see Chapter 7), "Ben Jalisco" (5:10, 11/18/61), and "The Waiting Room" (5:24, 2/24/62; see Chapter 7).

11. Paladin had advised Charley to put a drop of fat in his holster to make his draw smoother. It is, of course, totally incredible that Charley could have improved enough in these few days that the hopeless

fumbler of the trail could now outdraw a seasoned gunfighter. However, it makes a nice ending.

12. This is not an unfamiliar sentiment, but it appears to be an invented quotation, since there is no record of a philosopher, ancient or otherwise, named Herodius. There was Herodotus, but he did not write essays.

13. This detail, imagining cowboys "riding 80 miles to the next town," is one of many instances of the writers being unaware of realistic travel times and distances in the Old West. Eighty miles on horseback is a three- or four-day ride, unless the horse is specially bred for speed and endurance.

14. This aspect of the plot is wildly implausible, since the boy has been in jail in this same small town where he was tried and convicted for over eleven years. No lost file would cause them to forget his planned execution, especially when his name is so hated.

15. The remaining episodes with trials: "The Silver Queen" (1:33, 5/3/58); "Three Sons" (1:34, 5/10/58); "Deliver the Body" (1:38, 6/7/58); "Incident at Borrasca Bend" (2:27, 3/21/59); "Return to Fort Benjamin" (3:20, 1/30/60; see Chapter 7); "Justice in Hell" (5:18, 1/13/62; see Chapter 6); and "A Place for Abel Hix" (6:4, 10/6/62; see Chapter 6). The four episodes with important legal issues other than trials: "The Legacy" (4:13,12/10/60), which concerns legal wills; "Fandango" (4:24, 3/3/61), about age limits for the death penalty; "The Hanging of Aaron Gibbs" (5:8, 4/4/61; see Chapter 7); and "The Cage at McNab" (6:23, 2/16/63).

Chapter Six

1. Actually, "gunfighter" and "gunslinger" are early–20th century Hollywood terms; in the real Old West, such men were called gunmen, shootists, pistoleers, mankillers, or bad men, according to Wikipedia. The article goes on to note that the classic gun duels we know so well from movies and TV were invented by the dime novelists of the late 19th century. In real life, such duels were relatively rare. Many gunfighters lived on their reputations, and generally avoided confronting others with high reputations. Famous gunfighters were more often challenged by rising men hoping to build a reputation than by men of their own stature. Unlike the familiar iconography of the white-knuckle draw-down in the middle of the street, real-life gunfights often started spontaneously: one man draws and another responds; or they turn into a gun battle from cover, or one man takes advantage of another looking away to catch his opponent off-guard.

2. Danceman to Paladin, in "Everyman" (4:27, 3/25/61).

3. In "Birds of a Feather" (1:26, 3/8/58), however, Paladin demonstrated what it takes to refuse such a challenge, and without even losing his temper, merely pointing out to his rival that if they shoot each other, neither of them will get the chance to spend the money they are earning from their rival employers. Coe, unimpressed, insists that Paladin draw, but with a cigar in his right hand (so that he has no hand free for his gun), Paladin turns his back and walks away. Coe fires angrily at his rival's feet, and then at his cigar, but Paladin still refuses to fight. Despite the assumption of Coe and other observers that he is a coward, Paladin is confident enough in his own skill, his own manhood, that he does not need to prove it with a display of unnecessary violence.

4. See Chapter Five for a longer discussion of this episode.

5. Eileen Tuttle is a typical example of the kind of strong woman found so often in this series. Chapter 8 will examine these women in more detail.

6. Spruce's story will receive more analysis in Chapter 7, along with other sympathetic outlaws who belong to racial and ethnic minorities.

7. This episode was originally shot in August 1961, but the broadcast was delayed a full 18 months by controversy over the ending, Paladin's intentional shooting of Carl. In this period, Hollywood was under significant pressure from the federal government to tone down violence on TV, so Boone (as director of the episode) was urged to substitute what he called "a real soap opera ending," which he refused to do. Guy della Cioppa, head of CBS programs on the West Coast, supported Boone's position, so the original ending stayed when the episode was finally broadcast. As Boone later explained, "All I want is to do a television series which some of my adult friends could look at without being insulted" (Grams 461).

Chapter Seven

1. There is no consensus on the most appropriate term for the indigenous inhabitants of North America traditionally called "Indians," after Columbus's mistaken usage. In the days of political correctness, "Native American" gained considerable currency; some people now use "First People," a Canadian formulation. Current usage tends to prefer the specific tribal affiliation when it is known, with "Indian" as the most common non–tribally-specific or collective term. Taking my cue from the American Indian Movement (A.I.M.), the Center for American Indian Studies at UCLA, and *The American Indian Quarterly*, this is the usage I have adopted.

2. Yoggy, 319. In reality, Victor Sen Yung, the actor who played Hop Sing, spoke perfect English, since he was American-born and highly educated. According to the IMDb, he earned a degree in Economics from Berkeley in 1938 and eventually pursued graduate studies at UCLA and the University of Southern California, while during World War II he served as an intelligence officer in the Army Air Corps.

3. In "Day of the Dragon" (3:11, 12/3/61), Joe's winnings in a poker game include a beautiful young Chinese girl (played by Lisa Lu), the property of General Tsung. Joe tries to free her, but she insists on staying with him, even after Ben offers to pay her passage back to China.

4. Li Cheng is played by Korean-American actor,

Philip Ahn. According to traditional Chinese nomenclature, the patronymic precedes the personal name; so Li Cheng's son's name, even Americanized, should be Jimmy Li, not Jimmy Cheng. But the script identifies Cheng as the family name.

5. There is another brief discussion of this episode in Ch. 5, concerning Matt's behavior as a lawman. As the note in that chapter mentions, in the original radio script, the ruffians strangled Chen with his own queue. The radio script presumably emphasizes the lethal quality of such unreasoning prejudice.

6. Perhaps the pseudonym offers Hey Boy an anonymity that is advantageous in the often-hostile Anglo world. The "Hey, you!" incident is found in "The Singer" (1:22, 2/8/58). Paladin's knowledge of Hey Boy's real name is revealed in "Hey Boy's Revenge" (1:31, 4/12/58), though Paladin initially says "Kim Chan" but later shifts to "Kim Chang" without explanation—probably an uncorrected continuity error.

7. There is not one single Chinese language, of course, but many different ones, all mutually unintelligible in their spoken forms, though a common written form makes cross-communication possible. The official language of mainland China is Mandarin, as spoken in Beijing; Hong Kong and most of the Chinese diaspora (including the Chinese in America) use Cantonese, which is probably what Hey Boy uses.

8. Lisa Lu appeared as Hey Girl in 19 episodes in Season Four, and also played featured roles in two other *Have Gun* episodes, "Hey Boy's Revenge" and "The Hatchet Man," both discussed later.

9. The entire episode is historically anachronistic, as the high point of railroad building in the west occurred in the 1850s–'60s, largely ending with the completion of the transcontinental railroad in 1869. But "Hey Boy's Revenge" seems to be the first TV exposé of the mistreatment of Chinese workers, so an error of a decade or so in time perhaps matters less than the truth of the portrait.

10. The intent of such scenes is to signal both Paladin's basic knowledge of written and spoken Chinese, and the limits of his knowledge, but the details are occasionally implausible. For example, after successfully translating some fairly complex ideas in the letter, he needs Mr. Chung to translate the final line of the letter: "Please, my brother, you must help me."

11. Another historical inaccuracy, alas. In this time period (ca. 1850s–1870s), the law did not allow Chinese immigrants to testify in court against white Americans (Library of Congress website, "Chinese immigration").

12. A third episode includes a minor but positive Chinese character. Birdie, in "The Haunted Trees" (2:38, 6/13/59), is the Chinese cook for a large lumber ranch, and a skilled healer. Her race is incidental, but the character is treated with considerable dignity and no trace of stereotyping in language or behavior.

13. Another of those logical gaps that happen from time to time. Surely Loo Sam has many fighters available, not just one; but after his victory, Paladin does

challenge the Tong boss in front of witnesses to fight Joe Tsin in person. So perhaps we are to imagine that Loo Sam would now lose face if he sends a replacement.

14. A point made most clearly by William Stedman in *Shadows of the Indian*, 243ff.

15. Yoggy, 348.

16. Still, on *Have Gun* a few such men get screen credit, like Eddie Little Sky, while among the extras we see a number of faces whose features strongly suggest Indian heritage. Such extras can be found in the background on each of the other series from time to time, while I spotted apparently genuine Indian traditional singers at least once on *Bonanza* and once on *Wagon Train* in their first seasons.

For background on this issue, see *Reel Injuns*, a recent documentary by Cree filmmaker Neil Diamond, broadcast on PBS's *Independent Lens* series on Nov. 2, 2011.

17. MacDonald, *Who Shot the Sheriff?*, 114. The *Wagon Train* episodes are "The Nels Stack Story" (1:6, 10/23/57), "The Charles Avery Story" (1:9, 11/13/57), "The Cliff Grundy Story" (1:15, 12/25/57), "The Gabe Carswell Story" (1:18, 1/15/58), "The Dora Gray Story" (1:20, 1/29/58), and "The Sarah Drummond Story" (1:27, 4/2/58).

18. Renegades attacking without provocation: *Gunsmoke*, "Alarm at Pleasant Valley" (1:39, 8/25/56); *Have Gun*: "The Prophet" (3:16, 1/2/60) and "The Pledge" (3:18, 1/16/60).

Indians attacking after provocation: *Bonanza*, "The Paiute War" (1:4, 10/3/59); *Have Gun*, "The Englishman" (1:13, 12/7/57); "The Yuma Treasure" (1:14, 12/14/57); "The Solid Gold Patrol" (2:13, 12/13/58); "The Long Hunt" (2:25, 3/7/59); "Fight at Adobe Wells" (3:26, 3/12/60); "Crowbait" (4:10, 11/19/60); "Silent Death, Secret Death" (5:29, 3/31/61).

19. Major Adams insists it is a Sioux custom for a raiding party to abandon those too sickly or old to fight and leave them to die, but this is a calumny. Most Indians valued their elderly, took care of them, and would never have included such a man in a raiding party to begin with. He would have been left with the women and children.

20. For example, the chief's mother is played by Celia Lovsky, Peter Lorre's wife, with her mittel—European accent unaltered. A couple of years later, she plays an elderly Spanish aristocrat on *Bonanza*.

21. *Gunsmoke*: "Indian Scout" (1:23, 3/31/56), "Prairie Happy" (1:33, 7/7/56), "Indian White" (2:6, 10/27/56), "Sins of the Father" (2:17, 1/19/57), and "The Photographer" (2:28, 4/6/57). *Wagon Train*: "The Charles Avery Story" (1:9, 11/13/57), "The Clara Beauchamp Story" (1:13, 12/11/57), "The Bill Tawnee Story" (1:22, 2/12/58), and "The Sarah Drummond Story" (1:27, 4/2/58). *Bonanza*: "The Paiute War" (1:4, 10/3/59), and "The Last Hunt" (1:15, 12/19/59). The *Have Gun* episodes will be examined within the chapter.

22. The only real exception is "The Pledge" (3:18, 1/16/60). A renegade band of Paiutes, none of whom are individualized, takes a white woman hostage to

force her husband to bring them a Gatling gun. Paladin's problem is to rescue the woman without letting the Indians keep the gun, a solution which requires him to turn the gun on the renegades themselves in an orgy of casual mass violence otherwise unheard of in this series.

23. One other episode, "The Burning Tree" (6:22, 2/9/63), also includes Indians as a plot device, but in a most unsatisfactory way. According to the story, when an Osage Indian chief dies, he cannot go to the afterlife without a scalp. In earlier times, they used Pawnee scalps, but after the Pawnee left, the Osage began raiding the town and grabbing up the first person they saw. Now the town uses prisoners for this purpose, keeping them often for long periods of time till the next time a chief dies. But, given the pattern of the story, the Osage seem to lose a chief every six months or so—highly implausible.

24. Of course, this story is wildly anachronistic, as the Pawnee were settled on reservations by 1857, first in Nebraska and later in the Indian Territories, according to www.digital.library.okstate.edu/chronicles. So they would not still have been wandering like this in the 1870s.

25. Parker's mother, Cynthia Anne Parker, was originally kidnaped, but eventually adopted the Comanche way of life. Parker's father was a Comanche war chief. In the real history of Adobe Walls, in June 1874, Quanah Parker led 700 Indian warriors in an attack on 28 buffalo hunters sharing a fortified house near the Red River in Texas. Despite the Indians' vast advantage in numbers, the hunters' superior weapons ultimately doomed the attack. After fifteen dead and many wounded, the Indians withdrew, dispirited and demoralized, and the alliance collapsed. Within a year, Parker and his band surrendered and moved to the Kiowa-Comanche Reservation in southwest Oklahoma. See "Quanah Parker," website of the Texas State Historical Association [www.tshaonline.org].

26. The episode was written by Samuel A. Peeples and Frank Pierson, from a story by Peeples. The liner notes on the VHS version of the series identify Peeples as part Native American, though none of the on-line sources like IMDb or Wikipedia mention this fact. Grams notes that Peeples wrote the second pilot for *Star Trek*, and that Gene Roddenberry had consulted Peeples' extensive library of science fiction in conceiving his series.

There is one more *Have Gun* episode about doomed Indians, "The Race" (5:7, 10/28/61), but it is one of the weaker episodes. Unusually for the series, the Indians here are reduced to "pitiful victim" status, not allowed to speak in their own behalf. Instead, Paladin speaks for them, well-meaning but pre-emptive.

27. A point made only in the most oblique ways, this being the 1950s.

28. Far from being a central character, the young man has only one scene at the very end of the episode, while—in an episode that is intended to affirm the superiority of Indian culture—the only Indian character, the young mother, has neither a name nor a single line of dialogue. The bulk of the episode concerns the comic efforts of Hoss and Little Joe to help the young mother give birth when they find her alone on the mountain in a snowstorm. Once again, the official message of admiration for minority cultures is undercut by a dramatic structure that limits the agency of minority characters.

29. It is impossible to believe an Apache chief would have wanted his daughter to have a Western education, especially from a ladies' seminary, and harder still to explain how he could have paid the vast sums of money such schooling would have cost. Worse, why would an Apache woman with strong ties to her own people choose to marry a career Army man? And why would he marry her when having an Indian wife would likely destroy his chances of advancement?

30. Charley's activities as marshal are treated in more detail in Chapter Five.

31. Curiously, given this attitude, Jim chooses a traditional Indian woman for his wife, not one with a Western education.

32. There are serious issues with the script, however, many concealed (on first viewing) by Charles Bronson's strong performance as Abe, and some comic relief provided by a traveling paper goods salesman who gets caught up in the action. This happened with many episodes in Season 6, when Boone's energy was flagging.

33. Most white observers considered these tortures proof of the Indians' inhumanity—ignoring the fact that Europeans had practiced extreme and varied tortures of criminals, heretics, and other undesirables for many centuries. Another habit taken as a mark of Indians' "savagery"—cutting scalps from dead enemies—has been authoritatively traced to Europeans in North America, who paid bounties for dead Indians, and preferred the scalp as a proof of death over an ear or a hand, whose removal would not necessarily cause death.

34. I cannot discover any information about Pawnee attitudes toward suicide under such circumstances, but Quiet One is played with considerable dignity, so the scene works whether it is culturally accurate or not.

35. The remainder of the episode consists of Paladin's trial for murdering David. See Chapter Five for a discussion of this aspect of the episode.

36. Another mild anachronism. The phrase makes it sound like the Indian wars are concluded, but actually they have another decade to go, since the series is set around 1876.

37. Roland also provided the story for the episode, though not the screenplay. The story and characters are quite conventional, including the faithless Mexican femme fatale, but the story celebrates Juarez and his cause and manages to educate the audience briefly about the Mexican Revolution.

38. With curious inconsistency, in some episodes Paladin speaks at least a bit of Spanish, while in others he needs translations of even the simplest phrases. A typical problem of relying on a collection of freelance writers.

39. Respectively: "A Show of Force" (1:9, 11/9/57),

"The Long Hunt" (2:25, 3/7/59), "Saturday Night" (4:5, 10/8/60), "Death of a Gunfighter" (2:26, 3/14/59), "Squatter's Rights" (5:16, 12/30/61), "Beau Geste" (6:5, 10/13/62), "A Place for Abel Hix" (6:4, 10/6/62), "The Statue of San Sebastian" (1:39, 6/14/58), and "A Miracle for St. Francis" (6:10, 11/17/62).

40. One of the weakest episodes in the entire series, slipping unsteadily between comedy and melodrama, and further marred by a mute, subservient Indian character known as Dirty Dog. This story is redeemed only by an extraordinary performance by Hans Conried as the old knight.

41. Doroteo's story in this episode (aside from the Soledad plot) closely tracks the actual history, except the time frame has been shifted about 15 years. The real Doroteo/Pancho Villa was born in 1878, and so would have been at best a newborn at the time *Have Gun* is set.

42. Details about Ricky Vera are remarkably sketchy, except that he had 14 credits as a TV actor between 1954–1964, usually playing Hispanic characters, but occasionally (perhaps) an American Indian and once an East Indian on a episode of *Tales of The 77th Bengal Lancers*. I could find no birth or death dates, let alone any other information about him.

43. MacDonald, *Blacks*, 86.

44. Harbin, a native of Texas, parlayed a beauty contest title into small roles in a long string of black-themed films between 1941–1957, especially when there were musical numbers, appearing with Lena Horne in such classics as *Cabin in the Sky* and *Stormy Weather* (both 1943). Called "the black Marilyn Monroe," she was often featured on the covers of such magazines as *Jet*, and also entertained American troops in Korea. This appearance on *Wagon Train* was her last credit as an actress, though she lived till 1994.

45. MacDonald, *Blacks*, 88.

46. Boone and Hairston met on the set of *The Alamo* in 1960. Hairston was playing Jim Bowie's servant, Jethro, while Boone had a cameo as General Sam Houston. Boone was so impressed with Hairston that he insisted roles be found for him on the series.

47. In 1973, Capers won a Tony as Best Actress in a Musical for her role as Lena in *Raisin*, the musical version of Lorraine Hansberry's *Raisin in the Sun*.

48. A pleasingly Janus-like title that can refer both to the killings Jessie May commits, and to his own death in the episode. Grams lists the title as "The Shooting of Jessie May," based on certain primary documents he viewed. Though Hari Rhodes had an active career on TV and in film, he is best remembered for his roles in *Conquest of the Planet of the Apes* (1972) and *Battle for the Planet of the Apes* (1973).

49. However, since Jessie May also calls Jondill "Mr.," that strengthens the argument for a more innocent construction on the nonparallel usage.

50. Odetta's appearance was a great coup for the series, achieved by Peggy Rea, who had a personal connection to the singer. Though Odetta's agent was convinced the singer would never agree to the role, when Rea sent her the script, Odetta called the production office herself asking to play Sarah Gibbs. Eight years

after this performance, Crosse would become the first African-American to be nominated for an Oscar as Best Supporting Actor, for his role in *The Reivers* with Steve McQueen (1969).

51. According to Frank Pierson, there was a certain amount of anxiety about this episode during the planning, "but when they heard that we were going to use Odetta, it all quieted down." Grams, 398.

52. According to Shimon Wincelberg, the script's author. Wincelberg also recounts that, shortly after the episode was broadcast, Sammy Davis, Jr., confronted him, furious with disappointment at not getting a chance to play such a wonderful role (Grams, 369). Ivan Dixon was best known for his continuing role on *Hogan's Heroes* (1965–1971), though later was much more active as a director than an actor, frustrated by the limited roles available to black actors.

53. The most accessible and influential source for this explanation is Geneva Smitherman's classic *Talkin and Testifyin: The Language of Black America*. Boston: Houghton Mifflin, 1977.

54. Wincelberg might have supplied these features of black English; but more likely, Ivan Dixon's line readings are the source. The manuscript would reveal the truth, if I had been able to consult it.

55. Right: totally implausible. But the episode has some nice moments of acting.

56. A script which won its author, Gene Roddenberry, an Emmy.

57. See Rothel, 61.

58. Shotness was played by Martin Gabel, Boone's Broadway co-star in *The Rivalry*. Boone had been so impressed with Gabel's performance that he insisted a part be found for him on the series.

59. Reported by Wincelberg in Grams, 344.

60. The beloved ground-breaking musical about Russian Jews, *Fiddler on the Roof*, did not appear on Broadway until 1964, four years after "The Fatalist."

61. In fact, the authenticity of the ceremony was such that Wincelberg himself read the Hebrew prayers, as the actor playing the rabbi was not able to pronounce the words correctly. (Wincelberg: Grams, 402).

62. Grams, 402. It doesn't help that the script for "A Drop of Blood" is very uneven, nowhere near as effective as "The Fatalist." Rivka's character has changed: instead of the strong, forthright young teenager of the first episode, she is a much more conventional, even timid, young woman—screaming when a frog leaps out at her from one of her shopping baskets, placed there as a prank. And the relationship between Nathan and his neighbors is quite illogical: why would they come to the wedding party if they don't like him enough to defend him from Buckstone's hooligans? Finally, and most devastating of all, the script veers unsteadily between drama and comedy, not managing either very successfully.

63. This scenario has no close parallel in the actual history of Japan in this period.

64. My resident expert, Akina Miyata Morriss, watched this episode with me and verified that all of the Japanese dialogue is authentic and reasonably ac-

curate, though she observed that one of the actresses was clearly not very fluent in the language.

Chapter Eight

1. Weibel, "Preface," xx.

2. *Gunsmoke* expanded to one-hour episodes in 1961. The histories of these series indicate that there were few changes in *Gunsmoke*'s approaches to female characters except possibly much later, certainly long after *Have Gun* had gone off the air, while *Bonanza* never changed in this regard.

3. One test of women's importance in works of popular culture, developed a couple of decades ago, is to count how often women have significant interactions with other women, especially interactions about something other than a man. If there is only one major woman character in an episode, such interactions are obviously impossible.

4. The tabulated number of women in *Have Gun* episodes omits those in the introductory scenes in the Carlton, unless they also appear in the body of the episode, and, for the sake of fairness, also does not include the 14 episodes in Season Four where Hey Girl replaced Hey Boy at the Carlton Hotel.

5. It is impossible to know if a character like Kitty would have been included in the television series if she had not already been so popular on the radio version.

6. Consider, for example, the remarkable opening scene of "Twenty-Four Hours at North Fork" (1:36, 5/24/58). In the lobby of the San Francisco Opera House, a beautiful elegantly-gowned young blonde walks past Paladin and "accidentally" drops her program, carefully not making eye contact with him. He returns it to her, giving them an innocent excuse for a conversation. But the content of that conversation is anything but innocent. He asks accusingly, *sotto voce*: "Where were you last night?" She explains urgently that Uncle Ned arrived home yesterday, though he was supposed to be away till the following week. It seems that rumors about the two of them had reached Uncle Ned, and he was anxious to have "an important talk" with Paladin. Alarmed, Paladin inquires, "Were the rumors exaggerated?" She replies simply, "He insists upon killing you," and adds that she would be devastated at such an outcome. Paladin agrees mildly that this would not be acceptable to him either, nor is he anxious to kill Uncle Ned, even in self-defense. The young woman remarks that Uncle's business will not allow him to linger in town more than a few days. She is convinced that, given time, she can persuade Uncle Ned that her relationship with Paladin is "the most platonic of friendships, but it would be best if he couldn't find you till then." Paladin inquires, "Are you suggesting I leave the city?" She nods: "For your *health*."

Structurally, the scene has nothing to do with the plot of the episode; it merely serves to get Paladin out of San Francisco and on the road, where he can encounter a totally-unrelated adventure. But considered as a set piece, this scene is remarkable for a network series in 1958. Though there is not a single indelicate

word in the exchange, it is impossible to mistake the meaning: these two elegant well-bred people are having an affair. Though the lady is clearly not married (given that the troublesome relation is an uncle rather than a husband), she shows a complete lack of self-consciousness, let alone shame, about being engaged in an extramarital sexual relationship. For both characters, Uncle Ned's objections are simply an unfortunate nuisance, a practical problem to be solved, rather than a moral issue. It is impossible to imagine a similar scene on any other TV show of the time—or a woman in such a relationship being treated with no trace of moral objection. Though this scene is more explicit than any other in the series, the relationship revealed here is not the exception in Paladin's San Francisco life, but the rule.

7. He falls in love with Dr. Phyllis Thackeray of "No Visitors" (1:12, 11/30/57) and "The Return of Dr. Thackeray" (1:35, 5/17/58), and later with Princess Serafina of Montenegro in "The Princess and the Gunfighter" (4:19, 1/21/61). He is very attracted to a star trick shooter in "Ella West" (1:17, 1/4/58) but steps back to let her reconnect with her true love, while Sandy in "Bandit" (5:35, 5/12/62) is a doomed figure who compels his sympathy but is too angry and damaged to trust.

8. Because Indians play substantial roles in this episode, it is treated in more detail in Chapter Seven.

9. A point never made explicit in the script, perhaps because it seemed self-evident, or perhaps because the writer never considered that Elise might want to hold office in her own name.

10. The sheriffs in both "The Campaign of Billy Banjo" and "A Sense of Justice" are analyzed in more detail in Chapter Five.

11. There is one more woman teacher, a respectable but minor character in "The Kid" (5:15, 12/23/61).

12. Of course, according to the conventions of series TV, this outcome is inevitable: as the series protagonist, Paladin cannot be permitted to marry. However, unlike any love interest on *Bonanza*, Phyllis Thackeray is not required either to die or to marry someone else to save Paladin from marriage.

13. Ironically, by the 1950s, nursing was one of the few acceptable careers for women.

14. Her faith is expressed only in very general terms in the dialogue. Two or three times, she says "God" or "the Lord," but never mentions Jesus or quotes scripture; Melissa speaks only of love, peace, joy, and power and glory.

15. The script has serious problems of logic and coherence, because the problem of cultural misogyny is simply too great to be solved in 25 minutes. So Sandy's original complaint, that she was mistreated because she is a woman, is transformed into an argument that, if she behaved the way women were supposed to, men would treat her better. Therefore, if Paladin can teach her "how to act like a woman," her problem will be solved. Under close analysis, the script breaks down, though the actors manage to create genuine emotion between the characters; and the intent is clearly to present Sandy's situation as sympatheti-

cally as possible, without removing her responsibility for her previous actions.

16. Imagine any other Western character quoting the philosopher-emperor of Rome!

17. This is a very familiar story, of course; a similar relationship shapes that old classic, *The Prisoner of Zenda*, while the writers of this episode drew explicit inspiration from *Roman Holiday*, a 1953 film starring Audrey Hepburn as a bored young princess who escapes her minders and falls in love with an American newspaperman played by Gregory Peck (see Grams, 366). Robert E. Thompson creates an engaging script, while Arline Sax as Serafina is delightfully fresh and appealing. I confess: though not necessarily the best episode, this is one of my personal favorites.

18. Sheriff Dobbs is discussed in more detail in Chapter Five.

19. For discussion of the main issues in this episode, see Chapter Six.

20. For a discussion of the sheriff in this episode, see Chapter Five.

21. The genealogical details are highly inaccurate in this episode. Diana's title indicates that her father held a title just below that of Earl, which means that any brother would inherit the title on their father's death, even if the brother were younger than she. She also has an uncle who commands a regiment of Bengal Lancers, so it's not clear why she couldn't have gone to him. But this was American television, and nobody much cared about such details. The significant line concerns her limited options.

22. In fact, according to the laws of primogeniture, as a woman Charity would be unable to inherit a title, though she might inherit an estate if it were not entailed. Otherwise, both title and estate would have to pass to the nearest male relative, or, failing that, to the Crown. But only the most dedicated Anglophiles in the audience would have recognized, or cared about, this error.

23. For a discussion of the sheriff in this episode, see Chapter Five.

24. The sheriff in this episode is analyzed in more detail in Chapter Five, while the Widow Briggs is examined earlier in this chapter.

25. In short, despite its title, the episode is less about Sarah's dilemma than a critique of anti–Indian prejudice, though—typically—with no significant Indian characters, a most curious undertaking.

26. Casting is another clue here: while the male roles are played by well-known and established actors, the actresses playing Ella and Lucy are relative unknowns, pretty Hollywood ingenues that were, then as now, a dime a dozen.

27. There are problems with the script, a certain incoherence and some implausible details. The tone likewise shifts uneasily between comedy and seriousness; but as is so often the case, strong performances redeem the weaknesses.

28. For examination of the marshal in this episode, see Chapter Five.

Epilogue

1. Adler, 19.

2. Boone selected ten of the most versatile and gifted actors he could find to join him, four women and six men, and set out to perform a new original hour-long play every week about American life. Though occasionally the company brought in a guest performer, generally these eleven people played virtually all the parts among them—one week a lead, the next a bit part, in true repertory fashion. This exhilarating project represented the culmination of everything Boone believed about the theater, everything he had been striving for ever since he arrived at the Neighborhood Playhouse in 1946. It consumed all his energy and enthusiasm, and demanded every bit of his skills, with impressive results. The series was voted the "best dramatic program of the year," as well as the "most unique new program," while Boone himself was chosen one of the top two television performers of the year. Despite this artistic acclaim, halfway through the first season NBC announced that the show would not be renewed. Worse, they did not manage to notify Boone of the decision privately before the news appeared in *Variety*. This betrayal wounded him so deeply that he left Hollywood to move his family to Hawaii for the next six years, and never really forgave the industry. See Rothel, 241–45, for the full story.

3. Boone friend Peter Fithian: Rothel, 132.

4. Claire Boone: Rothel, 65. Peter Boone: Rothel, 79. B'Lou Boone Brown: Rothel, 39.

5. Peter Boone: Rothel, 74–75.

6. Smith, D1.

Works Cited

Adler, Dick. "Had Gun, Traveled, Is Back in TV." *TV Guide* (Sept. 25, 1971), 16–19.

Barabas, SuzAnne, and Gabor Barabas. *Gunsmoke: A Complete History and Analysis of the Legendary Broadcast Series.* Jefferson, NC: McFarland, 1990.

Barnouw, Erik. *The Image Empire: A History of Broadcasting in the United States. Volume 3: From 1953.* New York: Oxford University Press, 1970.

_____. *Tube of Plenty: The Evolution of American Television,* 2d ed. rev. New York: Oxford University Press, 1990.

Becker, Christine. *It's the Pictures That Got Small: Hollywood Film Stars on 1950s Television.* Middletown, CT: Wesleyan University Press, 2008.

Bobo, Jason W. "Comment: Following the Trend: Alabama Abandons the Duty to Retreat and Encourages Citizens to Stand Their Ground." *Cumberland Law Review* 38 (2007–2008), 339.

Boddy, William. *Fifties Television: The Industry and Its Critics.* Urbana: University of Illinois Press, 1990.

Brauer, Ralph. *The Horse, The Gun, and the Piece of Property: Changing Images of the TV Western.* Bowling Green, OH: Bowling Green State University Popular Press, 1975.

Brooks, Tim, and Earle Marsh. *The Complete Directory to Prime Time Network and Cable TV Shows, 1946-Present,* 6th ed. New York: Ballantine, 1995.

Cawelti, John G. *The Six-Gun Mystique.* Bowling Green, OH: Bowling Green State University Popular Press, 1970.

Coontz, Stephanie. *The Way We Never Were: American Families and the Nostalgia Trap.* New York: Harper-Collins, 1992.

Davidson, Bill. "Grumbling, Hollering and Shocking the Ladies." *TV Guide* (February 23, 1974), 25–30.

De Roos, Robert. "The Greta Garbo of Dodge City." *TV Guide* (December 10, 1966).

_____. "Private Life of *Gunsmoke*'s Star." *Saturday Evening Post* (April 12, 1958), 108.

Doherty, Thomas Patrick. *Cold War, Cool Medium: Television, McCarthyism, and American Culture.* New York: Columbia University Press, 2003.

Donati, William. *Ida Lupino: A Biography.* Lexington: University Press of Kentucky, 1996.

Dunning, John. *On the Air: The Encyclopedia of Old-Time Radio.* New York: Oxford University Press, 1978.

Edson, Lee. "TV's Rebellious Cowboy." *Saturday Evening Post* (August 6, 1960), 23, 82–84.

Flagg, Jeffrey B. "Frederick Jackson Turner 1861–1932." http://www.BGSU.edu/departments/acs/1890s/turner/turner.html. 1997.

Garfield, David. *A Player's Place: The Story of the Actors Studio.* New York: Macmillan, 1980.

Gehman, Richard. "The Paradox of Paladin." *TV Guide.* Part 1 (January 7, 1961), 9–11. Part 2 (January 14, 1961), 20–23. Part 3 (January 21, 1961), 24–27.

Grams, Martin, Jr., and Les Rayburn. *The Have Gun–Will Travel Companion.* Arlington, VA: UTR, 2000.

Halberstam, David. *The Fifties.* New York: Villard Books, 1993.

Hewlett, Sylvia Ann. *A Lesser Life: The Myth of Women's Liberation in America.* New York: Warner Books, 1986.

Hirsch, Foster. *A Method to Their Madness: The History of the Actors Studio.* New York: Norton, 1984.

Hobson, Dick. "The Cartwrights Never Order Mandarin Duck." *TV Guide* (October 9, 1971), 49–50.

Hollon, W. Eugene. *Frontier Violence: Another Look.* London: Oxford University Press, 1976.

Homans, Peter. "The Western. The Legend and the Cardboard Hero." *Look* (March 13,1962), 89.

Kimmel, Michael. *Manhood in America: A Cultural History.* New York: Free Press, 1996.

Kirkley, Donald H., Jr. *A Descriptive Study of the Network Television Western During the Seasons 1955–56–1962–63.* New York: Arno Press, 1979.

Kisseloff, Jeff. *The Box: An Oral History of Television, 1920–1961*. New York: Penguin, 1995.

Kraszewski, Jon. "Adapting Scripts in the 1950s: The Economic and Political Incentives for Television Anthology Writers." *Journal of Film and Video* 58:3 (Fall 2006).

Leiby, Bruce R. and Linda F. Leiby. *A Reference Guide to Television's Bonanza*. Jefferson, NC: McFarland, 2001.

MacDonald, J. Fred. *Blacks and White TV: African Americans in Television Since 1948*, 2d ed. Chicago: Nelson-Hall, 1992.

_____. *One Nation Under Television: The Rise and Decline of Network TV*. New York: Pantheon, 1990.

_____. *Who Shot the Sheriff? The Rise and Fall of the Television Western*. New York: Praeger, 1987.

Marill, Alvin. *Big Pictures on the Small Screen: Made-for-TV Movies and Anthology Dramas*. Westport, CT: Praeger, 2007.

Mills, C. Wright. *White Collar*. New York: Oxford University Press, 1953.

Mitchell, Lee Clark. *Westerns: Making the Man in Fiction and Film*. Chicago: University of Chicago Press, 1996.

Morhaim, Joe. "Why *Gunsmoke*'s Amanda Blake, James Arness Won't Kiss." *TV Guide* (March 15, 1958), 8–11.

Nachbar, Jack. "Introduction," *Focus on the Western*, ed. Jack Nachbar. Englewood Cliffs, NJ: Prentice-Hall, 1974.

Neal, Patricia. *As I Am: An Autobiography* with Richard DeNeut. New York: Simon & Schuster, 1988.

Newcomb, Horace. "From Old Frontier to New Frontier." In *The Revolution Wasn't Televised: Sixties Television and Social Conflict*, ed. Lynn Spiegel and Michael Curtin. New York: Routledge, 1997, pp. 286–302.

_____. *TV: The Most Popular Art*. New York: Anchor/Doubleday, 1974.

Nussbaum, Martin. "Sociological Symbolism of the 'Adult Western.'" *Social Forces* 39.1 (October 1960), 25–28.

Parks, Rita. *The Western Hero in Film and Television: Mass Media Mythology*. Ann Arbor UMI Research Press, 1982.

Peel, John. *Gunsmoke Years: The Behind-the-Scenes Story ...* Las Vegas: Pioneer Books, 1989.

Pleck, Joseph H. *The Myth of Masculinity*. Cambridge: MIT Press, 1981.

Press, Andrea L. *Women Watching Television: Gender, Class, and Generation in the American Television Experience*. Philadelphia: University of Pennsylvania Press, 1991.

Pumphrey, Martin. "The Games We Play(ed): TV Westerns, Memory, and 'Masculinity.'" In *Action TV: Tough Guys, Smooth Operators, and Foxy Chicks*. Eds. Bill Ogerby and Anne Gough-Yates. London: Routledge, 2001. pp. 145–158.

Orlick, Peter. "Have Gun, Will Travel." *Museum of Broadcast Communications*, www.museum.tv/archives/etv/H/htmlH/havgunwil/havegunwil.htm (4/10/2009).

"Richard Boone: Evolution of an Actor." *TV Guide* (February 28, 1959), 17–19.

"Richard Boone Has Gun, Will Travel." *TV Guide* (October 12, 1957), 12–14.

Rosin, James. *Wagon Train: The Television Series*. Philadelphia: Autumn Road, 2008.

Schickel, Richard. "TV's Angry Gun." *Show: The Magazine of the Arts* (November 1961), 53–55.

Shapiro, Melany. *Bonanza: The Definitive Ponderosa Companion*. Nipoma, CA: Cyclone Books, 1997.

Skolnick, Arlene. *Embattled Paradise: The American Family in an Age of Uncertainty*. New York: Basic Books, 1991.

Smith, Jack. "Hero Today and Gone Tomorrow." *Los Angeles Times* (May 27, 1963); D1.

Stedman, Raymond William. *Shadows of the Indian: Stereotypes in American Culture*. Norman: University of Oklahoma Press, 1982.

"Togetherness–Western Style." *TV Guide* (June 25, 1960), 18.

Turner, Frederick Jackson. "Significance of the Frontier in American History." Chicago, 1893. http://xroads.virginia.edu/~hyper/turner/.

Warshow, Robert. *Movie Chronicle: The Westerner*. 1954. Reprinted in *Focus on the Western*, ed. Jack Nachbar. Englewood Cliffs, NJ: Prentice-Hall, 1974.

Weibel, Kathryn. *Mirror Mirror: Images of Women Reflected in Popular Culture*. Garden City, NJ: Anchor Books, 1977.

Whitney, Dwight. "The Life and Good Times of Hollywood's Harry Julian (Bret) Fink." *TV Guide* (February 27, 1960), 23.

_____. "What a Bonanza!" *TV Guide* (September 8, 1962), 16.

_____. "Why *Gunsmoke* Keeps Blazing Away." *TV Guide* (December 6, 1958), 10–11.

Wilk, Max. *The Golden Age of Television: Notes from the Survivors*. New York: Delacorte Press, 1976.

Winick, Charles. *Taste and the Censor in Television*. New York: The Fund of the Republic. February 1959.

Winkler, Adam. *Gunfight: The Battle over the Right to Bear Arms in America*. New York: W. W. Norton, 2011.

Winters, Shelley. *Shelley, Also Known as Shirley*. New York: William Morrow, 1980.

Yoggy, Gary A. *Riding the Video Range: The Rise and Fall of the Western on Television*. Jefferson, NC: McFarland, 1994.

Index